Oxford AQA History

A LEVEL AND AS

Component 2

International Relations and Global Conflict c1890–1941

① 1890 - 1923
② 1923 - 1939

Kat Kearey

SERIES EDITOR
Sally Waller

OXFORD

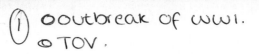

OXFORD
UNIVERSITY PRESS

Great Clarendon Street, Oxford, OX2 6DP, United Kingdom

Oxford University Press is a department of the University of Oxford. It furthers the University's objective of excellence in research, scholarship, and education by publishing worldwide. Oxford is a registered trade mark of Oxford University Press in the UK and in certain other countries

British Library Cataloguing in Publication Data
Data available

978-0-19-835454-3

Kindle edition: 978-0-19-836386-6

10 9 8 7 6 5 4 3 2

Paper used in the production of this book is a natural, recyclable product made from wood grown in sustainable forests. The manufacturing process conforms to the environmental regulations of the country of origin.

Printed in Great Britain by CPI Group (UK) Ltd., Croydon CR0 4YY

Links to third-party websites are provided by Oxford in good faith and for information only. Oxford disclaims any responsibility for the materials contained in any third-party website referenced in this work.

Approval message from AQA

This textbook has been approved by AQA for use with our qualification. This means that we have checked that it broadly covers the specification and we are satisfied with the overall quality. Full details of our approval process can be found on our website.

We approve textbooks because we know how important it is for teachers and students to have the right resources to support their teaching and learning. However, the publisher is ultimately responsible for the editorial control and quality of this book.

Please note that when teaching the AQA A Level History course, you must refer to AQA's specification as your definitive source of information. While this book has been written to match the specification, it does not provide complete coverage of every aspect of the course.

A wide range of other useful resources can be found on the relevant subject pages of our website: www.aqa.org.uk.

Please note that the Practice Questions in this book allow students a genuine attempt at practising exam skills, but they are not intended to replicate examination papers.

Contents

Contents (continued)

Introduction to features

The *Oxford AQA History* series has been developed by a team of expert history teachers and authors with examining experience. Written to match the new AQA specification, these new editions cover AS and A Level content together in each book.

How to use this book

The features in this book include:

TIMELINE

Key events are outlined at the beginning of the book to give you an overview of the chronology of this topic. Events are colour-coded so you can clearly see the categories of change.

LEARNING OBJECTIVES

At the beginning of each chapter, you will find a list of learning objectives linked to the requirements of the specification.

SOURCE   EXTRACT

Sources introduce you to material that is primary or contemporary to the period, and **Extracts** provide you with historical interpretations and the debate among historians on particular issues and developments. The accompanying activity questions support you in evaluating sources and extracts, analysing and assessing their value, and making judgements.

PRACTICE QUESTION

Focused questions to help you practise your history skills for both AS and A Level, including evaluating sources and extracts, and essay writing.

STUDY TIP

Hints to highlight key parts of **Practice Questions** or **Activities**.

ACTIVITY

Various activity types to provide you with opportunities to demonstrate both the content and skills you are learning. Some activities are designed to aid revision or to prompt further discussion; others are to stretch and challenge both your AS and A Level studies.

CROSS-REFERENCE

Links to related content within the book to offer you more detail on the subject in question.

A CLOSER LOOK

An in-depth look at a theme, event or development to deepen your understanding, or information to put further context around the subject under discussion.

KEY CHRONOLOGY

A short list of dates identifying key events to help you understand underlying developments.

KEY PROFILE

Details of a key person to extend your understanding and awareness of the individuals that have helped shape the period in question.

KEY TERM

A term that you will need to understand. The terms appear in bold, and they are also defined in the glossary.

AQA History specification overview

AS exam

Part One content

Great Power rivalries and entry
  into war, c1890–1900

1 Great Powers: Britain, Germany, France,
    Russia and Austria-Hungary, c1890–1900
2 The Great Powers and Crises, 1900–1911
3 The coming of war, 1911–1917

Part Two content

The failure of international
peace and the origins of the
Second World War, 1917–1941

4 The end of the First World War and the
    peace settlement, 1917–1923
5 Attempts at maintaining the peace,
    1923–1935
6 The coming of War, 1935–1941

A Level exam

AS examination papers will cover content from Part One only (you will only need to
know the content in the blue box). A Level examination papers will cover content
from both Part One and Part Two.

The examination papers

The grade you receive at the end of your AQA AS History course is based entirely on your
performance in two examination papers, covering Breadth (Paper 1) and Depth (Paper 2). For
your AQA A Level History course, you will also have to complete an Historical Investigation (Non-
examined assessment).

Paper 2 Depth Study

This book covers the content of a Depth Study (Paper 2). You are assessed on the study in depth
of a period of major historical change or development, and associated primary sources or sources
contemporary to the period.

Exam paper	Questions and marks	Assessment Objective (AO)*	Timing	Marks
AS Paper 2: Depth Study	**Section A: Evaluating primary sources** One compulsory question linked to two primary sources or sources contemporary to the period (25 marks) • The compulsory question will ask you: *'with reference to these sources and your understanding of the historical context, which of these sources is more valuable in explaining why...'*	AO2	Written exam: 1 hour 30 minutes	50 marks (50% of AS)
	Section B: Essay writing One from a choice of two essay questions (25 marks) • The essay questions will contain a quotation advancing a judgement and <u>could</u> be followed by: *'explain why you agree or disagree with this view'.*	AO1		
A Level Paper 2: Depth Study	**Section A: Evaluating primary sources** One compulsory question linked to three primary sources or sources contemporary to the period. The sources will be of different types and views (30 marks) • The compulsory question will ask you: *'with reference to these sources and your understanding of the historical context, assess the value of these three sources to an historian studying...'*	AO2	Written exam: 2 hours 30 minutes	80 marks (40% of A Level)
	Section B: Essay writing Two from a choice of three essay questions (2 x 25 marks) • The essay questions require analysis and judgement, and <u>could</u> include: *'How successful...'* or *'To what extent...'* or *'How far...'* or a quotation offering a judgement followed by *'Assess the validity of this view'.*	AO1		

*AQA History examinations will test your ability to:

AO1: Demonstrate, organise and communicate **knowledge and understanding** to analyse and evaluate the key features related to the periods studied, **making substantiated judgements and exploring concepts**, as relevant, of cause, consequence, change, continuity, similarity, difference and significance.

AO2: **Analyse and evaluate** appropriate source material, primary and/or contemporary to the period, within the historical context.

AO3: **Analyse and evaluate**, in relation to the historical context, different ways in which aspects of the past have been interpreted.

Visit **www.aqa.org.uk** to help you prepare for your examinations. The website includes specimen examination papers and mark schemes.

Introduction to the *Oxford AQA History* series

Depth studies

The exploration of a short but significant historical period provides an opportunity to develop an 'in-depth' historical awareness. This book will help you to acquire a detailed knowledge of an exciting period of historical change, enabling you to become familiar with the personalities and ideas which shaped and dominated the time. In-depth study, as presented here, allows you to develop the enthusiasm that comes from knowing something really well.

However, 'depth' is not just about knowledge. Understanding history requires the piecing together of many different strands or themes, and depth studies demand an awareness of the interrelationship of a variety of perspectives, such as the political, economic, social and religious – as well as the influence of individuals and

ideas within a relatively short period of time. Through an 'in-depth' study, a strong awareness of complex historical processes is developed, permitting deeper analysis, greater perception and well-informed judgement.

Whilst this book is therefore designed to impart a full and lively awareness of a significant period in history, far more is on offer from the pages that follow. With the help of the text and activities in this book, you will be encouraged to think historically, question developments in the past and undertake 'in-depth' analysis. You will develop your conceptual understanding and build up key historical skills that will increase your curiosity and prepare you, not only for A Level History examinations, but for any future studies.

Key Term, **Key Chronology** and **Key Profile** help you to consolidate historical knowledge about dates, events, people, and places

---

4 The state of international relations by 1900

LEARNING OBJECTIVES

In this chapter you will learn about:

- the extent of Anglo-French rivalry
- the state of Anglo-German relations
- the reasons for, terms and consequences of the Franco–Russian Alliance and the Dual Alliance of Germany and Austria-Hungary
- the potential for conflict between the Powers by 1900.

KEY CHRONOLOGY

1879 Germany and Austria form the Dual Alliance

1882 Germany, Austria and Italy form the Triple Alliance

1887 First Reinsurance Treaty between Germany and Russia

1890 Reinsurance Treaty not renewed

1894 France and Russia sign the Franco–Russian Alliance

CROSS-REFERENCE

The Crimean War is explained in the Introduction.

KEY TERM

Splendid Isolation: The British policy of remaining aloof from foreign affairs in Europe; it was viewed as splendid by British ministers as it avoided disadvantageous agreements with other countries and emphasised the British Empire's strength

Third Republic: the government established in France after the fall of Napoleon III in September 1870 while the Franco–Prussian War was still being fought. The Third Republic ended in 1940 following the Nazi invasion of France

revanchism: from the French for 'revenge', it was a policy that aimed to overturn the losses to French territory incurred as a result of the Franco–Prussian War

By the end of the nineteenth century, the Concert of Europe had almost completely collapsed, although most powers still professed a desire to maintain peace.

Anglo-French rivalry

Britain followed a deliberate policy of 'Splendid Isolation' from European affairs, preferring to focus on maintaining and building its empire; although politicians did take a greater interest in European relations when a risk was presented to the balance of power, a concern which grew with the creation and development of the German Empire. Tension between Britain and Russia was also well-established. Disputes over colonial possessions frequently threatened peaceful relations between Britain and the other powers in the 1890s. The Fashoda Incident in 1898 emphasised the increasing vulnerability of British dominance overseas.

SOURCE 1

The Secretary of State for India, Lord George Hamilton, recalled in his official comments the pessimism of Arthur Balfour, future Prime Minister, in 1901:

Balfour said the conviction was forced upon him that we were for all practical purposes at the present moment only a third-rate power; and we are a third-rate power with interests which are conflicting with and crossing those of the great powers of Europe. Put in this elementary form the weakness of the British Empire, as it at present exists, is brought home to one. We have enormous strength, both effective and latent, if we can concentrate, but the dispersion of our Imperial interests, renders it almost impossible.

Bismarck's plan to isolate France diplomatically, following the Franco–Prussian War was successful well into the 1890s: French politicians were too distracted by the teething problems of the **Third Republic** to focus much on foreign policy, and they needed to ensure that France recovered economically from the conflict. At the end of the nineteenth century, however, France sought suitable allies. Initially at least, France believed Russia and Britain would each require guarantees of support against the other before entering into a formal agreement. Germany was even considered, especially as the immediate consequences of the Franco–Prussian War and the *revanchism* stirred by the Alsace–Lorraine takeover began to fade from the memories of the French public. However, a committed minority of politicians refused to countenance an understanding with Germany as it would entail a formal renunciation of France's claim to Alsace–Lorraine. There was also much ground for pessimism when contemplating an Anglo–French agreement: for two centuries Britain and France had been imperial rivals, their colonial ambitions clashing in Canada, India, and – more recently – the African continent.

Colonial rivalry with Britain over Egypt, sparked by nationalist disorders there in 1881, prevented an Anglo–French understanding for several years. The Suez Canal in Egypt, a project jointly financed by the British and the French and completed in 1869, was threatened in 1882 by a nationalist uprising. As the Suez Canal was strategically vital for commerce, Britain was immediately concerned and sent troops to invade and occupy Egypt.

The potential for actual conflict between Britain and France was high, but there is also evidence of both sides reaching peaceful agreements

over disputed colonies. In June 1882 – just two months before Britain's occupation of Egypt – the Anglo–French Convention confirmed the territorial boundaries of each empire in West Africa, while the **Fashoda Incident** resulted in the formal agreement recognising spheres of influence in the north-east.

Anglo-German relations

The growth of Anglo-German rivalry in the years preceding the First World War was in many ways unexpected. The royal families of the two powers were closely related, their cultures shared many similarities, and both were suspicious of France. Britain had viewed Russia and France as the greatest threats to its imperial superiority for much of the nineteenth century, but the accession of Kaiser Wilhelm II, the departure of Bismarck and the subsequent demise of the **Bismarckian system**, which attempted to maintain the balance of power in Europe, gradually worsened relations between Britain and Germany.

A CLOSER LOOK

The Bismarckian system (1871–90)

Bismarck realised the other powers would view a unified, strong Germany as a threat to the balance of power after 1871. He stated that Germany had no plans for further European expansion: it would be 'folly beyond all political reason'. Bismarck developed a complex system of alliances – the Bismarckian system – so it appeared that the balance of power was being maintained while Germany developed economically without being challenged. Meanwhile he tried to keep France isolated from friendly alliances and to limit the potential for conflict between Austria-Hungary and Russia over the Balkans.

Germany was another colonial rival of Britain's during the **Scramble for Africa**. While Bismarck was determined to avoid any potential for conflict with Britain in Europe, overseas commercial interests were another matter entirely, and he even collaborated with the French in the 1880s against British interests in West Africa, the Congo and South West Africa. Two partition treaties were necessary in 1885 and 1890 to resolve Anglo-German disputes in Zanzibar. As a result, Germany established a protectorate known as German East Africa and a British **protectorate** was created in Zanzibar, calming relations between the two powers for the time being.

Hopes of an Anglo-German alliance

However, with the advent of *Weltpolitik* and the beginning of the **Anglo-German naval race** in 1890s, German politicians were well aware that they risked the hostility of the British. As such they sought an understanding with Britain which would secure its peaceful coexistence between the two powers while allowing Germany to seek its 'place in the sun' – imperial greatness. This goal was rather bungled by **Bernhard von Bülow**, the German foreign secretary, who was frequently complacent in his dealings with the British. He hoped that continued imperial rivalry with France would drive Britain into Germany's arms. News of the Fashoda Incident, therefore, was welcomed by Bülow, who believed that Britain would abandon its Splendid Isolation and enter into an alliance with Germany, thereby balancing out the 'encirclement' threat posed by the 1894 Franco–Russian Agreement (see pages 28–30). Given the long-term nature of Anglo-French rivalry, exacerbated by the Scramble

CHAPTER 4 | The state of international relations by 1900

CROSS-REFERENCE

The Fashoda Incident and its consequences for Anglo-French relations are explored in Chapter 3. Anglo-Russian rivalry is also explained in Chapter 3.

ACTIVITY

Explain why many British politicians were worried about Britain's status at the start of the twentieth century. You should also refer to Chapters 2 and 3.

ACTIVITY

Using information in this chapter and from Chapter 3, create two newspaper headlines following the resolution of the Fashoda Incident: one French and one British. Bear in mind that in 1899 the mainstream press of both powers was very nationalistic.

CROSS-REFERENCE

Britain's rivalry with other imperial powers, and the Scramble for Africa, are covered in Chapter 3.

You can find a definition of the term 'protectorate' in Chapter 3, page 18.

The causes and outcome of the Anglo-German naval race are explored in Chapter 5.

KEY PROFILE

Bernhard von Bülow (1849–1929) was German Foreign Secretary for three years before becoming Chancellor in 1900. A great debater, he spoke several languages and was quite ruthless in his treatment of his rivals. He resigned in 1909 over a tax debate in the Reichstag, but remained in Wilhelm's favour.

26 | 27

▲ International Relations and Global Conflict c1890–1941

Source features support you with assessing the value of primary materials

This book also incorporates primary source material in the **Source** features. Primary sources are the building blocks of history, and you will be encouraged to reflect on their value to historians in trying to recreate the past. The accompanying questions are designed to develop your own historical skills, whilst suggestions for **Activities** will help you to engage with the past in a lively and stimulating manner. Throughout the book, you are encouraged to think about the material you are studying and to research further, in order to appreciate the ways in which historians seek to understand and interpret past events.

The chapters which follow are laid out according to the content of the AQA specification in six sections. Obviously, a secure chronological awareness and understanding of each section of content will be the first step in appreciating the historical period covered in this book. However, you are also encouraged to make links and comparisons between aspects of the period studied, and the activities will help you to relate to the key focus of your study and the key concepts that apply to it. Through intelligent use of this book, a deep and rewarding appreciation of an important period of history and the many influences within it will emerge.

Developing your study skills

You will need to be equipped with a paper file or electronic means of storing notes. Organised notes help to produce organised essays and sensible filing provides for efficient use of time. This book uses **Cross-References** to indicate where material in one chapter has relevance to that in another. By employing the same technique, you should find it easier to make the final leap towards piecing together your material to produce a holistic historical picture. The individual, group and research activities in this book are intended to guide you towards making selective and relevant notes with a specific purpose. Copying out sections of the book is to be discouraged, but recording material with a particular theme or question in mind will considerably aid your understanding.

There are plenty of examples of examination-style 'depth' **Practice Questions** for both AS Level, in Part One, and A Level in Parts One and Two of this book. There are also **Study Tips** to encourage you to think about historical perspectives, individuals, groups, ideas and ideology. You should also create your own timelines, charts and diagrams, for example to illustrate causation and consequence, analyse the interrelationship of the differing perspectives, consider concepts, and identify historical processes.

It is particularly important for you to have your own opinions and to be able to make informed judgements about the material you have studied. Some of the activities in this book encourage pair discussion or class debate, and you should make the most of such opportunities to voice and refine your own ideas. The beauty of history is that there is rarely a right or wrong answer, so this supplementary oral work should enable you to share your own opinions.

Writing and planning your essays

At both AS and A Level, you will be required to write essays and, although A Level questions are likely to be more complex, the basic qualities of good essay writing remain the same:

- **read the question carefully** to identify the key words and dates
- **plan out a logical and organised answer** with a clear judgement or view (several views if there are a number of issues to consider). Your essay should advance this judgement in the introduction, while also acknowledging alternative views and clarifying terms of reference, including the time span
- use the opening sentences of your paragraphs as stepping stones to take an argument forward, which allows you to **develop an evolving and balanced argument** throughout the essay and also makes for good style
- **support your comment or analysis** with precise detail; using dates, where appropriate, helps logical organisation
- **write a conclusion** which matches the view of the introduction and flows naturally from what has gone before.

Whilst these suggestions will help you develop a good style, essays should never be too rigid or mechanical.

This book will have fulfilled its purposes if it produces, as intended, students who think for themselves!

Sally Waller

Series Editor

Timeline

The colours represent different types of events, legislation and changes as follows:

- Blue: Economic
- Red: Political
- Black: International (including foreign policy)

1894
- Accession of Tsar Nicholas II in Russia
- The Franco–Russian Alliance is ratified

1897
- Germany announces its pursuit of *Weltpolitik*
- Austro-Russian agreement over the Balkans

1898
- Germany passes the first Naval Law

1899–1902
- Second Boer War begins

1911
- Second Moroccan Crisis following revolt in Agadir
- Italy launches attack on Ottoman Empire at Tripoli

1912
- Balkan League formed
- **October–May** First Balkan War
- **May** Treaty of London reorganised the borders of the Balkan states

1913
- **July** Second Balkan War
- **August** Treaties of Bucharest and Constantinople

1914
- Outbreak of First World War in Europe

1919
- **January** Paris Peace Conference begins
- **28 June** Treaty of Versailles signed – peace settlement regarding Germany

1920
- **10 January** First meeting of the League of Nations
- **March** US senate refuses to ratify Treaty of Versailles or allow the USA to join the League of Nations

1922
- **16 April** Treaty of Rapallo between USSR and Germany
- **October** Benito Mussolini becomes Italian Prime Minister
- Russian Civil War between pro-Bolshevik forces (Reds) and anti-Bolsheviks (Whites) ends

1923
- **January** French and Belgian occupation of the Ruhr in Germany begins
- **24 July** Treaty of Lausanne signed – second peace settlement regarding the Ottoman Empire
- **August** Corfu incident between Greece and Italy

1931
- **June** Hoover Moratorium on reparations
- **18 September** Manchurian Incident and Japanese invasion

1932
- **January** Japanese troops reach Shanghai
- **June–July 1932** Lausanne Conference

1933
- **30 January** Adolf Hitler becomes Chancellor of Germany
- **March** Japan withdraws from the League of Nations
- **June–July** London Conference

1934
- **January** Germany signs Non-Aggression Pact with Poland

1939
- **March** Germany invades Czechoslovakia
- **April** Italy invades and annexes Albania
- **May** Pact of Steel signed between Germany and Italy

1939
- **23 August** Nazi–Soviet Pact signed
- **September** Germany invades Poland; Britain and France declare war on Germany; The USSR invades Poland

1940
- **10 June** Italy declares war on Britain and France

1941
- **22 June** Germany invades the USSR
- **7 December** The Japanese attack the American naval base at Pearl Harbor

1904
- Anglo-French Entente agreed

1905
- Schlieffen Plan completed
- First Moroccan Crisis

1907
- Anglo-Russian Agreement creates the Triple Entente between France, Russia and Britain

1908
- Young Turk Revolt
- Austria-Hungary annexes Bosnia–Herzegovina

1915
- **24 May** Italy declares war on Austria-Hungary

1917
- **2 March** Russian Revolution and abdication of Tsar Nicholas II
- **6 April** The USA enters the war on the side of the Allies

1917
- **25 October** Bolsheviks seize power in Russia
- **November** Russian Civil War between pro-Bolshevik forces (Reds) and anti-Bolsheviks (Whites) begins

1918
- **8 January** President Wilson of the USA announces the Fourteen Points
- **9 November** Abdication of Wilhelm II
- **11 November** German representatives sign armistice with the Allied powers; end of the First World War

1924
- **April** Dawes Plan created
- **October** Geneva Protocol approved by League of Nations

1925
- **August** End of French and Belgian occupation of the Ruhr
- **October** Locarno agreements signed

1928
- Kellogg–Briand Pact signed

1929
- **August** Young Plan created
- **October** Wall Street Crash

1935
- **January** Saar plebiscite returns Saarland to German rule
- **June** Anglo-German Naval Agreement
- **3 October** Italy invades Abyssinia
- **December** Hoare–Laval Pact discussed

1936
- **7 March** Germany remilitarises the Rhineland
- **November 1936** Germany and Japan sign the Anti-Comintern Pact

1936–39
- Spanish Civil War begins

1938
- **March** Germany annexes Austria
- **September** Czech Crisis and Munich Conference

Between 1890 and 1945, international relations – the conduct of relationships between the different nations of the world – were marked by two devastating global conflicts. This book explores the wide-ranging causes for the outbreak of the First and Second World Wars, including concepts such as nationalism, militarism and balance of power. The desire of citizens and politicians to free their own territories from foreign control, or to ensure their state did not fall into decline; the increasing influence of military staff on governments and the need to keep up with their rivals' military capabilities; and the threat to the existing balance of power brought about by these factors were key reasons for the failure of international relations at key points, but there were also notable successes in this period.

Europe and the wider world in the late nineteenth century

The emancipation of the serfs in Russia

For centuries, peasants in Russia were serfs: landless labourers with few legal rights. Serfdom hindered economic progress by discouraging the improvement of land, often preventing serfs from producing surplus crops, thwarting potential for an industrial workforce. Russian military prestige was dented by defeat in the 1854–6 Crimean War, and was attributed to the poor health of conscripted serfs. Tsar Alexander II 'freed' the serfs in 1861, but the wheels of industrial progress were only slowly set in motion.

EXTRACT 1

> The nineteenth century was an extraordinary time of progress in science, industry and education, much of it centred on an increasingly prosperous and powerful Europe. Its peoples were linked to each other and to the world through speedier communications, trade, investment, migration, and the spread of official and unofficial empires. International relations were no longer seen, as they had been in the eighteenth century, as a game where if someone won someone else had to lose. Instead, all could win when peace was maintained. The increasing use of arbitration to settle disputes among nations, the frequent occasions when the Great Powers in Europe worked together to deal with crises and potential conflicts seemed to show that, step by step, the foundations were being laid for a new and more efficient way of managing the world's affairs. War, it was hoped, would become obsolete.

Adapted from Margaret Macmillan, *The War that Ended Peace*, 2013

As Macmillan explains, the nineteenth century was a time of unprecedented change and development for the major countries of Europe. A key facilitator of this change was the Industrial Revolution, which began in Britain in the mid-eighteenth century. Trade between nations increased and people began to demand more political rights. France and Germany increased their industrial production from 1870, while the unwieldy Austro-Hungarian Empire made slower but solid progress thanks to rich reserves of natural resources. Towards the end of the century, the USA began to harness the potential of its abundant raw materials and land. Lagging behind was the sprawling Russian Empire. As you will discover in Chapter 2, Russia continued to face challenges in its industrial and military development, and appeared to be one of the weakest Great Powers.

The impact of socialism and communism

The Industrial Revolution caused huge social as well as economic change. Workers' living and working conditions were poor; as they lived and worked closer together than their ancestors had been, political ideas and agitation for change spread easily. Support for socialist parties increased in Britain, France, Germany and even Russia, where political parties were not yet legal. In 1848, the year of revolutions (see below), Karl Marx published the

Fig. 1 *Slums in London in the late nineteenth century*

Communist Manifesto, which predicted the destruction of capitalism and private property. His ideas had gained thousands of loyal followers by the start of the twentieth century. The impact of the growing popularity of socialism and communism was widespread. Socialists didn't necessarily advocate the overthrowing of governments, but some leaders, especially in Germany before the First World War and Italy after it, feared socialist uprisings and hoped to distract their people from domestic problems with ambitious foreign policies and empire-building. Communism, moreover, was to have a profound effect on Russian foreign policy. Russia, or the USSR as it became in 1922, turned to communism in late 1917 and the foreign policy of many powers after the First World War was based on the fear that communism would spread and suspicion of the world's first communist state. It could be argued that the fear of communism in the interwar period allowed fascist aggressors – Mussolini, Hitler and Franco – to commit acts of violence simply because they were the lesser of two evils.

Fig. 2   *During the 1848 Revolution in Berlin, German nationalism was a popular goal*

A CLOSER LOOK

New political ideologies in the nineteenth and twentieth centuries

Socialism advocated fairer distribution of wealth and better living and working conditions for the working classes, which had deteriorated since the Industrial Revolution. Communism, according to its proponent Karl Marx, was the next stage of socialism. Under this system there would be no private property: factories and farms would be owned and run by the state for the benefit of its workers and the state would then 'wither away'. **Fascism** was the ideological opposite of communism, as it asserted that the weak should be destroyed by the strong, and favoured a nationalistic, authoritarian government.

Nationalism and liberalism

Politically, the major powers of Europe covered a wide spectrum. None were truly democratic, but Britain, Germany and France had the largest **franchises** and the most powerful parliaments. The Russian people had the most limited political rights, closely followed by the Austro-Hungarians. The Austro-Hungarian Empire contained a great number of ethnicities, many of whom wanted to free themselves from the control of the Habsburgs, the ruling family. It is not surprising that the force of **nationalism** was fiercely resisted in the nineteenth century. European governments were greatly alarmed by the revolutions of 1848 which swept the continent in the name of liberalism and nationalism, and this was reflected in their foreign policies.

The governments of France, Italy, Prussia (the largest state of Germany, which was not yet unified) and Austria faced serious rebellions in 1848. The rebellion in the Prussian capital, Berlin, highlighted the people's desire not only for greater political freedom, but also for the Germanic states to be unified as a single country. Their hopes were dashed when King Friedrich Wilhelm IV reasserted his authority, and German unification would only be achieved after a series of wars orchestrated by the formidable Prussian statesman, Otto von Bismarck. That the creation of the German Empire was achieved by military means would have a profound effect on German policy in the years preceding the First World War. The German Empire was created without Austria, which was a power in decline by the late nineteenth century, even after it joined with Hungary to create the Dual Monarchy, or Austro-Hungarian Empire. The danger of the 1848 revolutions to authoritarian regimes convinced the new Austrian Emperor, Franz Joseph,

KEY TERM

fascism: a radical political ideology embracing the values of nationalism and authoritarianism; it is an extreme right-wing viewpoint and its traditional enemy is communism, the extreme left-wing equivalent

franchise: the right to vote in elections, or the portion of the population which is entitled to vote

nationalism: a strong, politicised form of patriotism; many nationalists' goals in the late nineteenth century were focused on gaining independence from an empire or dominant state

KEY TERM

liberalism: political view advocating greater freedoms for civilians, including freedom of speech and of the press, and limits to the power of rulers

that nationalism and **liberalism** were treacherous and poisonous ideals. Franz Joseph, who ruled long enough to sign Austria's declaration of war against Serbia in July 1914, was determined to maintain conservative and authoritarian ideals in Central Europe. This led to a natural alliance with similarly reactionary regimes: Austria-Hungary had ties to Germany and Russia, until clashes with the latter in the Balkan Peninsula made a continued alliance impossible.

Emerging and declining powers in the West and East

The USA and Japan were growing in wealth and importance in the second half of the nineteenth century. The industrial potential of the USA was increasingly exploited, challenging Britain's dominance over world trade. Its main language was English, but the USA was founded on immigration, primarily from Western Europe until the later 1800s, so the Americans did not have strong loyalties towards a single European power when it came to international affairs. In fact, one of its earliest principles was the avoidance of 'entangling alliances', which meant that the USA rarely involved itself in the disputes of other countries and therefore did not have a role in the collapse of peace in 1914. It is, however, arguable that the USA's policy of isolation, resumed after its short involvement in the First World War, contributed to the failure of the League of Nations which in turn enabled aggressors like Hitler to destroy the Versailles peace settlement unchallenged, and led to the Second World War.

Japan was ruled by an Emperor, who held a similar status to that of a god in the State **Shinto** religion. Unlike its larger but poorer neighbour, China, Japan had refused to allow itself to be 'opened up' to Western influences, but in 1854 signed a trade agreement with the USA. A Western-style political constitution was enacted in 1890, giving Japan a parliament, but the Emperor still retained a huge amount of power. With its growing economic strength and dramatic increase in population (it doubled to 70 million between 1873 and 1935), Japan sought to expand. The Japanese gained control of Taiwan and Korea but helped spark conflict with China (1894–5) and Russia (1904–5) as a result. Although Japan gave naval military support to the Allies during the First World War, anti-Western resentment grew among many Japanese in the early twentieth century. Disappointment with their gains under the Treaty of Versailles and the devastating impact of the Great Depression allowed militaristic and imperialist voices to gain strong influence over the Japanese government, leading it to acts of aggression from the 1930s onwards.

While Japanese imperialism was on the rise, the old empire of the Turkish Ottomans was firmly in decline. For much of the nineteenth century, European powers debated what was known as the 'Eastern Question' – what would happen to the Ottoman Empire's European possessions in the Balkans when it finally collapsed? This was to have a significant impact on international relations and bring Austria-Hungary and Russia into frequent dispute.

KEY TERM

Shinto: the state religion of Japan until 1945; centuries old, it involved the worship of ancestors, natural spirits and the Emperor

Themes in International Relations Before 1890

By the standards of the time, the century before the outbreak of war in 1914 was one of relative peace. The last major European conflict was the Napoleonic Wars (1803–15), during which France secured dominance over most of Europe but was defeated at Waterloo and forced to retreat. There are noteworthy comparisons to make between the treatment of France as a defeated aggressor at the Congress of Vienna in 1814–5, and the treatment of Germany at the Paris Peace Conference in 1919, following the First World War. Even after Napoleon returned from exile in 1815 to resume the war,

France was allowed to keep its borders before the conflict in 1792, whereas Germany had to surrender 10 per cent of its territory a century later.

Fig. 3 *The congress system had flaws, but by meeting to discuss potential disputes for the rest of the nineteenth century, it helped to prevent another large-scale European war until 1914*

The congress system

The Congress of Vienna also established the 'congress system', by which leading statesmen met regularly to discuss concerns affecting European relations, especially at times of potential conflict. Although the regularity of these congresses collapsed within a few years, there were notable successes of the congress method well into the later part of the century, such as the 1878 Congress of Berlin which (temporarily) resolved tension over the Balkans, and the 1884–5 Congress which enabled the European powers to establish colonies in Africa without provoking their imperial rivals.

The Crimean War, 1853–6

One of Russia's enduring foreign policy goals in the nineteenth century was the expansion southwards to gain access to the Black Sea, which would afford it warm-water ports and enable shipping trade all year round. This threatened British imperial interests as well as Turkish independence, provoking war between Russia and Britain, France and Turkey in 1854. Russia was defeated in 1856, hindering its restless expansionism, and partially blamed this on the lack of support from Austria, which Russia had considered to be a reliable ally. The beginning of mistrust between Russia and Austria-Hungary, exacerbated by the Eastern Question, would later become a primary cause of the First World War.

The Franco–Prussian War, 1870–1

The final step in Bismarck's plan to achieve the unification of Germany was war against France in 1870–71. The Prussian army won a speedy victory, sending the French Emperor Napoleon III into exile and causing political turmoil in Paris. The newly unified Germany forced a harsh settlement on the French, seizing from them the border territory of Alsace-Lorraine which contained lucrative iron ore and coal mines, and making them pay an 'indemnity' of 5,000 million francs. To add to France's humiliation, the Prussian King was crowned **Kaiser** of Germany in the Palace of Versailles. Afterwards, Bismarck was careful in his foreign policy to keep France isolated, knowing that the French would seek revenge, or *révanche*.

KEY TERM

Kaiser: the German Emperor

Fig. 4 *The Kaiser of the new German Empire, Wilhelm I, had himself crowned in the Hall of Mirrors at Versailles at the end of the Franco–Prussian War*

The conduct of international relations

International relations – the interaction between different countries – was conducted by a well-established system of ambassadors and diplomats. All developed powers had a Foreign Office or equivalent organisation responsible for their country's relationships with other countries and pursuit of foreign policy goals. Foreign secretaries, or foreign ministers in some countries, had the role of directing policy towards other countries, but the amount of autonomy they had from the head of government varied: for example, Edward Grey had considerable freedom to act as British Foreign Minister during the 1914 July Crisis, while German foreign ministers like Bernhard von Bülow took orders directly from the Kaiser at the turn of the century. Ambassadors represented their countries in person, assisted by diplomats, delivering messages and conveying sentiments of friendliness, firmness or hostility depending on the foreign policy of the day. When war broke out, custom dictated that a formal declaration of war be transmitted to the opposing country; when peace was agreed, treaties were used in an effort to maintain peace, but often also to settle upon the victor some 'spoils of war'.

This book will encourage you to reflect on what makes international diplomacy succeed or fail. As you will see in the opening chapters of this book, the foreign policies of each country were motivated by their own interests. Statesmen had to consider the economic, social and political disadvantages of their action or inaction abroad. After decades of relative peace, the decision-makers of the late nineteenth and early twentieth centuries had to manage many conflicting priorities, but there was a general consensus that a large-scale war ought to be avoided.

1 Great Powers: Britain, Germany, Russia, France and Austria-Hungary, c1890–1900

1 The political structures of the Great Powers

Europe's Liberal Democracies

Fig. 1   *Three of the monarchs of the Great Powers were closely related by blood or marriage: Edward VII of Britain (stood far left, third row), Nicholas II of Russia (stood second from left, first row) and Wilhelm II of Germany (seated left) are pictured here, with Queen Victoria (centre) and other members of the Royal Family at Palais Edinburgh, Coburg, in 1894*

In 1890 Europe had two loosely democratic powers: Britain and France. Neither state had **universal suffrage** but they stood apart from the other Great Powers because their heads of state had to work with Parliament. One impact of **democracy** was that the ruling political parties could not ignore public opinion and stay in power; the public mood and the press could, and often did, influence policymaking.

Britain

In 1900, Britain had a Parliament and a hereditary monarchy with limited power. As the British journalist and essayist Walter Bagehot described Queen Victoria's power in 1867, 'the Queen reigns but does not rule'. He also outlined the three rights of the British monarch in relation to their governments: 'the right to be consulted, the right to encourage, the right to warn'. Bagehot also made a distinction between the Queen's formal powers, such as signing state documents; and her 'symbolic and ceremonial' role, which promoted the illusion of greater power. Parliament, led by a Prime Minister, governed the country; the monarch did not have an active role in the day-to-day running of the country.

While Britain in 1900 was by no means a true democracy – suffrage was limited and the Head of State was unelected – its monarchy was limited in power and there was a strong system of **representative government**. The Rule

KEY CHRONOLOGY

1870–1	Franco–Prussian War; establishment of the French Third Republic
1888	Accession of Kaiser Wilhelm II in Germany
1890	Resignation of Bismarck, Chancellor of Germany
1894	Accession of Tsar Nicholas II in Russia

KEY TERM

universal suffrage: extending the right to vote in elections to all adult men and women

democracy: political system in which the people choose their own rulers; in modern states this is usually by electing representatives to sit in a National Assembly or Parliament

representative government: a government that is elected to serve the needs of its citizens

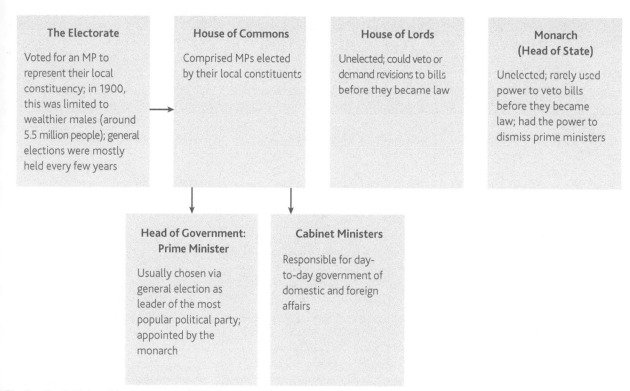

Fig. 2 *The British political system in 1900; the arrows denote the transfer of political power*

A CLOSER LOOK

The House of Lords

The House of Lords had the power to amend or reject legislation passed by the House of Commons. Lords were also allowed to serve as Cabinet Ministers or as Prime Minister. The monarch had the power to appoint new Lords on the advice of the Prime Minister, so while they were not elected by voters, some owed their position to someone who did at least depend on the support of the electorate for their own power, though a large number were hereditary. In 1911 the power of the Lords to amend or reject laws was restricted as a result of their rejection of the 1909 People's Budget.

KEY TERM

veto: the power to prevent a law being passed

foreign policy: a government's strategy in dealing with other nations

of Law ensured that both monarchs and elected representatives had to operate within legal limits; there was also a free press which, though more deferential to authority figures than today, was allowed to criticise policies. At the turn of the century newspapers were growing in circulation, which meant that politicians increasingly had to consider the opinions of a better-informed public.

Monarch and Prime Minister

Queen Victoria retained several powers known as the Royal Prerogatives, all of which were exercised by ministers who were accountable to Parliament. In principle, the monarch could **veto** Acts of Parliament, dissolve parliament, and would appoint and dismiss the Prime Minister. In addition, Victoria was the Commander-in-Chief of the British Army, but this power was delegated to ministers and military chiefs. Matters of foreign policy, including the formulation of treaties with other states, were conducted by the Prime Minister and the Cabinet.

The Prime Minister, although officially appointed by the monarch, obtained his office as leader of the political party that could command a majority in the House of Commons. This was mostly decided by a general election, but if a Prime Minister left office before an election, a new leader was chosen by the most influential members of the ruling party. Britain had an 'unwritten constitution', which meant the rules on how it was governed were not recorded in a legal document; instead the system adhered to a set of 'constitutional conventions', many of which were written down by Professor Albert Dicey in 1885. These 'conventions' expected that ministers resigned when they no longer had the confidence of the House of Commons, and that the monarch had to give their assent to any bill passed by both the Houses of Lords and Commons. The conventions had emerged over time and were traditionally respected.

The British Prime Minister was responsible for domestic and **foreign policy**, and for guiding legislation through the House of Commons and the House of Lords. He had the power to appoint Cabinet Ministers to undertake the day-to-day government of the country, and the power to declare war on other nations. By convention the Prime Minister needed the confidence of the House of

Commons, so he had to take the interests of the electorate – as represented by MPs in the Commons – into account, or risk losing the next general election.

General elections and law-making

The maximum length of a parliament (and therefore the longest amount of time between general elections) was set at seven years by the 1716 Septennial Act. Elections were generally called by the Prime Minister. The electorate voted for a person to represent their constituency in the House of Commons as an MP. MPs also represented one of the political parties. The party with the largest number of MPs usually became the ruling party.

Following the 1884 Representation of the People Act, around 5.5 million Britons (around 60 per cent of the male population) could vote in general elections. Only men were allowed to vote, and they had to be a homeowner, or pay at least £10 a year in rent. Although some working-class men now had political representation, most voters were middle class, so ruling parties tended to focus on representing the interests of the middle class.

Members of both the Houses of Commons and Lords were involved in the 'passage' of a **parliamentary bill** to an Act of Parliament, which then became law. As the franchise increased and the Commons became more democratic, the House of Lords was increasingly viewed as old-fashioned: government by the aristocracy and a burgeoning democracy grew more and more incompatible. The monarch and both Houses had to give their assent to an Act of Parliament for it to become law. Each institution could demand revisions of key terms in legislation, and there might be several passages of a Bill through the Houses, especially if the measure was controversial.

A CLOSER LOOK

British political parties

The two largest parties in 1900 were the Conservatives and the Liberals. The Conservatives had formed a political alliance with the Liberal Unionist party which opposed Irish Home Rule; together they won 402 out of 672 seats in the 1900 general election. The Liberals, who won 183 seats in 1900, favoured Irish Home Rule but became split in the 1890s over the Boer War (see Chapter 3). In other respects the foreign policy of the two parties was broadly similar: both favoured free trade and moderate expansion of the British Empire.

France

The decision-making power of French governments during the Third Republic (1870–1940) was weaker than Britain's. The tender age of the Third Republic was partly responsible for this, as a wide range of small political parties emerged with radically different views on France's future, and also because the ruling party changed frequently in the late nineteenth century. In the 1890s, France had no fewer than ten different prime ministers! Domestic and foreign policies changed regularly as a result.

The President

France was a republic: there was no monarch. The President was Head of State (Emile Loubet in 1900), and was elected (or re-elected) every seven years by the French National Assembly. The French political system was divided into executive and legislative powers. The French President wielded executive power, which meant he could propose laws, appoint ministers, and dissolve the Chamber of Deputies. He was also the commander-in-chief of the army, and undertook key duties in foreign affairs by receiving ambassadors and agreeing treaties with other nations.

A CLOSER LOOK

Many key decisions in domestic and foreign policy were made during Cabinet meetings, unless a change in the law or a popular vote was required, in which case the issue would be debated in the House of Commons and House of Lords.

A CLOSER LOOK

The People's Budget of 1909 aimed to raise taxes to pay for social reforms (such as old age pensions). When it was rejected by the House of Lords, the Commons passed the 1911 Parliament Act preventing the Lords from rejecting an act which had been passed three times in the Commons.

KEY TERM

parliamentary bill: the draft version of an Act of Parliament, often revised before receiving approval

ACTIVITY

Research

As you work through the rest of this chapter use Figure 2, the diagram of the British political system on page 2, to create similar diagrams for France, Russia, Austria-Hungary and Germany.

ACTIVITY

Revision

1. Compile a list of all the different factors that influenced the decision-making of British governments in 1900.
2. Explain the ways in which public opinion might influence policymakers.

France's turbulent recent history

Having become a republic in 1792, France executed its king in 1793. It subsequently became an empire under Napoleon Bonaparte. It restored its monarchy in 1815, and became a republic again in 1848. Napoleon's nephew, Napoleon III, claimed the title of emperor again four years later, only to lose his crown as a result of the Franco–Prussian War (1870–71). The French Third Republic was proclaimed in 1870 and would last until 1940. Against a backdrop of such frequent and sudden change, the political system established at the start of the Third Republic was to experience uncertainty and instability.

The legislature

Like Britain, France had a lower house (the Chamber of Deputies) and an upper house (the Senate) which together made up the National Assembly. One-third of senators remained in office for life, while the remaining two-thirds were elected for nine years by the **electoral college** system. The Chamber of Representatives, meanwhile, was elected every four years by universal male suffrage. Both the Senate and the Chamber could vote on laws and on the budget. The French Prime Minister, as leader of the Council of Ministers, had very similar powers to those of his British counterpart.

Autocracies

Austria-Hungary and Russia were ruled not by parliaments, but by absolute monarchs, making them **autocracies**. This meant that the power of the Austro-Hungarian emperor and of the Russian Tsar was almost unlimited by **constitutions** or strong parliaments: they appointed ministers of their choice, and there was no legal means to remove them from the throne. Germany, the 'odd one out', had elements of both autocracy and democracy.

Russia

Despite increasing pressure from the growing middle classes and intelligentsia, Russian tsars had refused to grant any political reform which would limit their power. Alexander II (who ruled 1855–81) had granted freedom to Russia's serfs and allowed the creation of rural councils (*zemstva*), local district and provincial councils (elected by an indirect system) which favoured landowners but did not exclude peasants. This key political development marked a shift away from the stricter autocracy of previous tsars, but the *zemstva* were often obstructed in their work by the Ministry of Internal Affairs.

Pressure for more political power at a national level was met with resistance from the Tsar. Just as Alexander was about to agree to discuss the beginnings of a possible constitution, he was assassinated by a terrorist group. His successors **Alexander III** (1881–94) and **Nicholas II** (1894–1917) interpreted the assassination as a warning against any further changes to the status quo.

electoral college: an elected body which votes on behalf of a larger group of voters

autocracy: a system of government by which all power is concentrated in the hands of the ruler and officials whom they appoint. Absolute monarchies are also autocracies

constitution: a set of rules on how a country should be governed. A constitutional monarch has their power limited by a constitution

reactionary: policies which demonstrate a negative response to change

Alexander III (1845–94)
Following the assassination of his father in 1881, Alexander III took strong action against opposition groups. His reign, though **reactionary**, was relatively stable. He also steered a careful path in foreign policy.

Fig. 3 *Alexander III*

Nicholas II (1868–1918) had little interest in the actual business of ruling Russia, but was determined not to give up any of his power. Nicholas' failure to address domestic issues, as well as a humiliating defeat in the Russo–Japanese War (1904–5), led to the first Russian Revolution in 1905.

Fig. 4 *Nicholas II*

The Tsar's autocratic rule

The government of Russia was entirely at the command of the Tsar. His imperial edicts (*ukase*) were the law of the land. He appointed and dismissed all ministers, and had no national parliament to answer to. Alexander III, alarmed by the response to his father's reforms, reaffirmed the autocratic power of the tsarist state. He reversed or diluted legislation from the previous reign and reinforced the influence of the Orthodox Church. The power of the *zemstva* was limited by the introduction of 'Land Captains' to the countryside to enforce law and order, as the Land Captains could override local elections and disregard the decisions of the *zemstva*.

By the end of the nineteenth century, several opposition groups, from liberals to Marxists, had emerged seeking a decisive change in Russia's political structure. They had no legal means to influence how Russia was ruled, so their methods were often violent: political assassinations increased in the late nineteenth century, including the Tsar himself in 1881. Alexander III relied on repression to control revolutionary groups. The powers of the police were extended: after 1882, agents could search, arrest, question, imprison or exile not only those who had committed a crime, but any who were thought likely to do so.

The tsars were reliant on the secret police force (*Okhrana*), which was responsible for 'security and investigation'. They intercepted mail and checked up on activities in factories, universities, the army and state, detaining suspects and resorting to torture and executions.

> ### SOURCE 1
>
> In his inaugural speech in 1894, Tsar Nicholas II declared:
>
> It has come to my knowledge that latterly, at some meetings of the *zemstva*, voices have been heard from people who have allowed themselves to be carried away by senseless dreams about the participation of representatives of the *zemstva* in the general administration of the internal affairs of the state. Let it be known that I devote all my strength to the good of my people, but that I shall uphold the principle of autocracy as firmly and unflinchingly as did my ever-lamented father.

ACTIVITY

Evaluating primary sources

Read Source 1.

1. What exactly do you think Nicholas means by the phrase 'senseless dreams'?
2. What can we infer from the fact that Nicholas emphasised these aims at the very beginning of his reign?

Austria-Hungary

Austria-Hungary is often referred to as the Habsburg Empire, after its royal family. It encompassed the modern-day Czech Republic, Slovakia, Slovenia, Croatia and Bosnia, and parts of Italy, Poland, Romania, Serbia and Ukraine. The **Dual Monarchy** of Austria-Hungary emerged as a result of the 1867 ***Ausgleich***, after which Austria and Hungary were ruled by the same Emperor, **Franz Josef** (before 1867, Hungary had been subordinate to the Austrian crown).

Government in Austria and Hungary

As a Dual Monarchy, the two states of shared the same foreign policy and army, and shared a budget for the latter. The two states had separate parliaments and ministers, and the Hungarians in particular were fiercely proud of their political customs and traditions. The agreement setting out the political

A CLOSER LOOK

The Orthodox Church

The Russian Orthodox Church reinforced the Russians' loyalty to the Tsar as a religious duty. The Tsar was head of the church and he ruled the country according to his own conscience, guided by God. In theory, this meant the Tsar's policies should have been unquestionable by his subjects. Meanwhile the strength of the Orthodox religion made Russians more sympathetic to other Orthodox Christians in the Balkans, making the ideals of pan-Slavism more influential on the Tsar (read more about this in Chapter 8).

CROSS-REFERENCE

Marxism, the political ideology behind the political practice of communism is discussed in the Introduction, page xiii.

STUDY TIP

When analysing a written source, remember to consider its context and provenance: who said it, when, and why? Who were they addressing? You should also consider the tone of the writing and whether you can make any inferences about the author's thinking.

KEY TERM

Dual Monarchy: rule of Austria and Hungary by a single monarch, under whom the two states had equal political status

Ausgleich: German for 'agreement' or 'compromise'. The Ausgleich of 1867 was the result of Hungarian attempts to win independence from the Habsburg Empire in 1848–49

CROSS-REFERENCE

The reasons for and implications of German unification are explored in the Introduction, pages xii–xv.

CROSS-REFERENCE

For a summary on socialism and liberalism in Europe at this time, return to the Introduction of this book, page xiv.

independence of each state guaranteed a lot of slow negotiation over issues that emerged later and affected both states, such as the building of railways.

The *Ausgleich* imposed some limits the Emperor's power, but he could still declare war, dismiss both parliaments and appoint ministers to the government. As such, the head of the Austrian government, the Minister-President, owed his position to the Emperor rather than Parliament. As the Emperor was resolutely conservative, no Minister-President could entertain ideas of political reform, and neither Parliament had any real power to influence policymaking. Emperor Franz Joseph was determined to assume as many governmental responsibilities as he could; often taking several months to replace ministers who left office.

The Imperial Council, Austria's legislative body, was divided into two houses: the House of Lords, which was made up of hereditary peers; and the House of Deputies, which, by 1896, was made up of 425 elected representatives. Reform in 1896 had extended the franchise by five million, but the system was strongly weighted in favour of the aristocracy. Only six per cent of the Austrian population could vote in House of Deputies elections. Austrian bills had to be approved by both Houses and the Emperor to become law. The Hungarian parliament, the **Diet**, also had a two-house system: an unelected House of Magnates and an elected House of Representatives. The franchise for electing the latter was even more indirect and complex than its Austrian counterpart, and was based on property qualifications. The electorate comprised only six per cent of the population, and the working classes and smaller nationalities were grossly under-represented.

Germany

After the unification of Germany in 1871, some Germans, particularly **liberals** and **socialists**, hoped that it might become a constitutional monarchy. The **Chancellor**, Otto von Bismarck, disagreed. The German constitution he shaped in 1871 enshrined the power of the Kaiser and the Chancellor, and limited the power of the German Parliament (the Reichstag).

The German constitution

In some ways, the constitution was surprisingly liberal. Approval for laws was needed not just from the Kaiser, his Chancellor and ministers, but also the upper and lower Houses of Parliament. Elections to the Reichstag, the lower house, were set every three years and members could debate laws proposed by the Chancellor. The franchise was easily the largest in Europe: all men over 25 could vote. The constitution guaranteed freedom of speech and law, leading to several political parties which acted like pressure groups, representing different interests.

However, in many ways the German political system was less liberal and democratic than France or Britain. The Kaiser, a hereditary monarch, was responsible for foreign policy and appointed the Chancellor – who did not have to be an elected member of the Reichstag – and other government ministers. He devised policies and laws in consultation with his ministers and the Bundesrat (Upper House), and had the final say in any dispute over the constitution. The limited power of the Reichstag was evident in policymaking: the government did not have to take the Reichstag's views into account, and ministers did not have to answer to it. Moreover, its members could not amend a law or demand the dismissal of any ministers. It did, however, have to approve the annual budget, so the Reichstag often won compromises from the government in exchange for budget increases.

The will of the Kaiser

Under Wilhelm I (1861–88), Bismarck as Chancellor had huge influence over policymaking, but the accession of **Wilhelm II** marked a shift in political power as he was determined to exercise more influence over the affairs of state. He was uninterested in public opinion and the Reichstag, only appointing chancellors he thought he could control, while seeking advice only from those whom he personally favoured. By 1900, Wilhelm was dictating policy, controlling all appointments, legislation and diplomatic moves and had provoked several confrontations with the Reichstag. Moreover, while Germany – like Britain – was a constitutional monarchy, the influence of the military was far greater. This was partly due to a strong tradition of militarism in Prussia (Germany's largest federal state) and a strong pride in the army felt by many Germans; but also Wilhelm's personal interest in the military. High-ranking military officers therefore had a greater influence over decision-making in Germany than their counterparts in Britain and France.

Because the Kaiser and his ministers needed the Reichstag's approval for legislation, government could only work through a system of agreement – or at least compromise – between the Reichstag majority and the Kaiser's ministers. However, as Wilhelm was determined to take a more active role in government, policymaking and diplomacy, while technically ordered by a constitution, he became unpredictable.

Fig. 5   *Kaiser Wilhelm II*

Kaiser Wilhelm II (1859–1941) proved that, as in Russia, the fortunes of authoritarian powers were heavily influenced by the personality of their rulers. He had little interest in working with the Reichstag, and while he left much of the day-to-day government to his ministers, he often intervened to change the course of German policy.

SOURCE 2

Wilhelm II, in his speech to the Reichstag during discussions over his first army bill in 1893:

The draft of the bill concerning the German army, through which a strengthening of our available force would have been achieved, was presented to the last Reichstag. To my great regret the project did not meet with the approval of the representatives of the people. The conviction, unanimously shared by my ministers, that in the face of the development of the other powers' military arrangements this government could no longer put off such a shaping of its military status as should guarantee its safety and its future, led to the decision to dissolve the Reichstag and the calling of new representatives.

Summary

No two political systems of the Great Powers were the same, and how each one was ruled affected how it responded to a crisis. This was further complicated, especially in Germany, by the difference between processes set down by constitutions and what rulers and ministers chose to do in practice. Russia, Germany and Austria-Hungary's political stability was also affected by the personality and effectiveness of their respective rulers. Each government had to take public opinion into account when making decisions, even the more autocratic rulers. They risked assassination or revolution if they failed to govern effectively, whereas the democratic political parties could be voted out of office.

You may come across texts which refer to Germany as an autocracy or even a military autocracy at this time. This is not strictly true, as the Reichstag had the power to approve legislation. The Kaiser, however, increasingly ignored constitutional government after 1900, although he had to rely on the Reichstag to approve the budget, and the military grew more powerful (see Chapters 2 and 5).

Pair discussion

1. In pairs, select one of the Great Powers each and compare their political systems. Discuss which power out of the two would be most effective at making decisions and responding quickly to events. When you've finished, compare another two powers.
2. Which of the two Great Powers do you think have the least in common politically?

Evaluating primary sources

What would be the value of Source 2 to an historian studying the relationship between Wilhelm II and the Reichstag?

ACTIVITY

Summary

Create a summary table of the decision-making processes of each of the Great Powers. You could use the following headings:

Power	Head of State	Head of Government	How were decisions made?	Other observations
Britain				
France				
Russia				
Austria-Hungary				
Germany				

STUDY TIP

It is important to provide a balanced response demonstrating how the judgement in the question can be supported and challenged, with a concluding paragraph that either supports or challenges the judgement. With 'agree/disagree' questions, try to avoid an answer that is too 'black and white', in other words one which either completely agrees or completely disagrees with the statement. There will always be points to both support and challenge the view, although some may be more subtle than others! It would also demonstrate high-quality analytical thinking if you can use the same point to argue both sides.

 PRACTICE QUESTION

'None of the Great Powers deserved to be called a democracy in 1900.' Explain why you agree or disagree with this view.

2 Economic strengths and armed forces

SOURCE 1

↱ RIGHT WING

From an article in the *Daily Mail*, a British tabloid newspaper, commenting on the naval review held to celebrate the coronation of Edward VII in August 1902:

To the casual eye this great fleet, as it lies peacefully at anchor in the historic harbour, makes the bravest of shows. But true wisdom demands that we must look beneath the surface and consider how far it is fit for the purpose for which it was designed. What cannot but strike the observer is that it is much weaker than the fleet assembled in 1897 for the late Queen's Jubilee. No doubt our squadrons are stronger than they were at that date, but there is also the fact that in the meantime a powerful navy has grown up in the North Sea which has to be considered in the balance of power.   *↳GERMANS.*

ACTIVITY

1. What is the author of this article in Source 1 calling for?
2. Which country do you think has 'a powerful navy' stationed in the North Sea?
3. How valuable is this source to an historian studying popular attitudes in Britain at the turn of the century? You should consider what you have learned about the popular press in Britain from Chapter 1.

Fig. 1   *The industrial capacities of most of the Great Powers had been transformed in the nineteenth century*

LEARNING OBJECTIVES

In this chapter you will learn about:

- the reasons for the erosion of Britain's economic supremacy

- the reasons for the rise of the German economy and Germany's increasing industrial strength

- the impact of economic reforms in Russia

- the strengths and weaknesses of the armed forces of the Great Powers.

KEY CHRONOLOGY

1889	Britain passes the Naval Defence Act
1893	Witte becomes Russian Finance Minister; oversees rapid industrialisation
1893	The German Reichstag votes to increase the size of the German army
1898	Germany passes the first Naval Law

– ECONOMIC
– MILITARY
– IMPERIALISM.

Economic strengths

The economies of the Great Powers, though all capitalist by 1900, were at varying stages of development. The global **depression** of the 1870s had a negative impact on Europe's economies, but most nations had recovered well. The Industrial Revolution, spearheaded by Britain in the eighteenth century, meant that the most successful economies were those that had plenty of raw materials; strong population growth to ensure a large workforce; efficient, mechanized methods of production; and good infrastructures to transport raw materials and finished products. Countries that still had a large rural and agricultural population, like Russia, were less developed and by 1890 were convinced of their need to catch up with the rest of Europe.

KEY TERM

depression: a downturn in economic activity, causing nations' economies to shrink. This leads to large-scale unemployment, and often a reduction in trade

Table 1 *The figures give indications of industrial production and capacity in each of the Great Powers, and how they changed around the turn of the century*

State	Year	Population (millions)	Iron and steel output (millions of tonnes)	Coal output (millions of tonnes)	Railway track (miles)
Britain	1890	37	8	184	15625 (1880)
	1900	41	8 (1914)	250	18,750 23,000 (1914)
Germany	1890	49	4	89	26,800
	1900	56	19	110	34,480
Russia	1890	116	1	6	19,000
	1900	130 (1897 census)	5 (1914)	16	31,000 (in 1905)
France	1890	38	2	26	13,750 (1880)
	1900	40 (1914)	5 (1914)	35 (1903)	23,450
Austria-Hungary	1890	42	1	24	3000 (Austria, 1884)
	1900	52 (1914)	3 (1914)	39 (1903)	14,210 (Hungary, 1910)

imperialism: the policy of creating and expanding an empire, or the desire to do so

ACTIVITY

1. As you read through this section, note the figures in Table 1. Which comparisons between years and nations are the most helpful for judging the strengths of each economy?
2. Looking at each of the key indicators in Table 1, how do you think they would help a country to fight a war?

ACTIVITY

Group work

1. Do you think Britain was right to feel frustrated by Germany's economic success?
2. Why do you think Britain remained committed to free trade until the early twentieth century?

The erosion of Britain's economic supremacy

Britain had pioneered the Industrial Revolution and the building of railways which had led to huge industrial and economic growth throughout the nineteenth century. As you will discover in Chapter 3, there was a great upsurge in **imperialism** in the late nineteenth century as the Great Powers rushed to secure the most profitable colonies for their empires. Britain had the largest empire by 1900, and had benefited economically from having greater access to new raw materials, and new markets in which to sell its manufactured goods.

As other powers expanded their own empires, however, Britain's dominance in world trade was challenged. France, Germany, Belgium, Portugal and Russia sought their share of lucrative materials from new colonies in Africa, Asia and South America. From their colonies, European powers bought raw materials such as rubber, palm oil and timber to facilitate their industrial growth. In return they were able to sell manufactured goods, such as chemicals, textiles and machinery, and offer services like banking and shipping to their colonies at a highly profitable rate. By 1900, British production levels were progressing, but it could not compete with the larger workforces and better access to raw materials of the USA and Germany.

Fig. 2 *A British dockyard unloading goods from the Empire in around 1900*

Another factor in Britain's relative industrial decline was its failure to develop new, technologically advanced industries like automobiles and chemicals, which the USA and Germany had embraced with more enthusiasm.

Unemployment increased in the 1890s, and a series of strikes affected industrial production as **trade unions** became more militant. In terms of industrial exports, Britain's share of world trade dropped to 10 per cent in 1910, half that of Germany's, and a quarter of the USA's. British industrialists put pressure on the government to abandon the principle of free trade and instead introduce tariffs to protect Britain's trade with the Empire from foreign competition.

The rise of the German economy

The output of heavy industry, particularly coal, iron and steel, were key indicators of a nation's industrial strength. Each of these commodities was necessary to power and supply factories and to produce a wide range of tools and goods. Heading into the twentieth century, German industrial output had already eclipsed Britain's, and was second only to the USA in terms of its production. This boom was brought about by a number of factors:

- Unification meant that raw materials could now be shared across the whole state. Manufactured goods could be transported more easily and there was a common currency and system of weights and measures, making business transactions easier.
- A substantial increase in population (from 41 million in 1871 to almost 50 million in 1891) provided both a ready workforce and a larger market for goods. Industry employed 60 per cent of the working population.
- The new colonies gained in the 1880s and 1890s gave Germany access to new raw materials and markets.
- Bismarck had reintroduced tariffs in 1878. This system of **protectionism** ensured that German goods, especially agricultural products, were cheaper for German consumers than foreign imports. The taxes placed on imports were a welcome source of income for the government.

Germany's combined iron and steel production stood at 4 million tonnes in 1890; although this was half that of Britain, the figure more than quadrupled by 1914. Its coal output was more than treble that of France, in part due to the German annexation of Alsace-Lorraine, an area rich in coal and iron ore. Germany's industrial success worried other powers: the French had been fearful of another German attack since their defeat in the Franco–Prussian war in 1871, and realised that Germany's booming industry would make its army even more formidable. The British also lamented the decline in their share of world trade. Hugo Stinnes, a German industrialist, said at the start of the twentieth century: 'Just let another three or four years of calm development go by and Germany will be the uncontested economic master in Europe.'

Economic reform in Russia

The transformation in the Russian economy had begun in the reign of Alexander II in response to the humiliation of defeat in the **Crimean War** (1854–6). A railway-building programme had started and there was some small-scale development of factories – some state-owned and geared to the manufacture of armaments, and others in the hands of foreigners. However, by 1881 Russia's economic development still lagged far behind that of Western Europe and there was a huge gulf between Russia's potential, given its vast supplies of natural resources and manpower, and the country's actual levels of achievement. It was not until the reign of Alexander III that a real 'industrial revolution' took off and its development owed much to Alexander's and Nicholas II's finance ministers, Ivan Vyshnegradsky and **Sergei Witte.**

KEY TERM

trade union: workers' organisations which campaign for better pay and conditions

protectionism: a policy designed to 'protect' domestic businesses from foreign competition by imposing a duty (or tariff)

CROSS-REFERENCE

The process of German unification is explored in the Introduction.

A CLOSER LOOK

Consequences of protectionism

Protectionism was increasingly used (France, Austria and Russia as well as Germany had imposed their own tariffs before 1900), and while helping the development of Europe's economies, it had significant consequences. As the price of many agricultural products, particularly bread, was artificially increased, the living conditions of the poor declined. In Germany and France, support for socialist parties amongst the working classes increased, while supporters of tariffs shifted their allegiance from liberal politicians to conservatives. Discouraging trade between countries also made them less likely to cooperate with each other on other matters. A key example of **tariffs** damaging international relationships was Russia's angry reaction to Germany's tariff on Russian grain imposed in 1892.

CROSS-REFERENCE

The issue of tariffs became serious for the global economy again during the Great Depression. See Chapter 18, page 154 for more details on this.

CROSS-REFERENCE

The Crimean War is explored in the Introduction on page xv.

Fig. 3   *Sergei Witte*

Sergei Witte (1849–1915) started
as a railway executive before serving
as a highly capable finance minister
from 1893. From 1905 to 1906 he
was Nicholas II's chief minister,
helping him to tame and then
suppress the first Russian Revolution.
He was sacked in 1906, and later
unsuccessfully warned Nicholas
against Russian involvement in the
First World War.

The causes and impact of the
emancipation of the serfs, including
redemption payments and the *mir*,
are explored in the Introduction.

mir: a peasant commune

You will find out more about
the Franco–Russian Alliance in
Chapter 4.

Russia's 'great spurt' of industrialisation

Ivan Vyshnegradsky and Sergei Witte adopted similar policies – improving
the Russian economy by increasing indirect taxes, negotiating loans,
reducing imports and expanding exports, particularly of grain. Through
the Tariff Act of 1891 Russian iron, industrial machinery and raw cotton
became heavily protected against outside competition. Witte was totally
committed to economic modernisation, believing it would raise standards
of living, thus curbing unrest and revolutionary activity and preserving
Russia's Great Power status. Witte also brought in engineers and managers
from Western Europe for advice and to encourage investment. Between
1880 and 1900, foreign investment increased tenfold to over 900 million
roubles.

The Russian rail network expanded dramatically at the end of the nineteenth
century: the state bought private companies in order to facilitate more
rapid construction. By 1890, the average annual railway construction was
568 miles per year. Meanwhile, heavy industry was also expanding as Witte
attempted to reorganise Russia's factories, concentrating industrial labour
in large factory units of over 1000 workers. One of the most successful
factories was the Putilov Works which reproduced its success in rail
production to machinery, artillery and steel goods. The factory's workforce
grew by 2000 in three years, and Putilov later competed successfully with
Krupp in Germany.

Russia's annual rate of growth stood at 8 per cent between 1894 and
1904, the highest of any industrial country. However, inhibitors of progress
persisted. Textiles rather than heavy industry still dominated by 1910, and
agricultural reforms were long overdue. Although the rural economy provided
a livelihood for 80–90 per cent of the Russian population, it was largely
ignored or sacrificed in the interests of industrialisation until around 1906.
Most farming was small-scale and in the hands of former serfs and state
peasants, tied to their local *mir* by the redemption dues they were repaying. In
the years of good harvest, farmers' incomes remained low because bread prices
were kept down – while in the bad years (1891–2, 1897, 1889, 1900), peasants
faced starvation.

Witte championed the improved efficiency of agriculture in order to
increase Russia's grain exports and raise the necessary capital for
industrialisation. He ensured that the Ukrainian coal and oil from the
Caucasus were exploited, and oversaw the beginnings and growth of industries
new to Russia: steel, petroleum and chemicals. Despite this impressive increase
in production and the modernisation of banking, however, the Russian state
had fallen into debt.

France and Austria-Hungary

French industrial progress was steady but slow compared to Germany's.
Fortunately for France, a new source of iron ore was discovered and her
heavy industry was maintained, albeit on a comparatively small scale.
However, France had a relatively small industrial workforce, with much of the
population working on the land. Of all the active French workers, 52 per cent
were in the agricultural sector in 1870, which declined to just over 40 per cent
by 1914 (by comparison, Britain and Germany's agricultural workers in
1910 made up 9 per cent and 37 per cent of their populations respectively).
The 1892 Méline Tariff introduced protective tariffs on all industrial and
agricultural imports, which contributed to France's self-sufficiency –

90 per cent at the turn of the century – and its place as the world's third biggest producer of wheat.

With the exception of the motor industry, France lagged well behind its competitors in the 'new' industries, however. New technological advances saw a boom in electricals, motorcars and chemicals. Near the start of the twentieth century, Germany was leading the way: companies such as Siemens and Mercedes were becoming household names.

Austria-Hungary had many economic benefits, including a strong agricultural sector and good access to resources. Its two capital cities, Vienna and Budapest, were centres of culture and education. Austria-Hungary had also, like Germany, begun production of new technologies: the Skoda engineering works, for example, was a well-known manufacturer of large guns. However, the Dual Monarchy had been slow to modernise and its economic growth was accordingly stunted at an average of 1.7 per cent per year, lower even than Russia's. It was a smaller player in world trade and the Austro-Hungarian government debt was on the rise. Moreover, although the output of agriculture, forests and fisheries was to rise by 85 per cent in the first 13 years of the twentieth century, the Habsburg Empire's agricultural strength had been threatened in the 1890s by the great influx of cheap American crops: only protective tariffs had prevented the irreversible decline of Hungary's wheat farming. Meanwhile, in Austria and Hungary around two thirds of the population still earned their living from the land, hampering the development of industry.

The relative strengths of the armed forces

As there had not been a major European war since 1870–1, the pressure on the Great Powers to maintain a large army was relatively low in the 1890s. Most conflicts in the late nineteenth century were fought in the colonies, either to defend or expand Europe's overseas territory. Fighting against native peoples was rarely an even contest, as the European nations had far more advanced weaponry. This led to a degree of complacency, especially amongst British military commanders. However, the advent of such deadly new equipment as the **Maxim machine gun** and barbed wire ensured that warfare now had the potential to inflict greater numbers of casualties than ever before.

Fig. 4 *The Great Powers, especially Britain, fought in several colonial conflicts in the late nineteenth century. In this painting of the Battle of Isandlwana, note the difference in technology between the two sides*

ACTIVITY

Thinking point

Why do you think new industries became so important at this time?

CROSS-REFERENCE

The Dual Monarchy is explained in Chapter 1.

ACTIVITY

Group discussion

Discuss in pairs or groups how you would rank the economies of the Great Powers by 1900. You could take into consideration their potential for future growth.

KEY TERM

Maxim machine gun: this was invented in 1884, and could fire up to 600 rounds per minute. This made shooting accuracy far less important as shots could be fired rapidly enough in the general direction of a target to hit it within seconds

KEY TERM

conscription: the compulsory drafting of all men of military age into the armed forces

battleship: a large, armoured war vessel equipped with heavy weaponry

CROSS-REFERENCE

The Second Boer War is discussed in relation to British imperialism in Chapter 3.

Fig. 5 HMS Majestic, built in 1895, was the largest battleship that had ever been made

British naval strength

With the advantage of the English Channel, Britain had less reason to fear invasion. As such the British army was relatively small given her imperial power (430,000 troops in 1901) and **conscription** was not used. Its role was to protect the British Empire around the world from local insurrections or invasions by competing empires, and as such the army in the second half of the nineteenth century had seen action in Egypt, the Zulu Kingdom and South Africa. These expeditionary campaigns, against armies whose weapons and training were inferior to Britain's, left the army relatively unprepared for large-scale campaigns against similarly equipped powers. Moreover, the British Army's performance in the **Second Boer War** had provided a shock for the government and the public: an anticipated easy victory over the Boer people in South Africa turned into a long and difficult conflict due to the poor condition of British recruits and ineffective tactics.

With the public mood generally opposed to high military spending, the British army had only increased in size to just over 730,000 in 1914 despite the arms race between other Great Powers in the preceding years. Despite its small size by contemporary standards, the army had been through a series of reforms in the 1870s and 1880s which reduced soldiers' length of service, improved conditions and based promotion on merit rather than wealth or connections.

The fact that Britain possessed both the largest empire and the largest navy in 1900 was no coincidence. **Battleships** were needed to defend the Empire, while merchant ships transported goods and materials to and from British colonies. Politicians and naval commanders recognised the necessity of a superior navy and for many years had followed the 'two power standard'. This meant that Britain had to maintain a fleet at least as big as the next two largest navies combined. The standard was enshrined in law with the passage of the Naval Defence Act in 1889, which authorised the spending of £21.5 million for the construction of ten battleships, 42 cruisers and 18 torpedo gunboats. Battleships were considered the most important and necessary of the new vessels: indeed Lord Hamilton, First Lord of the Admiralty, asserted that the 'two power standard' applied to battleships 'of the newest type'.

Unfortunately for Britain, however, the German Kaiser, Wilhelm II, had been able to admire the pre-eminence of the British navy at first hand. As a grandson of Queen Victoria, he visited the British naval dockyards and became convinced of Germany's need to catch up.

SOURCE 2

Speaking at a dinner party in 1904 to celebrate King Edward VII's visit to the German naval base at Kiel, Kaiser Wilhelm II said:

When, as a little boy, I was allowed to visit Portsmouth and Plymouth hand-in-hand with kind aunts and friendly admirals, I admired the proud English ships in those two superb harbours. Then there awoke in me the wish to build ships of my own like these someday, and when I was grown up to possess as fine a navy as the English.

CROSS-REFERENCE

The Anglo-German naval race intensified with the introduction of the dreadnought battleship, as explained in Chapter 5.

In 1897 Wilhelm II replaced the cautious German naval minister with the more aggressive Admiral von Tirpitz. Tirpitz convinced the Reichstag to pass the first of several naval bills which aimed to increase the German navy to the size of Britain's. This clashed directly with Britain's Naval Defence Act, and marked the beginning of the Anglo-German naval race.

German military strength

The most formidable power, in terms of its army, was Germany. There were a number of reasons for this:

- Germany's strong economy made high military spending possible. Its booming population also meant more potential soldiers.
- Prussia, the most powerful region within Germany, had a strong tradition of military success. Pride in the German army was extremely high amongst its citizens, and the defeat of France in 1870 provided recent propaganda to glorify the army. The Prussian officer class had a large amount of influence on government policy; this had continued since the eighteenth century when the Prussian army was described as 'an army with a state', rather than a state with an army.
- Wilhelm II, Kaiser since 1888, was very competitive and took a keen interest in military matters. When he came to the throne, his first speech was addressed to the army.

SOURCE 3

Kaiser Wilhelm II addressing the German Army in Berlin on 16 June 1888, the day after he became Kaiser (the speech was reported in newspapers around the world):

It is from a deeply moved heart I address my first words to my army, but the confidence with which I step in to the place to which God's will calls me is immovably strong. I refer you to my beloved father, who, as crown prince, already won a place of honour in the annals of the army, and to a long line of glorious ancestors, whose names shine brightly in history, whose hearts beat warmly for the army. We belong to each other, me and the army. We were born for each other, and will indissolubly cleave to each other, whether it be the will of God to send us calm or storm. You will soon swear allegiance and submission to me and I promise ever to bear in mind that from the world above, the eyes of my forefathers look down on me, and that I shall one day have to stand accountable to them for the glory and honour of the army.

ACTIVITY

Evaluating primary sources

1. Do you think the Kaiser's speech in Source 3 would worry Germany's neighbours?
2. Based on Source 3 only, what kind of ruler does Wilhelm II appear to have been?

With the Kaiser's support, the professional core of the army was allowed to expand, which was a key aim of high-ranking military officers worried about the recent agreement between its neighbours France and Russia, first established in 1892. Pressure from Chief of Staff von Schlieffen convinced Leo von Caprivi, Bismarck's successor as chancellor, to introduce a military bill, passed in 1893, to increase the size of the army by 84,000 soldiers.

Russian strength in numbers

By 1900, all of the Great Powers except Britain had a policy of conscription. This gave each of them access to millions of troops, as well as a core of professional soldiers and reservists (trained soldiers who had other jobs during peacetime). With the largest population – around 135.6 million – and conscription, the Russian army with around 1,162,000 soldiers was the largest in the late nineteenth century, but its reputation was poor. The soldiers' training was inferior to that of Germany and many of its recruits were peasants whose poor living conditions contributed to low levels of health and fitness. The Russian government, though overseeing long-awaited industrial development, could not yet afford to equip its soldiers as well as the other powers, despite the Putilov Works expanding its production to armaments.

French and Austro-Hungarian armed forces

In contrast to the German army, the military of both France and Austria-Hungary lacked a secure position in their respective cultures and societies,

CROSS-REFERENCE

The Franco–Russian Alliance and its origins are explored in Chapter 4.

The expansion of the German naval fleet was part of *Weltpolitik*, which is covered in Chapter 3.

which hampered possible improvements to training and efficiency. There were disagreements in French military circles as to what their army was for. Left-wing thinkers wanted an army for the people, used only for self-defence, while conservatives preferred a professional army akin to that of Germany. In the Habsburg Empire the army was a focus for rivalry between its two states. Traditionally the Austro-Hungarian army had been the preserve of German-speaking Austrians, who sought to emulate Prussian military success. By the start of the twentieth century a fierce political debate was looming over the role of Hungarians in the army.

Summary

- With its booming industry and superior army, Germany had the most reason to feel confident at the turn of the century.
- Britain relied on its navy to maintain its empire, but its share of world trade was falling as it competed with Germany and the USA.
- Russia was beginning to overcome centuries of economic underdevelopment, but its army and navy needed more investment.
- French and Austro-Hungarian industry was making steady, but comparatively slow progress. Both countries' armies lacked support from the majority of their populations.

ACTIVITY

Summary

Create a series of cards for each of the Great Powers to include a summary of the following information:
- population
- economic strength
- army strength
- naval strength.

Include statistics where possible. Arrange your card pack in order from the strongest to the weakest nation, and justify the order to your group.

STUDY TIP

When you need to consider two sides of an argument, plan your answer first. Identify multiple points for each side, and also plan precise evidence you can use to support each point you make.

 PRACTICE QUESTION

'Russia had a weak economy in 1900.'
Explain why you agree or disagree with this view.

STUDY TIP

When judging the value of a source, a key feature to consider is the authority of the author: were they in a position to know key information about the topic in question? Although the question asks you to consider a single source, when you progress to A level questions you are required to use multiple sources.

 PRACTICE QUESTION

With reference to your understanding of the historical context, assess the value of Source 3 to an historian studying the strength of the German army in the late nineteenth century.

3 Empires and rivalries

From a speech delivered to the British House of Commons on 20 March 1893 by **Joseph Chamberlain**, a Liberal Unionist MP:

The people of this country are determined they will take their full share in these new lands in Africa and in the work of civilisation they have to carry out there. They are justified in that determination – justified by the spirit of the past, justified by that spirit of adventure and enterprise which has made us, of all nations, particularly fitted to carry out the work of colonisation. We are the only nation which has been able to carry out this work without great cost to ourselves. Take the case of France: Algeria costs to the French exchequer large sums annually. The same is true with regard to Tunis, and also of the foreign possessions of Germany, and of Italy in Abyssinia. If we are not going to give up this mission of colonisation, let us be prepared for some sacrifice of life and money. This country has declared that it is our duty to take our share in the work of civilisation in Africa.

The 'Scramble for Africa'

Although Britain, France and Russia's empires had grown moderately in the first half of the nineteenth century, many policymakers and businessmen were beginning to question whether the income generated from imperial trade was worth the cost of maintaining control over their colonies. However, after 1870 this attitude began to change significantly, resulting in two 'scrambles' for territory in Africa and China, as well as creating considerable tension between the empire-builders. Britain sought to maintain her empire, while France and Germany hoped to increase theirs. Russia, meanwhile, aimed to expand her influence in three different areas.

Key
- Britain
- France
- Germany
- Russia

0   500 km

Fig. 1   *The territories and colonies of four of the Great Powers by 1914*

The beginning of the Scramble

Given the huge advantages imperialism offered by means of trading wealth, the Great Powers came to measure their status (and that of others) by the size of their empires. With the largest empire, Britain's status as an imperial power had been unchallenged for decades, but by the nineteenth century other

KEY PROFILE

Joseph Chamberlain (1836–1914) was Secretary of State for the Colonies between 1895 and 1903. A passionate believer in British imperialism and tariff reform, he commanded much influence. Chamberlain fiercely defended Britain's involvement in the Second Boer War (1899–1902), but failed to prevent his Liberal Unionist Party's defeat in the 1906 general election.

ACTIVITY

Evaluation primary sources

What can be learned from Chamberlain's speech in Source 1 about:

a. the attitude of the British government towards empire-building and colonisation?

b. the reasons why the Great Powers wanted to establish colonies in Africa?

c. the potential disadvantages of colonisation?

SOCIAL DARWINISM:
⤷ survival of the fittest
⤷ individuals + groups
   are subject to the same
   laws of natural selection

A CLOSER LOOK

Unlike the 'British Empire', the phrase 'German Empire' is potentially confusing. The German Empire is used to describe the different Germanic states that made up unified Germany from 1871 onwards, and does not refer to its collection of overseas colonies. This is also true of the Russian Empire and the Austro-Hungarian Empire, as each comprised different nationalities under one ruler. The distinction between these and colonial or overseas empires will be made clear in this book, but be wary when looking at other sources of the difference between the two.

ACTIVITY

Thinking point

Why do you think no African delegates were invited to the Berlin Conference?

KEY TERM

protectorate: territory over which a foreign power has political authority

powers began to envy the prestige Britain's Empire brought her. A large empire meant more than wealth: it also gave the mother country political influence overseas and strategically important military bases.

European control over Africa leapt from 10 per cent of the continent in 1880 to 90 per cent in 1900. The unprecedented rush to secure African possessions was triggered by a number of developments:

- The 1870s depression encouraged European businesses to seek new or cheaper raw materials overseas.
- The Ottoman Empire, which had contained North African regions on the Mediterranean coast for centuries, was now in decline. French and British rivalry over influence in Egypt then erupted, and came to a crisis point in 1882 when British forces invaded Egypt to crush unrest in the area. Egypt contained the Suez Canal, which was hugely important for world trade.
- King Leopold of Belgium initiated a new tactic of staking claims to overseas territory in the Congo. After making commercial treaties with tribal chiefs, the Belgians then claimed to have established an influence over the region. This prompted France, Britain, Portugal and Germany to dispute Belgium's claims.

An international conference was arranged in Berlin in 1884 to settle the matter. A relatively small proportion of Africa had been colonised in 1878, but in the following six years there were disputes over East and West Africa and the Congo.

ACTIVITY

Listen to the 'Berlin Conference' episode of the BBC Radio 4 programme *In Our Time*, available at: http://www.bbc.co.uk/programmes/b03ffkfd. Draw up a list of the main causes and consequences of the Scramble for Africa.

The Berlin Conference, 1884–5

Representatives of Britain, France, Germany, Portugal, Belgium, Austria-Hungary and Italy met between November 1884 and February 1885. Among the issues raised was the division of territories already disputed, and the process by which a country could stake its claim over territory in the future. The latter was resolved with the principle of 'effective occupation'. This ensured that countries already had an established physical presence in the prospective colony before they could claim it.

The formal division of much of the African continent was begun with very little regard for existing tribal structures. There were no Africans at the conference, and only two of the delegates had ever been in Africa. As Britain had the greatest established influence before the Scramble, by agreeing to the conference in the first place her dominance over the continent now ceased – Africa was 'up for grabs'. Much of Britain's African empire had been 'informal'; that is, it consisted of trade routes and trading posts rather than official **protectorates**.

The Berlin Conference did not end the scramble for territory in Africa; if anything, it tightened European control over the continent. Now that the accepted 'rules' of colonisation had been established, the powers hurried to make good on their claims. Britain's informal empire was formalised and extended: it could now count Egypt, Sudan, Somalia, British East Africa, Rhodesia and much of South Africa as colonial possessions. France secured a large swathe of territory around the Sahara Desert, including important trading posts in Morocco, the Ivory Coast and the French Congo. Germany, not yet in the thralls of *Weltpolitik*, secured the smaller total area of the Cameroons, German South West Africa, Togoland and German East Africa. Italy, like Germany a newcomer to empire-building, gained Italian Somaliland and Eritrea, but was humiliated by its failed attempt to conquer Abyssinia in 1895–6 when Italian forces were defeated at the Battle of Adwa. This is the only nineteenth-century example of an African state defeating a European colonising force.

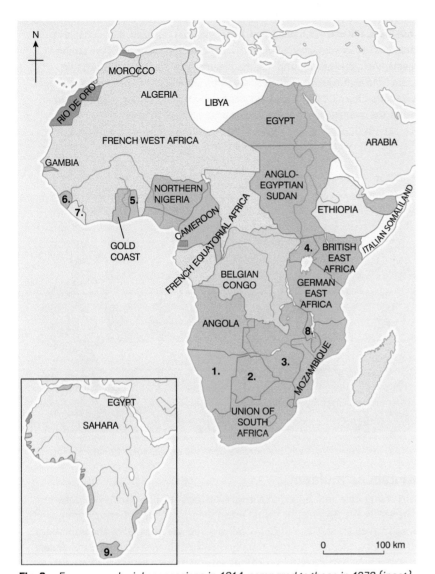

Fig. 2 *European colonial possessions in 1914, compared to those in 1870 (inset)*

The spread of influence over Africa as agreed at the Berlin Conference did help to prevent a European war breaking out over colonies, but their African empires gave the Great Powers new borders and more potential for disputes over them. Perceived expansion near to another country's colony often elicited huge concern and outraged condemnation by imperial rivals: businessmen often raised concerns about competition and disruption to trading routes, while politicians often stressed the potential loss of prestige by allowing such action to go unchallenged. Source 2 highlights one such dispute over Mozambique in East Africa:

ACTIVITY

Study Figure 2 and discuss with a partner where you think disputes over colonial rivalry were most likely to erupt.

SOURCE 2

Lord Salisbury in a letter to Queen Victoria, 23 December 1889. At this time Portugal had a sphere of influence in Mozambique which was challenged by the British. Zanzibar was a British protectorate:

Lord Salisbury with his humble duty to Your Majesty respectfully submits that, from the telegraph he has received this morning, it seems probable that the Portuguese Government will refuse to give the undertaking not to interfere with the settlements of British subjects, and the protected chiefs, which has been required of them. In that case, it has been agreed by the Cabinet to recommend

ACTIVITY

Evaluating primary sources

1. With reference to Source 2, what reason does Salisbury give for occupying Mozambique?
2. From this source, what can be learned about the potential for conflict created by imperial rivalries?

A CLOSER LOOK

Weltpolitik *WORLD POLICY.*

By 1890 Germany had colonies in East and South West Africa and with Bismarck's resignation came a new appetite for German imperial expansion. It was a hugely popular policy, and it had the emphatic support of Wilhelm II. Being so closely related to the British royal family, Wilhelm was keen to emulate Britain's large empire. He believed these two interlocking factors would secure Germany's destiny as a superior nation. *Weltpolitik* ('world policy') was supported by right-wing groups such as the Pan-German League, the Colonial League and the Navy League.

ACTIVITY

Pair discussion

Using this chapter, the map of colonised Africa, on page 19, and your own further research, discuss with a partner which of the Great Powers you think benefited the most and which benefited the least from the Scramble for Africa.

KEY TERM

Boers: the descendants of the Dutch who had settled in South Africa in the eighteenth century

that the island of Mozambique shall be temporarily occupied. It is probable that the Portuguese Government dare not give way on account of the strong feeling there is in Lisbon, and that they themselves would not be sorry that Great Britain should take some decisive step showing her to be in earnest over the matter. The negotiations are not yet concluded, but in case they should end badly, the requisite naval force is being assembled at Zanzibar.

Fig. 3 *In this French cartoon, Bismarck is depicted as slicing up the 'cake' of Africa*

The Fashoda Incident

Britain and France both hoped to consolidate their existing African colonies in the late 1890s. For Britain, this would mean securing a line of territory from South Africa to Egypt, and a 'Cape to Cairo' railway line was planned by the imperialist Cecil Rhodes to facilitate trade and stamp British influence on the area. France, meanwhile, aimed to expand its own influence eastwards from its colonies in West and Central Africa. These two policies clashed in the Sudan in 1898.

The governments of Britain and France sent troops to protect their claims in the Sudan. In the town of Fashoda on the River Nile, the two armies met but did not engage each other in combat. Despite a whirlwind of nationalistic fervour amongst the general public, the French realised that Britain's superior navy would ensure a British victory, and both sides backed down. In March 1899 the two powers agreed on the boundaries of each other's spheres of influence in the region. The Fashoda Incident marked the last major colonial clash between Britain and France.

The Second Boer War, 1899–1902

Tension between the British colonies of Cape Colony and Natal, and in the neighbouring **Boer** republics (Transvaal and the Orange Free State) had been increasing for decades. The Boer leaders resented the encroaching British influence in the region, and were determined to resist Britain's attempts to unify the South African region as one colony. The independent republics in South Africa were therefore a stumbling block to British imperial ambitions. In 1881 the First Boer War had forced Britain to recognise the independence of the Boers. The Boers continued to refuse any foreign political influence in their states, and the discovery of gold in the Transvaal frustrated the British even further: gold could transform the economy of the republic and make it more likely to resist future colonisation.

Cecil Rhodes, a British businessman who became Prime Minister of the neighbouring Cape Colony in 1890, was determined to help the British realise their aim of extending control over all of South Africa. When the government of Paul Kruger, President of the Transvaal, restricted the voting rights of 'uitlanders' (foreigners who had travelled to the region to take advantage of the gold discovery), many of whom were British, relations between the Boers and the British were further strained. In 1895 an uitlander uprising known as the Jameson Raid, planned by Rhodes and Chamberlain, only succeeded in convincing the Boers that their independence was seriously under threat.

With the Transvaal refusing to improve conditions for uitlanders, Britain resumed its conflict with the Boers in 1899, expecting its superior military resources to secure a quick and easy victory (as many did at the start of the First World War, soldiers went to war confidently predicting that it would be 'over by Christmas'). British confidence proved unfounded as the Boers resisted their attacks with **guerrilla** tactics. As the war dragged on, British commanders, including Lord Kitchener, who would serve as the Secretary of State for War in 1914, resorted to more desperate measures. The use of concentration camps to contain Boer civilians soon drew condemnation from the other European powers. Kaiser Wilhelm II was quick to capitalise on Britain's difficulties in the region by sending a message to Paul Kruger in 1896. Known as the Kruger telegram, it congratulated the president on resisting British ambitions in southern Africa. Wilhelm went on to make his support for the Boers very clear, to the great irritation of London.

KEY TERM

guerrilla: fighting involving 'undercover' methods of attacking a stronger enemy; guerrillas often set traps and used ambush tactics, rather than engaging their opponents using traditional methods, to give them a greater chance of victory

Fig. 4 *Although they eventually lost the Second Boer War, the Boers' avoidance of traditional tactics made the British victory much harder than anticipated*

SOURCE 3

Kaiser Wilhelm's telegram to President Kruger on 3 January 1896 following the Jameson Raid, a failed attempt by British troops to incite an uprising against the Boers:

I express to you my sincere congratulations that you and your people, without appealing to the help of friendly powers, have succeeded, by your own energetic action, against the armed bands which invaded your country as disturbers of the peace, in restoring peace and in maintaining the independence of the country against attack from without.

ACTIVITY

Evaluating primary sources

How valuable is Source 3 for an understanding of Anglo-German relations in 1896?

Russo–Austria-Hungary rivalry in the Balkans

The Balkan region in the south-east of Europe had seen dramatic change in the nineteenth century. As the power of the Ottoman Turks declined, individual nations including Greece, Montenegro and Serbia had achieved their independence by 1900. Two neighbours of the Balkans (a peninsula region in south-east Europe) saw this situation very differently:

- Austria-Hungary, already deeply concerned about the increase in **nationalism** within its empire, viewed the newly independent Balkan states as a potential threat. Emperor Franz Joseph ruled over a wide range of ethnicities, many of whom wanted independence and could now look to Serbs, Montenegrins and Bulgarians for inspiration. In the late nineteenth century, Austria-Hungary's policy was to maintain friendly relations with its Balkan neighbours.
- Russia saw a useful opportunity to increase its international political influence. Again, ethnicity was a vital factor: the majority of Russians were Slavs, as were many Balkan peoples. Russia hoped to set up the newly independent states as **client states**, and ensure their long-term loyalty to Russia.

CROSS-REFERENCE

The concept of nationalism is explained in the Introduction, page xiii.

KEY TERM

client states: smaller nations given economic, political and often military assistance by larger countries in return for their loyalty

CROSS-REFERENCE

The extent and status of the Ottoman Empire is explored later in this chapter: see page 24.

To read more about how pan-Slavism developed after Russia's defeat in the Russo–Japanese War, go to chapter 5, pages 35–36.

The very different aims of Russia and Austria-Hungary in the Balkans had already provoked two crises in the late nineteenth century. After its victory in the Russo–Turkish War in 1878, Russia imposed the harsh Treaty of San Stefano on the Turks which would have significantly increased Russia's territory and influence in the Balkans. This was unacceptable to the other powers and Austria-Hungary in particular. An international congress was arranged in Berlin to limit Russia's gains. Italian historian Luigi Albertini gave his perspective on the winners and losers of Congress of Berlin:

EXTRACT 1

Turkey had lost half her European territory; Bulgaria received only half of what was assigned to her by the Treaty of San Stefano; Serbia had been done out of Bosnia–Herzegovina. Russia had seen the fruits of her victory vanish, while Austria had won two large Slav provinces (Bosnia and Herzegovina) without sacrifice.

Adapted from Luigi Albertini, *The Origins of the War of 1914,* 1952

A CLOSER LOOK

Two significant conferences took place in Berlin in the late nineteenth century. The 1878 Conference decided the borders of the remaining Ottoman Empire and the newly independent Balkan states following the Russo–Turkish War of 1877–8. In 1884 the Great Powers met in Berlin to resolve imperial disputes over African colonies.

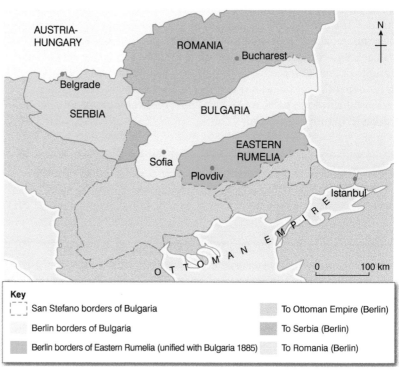

Fig. 5   *The new borders of the Balkan region following the Treaties of San Stefano and Berlin*

ACTIVITY

Thinking point

Germany and Britain were concerned about the situation in the Balkans. Why do you think this was?

The Berlin Conference did avert conflict between Russia and Austria-Hungary in the late nineteenth century, but failed to provide a long-term solution. Russian ministers were particularly aggrieved that the Treaty of Berlin allowed Austria-Hungary to occupy Bosnia and Herzegovina, an area home to a large number of Slavs. Slav nationalists too had hoped that the region would become part of Serbia.

Bulgaria had been Russia's most important client state following the Treaty of Berlin, but in 1885 the Bulgarians showed their resentment towards the terms of the treaty and Bulgaria's status as a satellite state of Russia. Prince Alexander of Bulgaria took the bold step of uniting with his country's neighbour, Eastern Rumelia, and forced Russian officials to leave. Tsar Alexander III was furious and forced Prince Alexander to abdicate. While the other powers, particularly Austria-Hungary, Germany and Britain, now viewed a strong Bulgaria as a useful buffer against further Russian expansion in the Balkans, Russia realised it needed to foster good relations with another Balkan state so its influence there didn't die out completely. It was Serbia, officially under Austrian 'protection', which now adopted a more pro-Russian stance.

The Russian and the Ottoman Empires

Russian expansionism

Despite its internal problems, Russia was committed to a policy of expansionism. The Russian Empire already comprised most of modern-day Poland, Ukraine, Lithuania, Estonia and Latvia, but its huge population lacked sufficient farmland. This problem, known as 'land hunger', not only made the condition of peasants decidedly miserable, but also continued to hinder Russian economic development well into the twentieth century. As such, successive tsars sought to expand their territory into Central Asia, their influence into the Balkans, and to establish secure trading posts in the Far East and gain access to the Straits to help facilitate trade.

Anglo-Russian rivalry over Central Asia was already a long-running problem by 1890. The diplomatic wrangling between Russia and Britain was termed 'the Great Game' and sparked a number of international crises and sometimes outright conflict in the nineteenth century. As Russia expanded towards Afghanistan and Britain increased its hold on the Indian subcontinent, the gap between the two powers' spheres of influence got smaller and smaller. The British had long perceived Russia's intentions in Central Asia as a direct threat to India, its most important colony. Afghanistan, it was hoped, would become a buffer state. The Anglo-Afghan War of 1878–80 was sparked when Russia sent diplomats to Kabul and the Afghan ruler Sher Ali refused to allow Britain to send its own diplomatic mission. The war ended to Britain's advantage.

Rivalry over the Straits

CROSS-REFERENCE

The implications of this new tension in the Balkans in 1887 are explored in Chapter 4, with the end of the second *Dreikaiserbund* and the Reinsurance Treaty between Russia and Germany.

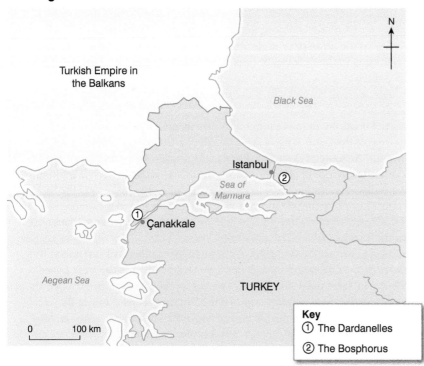

Fig. 6 *The Dardanelles and the Bosphorus were known collectively as the 'Turkish straits'*

Russia's coastline lay mostly on the Arctic Sea, which meant that most of her shipping and trading routes were frozen for large portions of the year. Securing a warm-water port in the Turkish Straits was a long-term goal, but it had helped to provoke the Crimean War with Britain and France in 1854–6. This resulted in the Black Sea clauses agreed at the Treaty of Paris in 1856, which said no warships of any navy could use the Black Sea in peacetime. This dashed Russia's plans to build an impressive naval fleet there.

Russia continued to pursue this objective, albeit more cautiously. In 1871 the Great Powers were prepared to allow a revision of the Black Sea clauses: warships could now sail through the straits of the Dardanelles and Bosphorus, but only if Turkish independence was threatened. Russia continued to push for further revisions in its favour well into the twentieth century. The decline of the Ottoman Empire seemed to present opportunities to secure the naval access to the Eastern Mediterranean that Russia longed for; but again, this raised the suspicions of Austria-Hungary as it affected the Balkan region, and Britain, who perceived this ambition as a threat to its Mediterranean trade and the security of its route to India – Britain's most profitable territory – via the Suez canal.

In 1887 Britain, Italy, Austria-Hungary and Spain signed a series of agreements, the Mediterranean Treaties, to protect the existing status quo in the Mediterranean Sea. The Treaties had the effect of limiting Russian hopes of greater influence over the Balkans by supporting the survival of the Ottoman Empire. Their terms also prevented Russia, once again, from gaining control of the Bosphorus and Dardanelles.

The Ottoman Empire in 1900

The Ottoman Empire comprised modern-day Turkey and its colonies, which had included most of the Balkan states since the fifteenth century, African regions on the Mediterranean coast, and territory in the Middle East including parts of modern-day Iraq, Iran and Syria. The Ottoman Empire ruled over peoples of different religions, languages and ethnicities, and had once been a formidable power: in terms of its territorial extent, the Empire's peak was in the mid-sixteenth century. Turkish control of Europe was concentrated in the Balkans, but the 1800s had witnessed a gradual erosion of its influence there. As the Empire shrank and internal problems grew more serious, it earned the nickname 'the sick man of Europe', a phrase first used by Tsar Nicholas I in 1853.

As the break-up of the Ottoman Empire seemed increasingly likely, statesmen of the Great Powers deliberated over the consequences in a debate known as 'the Eastern Question'. Russia and Austria-Hungary's rivalry in the Balkans often seemed poised to disturb the peace of Europe, while nationalism in the Balkans continued to weaken Turkish authority. Greece was the first Balkan state to overthrow Ottoman rule and declare its independence in 1830, and the Treaty of Berlin recognised Serbian and Montenegrin independence from the Turks.

Outside Europe, the Great Powers were bolder in their actions and willing to expedite the Ottoman Empire's decline. Algeria and Tunisia were seized by France in 1848 and 1881 respectively. Under the Treaty of Berlin, Cyprus became a British protectorate, and in 1882 Britain occupied Egypt. By 1900, Turkey had lost a large portion of its African territories, with only the northern coast of modern-day Libya still under its control.

By 1900 there were many sources of tension between the Great Powers of Europe, but they had also demonstrated that they had avoided going to war with each other when imperial rivalries surfaced. Since 1815, the balance of power had, with some notable exceptions, been effectively maintained and

CROSS-REFERENCE

The consequences of the decline of the Ottoman Empire are outlined in more detail in Chapter 7.

large-scale wars were circumvented by diplomacy. This period of relative harmony was known as the Concert of Europe, whereby representatives of the Great Powers met whenever potential conflict arose, and was a looser form of the Congress System introduced in 1815 after the Napoleonic Wars.

ACTIVITY

Summary

Compile a list of all the potential reasons for conflict explored in this section. How many appear to be due to the expansion of the Russian Empire; how many are due to the decline of the Ottoman Empire; and how many overlap?

 PRACTICE QUESTION

'The rivalry between Russia and Austria-Hungary was the greatest threat to European peace in 1900.'
Assess the validity of this view.

 PRACTICE QUESTION

With reference to Sources 1 and 2 and your understanding of the historical context, which of these two sources is more valuable in explaining why Britain aimed to expand its imperial possessions in the late nineteenth century?

STUDY TIP

Try to ensure that your writing is analytical, not descriptive. This means *explaining* and analysing different factors in detail, rather than 'telling the story'. For example, evaluate clearly the threat posed by the conflict between Russia and Austria-Hungary and then compare this degree of threat to the problems posed by other factors.

STUDY TIP

It is important to consider who the authors of the sources are, the time when they were produced and the type of source they are, for example, a speech compared to a letter. All of these considerations help form a judgement as to their value.

4 The state of international relations by 1900

LEARNING OBJECTIVES

In this chapter you will learn about:

- the extent of Anglo-French rivalry
- the state of Anglo-German relations
- the reasons for, terms and consequences of, the Franco–Russian Alliance and the Dual Alliance of Germany and Austria-Hungary
- the potential for conflict between the Powers by 1900.

KEY CHRONOLOGY

1879 Germany and Austria form the Dual Alliance

1882 Germany, Austria and Italy form the Triple Alliance

1887 First Reinsurance Treaty between Germany and Russia

1890 Reinsurance Treaty not renewed

1894 France and Russia sign the Franco–Russian Alliance

KEY TERM

Splendid Isolation: the British policy of remaining aloof from foreign affairs in Europe; it was viewed as splendid by British ministers as it avoided disadvantageous agreements with other countries and emphasised the British Empire's strength

Third Republic: the government established in France after the fall of Napoleon III in September 1870 while the Franco–Prussian War was still being fought. The Third Republic ended in 1940 following the Nazi invasion of France

revanchism: from the French for 'revenge', it was a policy that aimed to overturn the losses to French territory incurred as a result of the Franco–Prussian War

By the end of the nineteenth century, the Concert of Europe had almost completely collapsed, although most powers still professed a desire to maintain peace.

Anglo-French rivalry

Britain followed a deliberate policy of '**Splendid Isolation**' from European affairs, preferring to focus on maintaining and building its empire; although politicians did take a greater interest in European relations when a risk was presented to the balance of power, a concern which grew with the creation and development of the German Empire. Tension between Britain and Russia was also well-established. Disputes over colonial possessions frequently threatened peaceful relations between Britain and the other powers in the 1890s. The Fashoda Incident in 1898 emphasised the increasing vulnerability of British dominance overseas.

SOURCE 1

The Secretary of State for India, Lord George Hamilton, recalled in his official comments the pessimism of Arthur Balfour, future Prime Minister, in 1901:

Balfour said the conviction was forced upon him that we were for all practical purposes at the present moment only a third-rate power; and we are a third-rate power with interests which are conflicting with and crossing those of the great powers of Europe. Put in this elementary form the weakness of the British Empire, as it at present exists, is brought home to one. We have enormous strength, both effective and latent, if we can concentrate, but the dispersion of our Imperial interests, renders it almost impossible.

Bismarck's plan to isolate France diplomatically, following the Franco–Prussian War was successful well into the 1890s: French politicians were too distracted by the teething problems of the **Third Republic** to focus much on foreign policy, and they needed to ensure that France recovered economically from the conflict. At the end of the nineteenth century, however, France sought suitable allies. Initially at least, the French believed Russia and Britain would each require guarantees of support against the other before entering into a formal agreement. Germany was even considered, especially as the immediate consequences of the Franco–Prussian War and the *revanchism* stirred by the Alsace-Lorraine takeover began to fade from the memories of the French public. However, a committed minority of politicians refused to countenance an understanding with Germany as it would entail a formal renunciation of France's claim to Alsace-Lorraine. There was also much ground for pessimism when contemplating an Anglo-French agreement: for two centuries Britain and France had been imperial rivals, their colonial ambitions clashing in Canada, India, and – more recently – the African continent.

Colonial rivalry with Britain over Egypt, sparked by nationalist disorders there in 1882, prevented an Anglo-French understanding for several years. The Suez Canal in Egypt, a project jointly financed by the British and the French and completed in 1869, was threatened in 1882 by a nationalist uprising. As the Suez Canal was strategically vital for commerce, Britain was immediately concerned and sent troops to invade and occupy Egypt.

The potential for actual conflict between Britain and France was high, but there is also evidence of both sides reaching peaceful agreements over disputed colonies. In June 1882 – just two months before Britain's occupation of Egypt – the Anglo-French Convention confirmed the territorial boundaries of each empire in West Africa, while the **Fashoda Incident** resulted in the formal agreement recognising spheres of influence in the north-east.

Anglo-German relations

The growth of Anglo-German rivalry in the years preceding the First World War was in many ways unexpected. The royal families of the two powers were closely related, their cultures shared many similarities, and both were suspicious of France. Britain had viewed Russia and France as the greatest threats to its imperial superiority for much of the nineteenth century, but the accession of Kaiser Wilhelm II, the departure of Bismarck and the subsequent demise of the **Bismarckian system**, which attempted to maintain the balance of power in Europe, gradually worsened relations between Britain and Germany.

A CLOSER LOOK

The Bismarckian system (1871–90)

Bismarck realised the other powers would view a unified, strong Germany as a threat to the balance of power after 1871. He stated that Germany had no plans for further European expansion: it would be 'folly beyond all political reason'. Bismarck developed a complex system of alliances – the Bismarckian system – so it appeared that the balance of power was being maintained while Germany developed economically without being challenged. Meanwhile he tried to keep France isolated from friendly alliances and to limit the potential for conflict between Austria-Hungary and Russia over the Balkans.

Germany was another colonial rival of Britain's during the **Scramble for Africa**. While Bismarck was determined to avoid any potential for conflict with Britain in Europe, overseas commercial interests were another matter entirely, and he even collaborated with the French in the 1880s against British interests in West Africa, the Congo and South West Africa. Two partition treaties were necessary in 1885 and 1890 to resolve Anglo-German disputes in Zanzibar. As a result, Germany established a protectorate known as German East Africa and a British **protectorate** was created in Zanzibar, calming relations between the two powers for the time being.

Hopes of an Anglo-German alliance

However, with the advent of *Weltpolitik* and the beginning of the **Anglo-German naval race** in 1890s, German politicians were well aware that they risked the hostility of the British. As such they sought an understanding with Britain which would secure a peaceful coexistence between the two powers while allowing Germany to seek its 'place in the sun' – imperial greatness. This goal was rather bungled by **Bernhard von Bülow**, the German foreign secretary, who was frequently complacent in his dealings with the British. He hoped that continued imperial rivalry with France would drive Britain into Germany's arms. News of the Fashoda Incident, therefore, was welcomed by Bülow, who believed that Britain would abandon its Splendid Isolation and enter into an alliance with Germany, thereby balancing out the 'encirclement' threat posed by the 1894 Franco–Russian Agreement (see pages 28–30). Given the long-term nature of Anglo-French rivalry, exacerbated by the Scramble

CROSS-REFERENCE

The Fashoda Incident and its consequences for Anglo-French relations are explored in Chapter 3. Anglo-Russian rivalry is also explained in Chapter 3.

ACTIVITY

Explain why many British politicians were worried about Britain's status at the start of the twentieth century. You should also refer to Chapters 2 and 3.

ACTIVITY

Using information in this chapter and from Chapter 3, create two newspaper headlines following the resolution of the Fashoda Incident: one French and one British. Bear in mind that in 1899 the mainstream press of both powers was very nationalistic.

CROSS-REFERENCE

Britain's rivalry with other imperial powers, and the Scramble for Africa, are covered in Chapter 3.

You can find a definition of the term 'protectorate' in Chapter 3, page 18.

The causes and outcome of the Anglo-German naval race are explored in Chapter 5.

KEY PROFILE

Bernhard von Bülow (1849–1929) was German Foreign Secretary for three years before becoming Chancellor in 1900. A great debater, he spoke several languages and was quite ruthless in his treatment of his rivals. He resigned in 1909 over a tax debate in the Reichstag, but remained in Wilhelm's favour.

CROSS-REFERENCE

The Kaiser's support for the Boers is explored in Chapter 3.

ACTIVITY

In pairs, assume the roles of diplomatic advisers to the British in the 1890s and create two different reports for the Foreign Office. One of you should caution against an alliance with Germany, pointing out potential disadvantages and sources of tension; the other should recommend an alliance, explaining the expected benefits.

CROSS-REFERENCE

The Dual Alliance was the agreement between Germany and Austria-Hungary signed in October 1879, explored on page 30, and first mentioned in Chapter 2.

More reasons for the Reinsurance Treaty are explored in Chapter 3.

for Africa, the Germans had good reason to be optimistic – especially as the French had allied with Britain's other great imperial rival, Russia.

In 1898, 1899 and 1901, Joseph Chamberlain, the British Colonial Secretary, with the support of Lord Salisbury who was both Prime Minister and Foreign Secretary, proposed an alliance to Germany. However, Germany's response was less than encouraging. Britain was not prepared to ally herself to Austria-Hungary as well as Germany and so risk war with Russia in the Balkans. As these negotiations got underway in the spring of 1898, Germany began its naval building programme and pushed forward its plans for the Berlin–Baghdad railway. Both were outright challenges to Britain, which feared for its dominance at sea and was suspicious that the Germans had designs on Egypt and India. This resurgence in Anglo-German imperial rivalry was hardly helped by the **Kaiser's support of the Boers**. Britain would abandon Splendid Isolation, but as the century drew to a close, the likelihood that it would ally itself with another European power looked small.

Franco–Russian Alliance, 1894

In response to the **Dual Alliance** between Germany and Austria-Hungary, which was anti-Russian in character, and following a flare-up of tension in the Balkans in the 1870s, Russia sought a renewal of the *Dreikaiserbund* (Three Emperors' League) that had been agreed between Germany, Austria and Russia in 1873.

The lapse of the Reinsurance Treaties

The aftermath of the 1885 revolt in Bulgaria – in which Russia forced the abdication of the Prince of Bulgaria and threatened to greatly increase its influence over the Balkan state – damaged relations between Russia and Austria too badly for the *Dreikaiserbund* to continue, but Bismarck again was determined not to allow Russia to remain potentially hostile to Germany. In 1887 he arranged the **Reinsurance Treaty** with Russia, promising that:
- Russia should be allowed to be the prevailing influence in the Balkans
- both Germany and Russia would each remain neutral if the other became involved in a war with a third Great Power
- the above clause was not to apply if Germany attacked France, or if Russia attacked Austria-Hungary.

Kaiser Wilhelm II disagreed with this approach, however. He strongly disapproved of limiting German–Austrian influence in the Balkans, and after Bismarck's resignation in 1890 the Reinsurance Treaties were not renewed. Russian ministers now needed to seek alliances elsewhere, if they were to take the potential threat of the Triple Alliance (explored on pages 30–31) seriously.

French foreign policy

Since the 1870s, the German Empire's aim with regards to France was to keep it isolated. Bismarck hoped that if the French had no powerful friends they would be unable to seek revenge for their defeat in the Franco–Prussian War. However, the popular mood of *revanche* and the formation of the Dual Alliance forced the French government to seek friendly agreements with other powers. In the 1880s and 1890s Britain was following its policy of Splendid Isolation and had more common interests with Germany. Besides, Anglo-French imperial rivalry was still alive and well. It is rather remarkable then that Russia emerged as the most likely choice of ally: on the surface, the two nations had very little in common, especially in terms of their political systems.

Fig. 1 *This British cartoon shows Bismarck's control over the emperors of Austria, Germany and Russia*

The terms of the Franco–Russian Alliance

What brought France and Russia together was a growing mutual suspicion of Germany, continuing colonial disputes with Britain, and financial deals. Russia desperately needed foreign investment to develop its industry, and the French had money to give. The Franco–Russian Alliance (also known as the Dual Entente) formalised in 1894 paved the way for Russia to receive considerable French loans, and gave France military security.

SOURCE 2

The terms of the Franco–Russian Alliance Military Convention, 1894, were:

1. If France is attacked by Germany, or by Italy supported by Germany, Russia shall employ all her available forces to attack Germany. If Russia is attacked by Germany, or by Austria supported by Germany, France shall employ all her available forces to attack Germany.
2. In case the forces of the Triple Alliance, or of any one of the Powers belonging to it, should be **mobilised**, France and Russia shall mobilise immediately and simultaneously the whole of their forces.
3. The available forces to be employed against Germany shall engage to the full with such speed that Germany will have to fight simultaneously on the east and the west.
4. The General Staffs of the Armies of the two countries shall co-operate with each other at all times in the preparation and facilitation of the execution of the measures mentioned above.
5. France and Russia shall not conclude peace separately.
6. The present Convention shall have the same duration as the Triple Alliance.
7. All the clauses enumerated above shall be kept absolutely secret.

It is interesting to note in the exact terms of the alliance that both France and Russia were very aware of Germany's fear of encirclement by hostile powers, that the Triple Alliance (see below) had not remained secret as intended. Crucially, however, the exact terms of the two major alliance agreements at this point were not fully known by their opposing alliance. This allowed plenty of room for suspicion between the Great Powers, and a necessity for army **chiefs of staff** to prepare for the worst possible scenario.

Germany's Dual Alliance with Austria-Hungary, 1879

Under the chancellorship of Bismarck, Prussia had gone to war against Austria-Hungary in 1866 as part of the **German Wars of Unification**: he saw the Habsburg Empire as a decaying power and did not want to tie the new, united Germany to it. Concern over the potential aftermath of the **Ottoman Empire's decline**, however, helped bring about a change in policy towards Austria-Hungary. By 1878, though, German relations with Russia were particularly strained. At the Congress of Berlin that year Bismarck had been one of the most vocal opponents of Russian ambitions in the **Balkan region**, which even prompted a complaint from Tsar Alexander II to the Kaiser. Austria-Hungary was a natural choice of ally by this time, as it was equally concerned about Russian influence in the Balkans.

The terms of the Dual Alliance

The agreement between Germany and Austria-Hungary signed in October 1879 was directed specifically against Russia. It provided that:

- if either country was attacked by Russia, the other would provide full military support
- if either country was attacked by a country other than Russia, the other would observe 'benevolent neutrality' (it would not involve itself but might lend non-military support)
- the agreement would remain secret between the two powers
- the agreement would last five years with the expectation that it would be renewed every three years thereafter.

The Dual Alliance was indeed renewed, and remained in place when the First World War broke out in 1914. It naturally caused great concern for France and Russia in particular – who quickly became aware of the existence of a formal alliance but not its exact terms – both of whom faced a potentially hostile bloc of Germany and Austria-Hungary on its central European border.

Fig. 2 *This French cartoon depicts Germany, Austria-Hungary and Italy as unhappily tangled up in the Triple Alliance, while France and Russia stroll by*

The Triple Alliance, 1882

While the Dual Alliance was formed because Germany and Austria-Hungary had the same interests and common enemies, Italy joined the Dual Alliance in 1882 because they wanted to reduce the possibility of conflict with Austria. The existing territorial rivalry between Italy and Austria over Istria and the Tyrol on the border between the two states was exacerbated by the process of Italian unification (achieved, like German unification, in 1871). Nevertheless, the Dual Alliance recognised Italy as a useful ally against France, as it was now predicted that France would ally with Russia in response to the Dual Alliance. A dispute with France over Tunisia prompted Italy to begin discussions with Germany and Austria-Hungary, and the Triple Alliance was concluded in May 1882.

The terms of the Triple Alliance

As well as the existing agreements between Germany and Austria-Hungary, the terms of the Triple Alliance now recognised France as a likely enemy. The three powers agreed that:

- Germany and Italy would support each other if either was attacked by France

- if Germany, Austria or Italy was attacked by another power, they would give each other mutual support
- if Austria-Hungary went to war with Russia, Italy would remain neutral
- as with the Dual Alliance, the Triple Alliance was to be secret.

The potential for conflict

The impact of the formation of the Franco–Russian and Dual Alliances on international relations was significant. Their secret nature, which prevented other powers from knowing the specific terms of the agreements, effectively increased suspicion and tension between the newly-formed alliance blocs. The formation of the Dual Alliance marked a new era of international relations, which involved the gradual abandonment of congresses as a way of settling disputes and the pursuit of foreign policy aims by means of clandestine and defensive agreements between individual powers.

However, the existence of agreements between powers did add a further consideration for states ready to risk war: if they did so they were aware that they would be fighting against more than one country and reducing their chances of victory. Moreover, few statesmen – even in the increasingly militaristic 1890s – were prepared to knowingly ignite a large-scale war which would engulf most of Europe. In this way, the two opposing alliances acted as a deterrent, encouraging countries to de-escalate disputes with their neighbours.

There were nevertheless several potential sources of conflict by 1900. The decline of the Ottoman Empire increased territorial rivalry in the Balkans between Austria-Hungary and Russia; conflict between the two in the region, after the agreement of the Dual Alliance and Franco–Russian alliance, was far more likely to involve four Great Powers rather than two. Imperial rivalries, as we saw in Chapter 3, had been contained before 1900 but certainly not resolved, while the end of the Bismarckian alliance system and the pursuit of *Weltpolitik* made Germany's fellow states concerned about the upset it was causing to the balance of power as it sought to expand its overseas empire and create an impressive naval fleet to rival Britain's. The conclusion of two military alliances – defensive in nature but betraying their signatories' suspicion of their neighbours – was particularly significant as it highlights a shift away from international congresses and towards secret negotiations to defend their countries' own interests.

CROSS-REFERENCE

The Anglo-German naval race is explored in Chapter 5, pages 38–39.

ACTIVITY

On a large sheet of paper, create a diagram to show the changes in relations between the different powers as explained in this section. You could start with each of the main powers in different circles, and use arrows to show the agreements and rivalries between them.

SOURCE 3

Kaiser Wilhelm II wrote a private letter to his cousin, Tsar Nicholas II, on 26 September 1895. Wilhelm had just discovered that the French army was carrying out military manoeuvres on the French–German border. He wrote:

The proposed new Corps [an army subdivision] will increase the already overwhelming French forces to five Corps, and constitutes a threat as well as a serious danger to my country. This event happening in the moment your officers are being decorated has made people uneasy here and given affairs an ugly look, as if Russia would like France to be offensive against Germany with the hopes of help from the first named. Such a serious danger will cause me to strongly increase my army, to be able to cope with such fearful odds. God knows that I have done all in my power to preserve the European Peace, but if France goes on openly or secretly encouraged like this to violate all rules of international courtesy and Peace in peacetimes, one fine day my dearest Nicky you will find yourself suddenly embroiled in the most horrible of wars Europe ever saw! I hasten to you, if you are allied 'for better, for worse' with the French, well then, keep those damned rascals in order and make them sit still.

ACTIVITY

In what ways does Source 3 illustrate both the potential benefits of the alliance system and the potential for escalating conflicts between two powers?

Summary

By 1900 two opposing alliance blocs had been established, dividing Europe into two potentially hostile camps. However, although the terms of the Dual Alliance anticipated Austrian or German conflict with Russia, and the Franco–Russian Alliance committed each signatory to supporting each other against Germany, further understandings were still sought – especially by Germany – which would cut across these agreements and perhaps make them redundant. Meanwhile Britain was still contemplating which power was a strong enough potential ally to abandon Splendid Isolation for. The early 1900s saw new alliances formed and then tested in a series of crises.

ACTIVITY

Copy and complete the table to record the developments in relationships between the Great Powers. Colour-code the events to distinguish between those which had a positive effect and those which had a negative effect on relations.

	Austria	Britain	France	Germany	Russia
Austria					
Britain					
France					
Germany					
Russia					

STUDY TIP

When planning your response to this question, make sure you are very clear about what the question is asking you to consider, so that you can select the most relevant material to discuss. In this case, it is essential to analyse the tensions caused by Germany's growing strength and which powers in particular were concerned by it. To provide a balanced answer you should also consider the other causes of tension amongst the powers.

 PRACTICE QUESTION

'Suspicion of the growing strength of Germany was the main reason for tension between the Great Powers in the 1890s.'
Explain why you agree or disagree with this view.

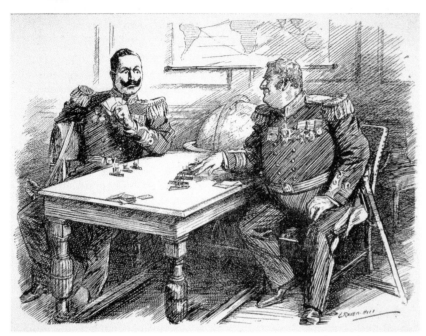

Fig. 1 *A 1908* Punch *cartoon showing Wilhelm II and 'John Bull' (Britain) playing poker with model dreadnoughts*

Balkan nationalism and its significance for Austria-Hungary and Russia

The Balkans had been a source of rivalry between Austria-Hungary and Russia for decades, as each power bordered the region and had conflicting interests there. However, by 1897 there was something of a **détente**. Both Russia and Austria-Hungary agreed to preserve the status quo in an agreement which stated that:

- neither power would attempt to alter the balance of power within the Balkans
- both powers would oppose any other power which tried to gain territory in the Balkans
- both accepted that the **Black Sea Straits** were closed to warships when Turkey was at peace
- if the Ottoman Empire (Turkey) collapsed, Austria-Hungary could annex the provinces of Bosnia and Herzegovina, as formally agreed in 1878.

KEY CHRONOLOGY	
1897	Austro-Russian agreement over the Balkans
1903	Military coup in Serbia
1905	Schlieffen Plan completed
1906	Britain launches the first dreadnought battleship
1906–8	'Pig War' between Austria-Hungary and Serbia

LEARNING OBJECTIVES

In this chapter you will learn about:

- why Balkan nationalism increased after 1903 and its significance for Austria-Hungary and Russia
- the reasons for and impact of increasing militarism and the status of the army in Germany
- the causes and outcomes of the arms and naval races
- the military plans of the Great Powers.

A CLOSER LOOK

Punch was a humorous magazine published between 1841 and 2002. It featured satirical cartoons about British current affairs as well as big topics in international relations. Its irreverant views on the actions of politicians and statesmen give historians an insight into popular British contemporary attitudes.

KEY TERM

détente: improvement in relations between countries which had previously been strained

CROSS-REFERENCE

Russia's ambition to control the Black Sea Straits for use as warm-water ports is explained in Chapter 3.

Nationalism is a strong pride in one's country. Nationalism took two different, but equally significant forms in European thought in the late 1800s and early 1900s:

- In independent countries such as Germany and France, strong patriotism was evident in patriotic songs, images and newspaper articles. It usually celebrated the apparently uniquely superior attributes of the country while heaping scorn or pity on others. Nationalism was often a powerful force in foreign policy: for example, the French desire for *revanche* made formal agreements with Germany during this period almost impossible.

- For people who felt that their sense of nationhood was being suppressed (in colonial countries belonging to an empire), nationalism was a force attempting to lead their country to independence and to the creation of a nation state. This was true of many inhabitants of the Balkan region: Serbia, Bulgaria and Greece had emerged from the crumbling Ottoman Empire; now Slav nationalists (among others) living in the Habsburg Empire strived for independence from Austria-Hungary. Meanwhile, Poles and Ukrainians in the Russian Empire also wanted independence for their nations, as did Republicans in Southern Ireland who advocated separation from Great Britain.

CROSS-REFERENCE

The origins of French *revanchism* are explored in Chapter 4.

Tension between Austria-Hungary and Russia over the Balkans is introduced in Chapter 3, and further consequences are explored in more depth in Chapters 7 and 8.

KEY TERM

coup: a violent seizure of power

The Serbian military coup

In May 1903 the pro-Austrian King and Queen of Serbia were gruesomely murdered by a group of Serbian army officers. The king was replaced by Paul I of the pro-Russian Karageorgevic dynasty. This **coup**, and the new ruler, marked the beginning of a far more aggressive Serbian foreign policy. Paul and his government encouraged the growth of Serb nationalism and were far less concerned about maintaining friendly relations with Austria-Hungary than their predecessors.

The Serbs saw themselves as champions of the Southern Slavs and wanted to form a united Slav state – Yugoslavia – including Croats, Slovenes and Slavs. Their ambitions extended to incorporating Bosnia, Herzegovina and Montenegro into a Greater Serbia. While not all the inhabitants of these territories favoured such a move, all contained active nationalist groups. One movement within Serbia, **the Black Hand**, emerged at this time. This group had unofficial links to the Serbian military and were willing to use terrorism and assassination to achieve their aims.

CROSS-REFERENCE

The aims, methods and actions of the Black Hand are explored in more detail in Chapters 10 and 11.

Significance for Austria-Hungary

The Austro-Hungarians saw the growth of Serbian nationalism as a threat to the integrity of their Empire, which contained around seven million Serbs and Croats. They were particularly concerned about Serbia's ambitions for the two provinces of Bosnia and Herzegovina, which the Austro-Hungarian Empire itself was hoping to incorporate. Modern-day Croatia and Slovenia were part of the Habsburg Empire, and Croat and Slovene nationalists called for independence. Austria-Hungary feared that a strong, increasingly assertive Serbia would inspire, and even directly support, Croatian and Slovene nationalism.

Austro-Hungarian policy towards Serbia became increasingly hostile after the 1903 coup, in the hopes of crushing Balkan nationalism once and for all, while bolstering the prestige of the Habsburg monarchy. In Vienna, a faction led by the Chief of General Staff, **Conrad von Hötzendorf**, championed an unashamedly aggressive approach towards Serbia. By the time of **Franz Ferdinand's assassination** in 1914, Hötzendorf had advocated war against Serbia no fewer than 20 times.

CROSS-REFERENCE

The reasons for the assassination of Franz Ferdinand and its impact on Austria-Hungary's relations with Serbia are explored as part of the July Crisis in Chapter 10.

Count Aehrenthal became Foreign Minister of Austria-Hungary in 1906 and, in an attempt to curb Serbian ambitions, the tariff arrangements between the two countries were not renewed that year. This led to the so-called 'Pig War' of 1906–8. Austria-Hungary tried to strangle the Serbian economy by banning imports of meat from Serbia and depriving that country of an important source of revenue. However, instead of crippling Serbia's agricultural trade, the Serbs found other export markets, most notably in France and Germany, and increased their agricultural output. Austro-Hungarian policy had proved counterproductive: by suspending trade with Serbia it actually decreased the Serbs' dependence on the Habsburg Empire and encouraged hopes that Serbia would soon be strong enough to lead the South Slav nationalities in a bid for independence away from Austria-Hungary.

ACTIVITY

In pairs, each take the role of either Serbia or Austria-Hungary. Write a headline and a short newspaper article announcing the beginning of the Pig War from your country's perspective, then swap to identify the differences.

KEY PROFILE

Fig. 2   Alois Lexa von Aehrenthal

Alois Lexa von Aehrenthal (1854–1912) became Foreign Minister in October 1906. He tried to preserve Austria-Hungary's interests in the Balkans, but was prepared to negotiate with Russia over the annexation of Bosnia–Herzegovina in 1908. Aehrenthal gained international acceptance of the annexation despite Russian objections. He sought a diplomatic approach to Serbia and the strengthening of Austria's German Alliance. He died of leukaemia in February 1912.

KEY TERM

pan-Slavism: the nationalist ambition to unite all Slavs and win independence from non-Slav empires; south Slav nationalism refers to pan-Slavism in the Balkans

KEY PROFILE

Fig. 3   Franz Conrad von Hötzendorf

Significance for Russia

Pan-Slavism, already popular in Russia, became a more powerful force after Russia's defeat in the Russo–Japanese War. The Karageorgevic dynasty in Serbia was strongly pro-Russian, as was Prince Boris of Bulgaria, who signed a military agreement with Russia in 1902. Russia appeared to be in a strong position in the area until its defeat in the Far East during the Russo–Japanese War, 1904–5, when Russia's credibility as a military power suffered: it was the first major defeat of a Great Power by a Far Eastern power in modern times, and Russian military chiefs had made some embarrassing mistakes. It would take some years before Russia recovered its military strength.

A CLOSER LOOK

Pan-Slavism was a cultural and political movement advocating the union of people of Slav ethnicity in the Balkans and Eastern Europe under the same rule. The movement became very popular in Russia from the 1860s, where pan-Slavists began to view Russia as the 'protector of Slavs', and many Slav nationalists in the Balkans saw Russia as a leader and protector from the rule of the declining Ottoman Empire and encroaching Austro-Hungarian Empire. Many Russians in turn felt a strong sense of affinity with Balkan Slavs, who also shared the same Orthodox Christian religion. Mistreatment – real or perceived – of Orthodox Christians by the Muslim rulers sparked several disputes between Russia and Turkey in the nineteenth century, most notably the 1878–8 Russo–Turkish War.

Franz Conrad von Hötzendorf (1852–1925) was Austrian Chief of General Staff from 1906 to 1916 (he is referred to as Conrad in some other texts). A passionate defender of the Austro-Hungarian Empire, he recognized the threat of independent Serbia and Slav nationalism to its survival. He advocated war against Serbia 20 times before 1914, bringing him into regular conflict with the foreign ministry. He struggled to command Austrian forces effectively in the First World War and was dismissed by the new emperor, Karl I.

In its role as 'protector of Slavs', the Russian government knew that Serbia would expect support for its Yugoslav ambitions. Russian foreign ministers also realised, however, that lending such support would lead to further disputes, and perhaps conflict, with Austria-Hungary. With the Austrians now drawing closer to Germany in response to Serbia's rise, and the exposure of Russian military weakness in the war against Japan, it was clear that they would need to proceed with caution. In 1907 there was some discussion within Russia of reaching a new agreement with Austria-Hungary, but the **Bosnian Crisis** of 1908 promptly ended such ideas. Russia's failure to resolve the crisis in Serbia's favour damaged its reputation in the Balkans, as did the resolution of the Pig War: German intervention forced Russia to cease sending aid to Serbia while Austria-Hungary's customs blockade continued.

The mounting problems for Russia in the Balkans encouraged its government to resolve its colonial rivalry with Britain in order to attain further security. The Anglo-Russian Agreement, signed in 1907, formed the basis of the Triple Entente of Russia, Britain and France. With the existing Triple Alliance of Germany, Austria-Hungary and Italy, Europe contained two rival alliance blocs, but it is important to recognise that the Triple Alliance was defensive in its aims (countries would only join a war if their allies were attacked by other powers), while Britain's agreements with France and Russia in the Entente involved no military commitments.

Militarism and the position of the German army

Nationalism and militarism were frequently interlinked: intense patriotism led people to believe they required a strong military for defence and to win respect from other nations. The growth of militarism and prestige attached to their armies ensured that many powers, especially Germany, allowed the influence of their armed forces to increase and expand; this influence would later encourage governments to spend more on defence, increase the size of their armies and navies, and to nurture military values like discipline, physical strength and respect for authority. The concurrent increase in nationalism gave many armies an inflated sense of importance.

The status of the German army

The power with the most respected army, amongst its own people as well as the other powers, was Germany. German military chiefs often boasted that the German Army was above the scrutiny of civilian authorities and that it answered only to the Kaiser, not the Reichstag. They also believed strongly in the army as a driving force behind achieving German glory, which attracted comment from the other powers, including Britain.

CROSS-REFERENCE

The Russo–Japanese War and its link to the Triple Entente are explained in Chapter 6.

The Bosnian Crisis and its consequences for the Balkans are explored in Chapter 8.

CROSS-REFERENCE

The political system of Germany and its impact on decision-making is explored in Chapter 1.

ACTIVITY

Evaluating primary sources

1. List the strengths of the German army according to Steevens in Source 1.
2. How valuable is Source 1 in understanding the position of other powers towards the German army at this time? Consider the provenance of the source in your answer.

SOURCE 1

From the British tabloid newspaper the *Daily Mail* in an 1897 article by the war correspondent George W. Steevens:

The German Army is the most perfectly adapted, perfectly running machine. Never can there have been a more signal triumph of organisation over complexity. The armies of other nations are not so completely organised. The German Army is the finest thing of its kind in the world; it is the finest thing in Germany of any kind. Briefly, the difference between the German and, for instance, the English armies is a simple one. The German Army is organised with a view to war, with the cold, hard, practical, business-like purpose of winning victories. And what should we ever do if 100,000 of this kind of army got loose in England?

The German army had the loyal support of the Kaiser, who was rarely seen out of military uniform in public. In many ways he was exploiting the constitutional status of the army, which swore its oath not to the people, but to the Kaiser. Military elites did not have to answer to the Reichstag, and Wilhelm was later as much influenced by generals as his civilian ministers. The conscription of young German men for two to three years instilled in future generations the Prussian military values, while in 1911 Kaiser Wilhelm allowed the Prussian army officer General Goltz to set up a league for German youth encouraging physical fitness and German pride, 'so that they will recognise that service to the fatherland is the highest honour of the German man'.

Military personnel were held in such high esteem in Germany that in 1906 a confidence trickster named Wilhelm Voigt was able to pull off an elaborate con by dressing as a Prussian military officer. His uniform alone commanded so much respect amongst the people he encountered that he was able to take command of a group of soldiers in Köpenick and 'confiscate' 4000 marks from a bank. Sentenced to four years in prison after his discovery, Voigt became something of a folk hero, nicknamed the 'Captain of Köpenick'. The episode was deeply embarrassing for Germany, and many opponents of German militarism viewed it as a warning of the dangers of the military having too strong an influence over German politics and society.

Fig. 4 *The German army practising a military drill in the early twentieth century*

A CLOSER LOOK

Militarism in Germany

The Garrison Church (Garnisonkirche) in Potsdam was a strong example of militarism in Germany. Built by the 'soldier king' Kaiser Friedrich Wilhelm I in 1723, the Garnisonkirche infused the high Prussian values of militarism and Protestantism. Potsdam was the location of both the royal court and a large army garrison, and the Church was frequented by Wilhelm II who added improvements to the building. The Kaiser had also spent many hours in his youth involved in the daily military ceremonies of the army garrison, becoming almost obsessive about military uniforms and routines.

SOURCE 2

From the German newspaper *Berliner Volkszeitung*, published 17 October 1906; the *Berliner Volkszeitung* was a daily publication with a liberal, democratic agenda:

As incredibly funny, as indescribably ridiculous as this story is, it has a serious, an embarrassing side. The Köpenick farce shows itself as the most glorious victory the militaristic ideal in its most extreme culmination has ever carried off. Yesterday's episode shows us quite clearly: encase yourself in a uniform in Prussian Germany, and you are almighty. The uniform is an irresistible charm. A military squad you meet on the street is yours to do with as you please. You can occupy the town hall like a conquered fort. You can arrest whomever you like, and steal whatever money there is. Then, you can get away untouched. The Captain of Köpenick has correctly interpreted the Zeitgeist. He is intelligent enough to understand and respect modern power structures. The victory of blind military obedience over common sense, over the state, over the personality of the individual — that is what yesterday's comedy showed us, in its horribly grotesque manner.

KEY TERM

autonomous: acting independently without reference to other authorities; in this case the Reichstag and civilian authorities

CROSS-REFERENCE

Mobilisation is explored in Chapter 4.

Railway lines and timetables were key to enabling a quick and efficient mobilisation, which in turn was crucial to securing an early advantage against the enemy on the battlefield. Alan J.P. Taylor's evaluation of the role of railways in August 1914 is explored in Chapter 11.

KEY TERM

tribunal: a committee set up to settle a dispute

arms race: a competition between countries to produce the most armaments. This often included the rapid development of military technology. The same concept applies to a naval race: battleships were produced, often with increasingly destructive capabilities

CROSS-REFERENCE

The nature and aims of *Weltpolitik* are explored in Chapter 3.

Britain's determination to maintain naval supremacy was formalised in the 1889 Naval Defence Act, explored in Chapter 2.

The arms and naval race

From around 1907, there was an increase in military influence on policymaking, particularly in Germany and Russia: ministers in both states were concerned about the growing tension between Austria-Hungary, as highlighted by the Pig War, while Russian ministers were determined to recover from the military weaknesses exposed by the Russo–Japanese War. The German army was virtually **autonomous**, while in Russia, generals became sufficiently powerful that in 1914 they were able to threaten the Tsar with defeat if he did not allow their orders for **mobilisation** to go ahead. This growing militarism was reflected in the amassing of weapons, an increase in the size of armies and navies, an increase in military spending and the development of elaborate military planning.

Weaponry

The growth of industry in the nineteenth century was also associated with the growth of weaponry. By the 1880s, the development of modern machines and chemicals had permitted the advent of high explosives, the machine gun and long-range artillery. Such weapons promised to transform war, as did the growing railway network that could be harnessed to carry troops to the front line.

The increasing production of weapons concerned Tsar Nicholas II enough for him to suggest a conference at The Hague in 1899 to consider disarmament, but although the Great Powers met for discussions, nothing was achieved. Germany argued that Britain's demand to stabilise arms production at existing levels was simply a ploy to keep German armaments permanently inferior to Britain's own. The only achievement was the setting up of a **tribunal** at The Hague to mediate between powers in case of a dispute. A second conference in 1907 similarly achieved little. International rivalry caused the **arms race** to continue to feed on itself.

Germany, home to the powerful Krupp Empire (a hugely successful manufacturer of weapons and steel), led the way in the production of weapons, but in the years from 1908, both France and Russia strove to equal or outpace the German advances. In 1908, a bill was passed to strengthen the French artillery. Meanwhile the Russian Minister of War, Vladimir Sukhomlinov, pressed for increased military spending to build up the Russian artillery. By 1914, Russian army expenditure was equivalent to 1577 million German marks, compared to the German army expenditure of 1496 million marks.

Armies

Not only did the numbers of weapons increase, but so did the size of armies. All the continental European powers relied on compulsory conscription. In Germany, although the length of military conscription was reduced from three to two years in 1893, the total size of the army was increased, particularly after 1907, to provide an army of five million men in wartime. Even Britain organised a small but strong British Expeditionary Force (BEF) for service on the continent and a Territorial Army for home defence. The BEF originated from army reforms of 1907 and was developed on the military advice of Douglas Haig.

The naval race

Since the impetus of *Weltpolitik* and the first German naval laws, the Anglo-German naval race had got well underway. When the details of the naval laws were reported in British newspapers and Germany's intentions became clear, the response among the British press and public was one of angry alarm. The British viewed their **naval superiority** not only as a matter of national pride, but also vital to the defence of their overseas empire and trade, especially as the British army was relatively small compared to the other Great Powers. The German Admiral, Von Tirpitz, however, viewed the British fleet as a direct threat to Germany's own interests.

In a memorandum to the Kaiser in 1897, Admiral Von Tirpitz made it clear that he felt a superior German fleet was essential for Germany's defence:

For Germany the most dangerous naval enemy at the present time is England. It is also the enemy against which we most urgently require a certain measure of force as a political power factor. Commerce raiding and transatlantic war against England is so hopeless, because of the shortage of bases on our side and the superfluity on England's side, that we must ignore this type of war against England in our plans for the constitution of the fleet. Our fleet must be so constructed that it can unfold its greatest military potential between Heligoland and the Thames. The military situation against England demands battleships in as great a number as possible. Given the measure of our powers of development, which are limited by the capacity of our shipbuilding industries, we cannot create in the near future, that is up to 1905, more than two full squadrons of eight battleships each.

ACTIVITY

How far do you think Source 3, Tirpitz's memorandum, would have calmed British fears, if it had been made public in the early 1900s?

The impact of the dreadnought

In 1900, the second German Navy Law was passed, which provided for a 20-year building programme and the construction of a high seas fleet of 38 battleships, eight battle cruisers and 24 cruisers. Britain responded with a new naval base at Rosyth in 1903 and, determined to meet the threat from Germany, Parliament approved plans for the formation of a North Sea Fleet. It was also decided to adopt the revolutionary design for a new **dreadnought** class of battleships, superior to previous battleships as they had ten 12-inch guns rather than the usual four. These new faster ships would cost £1 million each (roughly equivalent to £60 million today) but they would make the German fleet obsolete. The first dreadnought was launched in February 1906.

The British believed that they had secured superiority because the Germans could not manufacture an equivalent ship without first widening and deepening the Kiel Canal. However, in May 1906, the German government laid down plans to extend the number of German ships under construction, add six cruisers, and widen and deepen the canal. In 1909, Britain then increased the planned number of dreadnoughts. The naval arms race was hugely expensive for both powers, and by 1914 it was clear that Britain had 'won' – it had 29 dreadnoughts to Germany's 17. The race also did severe damage to Anglo-German relations, and public antagonism between the two countries was egged on by the press.

A CLOSER LOOK

Dreadnoughts became something of a national obsession in Britain. The Liberal Party had come to power in 1906 promising to improve social welfare and cut the defence bill. However, pressure from the public forced them to reconsider the production of more dreadnoughts. 'We want eight and we won't wait!' became a popular slogan.

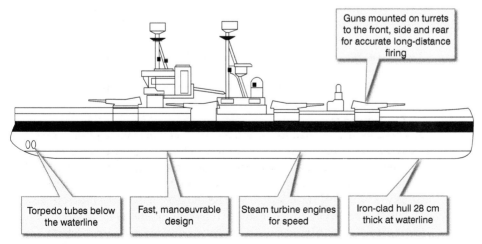

Guns mounted on turrets to the front, side and rear for accurate long-distance firing

Torpedo tubes below the waterline

Fast, manoeuvrable design

Steam turbine engines for speed

Iron-clad hull 28 cm thick at waterline

Fig. 5 *Diagram of a dreadnought*

Military plans

Conscription and large reserves were accompanied by detailed planning for both war and mobilisation. Technological and organisational developments led to the formulation of precise plans that often could not be reversed once they had begun, especially as they involved detailed procedures for mobilisation including the complicated timetabling of trains to transport troops and equipment.

It would be wrong to assume that, because the opposing Triple Entente and Triple Alliances were formed by this point, a war was inevitable from 1894. Several crises were avoided before 1914, and often diplomacy was still an effective means of resolving disputes. It is perhaps telling, however, that as well as continuing to pursue diplomatic methods, Germany's main solution to the problem of **encirclement** (now exacerbated by the formation of the new Franco–Russian Alliance) was arrived at by its military planners.

Work on what became known as the Schlieffen Plan began in 1897 under the leadership of Count Alfred von Schlieffen, then Chief of the German General Staff. Despite Germany's increasing industrial strength and its formidable army, it was clear that fighting France and Russia simultaneously ran the very high risk of stretching her resources too thin. The plan was so detailed that it was not finished until 1905, and was modified several times before it was put into place in August 1914. It planned to allow Germany to win a war on two fronts. By invading France through Belgium and Luxembourg where there would be minimal defences, Germany hoped to knock the French out of the war quickly and then focus the strength of its armies on fighting Russia, who it was assumed would take at least six weeks to mobilise its troops.

After Germany offered Austria-Hungary support against Russia in 1908–9 as a result of the **Bosnian Crisis**, the Russian War Ministry drew up their own war plan – Plan No. 19. This provided for a speedy attack on East Prussia during the critical opening phase of a potential conflict, so diverting German troops from France. The French provided a loan for the construction of railways needed to implement **Plan No. 19.**

Military spending

There was a huge rise in military spending to support the military plans and the arms race. The total defence expenditure of the Great Powers rose from £268 million in 1900, to £289 million in 1910 and to £398 million in 1914. While France increased defence spending by 10 per cent, Britain increased military expenditure by 13 per cent, Russia by 39 per cent and Germany by 73 per cent in the years 1870–1914.

Summary

By 1911, existing sources of tension had been exacerbated:
- Mistrust between Austria-Hungary and Russia over the Balkans deepened following the Serbian coup in 1903 and the increase in Slav nationalism.
- The German fear of encirclement, apparently confirmed by the conclusion of the Franco–Russian Alliance, led to the creation of the Schlieffen Plan which committed Germany to war against both opposing powers. In the resulting arms race, Russia, Austria-Hungary and France also increased their military spending.
- To the British, German *Weltpolitik* and the start of the naval race increased their suspicion of German motives. This was a crucial factor in the formation of Britain's alliances with Japan and France, which will be discussed in Chapter 6.

CROSS-REFERENCE

Germany's fear of encirclement is first explored in Chapter 4.

There is a map of the Schlieffen Plan in Chapter 11, page 91.

CROSS-REFERENCE

The Bosnian Crisis is explored in Chapter 8; while the development of Russian war planning is outlined in Chapter 9.

After the Bosnian Crisis in 1908, other Great Powers developed their own military plans. Find out more about the plans of Austria-Hungary and France in Chapter 8.

ACTIVITY

Research

1. Research the effect of the arms race on the Great Powers in the years 1900–11. Present the state of their military preparedness as a report for their respective heads of government.
2. As you read through the next few chapters, see if you can identify which events helped to provoke a dramatic increase in military spending between 1910 and 1914.

PRACTICE QUESTION

With reference to Sources 1 and 3, and your understanding of the historical context, which of these two sources is more valuable in explaining why German militarism caused concern to Britain between 1900 and 1911?

 PRACTICE QUESTION

'Britain was to blame for the naval rivalry between Britain and Germany in the years 1908–14.'
Assess the validity of this view.

6 Evolving alliances

LEARNING OBJECTIVES

In this chapter you will learn about:

- the influence of the Moroccan Crises on the alliances of Europe

- why Britain abandoned Splendid Isolation to form the Anglo-French Entente

- how Britain and Russia came to agree the Anglo-Russian Convention and form the Triple Entente

KEY CHRONOLOGY

Diplomatic relations 1902–11

1902	Anglo-Japanese agreement
1904	Entente Cordiale agreed
1904–5	Russo–Japanese War
1905	First Moroccan Crisis
1906	Algeciras Conference
1907	Anglo-Russian Agreement
1911	Second Moroccan Crisis

CROSS-REFERENCE

The Second Boer War is explored in Chapter 3.

The Fashoda Incident, an example of deep-rooted Anglo-French imperial rivalry, is explained in Chapter 3.

KEY TERM

entente: an understanding; it is not an alliance and does not bind either party to support the other in the event of a general war

The first decade of the twentieth century saw a degree of fluctuation between the alliances of Europe. Those that already existed, the Triple Alliance (Austria-Hungary, Germany and Italy) and the Franco–Russian Agreement, were still in place by 1914, but there was still a great deal of bargaining, manoeuvering and manipulation to be done, especially as Britain abandoned its Splendid Isolation and became a potential ally to the other Powers.

By 1900 Britain's policy of Splendid Isolation – avoiding the 'entanglement' of European alliances and focusing instead on its empire – was looking less beneficial to its politicians. A decline in world trade and industrial production, coupled with frequent disputes over colonial territories, made the avoidance of binding agreements with other powers appear increasingly risky. Britain's experience in the **Boer War** was also a catalyst, encouraging ministers to consider the abandonment of Splendid Isolation: it had exposed the weaknesses and inefficiencies of the British Army and made alliances appear more useful.

There were powerful voices within Britain who preferred an agreement with Germany at the turn of the century: Queen Victoria (grandmother to Kaiser Wilhelm II), Prime Minister Lord Salisbury and Secretary of State for the Colonies Joseph Chamberlain were all in favour. However, Germany's response was lukewarm. Britain was reluctant to join the Triple Alliance, as its ministers foresaw the potential for conflict between Austria-Hungary and Russia in the Balkans. Chancellor Bülow expected more imperial clashes between Britain and its colonial rivals France and Russia, and bided his time, hoping another incident like **Fashoda** would scare Britain into allying with Germany on his terms. None of these circumstances were helped by the construction of Germany's rival naval fleet, which started in 1898. As the Anglo-German naval race heated up, an agreement between the two powers grew ever more unlikely.

The Anglo-Japanese agreement, 1902

Britain and Japan had common interests in the Far East. Both sought to defend their empire and trade routes from the encroaching empires of France, Russia and Germany. The Anglo-Japanese agreement of 1902 is notable for being the first military alliance signed between a European power with an Asian country against another Western nation. Its terms stated that both would support one another if either was attacked by two or more powers in the Far East, but if either was attacked by one power, the other would remain neutral. The Anglo-Japanese agreement was still in force in 1914.

The Anglo-French Entente of 1904

Détente with France

The British agreements with France over colonial disputes in West and East Africa marked a softening of mood in one of Europe's longest-running rivalries. After the death of Queen Victoria, negotiations for an '**entente**' between Britain and France began. Victoria's successor **Edward VII**, who was personally suspicious of the Kaiser's intentions, proved quite popular with the French. His visit to Paris in 1903 began with hostile reports in the French press, but Edward's charm helped to win over public opinion. These developments, along with Edward's pro-French tendencies, all smoothed the path towards a formal understanding between the two countries.

The Anglo-French entente is often referred to as the Entente Cordiale, which translates as 'cordial understanding'. This highlights the nature of the agreement between Britain and France, which was not a military alliance as many often assume.

The agreement, signed in 1904, stipulated that:

- Britain and France settled their old disputes and the French recognised the British occupation of Egypt, while Britain agreed not to oppose the French in Morocco (the latter being kept as a secret term, since by an agreement of the Great Powers made in 1880, France had no right to assume control there).
- both countries agreed to help the other against outside powers in the event of any disputes over Egypt or Morocco.
- regular consultation on naval and military matters was arranged.

Members of the Triple Alliance, especially Germany, saw the Entente Cordiale as a very worrying development. The Germans were already worried about 'encirclement' by France and Russia; now France had more freedom for manoeuvre in its foreign policy without risking upsetting Britain.

Fig. 2 *A* Daily Mirror *cartoon celebrating the Entente Cordiale; the caption reads 'Heavy Villain (in the background): I wish I could think of some scheme to spoil their dance!'*

The formation of the Triple Entente by 1907

If Britain and France resolving their differences would have been almost unthinkable 50 years earlier, Britain also coming to terms with Russia, its other great imperial rival, looked even less likely. However, events in the Far East eventually changed the minds of ministers in London and St Petersburg, leading to the formation of the 'Triple Entente'.

CROSS-REFERENCE

The rivalry between Britain and France over Egypt is explored in Chapter 3; while the consequences of the Entente's Moroccan terms are explained in Chapter 6, pages 45–46.

ACTIVITY

Thinking point

Why do you think Britain agreed to an entente with France, rather than a binding military agreement like the Franco–Russian Alliance?

KEY PROFILE

Fig. 1   *Edward VII*

Edward VII (1841–1910) reigned as King of the United Kingdom between 1901 and 1910. He had little political power as British monarch but played a significant role in foreign affairs: he earned the nicknames 'Peacemaker' and 'Uncle of Europe' by fostering good relations with most European powers, but he disliked his nephew, Kaiser Wilhelm II.

ACTIVITY

Study the cartoon in Fig. 2. Note that Britain is represented by a sailor (usually Britain was personified by John Bull, wearing a suit) and that Germany looks like a cartoon villain. How does this fit with your understanding of the aims of the treaty?

The Russo–Japanese War, 1904–5

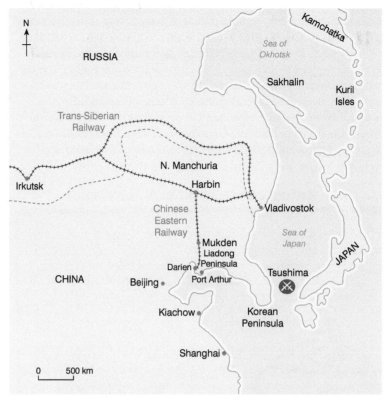

Fig. 3 *The location of engagements of the Russo–Japanese War, 1904–5*

Russia's expansion in the Far East brought it into conflict with Japan. In 1898, and again in 1903, the Japanese had tried to reach an agreement with the Russians whereby Japan would retain influence over Korea in return for Russia's influence over Manchuria. Russia's refusal to make such a deal provoked the Japanese attack on Port Arthur in February 1904. With the advent of war, serious concerns were raised in London about Britain's diplomatic position: it had a military alliance with Japan, but also a hard-won agreement with France, Russia's ally. However, Britain stuck rigidly to the terms of the Anglo-Japanese Agreement, which did not draw it into the conflict.

The war was a humiliating defeat for Russia for a number of reasons:
- The Japanese navy almost destroyed the Russian fleet, all its battleships and most of its cruisers were lost.
- The defeat of a European power by an Asian force won the Japanese new respect from Western powers.
- It helped to spark the 1905 Revolution in Russia.
- It prompted the rise of Japan as a world power.
- Russia was determined not to suffer such a defeat again, and began to build up her armaments and improve military training.

The war was ended by the Treaty of Portsmouth (USA) by which Russia handed over South Sakhalin and the lease of Port Arthur to Japan, evacuated Manchuria and recognised Korea as a Japanese sphere of influence.

Russia's military weaknesses worried France, especially in view of the growing strength of Germany, while Britain became less anxious about Russian expansion in the Far East. In 1907, the Russian Foreign Minister Izvolsky made an agreement with Japan to guarantee the independence of China, and to settle their differences over Korea and Manchuria. It seemed that the issues which had divided the two countries in the Far East were no longer of relevance. Consequently, Britain, France and Russia grew closer together.

ACTIVITY

Compare the terms of the Anglo-French Entente and the Anglo-Russian Agreement. How similar are their aims?

The terms of the 1907 Anglo-Russian Agreement

Just as the Anglo-French Entente was aimed at resolving imperial rivalry between Britain and France, the Anglo-Russian Agreement was deemed a useful way to prevent conflict between Britain and Russia over their influence in Afghanistan and Persia; the rivalry between the two in the Middle East had hindered relations between them in the nineteenth century. Furthermore, Britain's 1902 agreement with Japan had threatened to bring it into conflict against Russia in the Russo–Japanese War, a possibility the Russians were determined to avoid even after 1905. An agreement was signed between Britain and Russia in 1907 by which:

- agreement was reached on the Afghanistan–Indian border; Britain was given control over the foreign policy of Afghanistan while Britain and Russia were given equal trading rights.
- Russia was given control over Northern Persia while Britain controlled the south and the Persian Gulf. The central section remained neutral.

From 1907, Britain's foreign policy involved friendlier relations with both France and Russia, but their agreements only amounted to a 'Triple Entente' rather than a definite alliance. When war finally came in 1914, it was by no means certain that Britain would fight on the Franco–Russian side and it was under no legal obligation to do so. Furthermore, Germany was given assurances that the Anglo-Russian Convention was not intended to damage them, and on the whole, with the exception of the Bosnian Crisis, Russo–German relations showed some (at least superficial) improvement in the years up to 1914.

The Moroccan Crises

The Anglo-French alliance of 1904 became more firmly defined as a result of the colonial clashes over Morocco that occurred in 1905 and 1908–11.

The First Moroccan Crisis: 1905–6

[handwritten: USED TO BE RULED BY OTTOMAN EMPIRE.]

At the Madrid Conference in 1880, all major European countries as well as the USA had agreed that all powers had equal trading rights in the independent state of Morocco. Since that date, both French and German traders were active there, but France hoped to procure a more secure political influence in Morocco too, which would undermine the earlier agreements made in Madrid. In January 1905 a French delegation travelled to meet with the Moroccan Sultan, with the aim of persuading him to agree to a series of reforms. This mission had been approved by Britain, which by this point had agreed the Anglo-French Entente, but Germany feared that Morocco was about to become another French protectorate, just as Tunisia had in 1881. German merchants feared that this would threaten their commercial interests in the area.

While on a Mediterranean cruise, Kaiser Wilhelm sailed into the Moroccan capital, Tangiers, on 31 March 1905, supposedly in support of German business interests in the area. Here, he gave outspoken speeches in which he recognised the Sultan of Morocco as an independent ruler and questioned the (originally secret) agreements between France and Britain which had been subsequently 'leaked'. Wilhelm, who had resolved to carry out the plan of his Chancellor and Foreign Minister, hoped that his outspokenness would persuade the French to back down and show the British the weakness of their new ally, perhaps also signalling to the British that their friendship with France was likely to pull them into imperial disputes.

Wilhelm's presence in Tangiers provoked a crisis between France, Germany and – to a lesser extent – Britain. It appeared from Wilhelm's speeches that Germany would help the Moroccans resist French domination which, if followed through, would lead to an imperial conflict between France and Germany – possibly even drawing in the other Great Powers in support of their respective allies.

CROSS-REFERENCE

The British Ambassador was referring to the rivalry between Britain and France over Egypt, which is explored in Chapter 3.

Fig. 4 *The Kaiser meets with the Moroccan Sultan in 1905*

KEY PROFILE

Fig. 5 *Théophile Delcassé*

Théophile Delcassé (1852–1923) was the French Foreign Minister between 1898 and 1905. He was pro-British and deeply suspicious of Germany. By engineering the Anglo-French Entente and paving the way for the Anglo-Russian Agreement, he incurred the wrath of German ministers and there were repeated calls from Berlin for his dismissal.

The British were outraged by what they saw as the impertinence of the Kaiser and his ministers. The British Ambassador to Paris told the French that the Germans would live to regret the incident: 'Let Morocco be an open sore between France and Germany as Egypt was between France and ourselves.' His words highlight the remarkable shift in relations between the three powers. Edward VII, who had always found his German nephew highly irritating, remarked: 'The Tangiers incident was the most mischievous and uncalled-for event which the German Emperor has ever been engaged in since he came to the throne. It was also a political theatrical fiasco, and if he thinks he has done himself good in the eyes of the world he is very much mistaken.'

ACTIVITY

Summary

Do you think Edward VII's assessment of Wilhelm II's reputation as a result of the Moroccan Crisis is valid?

SOURCE 1

From the memoirs of German Chancellor von Bülow, published in 1931, two years after his death; his memoirs have been criticised for trying to exonerate himself from blame for the increasing tension in Europe before 1914:

It was not only the extent of our economic and political interest in and about Morocco which persuaded me to advise the Kaiser to set his face against France. In the interests of peace, we must no longer permit such provocations. I do not desire war with France, but I did not hesitate to confront France with the possibility of war. I felt that I could prevent matters coming to a head, cause **Théophile Delcassé**'s fall, break the continuity of aggressive French policy, knock the continental dagger out of the hands of Edward VII and the war group in England, and simultaneously ensure peace, preserve German honour and improve German prestige.

ACTIVITY

Evaluating primary sources

1. What impression of the German interests in Morocco is given by Source 1?
2. What else would you want to know about the context and provenance of Bülow's comments before judging the reliability of Source 1 for an historian studying the causes of the first Moroccan Crisis?

The Algeciras Conference, 1906

Delcassé urged the French to resist Germany's demands in Morocco, but his colleagues in government believed that a more conciliatory approach was necessary. While they were determined not to fully concede, the French realised that if a war with Germany did ensue, they could hardly count on support from the Russians who were still fighting against Japan in spring 1905. To placate the Germans, the French forced Delcassé to resign as foreign minister in 1905, and they agreed to an international conference in Algeciras, Spain. It appeared that Germany's *coup d'état* of Morocco had succeeded.

The conference of 13 nations met at Algeçiras in Spain between January and March 1906, but the Germans found the British, Russians, Italians, Spanish and even the Americans all supporting the French claims. Germany's only ally was Austria-Hungary and the country suffered a major diplomatic defeat. The Kaiser

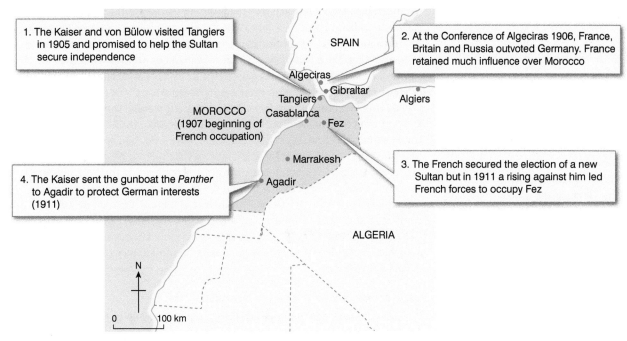

Fig. 6 *The Moroccan crises of 1905–6 and 1911*

was deeply frustrated by the conference, believing that he – and Germany – had been treated disrespectfully by the other powers. A key aim of Germany was to prompt Britain into reconsidering its entente with France; in this respect, German intervention in Morocco had been a disaster. A Liberal government came to power in Britain in 1906 and Edward Grey, the new foreign minister, was far more suspicious of Germany than his predecessor. As a result he advocated total support for France during the conference, even when French delegates appeared unreasonable. The Anglo-French Entente remained firm.

It was agreed at Algeciras that France would be allowed extensive control over the Moroccan police and the Moroccan state bank. Germany had to be satisfied with the reaffirmed guarantees of freedom for all powers to trade in the region, and the independence of the Moroccan Sultan.

The impact on Germany's foreign policy

Whether the Algeciras Conference was as important as is sometimes suggested has been questioned by the historian Alan J.P. Taylor, who pointed out that the British made no military preparations to back the French and that subsequent military talks were ineffectual. Nevertheless the rebuff did have the effect of increasing Wilhelm II's fears and discouraging Germany from using international conferences as a means of settling disputes. Furthermore, by allowing the British and Russians to come together, it opened the way for the Anglo-Russian Agreement of 1907, which further contributed to German fear of encirclement by hostile powers. Although the agreement involved no guarantees of military support for each other, it made Britain far less likely to support any German foreign policy which acted against Russia's interests.

The second Moroccan Crisis: Agadir, 1911

Morocco was again the centre of European tension in 1911 when the French provoked a renewed crisis by sending troops to the Moroccan capital, Fez. The official reason given by France was that the troops were there to help the Sultan defeat some local rebel tribesmen, but the Germans, with some justification, claimed that France had breached the earlier agreements. The Germans reacted

CROSS-REFERENCE

The aims of the Pan-German League and its connection to *Weltpolitik* are explored in Chapter 3.

ACTIVITY

Explain why the Anglo-French Entente held firm despite the two crises in Morocco. You should also consider other factors in the relationship between Britain, Germany in France explored in previous chapters.

Fig. 7 *This* Punch *cartoon satirises the attempt by the Germans to break up the* Entente Cordiale *with its Moroccan policy. The original caption reads, 'Germany: "Donnerwetter! It's rock. I thought it was going to be paper."'*

CROSS-REFERENCE

Many nationalists in the Balkans hoped to create an independent Slav state. Pan-Slavism is introduced in Chapter 5 and further consequences are explored in Chapters 8, 9 and 10.

ACTIVITY

Germany viewed Lloyd George's speech as a threat. Which phrases in Source 2 do you think alarmed them most?

in an extreme manner by sending the gunboat *Panther* to the Moroccan port of Agadir. *Panther* docked on 1 July 1911. This was supposedly to protect German interests and seems to have been the work of the nationalistic German Foreign Minister, Alfred von Kiderlen-Wächter, who had connections with the Pan-German League. It has been suggested that he and his associates had hopes of establishing a greater German presence in North Africa.

The British were immediately alarmed by the potential threat to Gibraltar, at the entrance to the Mediterranean next to Morocco. On 21 July, Britain's Chancellor of the Exchequer, Lloyd George, gave a pointed speech at the Mansion House, indicating Britain's desire for stability in Morocco and expressing a determination to support France, reaffirming the Entente. Faced with such resolution, Germany backed down and a compromise was agreed whereby Germany received some territory in the French Congo by way of compensation. The French were able to establish a formal French protectorate in Morocco in March 1912. All that the crisis seemed to have achieved was a further weakening of Anglo-German relations and a strengthening of Anglo-French ones.

The consequences of the Second Moroccan Crisis

It was no coincidence that the Naval Race was stepped up in the next two years. In France, those elements favourable to a compromise settlement with Germany were lost to the more nationalistic politicians and Raymond Poincaré, who was strongly anti-German, came to power as prime minister. Furthermore, from 1912, Britain and France undertook a series of military conventions, beginning with a naval agreement in March 1912 whereby Britain undertook to allow the French navy to dominate the Mediterranean, whilst Britain would confine itself to Gibraltar and the North Sea.

The second Moroccan crisis did not affect Russia. Indeed, the Russian foreign minister Alexander Izvolsky claimed, 'Russian public opinion could not see in a colonial dispute, the cause for a general conflict'. However, the crisis had created a new level of tension in Europe and it was to have a direct link to the outbreak of war. In 1911, Italy chose to copy the French example with an unprovoked attack on Turkish Tripoli. This, in turn, encouraged the Balkan States to renew their quest for greater power and it was out of this turmoil that the First World War erupted.

SOURCE 2

From a speech by the British Chancellor of the Exchequer, David Lloyd George, given at Mansion House, the official residence of the Mayor of London, on 21 July 1911 and later reported in *The Times* newspaper:

I am a sincere advocate of the settlement of international disputes by methods such as those which civilisation has so successfully set up for the adjustment of differences between individuals. But I believe it is essential in the highest interests, not merely of this country, but of the world, that Britain should at all hazards maintain her place and her prestige amongst the Great Powers of the world. It has in the past redeemed continental nations, who are sometimes too apt to forget that service, from overwhelming disaster and even from national extinction. I would make great sacrifices to preserve peace. But if a situation were to be forced upon us in which peace could only be preserved by the surrender of the great and beneficent position Britain has won by centuries of heroism and achievement, by allowing Britain to be treated where her interests were vitally affected, then I say emphatically that peace at that price would be a humiliation intolerable for a great country like ours to endure.

Summary

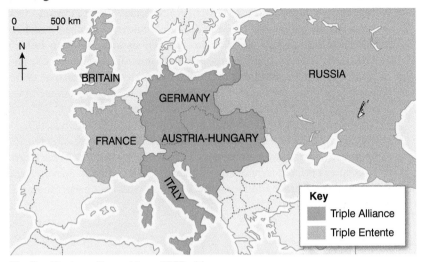

Fig. 8 *The two alliance blocs, 1907–14*

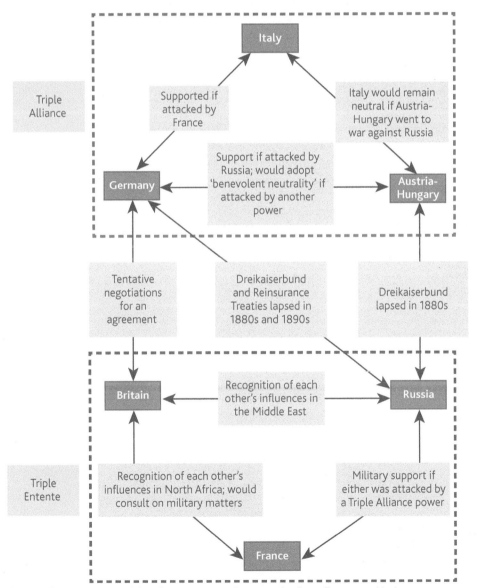

Fig. 9 *Diagram summarising the agreements between the Great Powers and Italy*

Extension

Assume the role of the German Chancellor, Theobald von Bethmann Hollweg, after the Second Moroccan crisis. What advice would you give to Wilhelm II on how to proceed with his foreign policy towards the Triple Entente powers?

STUDY TIP

Note that this is a broad question concerning the Moroccan Crises. Source 1, by von Bülow in his memoirs, raises issues of value, since this was written with hindsight for a particular purpose. Source 2 is a speech by Lloyd George; consider what the strengths and weaknesses of a speech such as this may be. Try to comment on tone, which both adds and detracts from the value.

STUDY TIP

When comparing the consequences of two events, you should plan your answer carefully first to identify multiple points for each side. Some evidence, however, may be 'weightier' than others, i.e. one or two consequences of one event could be far more significant than all the relevant consequences of the other. Make sure your explanations of the points you include are developed accordingly.

Glancing at the map of alliances formed by 1914, the Triple Entente appears to have existed in resistance to the Triple Alliance. While the Franco–Russian Alliance had indeed identified Germany as each power's greatest threat, it is important to remember that Britain's agreements with France in 1904 and Russia in 1907 did not commit Britain to the military support of either country. Nevertheless, Britain's rejection of Germany's half-hearted attempts at forming an alliance in favour of French and Russian interests helped to inspire a more passive-aggressive German approach to Morocco.

The Moroccan Crises have often been blamed for creating and strengthening the opposing alliances in Europe, thereby increasing tension to crisis point. Others have pointed out that Germany was quick to back down in both situations, but the impact of the second Moroccan incident in Agadir was significant: Britain and France both committed to increasing their military preparedness.

 PRACTICE QUESTION

Evaluating primary sources

With reference to Sources 1 and 2, and your understanding of the historical context, which of these two sources is more valuable to an historian studying the causes of the Moroccan Crises?

 PRACTICE QUESTION

'The first Moroccan crisis in 1905–6 was a bigger cause of international tension than the second crisis of 1911.'
Assess the validity of this view.

7 The decline of the Ottoman Empire

Fig. 1 *Crowds gather to hear the proclamation of the Young Turk Revolution in July 1908, declared by leaders of different religious communities within the Ottoman Empire; The Revolution exacerbated the Empire's decline*

KEY CHRONOLOGY

1889	Origins of Young Turk movement
1897	Greco–Turkish War
August 1903	Ilinden uprising in Macedonia
1907	Committee of Union and Progress (CUP) of the Ottoman Empire was formed
July 1908	Beginning of the Young Turk revolution
5 October 1908	Bulgaria proclaims full independence from Ottoman Empire
6 October 1908	Annexation of Bosnia–Herzegovina by Austria-Hungary
April 1909	Conservative counter-revolution against the Young Turks

ACTIVITY

Pair discussion

Discuss the features of the image in Fig. 1 with your partner and answer the following questions:
1. What might the female figure in the centre represent?
2. What is symbolised by the men breaking chains on the far right?
3. In what ways does the image demonstrate high hopes for equality among Ottoman subjects?
4. What do you think is the overall message of the image?

The Ottoman Empire in 1900

To some extent, the Great Powers of Europe played a key role in hastening the decline of the Ottoman Empire by gaining influence and control over Ottoman lands, and by pursuing their own economic interests in Turkey. Moreover, the Empire's decline and the consequences of the **Young Turk revolution** in 1908 also contributed to the destabilisation of peace in Europe.

The economic and political condition of the Ottoman Empire

The Ottoman Empire's geographical location, on lucrative routes to India and China, ensured it had remained a significant trading partner in the nineteenth century, but there had been little effort to modernise industry in its territories. With the railway boom of the 1850s however, the Ottoman Empire became a focus of international rivalry as European investors and financiers sought to profit from railway-building in the region. In the 1890s, Germany's increased interest in Turkey led to plans for a railway from Berlin to Baghdad. The 'opening up' of the Ottoman Empire to foreign investment highlighted

CROSS-REFERENCE

The Ottoman Empire is introduced in Chapter 3, pages 23–24.

You can find out more about the consequences of the Young Turk revolution on European peace (especially concerning the Balkans) in Chapter 8.

CROSS-REFERENCE

The Crimean War is explored in the Introduction, page xv.

KEY PROFILE

Abdul Hamid II (1842–1918)

Fig. 2   *Abdul Hamid II*

Sultan of the Ottoman Empire between 1876 and 1909, the Young Turk revolution severely undermined Abdul Hamid's rule. He reluctantly gave up his absolute power by restoring the 1876 constitution, but the leaders of a counter-coup in 1909 decided to remove him.

KEY TERM

intellectualism: the pursuit of intellectual development and learning; academic and scientific and cultural study are signs of intellectualism

pan-Turkism: a movement advocating the union of Turkish-speaking peoples within and outside the borders of the Ottoman Empire

its weakened economic state in relation to the Great Powers of Europe. Meanwhile, the Ottoman economy was heavily in debt to British and French creditors, partly as a result of the **Crimean War**.

At the beginning of the twentieth century the Empire was an autocracy ruled by **Sultan Abdul Hamid**. The Hamidian regime was increasingly unpopular, and Abdul Hamid earned the nickname the 'Red Sultan' on account of his repressive policies and severe treatment of rebels. One of the most infamous examples was the Armenian massacres of 1894–1896, triggered by the Sultan's suspicion of Christian Armenian nationalists in the region. Estimates of the death toll vary, but it is likely that around 200,000 Armenians were killed under the Hamidian government, attracting the attention of the Great Powers and leading to further fears that the Ottoman Empire would be dismantled by foreigners who believed that the Turks were incapable of running their empire justly and fairly.

Another feature of the Sultan's autocratic rule was its stifling of **intellectualism**. The Empire did not have a university until 1900, which encouraged intellectuals to study in Western European institutions, exposing them to the ideals of parliamentary government and written constitutions. Many of these 'students-in-exile' later joined reformist opposition groups, such as **the Young Ottomans** – a forerunner of the Young Turks – which emerged in the 1860s. In 1876 their influence bore fruit when Sultan Abdul Hamid granted a constitution, but this was quickly overturned and the Empire returned to autocratic rule.

A CLOSER LOOK

The First Constitutional Era (1876–8)

The Young Ottomans believed in Western-style liberal democracy with a representative parliament. They also advocated 'Ottomanism', the equal treatment of all citizens of the Ottoman Empire, regardless of nationality. Although reformists persuaded the Sultan to grant a constitution in 1876 which allowed an elected parliament and religious freedom and removed many aspects of censorship, he quickly dissolved the first parliament. In 1878 the constitution was suspended, ending the short-lived First Constitutional Era.

By 1900 the Turkish intellectuals and liberals were increasingly disaffected. However there was disunity among those who opposed the Sultan's rule. Some wanted an emphasis on social reform and insisted that all Ottoman subjects should have equality, while others wanted **pan-Turkism**. Damascus (now in Syria) and Salonika (now Thessaloniki in Greece) became centres of opposition to the Hamidian regime. As opposition grew, the Sultan deployed up to 40,000 agents in Macedonia to limit the spread of such groups. In 1903, events in this region were to highlight the vulnerability of the Sultan's rule and the potential violence of competing national identities.

ACTIVITY

Revision

Create a list of all the problems faced by the Ottoman Empire by the early twentieth century under two headings: internal and external. Add more to the external column after you have read the section below.

The Balkan States in 1900

Fig. 3 *The Balkans in 1900*

Another significant feature of the **Ottoman Empire's** decline was its increasing loss of territory in the Balkan region. Greece was the first Balkan state to gain its independence following the war of 1821–32, although the Serbs had been fighting to remove themselves from Turkish control since 1804. At the Treaty of Berlin in 1878 Greece, Serbia, Montenegro and Romania were all recognised as independent states. Bosnia and Herzegovina, though officially still Ottoman territories, were occupied and administered by, and Bulgaria was granted internal autonomy but remained under Ottoman **suzerainty**. As nationalist feeling within each Balkan state – independent or otherwise – grew at the end of the nineteenth century, the region was faced with two problems: how to push back Turkish control altogether, and how to peacefully settle strong tensions and rivalries between the Balkan countries themselves.

Greece, Serbia and Bulgaria were growing in wealth and population, and their increasing military strength began to pose another threat to the Ottoman

CROSS-REFERENCE

The Ottoman Empire's loss of control over the Balkans is introduced in Chapter 5.

KEY TERM

suzerainty: a status under which a country has control over its own domestic affairs, but its foreign policy is under the influence of another state, to which it owes formal allegiance

CROSS-REFERENCE

Militarism – the strong influence of military staff over government policy, especially foreign policy – is explored in Chapter 5, pages 36–37.

A CLOSER LOOK

Macedonian-Adrianople Revolutionary Organisation (SMARO)

Adrianople was a region in Eastern Thrace which bordered Greece and Bulgaria and was then part of the Ottoman Empire. The Organisation was a revolutionary national liberation movement which was later involved in the Ilinden Uprising.

ACTIVITY

Evaluating primary sources

How valuable is Source 1 for an understanding of revolutionary opposition to Turkish control at the beginning of the twentieth century?

CROSS-REFERENCE

The coup in Serbia, which had a strong impact on Serbia's foreign policy and its status in the Balkans, is explored in Chapter 5.

ACTIVITY

Pair discussion

Using your list of the problems facing the Ottoman Empire, discuss with a partner how you would rank them in order of most to least serious. Do you think internal or external problems were more serious overall?

Empire. Bulgarian foreign policy became more aggressive in response to its lengthy struggles against Ottoman rule, and its governments more militaristic in character. The Greeks were developing their navy, but a war against Turkey in 1897 ended in humiliation. However, the European powers (influenced by the pro-Greek British) were unwilling to allow Turkey to profit as a result and ensured that Greece lost no territory to its former rulers. Despite the Ottoman Empire militarily having the upper hand in the Greco–Turkish War, this was one of many examples of European leaders intervening to ensure the Empire did not regain its losses in the Balkans.

Macedonia, the only region of the Balkan Peninsula still under full Ottoman control, caused grave problems for the Empire in the early twentieth century. It was home to Turks, Jews, Greeks, Albanians, Bulgarians and Serbs. As such there were several states keen to foster nationalism in Macedonia and secure more territory for themselves by encouraging its dismantling. Religious divisions further destabilised the region: in laying claim to Macedonia, Greece, Bulgaria and Serbia could present themselves as co-religionists to those Christian peoples in Macedonia desiring independence from the Ottoman Empire. In response, Abdul Hamid aimed to maintain the loyalty of the Muslims of the region while seeking to 'divide and rule' the Christian population.

SOURCE 1

From The Statute of the Secret Macedonian-Adrianople Revolutionary Organisation (SMARO), written in 1902:

Statute of the Secret Macedonian-Adrianople Revolutionary Organisation
Chapter I – Goal
Art. 1. The Secret Macedonian-Adrianople organisation has the goal of uniting all the disgruntled elements in Macedonia and the Adrianople region, regardless of their nationality, to win, through a revolution, a full political autonomy for these two regions.

Art. 2. To achieve this goal the organisation fights to throw over the chauvinist propagandas and nationalist quarrels that are splintering and discouraging the Macedonian and Adrianople populations in his struggle against the common enemy; acts to bring in a revolutionary spirit and consciousness among the population, and uses all the means and efforts for the forthcoming and timely armament of the population with all that is needed for a general and universal uprising.

Chapter II – Structure and Organisation
Art. 3. The Secret Macedonian-Adrianople revolutionary organisation consists of local revolutionary organisations (bands) consisting of the members of local towns or villages.

Art. 4. A member of SMARO can be any Macedonian, or Adrianoplitan.

In August 1903 the uprising of Macedonians, known as the Ilinden uprising, was brutally crushed by the Hamidian regime. In the wake of the violence in Macedonia, Russia and Austria-Hungary created the Mürzsteg agreement in November 1903, under which non-Ottoman officers from foreign countries were dispatched to Macedonia to keep the peace impartially. The Mürzsteg agreement blurred the boundaries of the Ottoman Empire's political authority in the region as well as highlighting the Sultan's lack of strength internationally, hastening its decline.

The causes of the Young Turk Movement

Long-term reasons

The wide range of problems faced by the Ottoman Empire caused increasing disaffection amongst Turkish liberals and intellectuals. They were frustrated by the Empire's increasing loss of territory and influence – most severely as a result of the Treaty of Berlin, which dramatically decreased 'Turkey-in-Europe', as the Ottoman Balkan states were also known. The liberals and intellectuals also viewed the increasing foreign involvement in the Empire's finances as a sign of its inherent weaknesses, but rather than blaming the European powers for their role, they saw the repressive policies of the Hamidian regime as the greatest cause of Ottoman decline.

Nationalism was a threat to every European empire at the beginning of the twentieth century, but the Sultan's opponents believed it would pose less of a danger to the Ottoman Empire if the wide range of nationalities (known as *millats*) within it were represented in a Western-style parliament. As such they advocated the revival of the 1876 constitution which they hoped would lead to a more efficient and representative government, much better placed to maintain the loyalty of its peoples.

Short-term reasons

What became known as the Macedonian Question – the threats of nationalism and rebellion against the Ottomans as seen during the Ilinden Uprising – highlighted two of the Empire's major problems and helped to cause another more immediate threat. Firstly, the Sultan's fierce and brutal response to the Ilinden revolt highlighted the cruelty of his policy towards the *millats*, and went on to breed more determined and ambitious nationalist groups and revolts. Serbian nationalists, for example, increased their guerrilla activities in Macedonia, convinced that its people must be freed from Ottoman oppression. According to liberal Turks, the need to gain the loyalty of Ottoman subjects through a representative parliament gained more urgency after the Macedonian crisis.

Secondly, the harsh actions of the Sultan attracted international attention, which resulted in the further loss of Ottoman control and influence in the Balkans, as exemplified by the Mürzsteg agreement. Again, his opponents blamed him for allowing – perhaps inadvertently encouraging – the dismantling of the Empire by foreign powers who seemed convinced of Turkey's inability to rule their empire fairly. Additional pressure on the Sultan came from disgruntled army officers stationed in Macedonia, who often went for months without pay.

As threatened as the Sultan was, his opponents were far from united. From a range of different political views on the best future for Turkey amongst the **émigrés**, two emerged at this time: those who believed the Empire should be divided along ethnic and religious lines; and those who believed the Empire should be retained with a strong government in central control. In 1906 the young army officer **Mustafa Kemal** (later known as Atatürk) was instrumental in founding a secret society in Damascus called *Vatan* ('Fatherland'). This merged with existing reformist and nationalist groups, which led to the formation of the Committee of Union and Progress (CUP) in 1907 and a meeting in Paris of Ottoman émigrés in December the same year, but the latter achieved little agreement on how to achieve their aims.

One factor which finally stirred the CUP into action was a meeting by the Entente powers in Reval (modern-day Estonia). The British, French and Russians discussed further intervention in Macedonia to help calm the region, and the Young Turks feared the imminent loss of further territory if they remained inactive.

The Ilinden Uprising

The August 1903 revolt was organised by the Internal Macedonian Revolutionary Organisation (IMRO), Macedonian nationalist who also hoped to further Bulgaria's political interests. IMRO had the support of much of the local Slav Christian population.

CROSS-REFERENCE

Nationalism and its influence in the Balkan region are explored in Chapter 5.

KEY TERM

émigré: a person who has fled their country for fear of oppression

KEY PROFILE

Fig. 4   *Mustafa Kemal Atatürk*

Mustafa Kemal Atatürk (1881–1938) was born in Salonika and entered the military. He was a key player in the Young Turk Revolution and led a nationalist revolution in 1919 in opposition to the peace treaty imposed by the Allies. Following the final collapse of the Ottoman Empire in 1922 and Atatürk established a one-party secular republic in Turkey, which he ruled until his death in 1938 having earned the name 'Father of the Turks'.

The Young Turk Revolution and its consequences for the Ottoman Empire

The revolution began in Salonika in July 1908 with an army mutiny, triggered by long-term frustration of the Turkish troops stationed there who had not been paid for months. This action was spontaneous in nature, rather than planned by the Young Turks, but the chaos it unleashed played directly into their hands. On 6 July, rebel soldiers and their officers demanded the restoration of the 1876 constitution, prompting further mutinies across Macedonia, and by 21 July the rebels had control of most of the region. A march on Constantinople itself was threatened if their demands for the restoration of the 1878 parliament were not addressed. The Sultan had little choice but to yield, which he did three days later.

By the end of July 1908, the streets of Istanbul were filled with joyous citizens who expected the revolution to instigate a glorious new era for the Empire. Slogans from the French Revolution over a century earlier were adopted and proclaimed, chiefly 'Liberty, Equality and Fraternity'. The ideal of equality and brotherhood amongst all Ottoman peoples was extremely popular in these heady days, and in Salonika, national groups who had been rivals and even enemies weeks earlier now seemed happy and willing to lay their hostilities aside for the greater cause of the revolution.

SOURCE 2

The words of Sandanski, a former Macedonian guerrilla fighter, in his 'Proclamation to All Nations of the Empire', in July 1908. He had been fighting against Ottoman rule in Macedonia for years:

Our fatherland, so sorely tried, is now celebrating its rebirth. The revolutionary appeal of our Young Turkish brothers has echoed joyously in the souls of its equally sorely tried people. To my Turkish compatriots! You represent the great majority of the people and you have therefore carried the greatest weight of our mutual enemy's oppression. In your Turkish Empire, you were no less slaves than your Christian counterparts. Dear Christian compatriots! You were also cruelly deceived in your belief that your suffering at the hands of tyranny was caused by the entire Turkish people. Dear Friends! Do not allow yourself to be influenced by the criminal agitation which may be used by the official Bulgarian government to undermine your joint struggle with the Turkish people and the peaceful continuation of this struggle.

ACTIVITY

Evaluating primary sources

How valuable is Source 2 to an historian studying reactions to the Young Turk Revolution? Focus in particular on the date of the source.

The election in November 1908 produced an overwhelming result in favour of the CUP which won every seat except one. However, the Young Turks – as they had come to be known by European observers – faced severe problems before being able to form a government. They remained inexperienced and disunited: there was much internal disagreement on what action they should take next. Meanwhile the Sultan, though now a constitutional monarch, remained as Head of State and could rely on the support of Muslim religious conservatives to challenge the new secular regime.

A CLOSER LOOK

A new political system

The political system of the Ottoman Empire during the Second Constitutional Era (1908–1920) was formed along Western parliamentary lines. The Senate was the Upper House, and was made up of officials appointed by the Sultan.

The Chamber of Deputies, however, consisted of elected representatives; together the two houses made up the General Assembly.

These two issues were still unresolved in early 1909, by which time liberal opinion had been alienated by an increasing shift towards Turkish nationalism. In Constantinople on 12 April, conservative Muslims led an uprising against the Young Turk government which was replicated across Turkey (this was known as the 31 March incident, as the Ottoman calendar ran several days behind that of Europe). This counter-revolution was quashed on the 23 April by Macedonian forces which occupied the Turkish capital and deposed Abdul Hamid, who was sent into exile. He was succeeded by his brother Mehmet V. The CUP was left in control of the government, led by Ahmed Rıza as President of the Chamber of Deputies and of the Upper House and Hilmi Pasha as **grand vizier**, having adopted a more militaristic and nationalist character. They advocated 'Ottomanism', which meant that all the peoples of the Empire should remain loyal to it regardless of their own culture and nationality.

KEY TERM

grand vizier: a long-established position in the Ottoman government, roughly equivalent to a British prime minister

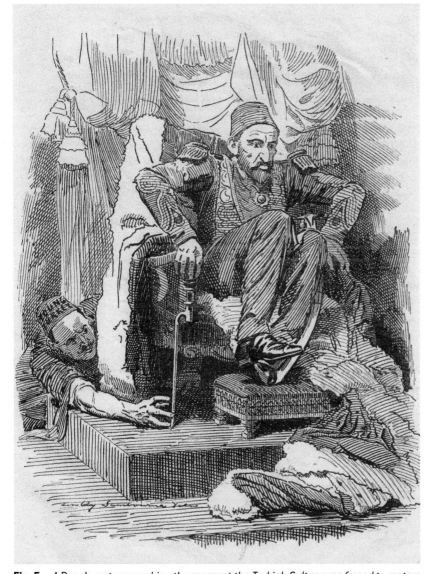

Fig. 5 *A* Punch *cartoon marking the moment the Turkish Sultan was forced to restore the 1876 constitution in 1908*

The reality of the new regime fell far short of the high expectations of its inception. Within three years of the Young Turk revolution, many of the repressive policies of the Sultan's rule were once again in force: secret police returned, non-Muslims faced oppression and freedoms were restricted. In August 1909 the Law of Associations was passed, which banned any political organisation founded on the basis of ethnicity or nationalism. This legislation highlights how the advocates of government centralisation of the Empire under Turkish nationalism had prevailed, instead of Ottoman brotherhood. It was believed – especially after Abdul Hamid's attempted counter-coup – that decentralisation and increased powers for the different ethnicities within the Empire would only weaken it and hasten its collapse.

The consequences of the Young Turk Revolution for the Balkans

The revolutionaries blamed the Sultan for the disloyalty of the *millats* and erosion of the Empire's authority by foreign powers, but the Young Turks also proved incapable of preventing nationalism from threatening its existence. Even in July 1908, at the height of people's hopes for the revolution, Greece, Serbia and Bulgaria viewed the Young Turk movement as a symptom of Ottoman weakness and sought to capitalise on this.

Bulgaria

It is perhaps unsurprising that the Bulgarians seized the early opportunity to proclaim its full independence from the Ottoman Empire on 5 October 1908. Bulgarian activists had played a prominent role in the Ilinden Uprising and in the Macedonian Question as a whole; after the Young Turk Revolution, Bulgarian ministers were concerned that Macedonia would no longer receive the attention and protection of the Great Powers. The Bulgarian diplomat in Constantinople, Ivan Geshov, argued on 1 August 1908 that Bulgaria needed to take action sooner rather than later: 'My conclusion is that in the final analysis, we, as a state, lose from the revolution because it has displaced the Macedonian question and our position in it has been significantly weakened. As we lose by the Young Turk coup, we are obliged to seek some revenge. At today's time, this cannot be other than the full independence of Bulgaria.'

The shrinkage of Turkey-in-Europe had been one of the primary factors behind the Young Turk movement, but the instability the revolution caused in Istanbul only encouraged Bulgaria to finally rid itself completely from Turkish rule. Prince Ferdinand of Bulgaria proclaimed himself Tsar on 5 October and mobilised around 110,000 men; rumours reached Constantinople that full military preparations were underway in case of a hostile Turkish reaction to the declaration of independence. The Ottomans realised that they were at risk of a humiliating defeat if they engaged Bulgaria's surprisingly strong and efficient army and put up little diplomatic resistance.

CROSS-REFERENCE

The most significant consequence for the Balkans of the Young Turk revolution was Austria-Hungary's annexation of Bosnia–Herzegovina on 6 October 1908. The event is explored in depth in Chapter 8.

SOURCE 3

Bulgaria's declaration of independence, proclaimed on 5 October and written by Prince Ferdinand:

In this endeavour, nothing shall stop the progress of Bulgaria, nothing shall hinder her success. This is the desire of my people, this is their will. Let it be as they wish! The Bulgarian people and their leader cannot think and feel differently. Being semi-independent, the Bulgarian state is impeded in her normal and peaceful development by certain illusions and formal limitations, which as a result cool the relations between Turkey and Bulgaria. The people and I sincerely rejoice in the political revival of Turkey!

Turkey and Bulgaria, free and completely independent from each other, may exist under conditions which promote their friendly relationship and may devote themselves to peaceful internal development. Inspired by this sacred deed and to respond to the national exigencies and in harmony with the will of the Bulgarian people, I proclaim, in the name of the God Almighty, Bulgaria as an independent Kingdom. Together with my people I profoundly believe that this act will meet the approval of the Great Powers. Long live independent Bulgaria! Long live the Bulgarian people!

Greece and Crete

Greece also took the opportunity to fulfil its expansionist aims in the wake of the Young Turk revolution. The Greco–Turkish War of 1897 had been triggered by Greek involvement in nationalist movements in Crete. Greece hoped to reverse their failure to secure *enosis* (union) with the island as Istanbul was distracted by its internal difficulties. Following the Bulgarian declaration of independence and the annexation of Bosnia–Herzegovina, Crete declared its formal union with Greece in October 1908.

As the new government of the Ottoman Empire became more heavily influenced by Turkish nationalism, the Balkan states became increasingly alienated from it. The Macedonian Question remained, and the governments of Bulgaria and Serbia in particular were increasingly militaristic with more aggressive foreign policies. The further decline of Turkey-in-Europe made the issue of continued Turkish rule in Macedonia a more urgent anomaly, and exposed the Balkans to the ongoing rivalry in the region between Austria-Hungary and Russia.

Summary

In his highly significant study of the Balkans, Misha Glenny argued that Western historians have tended to overlook the importance of the Young Turk revolution, when in fact it should be regarded as being as significant as the Russian Revolution to the twentieth century.

Causes

- The Sultan provoked opposition both within Turkey and amongst his subject peoples with his repressive policies, most obviously highlighted by the Armenian massacres of the 1890s and his brutal response to the Ilinden Uprising. Intellectuals, unable to attend a university within the Empire until 1900, went abroad to study where they were exposed to Western, constitutional governments.
- The First Constitutional Era of 1876–8 was short-lived, but it gave the Sultan's opponents something to aspire to. Although reformers disagreed on how to arrest the decline of the Empire, they all blamed the Hamidian regime's autocratic nature, repressive policies and weak government for its ills.
- The Great Powers seemed poised to dismantle the Empire, often prompted by the clear injustices of the Hamidian regime. The Macedonian Question in particular led to direct foreign involvement in the policing of the Empire.

Consequences

- The revolution was widely celebrated in Turkey, but following the attempted counter-revolution of Abdul Hamid, the government of CUP members followed a Turkish nationalist agenda and also used repression to keep control of the Empire.

Remember to consider the content of each source as well as the provenance. For example, some authors may be more representative (speak for more people) than others; while other authors may be in a position of authority and, in some cases, more informed about what is going on, depending on the circumstances. Consider the purpose of the author in creating the source, its nature (for example, whether it is a private letter, a public speech, or a government document), the date it was written and its intended audience.

Try to identify different movements and comment on their aims. In this way you will be able to reach a judgement about their success, although you may also wish to include further comment on 'success' from a broader perspective.

- Three months after the initial revolution, Bulgaria seized the opportunity to declare its full independence. Its considerable military strength meant this was accepted by Istanbul.
- Bosnia–Herzegovina was annexed by Austria-Hungary, while Greece reversed defeat by Turkey in 1897 by uniting with Crete in October 1908.

 PRACTICE QUESTION

Evaluating historical sources

Study Sources 2 and 3. With reference to these sources and your understanding of the historical context, which of these two sources is more valuable in explaining why some regions wanted to break from Ottoman rule?

 PRACTICE QUESTION

How successful were revolutionary movements within the Ottoman Empire in the years 1900 to 1911?

8 Pan-Slavism and the Bosnian Crisis

Aims of pan-Slavism

Pan-Slavism, the nationalist ideal of uniting all Slavs, who shared ethnic, religious and cultural identities, had been a political force in Russia and the Balkans for decades. As the number of Balkans states declaring independence from the Ottoman Empire increased from the late nineteenth century onwards, this ambition grew even stronger. The creation of a South Slav state, also known as Yugoslavia, became the ultimate goal for Slav nationalists, especially in Serbia and Croatia.

Russia, in its self-appointed role as 'Protector of Slavs', offered support to Balkan nations like Serbia and Bulgaria, however, Austria-Hungary decided to take a more proactive approach to defending its own interests in the region. This was fostered by two appointments in the empire: **Alois von Aehrenthal** as Foreign Minister and Franz von Hötzendorf as Chief of the General Staff. Both men had the same goal of halting the Habsburg Empire's decline, although Hötzendorf's methods were more aggressive. Nonetheless, the Slav nationalists of the Balkans now had three empires to bear in mind when pursuing their Yugoslav objective: the decaying Ottoman Empire, which still had control of Macedonia and Albania; the Austro-Hungarian Empire, which had occupied and administered Bosnia–Herzegovina since 1878 and made it clear that they wanted a full annexation of the provinces; and the Russian Empire, which promised support but had been badly weakened by its defeat in the Russo–Japanese War in 1905.

Russia's defeat had helped to spark the first Russian Revolution in January 1905, after which pan-Slavism grew in Russia as politicians and intelligentsia searched for solutions to Russia's apparent decline.

EXTRACT 1

There was one point, however, at which the interests of all those Slavic peoples met. They all found themselves in the subjection of other nations who despised them. To German, Hungarian, and even Turk, the Slav seemed an inferior being who had achieved nothing in politics or in the arts of life. The reaction against this was a desire on the part of the Slavs to assert the value, not of this or that particular Slav people, but of the Slav race as a whole. The leaders of the nationalist movements pointed with equal pride to the political greatness of Russia, to the poetic genius of the Serbs, to the missionary zeal of the early Bulgarians, or to the cultural acquisitions of the Czechs. They interpreted them as illustrations of the common genius of the race. This naturally led to emphasis on the common origin of the Slavs and their bonds of kinship. It resulted in a vague, semi-poetic, semi-philosophical idea of a great Slav race with a common life in the remote past and with a great common destiny in the more or less misty future.

Louis Levine, "Panslavism and European Politics" in *Political Science Quarterly*, December 1914.

ACTIVITY

What interpretation of pan-Slavism is advanced by Levine in Extract 1?

LEARNING OBJECTIVES

In this chapter you will learn about:

- the influence of pan-Slavism in foreign policy at the start of the twentieth century

- the causes of the Bosnian Crisis

- the course and consequences of the Bosnian Crisis.

KEY CHRONOLOGY

The Bosnian Crisis

1878	Austria-Hungary occupies and administers Bosnia and Herzegovina under the Treaty of Berlin
September 1908	Meetings between Izvolsky and Aehrenthal
5 October 1908	Austro-Hungarian troops march into Bosnia and Herzegovina; Bulgaria declares independence from Ottoman Empire
6 October 1908	Austria-Hungary formally announces its annexation
March 1909	Russia and Serbia end their protests against the annexation

CROSS-REFERENCE

The development of Serb nationalism at the turn of the century is explored in Chapter 5.

A Key Profile of Alois von Aehrenthal is in Chapter 5, page 35.

ACTIVITY

Compare the ideals of pan-Slavism with those of other nationalist movements like the Pan-German League (explored in Chapter 3). Do you think that pan-Slavism was more or less of a threat to European peace? Explain your reasons.

The causes and course of the Bosnian Crisis

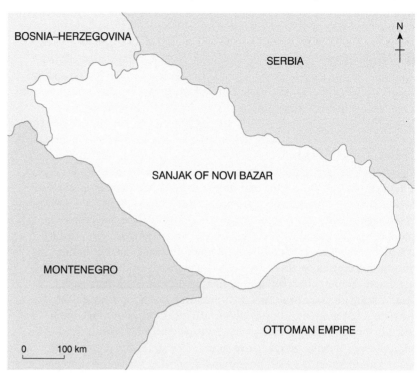

Fig. 1 *Map of the Sanjak of Novi Bazar. This region was a focus for rivalry between Serbia and Austria-Hungary in the early 1900s.*

CROSS-REFERENCE

The agreements made at the 1878 Congress of Berlin and their consequences are explored in Chapter 3.

Although relations between Austria-Hungary and Russia over the Balkans were improving, as documented in the 1897 agreement between them, new developments ensured that this would not last. The Serbian coup in 1903 was deeply worrying for the Austrians, as Serbia now had an aggressively pro-Russian monarch and government. In early 1908 the Habsburg Empire also risked damaging relations with Russia over its plans for the Sanjak of Novi Bazar, another territory it had been given permission to occupy under the **1878 Berlin Treaty**. The Sanjak was a province located between Serbia and Montenegro, providing a convenient barrier for Austria-Hungary – it was unlikely that the independent and nationalist Serbia and Montenegro would be able to unite and mount a challenge to Austro-Hungarian influence. To cement its authority in the Sanjak and extend its influence further into the remainder of the Ottoman Empire, Austria planned a railway through the region, which angered Russia.

ACTIVITY

Revision

On a blank map of the Balkan region, add labels, arrows and dates to create a visual guide to the tensions and developments there around 1908. Use your knowledge from this chapter as well as Chapters 3 and 7.

CROSS-REFERENCE

The causes and events of the Young Turk revolution are explained in Chapter 7.

The Anglo-Russian Agreement, which ended rivalry between Russia and Britain in the Middle East, is explained in Chapter 5.

Causes of the crisis

The Young Turk Revolution in Constantinople sparked Austro-Hungarian fears of a resurgence of Turkish power, which could threaten their ambition to absorb Bosnia–Herzegovina. When these two provinces were invited to send representatives to the Turkish Parliament, this seemed to undermine the justification Austria-Hungary had hoped to offer for their annexation – namely the need to protect them. Serbia, meanwhile, regarded Bosnia–Herzegovina as Slav states waiting to be liberated from foreign rule. The two provinces contained a large number of Slavs (44 per cent of their combined population were Serbian), and therefore would belong to the future Yugoslavia, according to Serb nationalists.

Aehrenthal believed that the Habsburg Empire's only hope was to act quickly and take full control of Bosnia–Herzegovina before the Turks were ready to mount a challenge. His anxiety to incorporate them was inflamed by the desire to forestall Serbia's ambition of forming a union with them. There were also other influential voices within Austria who hoped that the action might provoke Serbia into a war, thereby giving Austria an opportunity to crush Serbia once and for all.

Meanwhile, Russia also fostered hopes for a revision to one international agreement in particular that, without careful negotiation, risked provoking war: this was the granting of access to the Black Sea Straits. The hopes of the Foreign Minister, **Aleksandr Izvolsky,** were raised by the Anglo-Russian Agreement of 1907. While discussing the agreement, the British were positive about the idea of ending their traditional policy of blocking Russia's access to the Straits. Meanwhile Izvolsky and Tsar Nicholas II discussed making concessions to Austria-Hungary in the Balkans in return for Austro-Hungarian support for access to the Straits.

A diplomatic *coup d'état*?

Before risking war with Serbia over Bosnia–Herzegovina, the Austrians needed to be sure that Russia would not intervene against them, in defence of its ally and of pan-Slav interests. Although the Tsar and Izvolsky were prepared to make concessions to Austria-Hungary, Franz Joseph and his government could not be sure of Russia's reaction, particularly since the resurgence of Russian pan-Slavism after the 1905 **revolution in Russia**.

On 15 and 16 September, Aehrenthal held discussions with Izvolsky at Buchlau Castle in Moravia. No records have been preserved of the discussions, which allowed both ministers to put forward different versions of what happened. However, it would seem that the two ministers did agree some terms. Aehrenthal was granted Russian approval for the annexation, in return for a promise to bring about a revision of the Black Sea Straits agreement in Russia's favour. Both men took some steps towards fulfilling this deal but on 5 October 1908, Austro-Hungarian troops marched into the provinces and on 6 October Aehrenthal announced the annexation, without any further reference to Russia.

Fig. 2   *Aleksandr Izvolsky*

Aleksandr Izvolsky (1856–1919) was the Russian Foreign Minister (1906–1910). He was pro-British and a key architect of the 1907 Anglo-Russian Agreement. He also sought to mend diplomatic relations with Japan following Russia's defeat in war against them. In 1908, following his out-manoeuvring by Aehrenthal and Russia's embarrassing climb-down in the Bosnian Crisis, Izvolsky was accused of betraying his fellow Slavs. He was demoted and sent to France as a diplomat, where he strengthened the alliances with Britain and France before and during the First World War.

The Russian Revolution of 1905 was partly the result of defeat in the Russo–Japanese War, more implications of which are explored in Chapter 6.

The Buchlau negotiations

It is difficult for historians to piece together exactly what Aehrenthal and Izvolsky discussed in September 1908 because almost no evidence exists of their meeting. Izvolsky knew he was foregoing the interests of Britain and France by canvassing support for a revision of the Black Sea Clauses made in 1841. Aehrenthal may have been planning to secure Izvolsky's agreement by promising to support Russia's aims. When he failed to fulfil his side of the 'bargain', there was no written record of him agreeing to anything at all. The annexation was presented as a **fait accompli**.

fait accompli: an action already completed, and which therefore must be accepted, even if inconvenient

ACTIVITY

What does Franz Joseph mean by his reference to 'the altered state of affairs in the Ottoman Empire'?

SOURCE 1

Emperor Franz Joseph's private letter to Kaiser Wilhelm II on 29 September 1908, advising him of the imminent annexation of Bosnia and Herzegovina by Austria-Hungary.

While Bosnia and Herzegovina have expressed a desire for some time to establish a constitution, these aims now, because of the altered state of affairs in the Ottoman Empire, have asserted themselves so vigorously that my Government no longer feels that it can oppose them, especially if the southern borders of the monarchy are to be free of disturbances. Since a constitution can be granted only by a sovereign power, I shall find myself forced to announce the annexation of Bosnia and Herzegovina. We shall inform the Ottoman Empire of this and, as proof of our policy of peace and our rejection of any thought of acquiring territory in the Balkans, we shall withdraw our troops stationed in the Sanjak of Novi Bazar and in the future shall renounce the privileges granted to us in the Sanjak by the Treaty of Berlin. I am certain that you will judge this with friendly goodwill and that you will not fail to understand that we are acting under the pressure of urgent necessity.

ACTIVITY

Pair discussion

In pairs, role play how you think the discussions at Buchlau might have gone between Izvolsky and Aehrenthal. Make sure you prepare first by researching the aims and motivations of each statesman, using information in this chapter as well as further research.

Fig. 3 *This cartoon gives us some idea of Turkey's reaction to the annexation; the caption reads, 'Advance of civilisation in Bosnia and Herzegovina'*

The consequences of the Bosnian Crisis

There was deep concern throughout Europe following the annexation. The Russian government, which had not at that stage been fully informed of Izvolsky's negotiations, condemned Austria's action outright and threatened to send troops in support of the outraged Serbia. Izvolsky tried to save face by demanding an international conference. For weeks it was unclear how Russia and Serbia would respond to the annexation, and tension increased when Serbia mobilised its army.

In January 1909, Austria-Hungary reached an agreement with Turkey, whereby the Turks accepted the annexation in return for two million pounds in compensation. Serbia's troops, however, remained mobilised, awaiting Russian support to force the Austrians out of Bosnia–Herzegovina. Bülow announced Germany's intention to support Austria and General Moltke, Chief of the German General Staff, wrote to Hötzendorf on 19 March 1909 declaring: 'As long as Austria and Germany stand should to shoulder we will be strong enough to break any ring around us.'

Kaiser Wilhelm II was annoyed with Aehrenthal for provoking Russian hostility and risking Germany's influence in Turkey. Nevertheless, in the wake of the first **Moroccan Crisis**, Germany realised it could not afford to alienate Austria-Hungary. Wilhelm put Germany's support for its ally rather more flamboyantly when he promised that if Austria were attacked, 'a knight in shining armour' would be found at her side. This was the first time Germany had made such a promise to its ally and it placed Russia in an extremely difficult position. Although Russia had begun a major rearmament programme in 1906, in the wake of defeat in the Russo–Japanese War, the country was not yet ready to face both Austria and Germany. ᵗᵉ; Russia

Germany went on to take the initiative on 21 March, sending Russia a note warning that if it did not accept the annexation and end support for Serbia, events would 'run their course'. Ten days later, under pressure from Russia, Serbia withdrew its objections and made promises of good behaviour to Austria-Hungary. Russia had been forced to back down completely and Izvolsky was forced to resign.

CROSS-REFERENCE

The consequences of the Moroccan Crisis of 1905–6 are explored in Chapter 6.

SOURCE 2

Serbia's official response to the annexation of Bosnia–Herzegovina, written in negotiation with Austria-Hungary on 26 March 1909:

Serbia recognises that she has not been injured in her right by the fait accompli created in Bosnia–Herzegovina and that consequently she will conform to such decision as the Powers shall take in regard to Article 25 of the Treaty of Berlin. Submitting to the advice of the Great Powers, Serbia undertakes already now to abandon the attitude of protest and opposition which she has maintained in regard to the annexation since last autumn and undertakes further to change the course of her present policy towards Austria-Hungary to live henceforward with the latter on a footing of good-neighbourliness. Conformable to these declarations and confident of the pacific intentions of Austria-Hungary, Serbia will reduce her army to the position of spring 1908 as regards its organisation, its distribution and its effectives.

Consequences of the crisis for international relations

The crisis fuelled the ambitions of the Balkan States. Serbia, in particular, was determined to fight back from the humiliation, viewing the annexation as a deliberate act of hostility towards their 'legitimate' ambitions. They set about

ACTIVITY

Evaluating primary sources

1. Discuss Source 2 with your partner. What predictions could you make about how the Kaiser might have responded to the annexation itself, and of Franz Joseph's stated reasons for it?

2. What would an historian have to consider when using this source as evidence of reasons for the annexation of Bosnia–Herzegovina by Austria-Hungary?

ACTIVITY

Evaluating primary sources

1. Like most diplomatic documents, Serbia's response in Source 2 to the annexation is carefully worded to maintain good relations, and it has glossed over some controversial events. Explain what the Serbians were referring to with the following phrases:
   a. 'Submitting to the advice of the Great Powers'
   b. 'To change the course of her present policy towards Austria-Hungary'
   c. 'Confident of the pacific intentions of Austria-Hungary'

2. What is the value of this source to an historian investigating relations between Serbia and Austria-Hungary between 1903 and 1909?

HON OR DEATH"
- Black Hand.

borrowing money for railway-building from France and laid track to the Austro-Hungarian border. Artillery guns were also purchased from the French, increasing the strength of the Serbian army. Serbia grew more open in her support of South Slavs and did nothing to stop terrorist organisations forming within its borders and acting in the southern provinces of the Habsburg Empire. Among these extreme nationalist groups was 'Union or Death!', also known as the **Black Hand**. In Austria some, including Hötzendorf, argued that Austria should launch a pre-emptive war against Serbia.

A CLOSER LOOK

The Black Hand was a secret terrorist organisation. Its origins can be traced back to 1901, but it became far more active from 1911 onwards. In that year the group attempted, unsuccessfully, to assassinate Emperor Franz Joseph. Some of its members were high-ranking Serbian officials, including its influential founder Captain Dragutin Dimitrijevic, better known as 'Apis', who was also the Serb Chief of Military Intelligence. The full extent of the group's connections to the Serbian government have not been established, and the issue has been clouded by the group's assassination of Franz Ferdinand in June 1914.

Bulgaria also sought to profit from this demonstration of Turkish weakness. Since Russia was keen to create a barrier against further Austrian expansion, it fostered closer relations with Bulgaria, which accepted Russian money to help pay Turkey the compensation agreed as a result of its declaration of independence. Russia also encouraged an alliance between Serbia and Bulgaria, and this was signed in March 1912 when the powers agreed their future stakes to Macedonia. Meanwhile, in its agreement with Turkey, Austria-Hungary gave up its occupation of the Sanjak of Novi Bazar, which ended one of the many smaller sources of tension between the Austrians and the Russians.

ACTIVITY

Thinking point

If you were Emperor Franz Joseph in April 1909, would you have been impressed with Aehrenthal's handling of the annexation? Explain your reasons.

KEY TERM

Sublime Porte: the location of the central government of the Ottoman Empire, therefore the name is used to refer to the Ottoman Empire

ACTIVITY

1. With reference to articles of the Protocol in Source 3, which government do you think gained most from the agreement?
2. Why do you think Austria-Hungary was willing to give up the Sanjak at this point?

SOURCE 3

The Protocol between Austria-Hungary and Turkey, signed in Constantinople on 26 February 1909 by the Turkish Prime Minister Hussein Himil, the Turkish Foreign Minister, Gabriel Noradounghian, and the Austro-Hungarian Ambassador, Marquis Pallavicin:

ART. 1: Austria-Hungary declares that it expressly renounces all the rights conferred on it by the Treaty of Berlin and the convention of Constantinople of 21 April 1879, regarding the former Sanjak of Novi Bazar.

ART. 2: The protest of the **Sublime Porte** against the decision of the dual government of Austria-Hungary concerning Bosnia and Herzegovina is ended and replaced by the present protocol which states that every disagreement on the subject of these two provinces is cleared up between them, and that the Ottoman government expressly recognises the new state of affairs in Bosnia–Herzegovina created by the said decision.

ART. 8: The Sublime Porte proposing to open negotiations with the Great Powers with a view to contracting more international treaties, Austria-Hungary, in recognising that the intentions of the Sublime Porte are well founded declares that it is willing from this moment to lend the Porte its entire and sincere support for this purpose.

The Bosnian Crisis had a major impact on the future division of Europe. Germany had shown its total commitment to Austria-Hungary, while the Russians were determined never to give in again: if they did they risked losing all their influence in the Balkan region, as well as their reputation as 'Protector of Slavs'. It indirectly drove Italy, although a member of the Triple Alliance, further from Austria. Italy's ambitions were, in part, contrary to those of its supposed 'ally' as it wanted border areas in the Tyrol which fell within the Austrian Empire but were largely Italian-speaking. Thus, it was prepared to respond to Russia's request for support in 1911, and signed an agreement with Russia whereby each agreed to consult with the other on any future settlement in the Balkans. The agreement was limited but was a pointer to Italy's future loyalties.

CROSS-REFERENCE

You can remind yourself of the terms of the Triple Alliance in Chapter 5.

The impact on Russian foreign policy

One of the most significant consequences of the Bosnian Crisis was a result of the damage it caused to Russia's reputation as 'Protector of Slavs'. Pan-Slavism remained a strong goal for Russians, yet through naivety or incompetence they had allow a region with a majority Slav population, coveted by its fellow Slav nation Serbia, to be absorbed under Austro-Hungarian rule. The Russian government knew it could not afford to back down again in a future dispute in the Balkans, or its influence in the region – perhaps even its Great Power status – would be finished. Within Russia itself, the ambitions of pan-Slavism were also a useful distraction from severe internal problems.

The Russian military had been humiliated in the Russo–Japanese War of 1904–5. Its weakened state had both prevented it from responding more effectively to the Bosnian annexation, and highlighted the drastic and urgent need for its improvement. Despite Izvolsky risking French disapproval by asking Aerenthal for help in revising the Black Sea Clauses at Buchlau, the Bosnian Crisis helped to bring France and Russia into closer alignment. News of Germany's support for Austria-Hungary's actions was welcomed in France, as it made Russia more likely to develop plans for war against Germany on Germany's eastern border.

Russia was not ready to adopt a more openly hostile stance towards Germany, however; in 1910 at Potsdam, Sazonov – Izvolsky's replacement as Foreign Minister – formally ended Russia's long-held objections to Germany building a railway linking Berlin to Baghdad. Russia then signed a secret agreement with Japan on 8 July 1912 (the Russo–Japanese Agreement), separate to either party's agreements with Britain, but which would allow Russia to focus on relations with the European powers.

ACTIVITY

How might a German or French newspaper have reported on the Bosnian Crisis? Remember to consider how their own interests were at stake.

Summary

Causes of the crisis	Events	Consequences
• Pan-Slavism in Russia and the Slav Baltic states, especially Serbia • Occupation and administration of Bosnia–Herzegovina since 1878 • Austro-Hungarian concerns about nationalism • Growing tension between Austria and Serbia; concerns over the Sanjak of Novi Bazar • Decline of Ottoman Empire exacerbated by Young Turk revolution in 1908	• Buchlau negotiations, 1908 • Aerenthal's manoeuvrings • Izvolsky's calls for international conference ignored • Germany's support for Austria-Hungary • Turkey, Russia and Serbia's formal acceptance of the annexation, 1909	• Humiliation of Russia as 'Protector of Slavs' • Italian alienation from Triple Alliance • Development of Serbian nationalism; formation of the Black Hand

STUDY TIP

As well as exploring the provenance of each source, remember to analyse their content carefully and compare it to your own knowledge. Due to the nature and purpose of these two sources, neither gives an honest account of how Serbia and Turkey felt about the annexation, which you can explain using your knowledge of the context.

STUDY TIP

Try to select your supporting evidence carefully and pay careful attention to key words like 'total'. There will be at least some points to support the view given and some to challenge it – but one side might be far stronger than the other. Make sure you consider the whole topic carefully so you can identify strong evidence for both sides.

 PRACTICE QUESTION

Evaluating primary sources

With reference to Sources 2 and 3, and your understanding of the historical context, which of these two sources is more valuable in explaining the response of other countries to Austria-Hungary's annexation of Bosnia?

 PRACTICE QUESTION

'The Bosnian Crisis was a total defeat for the pan-Slav movement.' Assess the validity of this view, with reference to the years 1900–8.

9 The First and Second Balkan Wars

SOURCE 1

From an interview given by an anonymous Bulgarian statesman to Leon Trotsky, a Russian revolutionary leader, recorded soon after the First Balkan War broke out at the end of 1912:

We Balkan peoples will settle with Turkey, without any interference from Europe, which puts on an air of being afraid that we shall be excessively demanding. And this from Europe – that is to say, from Austria-Hungary, who annexed Bosnia; from Italy, who seized Tripoli, from Russia, who never takes her eyes off Constantinople. This is the Europe that comes to us preaching moderation and restraint. Your diplomats would not be averse to freezing the Balkans for another ten years, in expectation of better days sometime. How is it that they cannot understand it is increasingly possible in our epoch to direct the destinies of the Balkans from the outside? We are growing up, gaining confidence, and becoming independent. In the very first years of our present phase of existence as a state, we told our would-be guardians: 'Bulgaria will follow her own line.' And so foreign diplomats would do well to get used to the idea that the Balkan Peninsula 'will follow its own line'.

ACTIVITY

Evaluating historical sources

1. Read Source 1. What does the Bulgarian statesman mean by the phrase 'settle with Turkey'? It may help to look back to Chapters 7 and 8 before you answer this.
2. How would you describe the tone of the statesman's remarks, especially phrases like 'the Europe that comes to us preaching moderation and restraint'?
3. After reading this chapter, discuss with a partner how valuable you think this source is as an overview of the Bulgarian point of view in late 1912.

Causes of the First Balkan War

By 1911 the independent Balkan nations had grown in confidence and military strength. Furthermore, as Source 1 suggests, they were determined to engineer the future of the Balkans themselves.

After the tremors caused by the Bosnian Crisis, the Balkan region enjoyed a brief period of relative calm from 1911. It was, however, also a time during which the newly independent Balkan states could develop their goals, which for many nationalist groups revolved around **pan-Slavism**. Moreover, although the Young Turk revolution indirectly led to the annexation of Bosnia–Herzegovina by Austria-Hungary and Bulgaria's declaration of independence, the Macedonian Question still remained. This was of increasing concern to the independent Balkan states rather than the Great Powers, as it was the Bulgarians, Greeks and Serbs who sought to champion the ethnic minorities they believed to be living under Turkish oppression in Macedonia. While Britain, France and Germany were distracted by the second Moroccan Crisis, the Balkan states' desire to force Turkey out of Europe for good grew.

LEARNING OBJECTIVES

In this chapter you will learn about:

- the causes of the First and Second Balkan Wars
- how the Great Powers tried to impose peace on the Balkans
- the impact of the Balkan Wars on the Great Powers and on Serbia.

KEY CHRONOLOGY

1911	Italy launches attack on Ottoman Empire at Tripoli
1912	Balkan League formed
October 1912– May 1913	First Balkan War
May 1913	Treaty of London
July 1913	Second Balkan War
August 1913	Treaties of Bucharest and Constantinople

CROSS-REFERENCE

The Balkans are introduced in Chapter 7, pages 53–54, and Chapter 8, page 61.

To remind yourself about pan-Slavism, turn to page 35.

CROSS-REFERENCE

The second Moroccan Crisis and the concerns of Britain, France and Germany in 1911 are explored in Chapter 6, pages 47–48.

The status of the Ottoman Empire following the Young Turk revolution and its loss of territory by 1911 are explained in Chapter 7, pages 56–58.

The Bosnian Crisis and its impact on the Balkans are explored in Chapter 8.

Fig. 1   *Italian artillery in the attack on Tripoli*

CROSS-REFERENCE

Relations between Austria-Hungary and Russia at this point are explored in Chapters 5 and 8.

The Italian attack on Tripoli

Italy had long wanted a colony in North Africa, having been disappointed by their lack of imperial gains at Berlin in 1878. In the summer of 1911, taking advantage of the instability in Constantinople following the Young Turk revolution, the Italians attacked and occupied the Ottoman province of Tripoli (in modern-day Libya); on 29 September, Turkey declared war on Italy. In response, the Ottoman Government diverted many of its forces to North Africa, leaving its remaining Balkan territories exposed. The Italian navy then threatened Turkey's islands in the Aegean Sea, and by May 1912 the Italo–Turkish war was at a stalemate. This encouraged the Balkan states to advance their own positions while the Turkish Government and its resources were focused elsewhere, especially as war with Italy had revealed the poor state of the Ottoman military.

Fig. 2   *Italian offensives during the Italo–Turkish War, 1911–12*

The Balkan League

Two figures were instrumental in forming the Balkan League. One was the Greek Prime Minister, Eleutherios Venizelos, who hoped to make Greece's neighbours into firm allies. The other figure was Nicholas Hartwig, the Russian ambassador to Serbia, stationed in its capital, Belgrade. He recognised the opportunity posed by the Italian attack on the Ottoman Empire and encouraged the Serbs to agree to an alliance with Bulgaria. By fostering strong relations between Serbia and Bulgaria, Hartwig hoped to deter Austro-Hungarian and German ambitions in the region, thereby securing Russia's interests in the Balkans. He was partly acting on his own initiative, rather than following orders from St Petersburg.

In the event Serbia and Bulgaria joined together with an agreement in spring 1912. Both countries felt frustrated with the lack of readiness of the Great Powers to protect their fellow Christian peoples from Ottoman aggression, and felt it was time for them to take the situation in the Balkans into their own hands. Hartwig was not the only Russian to see the benefits of this, indeed Russian encouragement was instrumental in the formation of a Balkan collaboration.

At the instigation of Venizelos, Greece and Montenegro joined to form the Balkan League in May 1912, which was committed to driving the Ottomans out of the Balkan region for good. This, however, was as far as their agreement went, for each power had a different view of the future of the Balkans. Bulgaria, for example, wanted an independent Macedonia that would look to Bulgaria for protection and the port of Salonika on the Aegean Sea, while Serbia favoured dividing up Macedonia and was primarily interested in gaining Albania and an outlet to the Adriatic Sea. Serbian and Bulgarian diplomats disagreed on exactly how Macedonia would be divided following a Balkan League victory: in the final document only rough borders were agreed upon, while the fate of area in the middle of Macedonia would be decided by Tsar Nicholas II.

Albanian riots spread throughout Macedonia in the summer of 1912 which the Turks were unable to control. In September, the League's members took advantage of the situation by mobilising their forces. However, it was Bulgaria which, without consulting its allies, first declared war on the Ottoman Empire on 7 September.

The events of the First Balkan War

Montenegro followed Bulgaria's declaration of war on Turkey on 8 October, as did Serbia and Greece on 18 October. The Turks were in no position to resist, but the rivalry between the Balkan powers was evident from the beginning. The Bulgarian forces rushed to Macedonia to seize the area before the Greeks could do so and went on to press southwards and, in a series of brilliant victories, forced the Ottomans out of Eastern Thrace and back to Constantinople. However, following warnings from Russia about the possible consequences, they did not follow up their victory and move on to the Turkish capital.

> **ACTIVITY**
>
> Prepare a table showing the different ambitions of the Balkan states before and during the two Balkan Wars. Add to this as you read through this chapter.

Fig. 3 *Troop movement during the First Balkan War*

Fig. 5 *Bulgarian officers on the battlefield after capturing the Turkish fort of Aidjolou, October 1912*

Yugoslav empire: a country for the southern Slavs

Fig. 4   *Leopold von Berchtold*

Leopold von Berchtold (1863–1942) succeeded Aehrenthal as the Austrian Foreign Minister in 1912. Before the Balkan Wars he had hoped to preserve the status quo in the Balkans and avoid war. However, he became far less sympathetic to Serbia following its successes in the two Balkan Wars. He came to agree more with Hötzendorf, collaborating with him on the issuing of the ultimatum to Serbia in July 1914. Berchtold was dismissed in 1915.

Balkan League success

While Bulgaria was fully occupied, their 'allies' were able to seize land for themselves. In the west, Serbia took Northern Albania while in the south the Greeks seized Salonika. Virtually all of European Turkey fell to the Balkan League. Four small countries with a population of 10 million had defeated a power of 25 million. On 3 December 1912, an armistice was signed between Turkey, Serbia and Bulgaria. Fighting was renewed in early 1913, but eventually the Turks conceded defeat after the loss of Adrianople in April 1913.

As the strength and ambitions of the Balkan nations grew, so did Austria-Hungary's fear of a multi-national **Yugoslav empire**. Hötzendorf, the Austrian Chief of General Staff, had advocated a pre-emptive strike against Serbia for some time, and when the Balkan War broke he argued for Austrian intervention. Once again the situation in the Balkans looked likely to flare up into a wider European conflict. From previous commitments made by the Great Powers, it was entirely possible that Russia would support its Balkan clients Serbia and Bulgaria against Turkey, while Germany would fight alongside Austria-Hungary and France would support Russia. The division between the standpoints of the Austrian military and the Austrian civilian leadership widened, as Foreign Minister **Berchtold** argued for caution.

Group work

In pairs, draw up a list of the main causes of the Balkan Wars. Group them according to the following categories: Balkan Strength, Ottoman Weakness, Involvement of the European Powers.

Attempts to impose peace

Although Germany, Austria and Russia had initially avoided intervening in the war (the former believing, wrongly, that the Turks would defeat their rebellious subjects) by November 1912 both Austria and Russia, alarmed by the Ottoman Empire's rapid disintegration, had begun to mobilise. Their allies instructed their diplomats and ambassadors to seek assurances that the alliance treaties signed years before would be honoured if a dispute broke out in the Balkans: the French Prime Minister Poincaré tried to reassure Russia of its support and apparently promised that Britain would commit to backing France in the event of war with Germany. As the crisis deepened, the British Foreign Secretary, **Edward Grey**, instigated talks between the other Great Powers great powers in London in December 1912.

While Grey maintained that Britain's commitments to France and Russia were limited and Britain still had freedom of action in relation to the Balkan crisis, he had been disturbed enough by the war against Turkey to discuss plans to mobilise the army should France be threatened by Germany. This suggests that a Balkan war which had the capacity to trigger the alliance system was already anticipated in 1912, and Grey was keen to avert this.

The Great Powers gathered in London at the start of 1913 to discuss a new settlement for the Balkans. The status of the Balkan states had changed dramatically since the 1878 Berlin conference, at which strenuous efforts were made by Britain and Austria to ensure that the Ottoman Empire retained some power in the Balkans to prevent Russia from expanding her influence. In 1913, it was clear that this was no longer a realistic aim, and attention now turned to managing the ambitions of the individual Balkan powers carefully so that none of them could become too aggressive – and to ensuring that Slav nationalism did not engulf the region in further conflict.

At the London conference, the British and German representatives attempted to mediate between the conflicting Balkan interests. They persuaded the Russians and Austrians to compromise: the former could not realise all its expansionist aims for its **client states,** especially Serbia; while the latter could not dictate the borders of its new neighbours.

The Treaty of London, 30 May 1913

The peace treaty was a result of the negotiations between the Great Powers rather than the Balkan states and the terms were not well-received by those whom they affected. It was decided that:

- Greece would receive Crete, Salonika and Southern Macedonia (even though it was mainly peopled by Bulgarians)
- Bulgaria would keep Thrace
- Serbia would receive Central and Northern Macedonia
- Albania would become an independent state on the Adriatic coast.

Serbia was very resentful of the Austrian insistence on the creation of an independent Albania. This closed a stretch of coastline to possible Serbian expansion and kept Serbia a landlocked state. Serbia also felt entitled to a greater share of Macedonia and resented Bulgaria's support for Austria. A Serbian diplomat complained: 'Bulgaria, her shores washed by two seas, denies us a single port.' However, the Bulgarians felt that, as they had borne the largest share of the fighting, more of Macedonia should be theirs. Both Serbia and Bulgaria were determined to win back what they felt they rightly deserved and on 1 June 1913, Serbia formed an alliance with Greece to this end.

The apparent success of the London conference – at least from the perspective of the Great Powers – may have contributed to the later mismanagement of the **July Crisis** following the assassination of Franz Ferdinand. Leading statesman like Grey showed signs of complacency in 1914, perhaps confident that if a major war triggered by crisis in the Balkans could be avoided by diplomacy once, it would be straightforward to ensure this happened in the future.

Causes of the Second Balkan War

The military strength of the independent Balkan states had already increased enough to threaten and defeat the Ottoman Empire when working together as the Balkan League: a Bulgarian general remarked in 1910 that 'We have

KEY PROFILE

Fig. 6   *Edward Grey*

Edward Grey (1862–1933) was British Foreign Secretary from 1905 to 1916. His attempts at crisis management in 1914 failed: although he attempted to limit the impact of the conflict between Austria and Serbia in July, his vagueness in discussions with foreign ambassadors allowed for misunderstandings (for example, during the July Crisis). He resigned as foreign secretary and later became ambassador to the USA.

KEY TERM

July Crisis: the collective term for the diplomatic and military action taken by European powers in response to the assassination of Franz Ferdinand on 28 June 1914 which is explored in depth in Chapters 10 and 11.

CROSS-REFERENCE

Read Chapter 3, page 21, for more information on the client states.

ACTIVITY

Research

Split into two groups, and research arguments for or against the following statement: 'The Balkan Wars were an inevitable consequence of the European Powers' determination to maintain Ottoman authority in the Balkan region.' Use Chapters 3, 5, 7 and 8 of this book, and other sources to help you prepare your argument.

become the most militaristic state in the world' (a strong claim considering the militarism of Germany at the same time). In the Second Balkan War, however, their formidable armies would be turned against each other.

With further conflict on the horizon, Tsar Nicholas II of Russia attempted to organise negotiations between the Balkan states, and on 8 June 1913 contacted the rulers of Serbia and Bulgaria, offering his services as an arbitrator. This attempt was ruined, however, by the orders of the Bulgarian General Savov on 28 June to launch surprise attacks on Serbia. This was viewed as a pre-emptive strike by the Bulgarians, who were convinced that the Greeks and the Serbs would attack before long. Bulgaria did not declare war on Serbia or Greece before attacking, hoping instead to make solid advances into Macedonia before the Great Powers could intervene.

A CLOSER LOOK

Interpretation of the Balkan Wars

The journalist Misha Glenny has argued that while the aims of the First Balkan War can be viewed as reasonable, the second was 'motivated by sheer greed and nothing else.' Though acknowledging Bulgarian forces were the first to attack, he asserts that Greece and Serbia's war plans were primarily responsible: they 'simply decided to attack Bulgaria in its moment of maximum weakness, exhausted by its sacrifices the previous winter.' The increasing militarism of the Balkan states – especially Bulgaria – and the growth in nationalism following the decline of Turkey-in-Europe and disputes over the diverse peoples of Macedonia were also long-term reasons for the renewed Balkan conflict.

Defeat for Bulgaria

Although public opinion in Bulgaria had become increasingly militaristic and the resumption of hostilities was overwhelmingly popular, the Bulgarian army was outnumbered by mid-July as Romania (which had stayed neutral in the first war) and Turkey joined in on Serbia's side. The Turks were hoping to be able to use this dispute between their former enemies as an opportunity to win back something of what they had lost. They succeeded in regaining Adrianople, and in August Bulgaria asked for peace terms.

Under the Treaty of Bucharest, signed on 10 August 1913 by Bulgaria, Romania, Greece, Montenegro and Serbia, Bulgaria lost most of its recent gains. It surrendered territory to Greece and Serbia, and the latter almost doubled in size. Romania was given a small amount of territory in Northern Bulgaria in recognition for its part in the fighting. A further agreement – the Treaty of Constantinople, signed on 13 August – required Bulgaria to return Adrianople to Turkey.

ACTIVITY

Summary

Compare the territorial gains of the Balkan states above with their aims before and after the First Balkan War. Which nation seems to have got the most of what they wanted? Which nation got the least?

Table 1 *The partition of Turkey, 1913.*

Gain	Territory	Population (millions)	Area (sq. miles)
Greece	Epirus, South Macedonia, Salonika, Crete	1.7	17,000
Serbia	Central Macedonia	1.5	17,000
Romania	South Dobruja	0.25	10,000
Bulgaria	Eastern Macedonia	0.15	2,700
Montenegro	Novi Bazar	0.2m	2,100

Fig. 7 *Map of the Balkans following the two Balkan Wars*

The humiliation of Bulgaria boosted the Serbs' confidence and in September they invaded Albania in the hope of fulfilling their ambition to take a coastal strip. Only when Austria-Hungary threatened intervention did they withdraw, and some Greek troops remained stationed in this area until 1914.

The impact of the wars on the Balkans

SOURCE 2

The following are some of the terms of the Treaty of Bucharest, signed to conclude peace between the Balkan states following Bulgaria's defeat in the Second Balkan War, 1913:

- A mixed commission shall supervise the division of the lands and funds which up to the present time may have belonged in common to districts, communes, or communities separated by the new frontier. In case of disagreement as to the line or as to the method of marking it, the signatories agree to request a friendly government to appoint an arbitrator, whose decision upon the points at issue shall be considered final.
- Questions relating to the old Serbo–Bulgarian frontier shall be settled according to the understanding reached by the two High Contracting Parties.
- The headquarters of the respective armies shall be immediately informed of the signing of the present treaty. The Bulgarian government engages to begin to reduce its army to a **peace footing** on the day after such notification.
- The evacuation of Bulgarian territory, both old and new, shall begin immediately after the **demobilisation** of the Bulgarian army and shall be completed within a period of not more than fifteen days.

KEY TERM

peace footing: the status of an army whose country is at peace and which is needed only for self-defence; usually the number of active soldiers is reduced

demobilisation: the process by which armed forces are disbanded

ACTIVITY

Evaluating primary sources

1. How easy do you think it would have been for the Balkan states to agree on a 'friendly government' to act as an arbitrator?
2. What is the value of Source 2 to an historian investigating the consequences of both Balkan Wars?

The wars had divided the Balkan states more than ever before. Serbian prestige had grown while the Bulgarians had emerged frustrated and embittered, especially after their early military successes in the First Balkan War. Bulgaria had incurred heavy losses for little reward and resented Greece's acquisition of Salonika. By 1913, it was clear that Bulgaria would never assist Serbia in any future conflict.

The wars also worsened relations between the Austro-Hungarian Empire and Serbia. Serbia had been angered and frustrated by the Austrian insistence on the creation of Albania at the Treaty of London, as it prevented Serbia from maintaining its access to the sea gained with its brief occupation of the port of Durazzo. To Serbian ministers, it seemed that Austria-Hungary was deliberately blocking its ambitions. Nevertheless, Serbia did gain a large amount of territory, including the former Ottoman province of Kosovo and land in Macedonia. Even this, however, caused problems: these territories included minority populations of Albanian Muslims who rebelled against Serbian rule. The response of Belgrade was quick and appallingly savage, to an extent that it has marred relations between Serbia and Albania ever since.

Serbia's increased confidence, boosted by its territorial growth and its double success on the battlefield, was so remarkable that a correspondent for *The Times* commented on it: 'The Serbs listened to nothing and were capable of all sorts of follies.' This confidence, in turn, encouraged nationalist movements – most notably the Black Hand – to further their ambitions for the creation of a Greater Serbia and the union of the South Slavs.

Bulgaria was deeply frustrated not only by its losses in the second war, but by the lack of support from Russia. Bulgaria had long been a client state of Russia's but after 1913 it grew closer to Austria-Hungary; after all, they now shared the common goal of restraining and even crushing Serbian ambitions. Bulgaria would later fight with Germany and Austria-Hungary in the First World War.

Since further conflict seemed likely, all the powers tried to manoeuvre to improve their positions. To the dismay of France and Russia, in November 1913 the Turks invited a German general, Liman von Sanders, to undertake the reorganisation of the Turkish army in Constantinople. With military and economic assistance from Germany, the Young Turk government prepared for retaliation for the loss of more than 90 per cent of its European empire.

The impact of the wars on the Great Powers

Military preparations and planning

Before the Balkan Wars, many German politicians and military staff could easily see the danger of being dragged into further trouble in the Balkans. This even included the Kaiser, who stated at the beginning of the First Balkan War: 'I will keep out of it. Let them get on with their war undisturbed.' However, the Second Balkan War broke out even after the hard-negotiated Treaty of London had been signed. In July 1913 the German army was increased to its largest size in its history when the Reichstag agreed to a further 130,000 troops.

Germany's Schlieffen Plan, completed in 1905, later went through a series of amendments by military staff, including a reduction in the number of attacking troops, and altering their course so they would not attack via Holland. Meanwhile, other powers began to develop their own detailed military strategies in response to growing concerns over the Balkans:

- After Germany offered Austria-Hungary support against Russia, in 1908–9 the Russian War Ministry drew up a new war plan, Plan No. 19. This provided for a speedy attack on East Prussia during the critical opening phase of war, so diverting German troops from France, and the French provided capital for railway-building to implement it. However, in May 1912 Russian traditionalists, more concerned about Russian expansion in the Balkans, forced an alteration by which Russian forces were to be divided and half sent to the Southern Front, to attack Austria-Hungary through Galicia. This was to prove to Germany's advantage in 1914.

- The Austrians had two plans, **Plan R (Russia) and Plan B (Balkans)** – designed to cover different eventualities. Plan B ran directly counter to the Schlieffen Plan (which the Germans had shared with the Austrians in 1909). The mobilisation order had to be written in 27 different languages and the military command structure of the Habsburg Monarchy – with its dual authority – was slower and less well-organised, making the Austrian war plans difficult to implement.

- France developed the highly aggressive 'Plan XVII' in the wake of its Three Year Service law of 1913. This involved an all-out offensive in Lorraine and was a mark of the confidence of the French High Command at this time. The French mobilisation was centred on precise use of railway timetables, which necessitated trains being in position to move soldiers with meticulous implement.

The effect on the alliances

When Austria forced Serbia to give up its plans of annexing Albania, the Kaiser assured his Austrian ally that it had Germany's full support, as it had done during the Bosnian Crisis. Meanwhile the Entente powers also strengthened their commitments to each other as a result of the Balkan Wars. The French President Poincaré confirmed his support for Russia if they were attacked by Germany due to Austria-Hungary's actions in the Balkans. In 1912, the Anglo-French Naval Agreement was concluded, which guaranteed British naval protection of France's coastline in case of an attack by Germany, and the French navy to protect British interests in the Mediterranean, which made this a highly significant agreement. Both the arms race and the system of alliances seemed primed for war.

THE BOILING POINT

Fig. 8 *This* Punch *cartoon from October 1912 gives a British perspective on turbulence in the Balkans*

CROSS-REFERENCE

For more on the military plans, turn to Chapter 5, page 40.

A CLOSER LOOK

Conflicts between military planning and diplomacy

In the months directly preceding the outbreak of war, the military staff of each country, especially Germany, grew in influence. Diplomacy and even foreign policy itself could be influenced by the detailed forward planning of chiefs of staff, even though foreign policy was technically the responsibility of civilian governments. A key example of this was the different aims pursued by the German foreign office and German army towards France. As tensions between Germany and the Western powers simmered down thanks to careful diplomacy, the Kaiser hoped to avoid war with France altogether. However, the success of the Schlieffen Plan, the only plan Germany had in the result of war with Russia, dictated that France had to be invaded and defeated first before Russia could be engaged in battle.

ACTIVITY

Thinking point

Explain how the two Balkan Wars encouraged the growth of militarism and strengthening of the alliances among the Great Powers.

ACTIVITY

Can you identify the figures depicted in Fig. 8? What message is the cartoonist trying to get across?

Summary

- The 1911–12 Italo–Turkish War both exposed the weakness of the Ottoman army and gave the Balkan states the ideal opportunity to launch their own attack to drive the Turks out of Europe in October 1912.
- The Balkan League, partly formed at the instigation of Russia, had grown in military strength. The combined forces of the Serbian, Greek, Bulgarian and Montenegrin armies removed Turkish influence in the Balkans with considerable ease.
- The First Balkan War was bloody and serious enough to attract the attention of the rest of Europe, which feared an escalation in the conflict. The Great Powers imposed a peace settlement, the Treaty of London, in May 1913 which left the ambitions of Serbia, Greece and Bulgaria unrealised. Serbia and Greece in particular viewed Bulgaria's gains as unfair, but it was Bulgaria who renewed the conflict.
- The very short Second Balkan War led to humiliation for Bulgaria and doubling in size of Serbia. Serbia's confidence grew significantly, as did the activities of nationalist groups like the Black Hand.
- The realisation that another Balkan crisis could easily pull other powers into a wider war led Germany, France, Russia and Austria-Hungary to increase their military expenditure and planning.

> **STUDY TIP**
>
> Consider the aims of the Great Powers in the period and decide the ways in which they failed to understand the ambitions of the Balkan people, or whether different reasons existed, such as the desire to prevent the Great Powers themselves falling out over the Balkans.

 PRACTICE QUESTION

'The Great Powers failed to understand the ambitions of the Balkan peoples in the crises of 1912–13'.
Explain why you agree or disagree with this verdict.

> **STUDY TIP**
>
> Choose your evidence carefully; show that you have a wide range of knowledge and that you are able to pick the most useful points. You should consider what the different aims were of the Balkan states, how they developed and why they clashed with reference to the motives of Serbia and Greece and to other reasons for the outbreak of war.

A **LEVEL** **PRACTICE QUESTION**

'The outbreak of the Second Balkan War was mostly due to greed on the part of Serbia and Greece.'
Assess the validity of this view.

The outbreak of war in the Balkans and the July Crisis

The assassination of Franz Ferdinand

Franz Ferdinand's bodyguard, Franz Von Harrach, recounting the moment of Ferdinand's assassination. Harrach was riding in the same car as Franz Ferdinand and his wife Sophie at the time:

As the car quickly reversed, a thin stream of blood spurted from His Highness's mouth onto my right cheek. The Duchess cried out to him, 'For God's sake, what has happened to you?!' At that she slid off the seat and lay on the floor of the car. I had no idea that she too was hit, and thought she had simply fainted with fright. Then I heard His Imperial Highness say, 'Sophie, Sophie! Don't die; stay alive for the children.' At that I seized the Archduke by the collar of his uniform to stop his head dropping forwards, and asked him if he was in great pain. He answered me quite distinctly, 'It is nothing.' His face began to twist somewhat, but he went on repeating six or seven times, ever more faintly as he gradually lost consciousness, 'It's nothing.'

On the morning of 28 June 1914, eight men lined the route of the Archduke Franz Ferdinand's car as it drove through the streets of Sarajevo. Despite concerns about security in the Bosnian capital, and even a vague warning from the Serbian government about an assassination plot, the local crowds gave the Archduke and his wife a warm, enthusiastic reception. The eight men, however, were all members of the **Black Hand movement**. They carried with them pistols and bombs, and vials of cyanide to swallow after completing their mission. After one assassin injured some of Franz Ferdinand's advisers by throwing a grenade, the Archduke insisted on visiting them in hospital later that morning. On the way there his driver took a wrong turn at a corner outside Schiller's Delicatessen, and the car pulled up next to **Gavrilo Princip**. He fired two shots, hitting Franz Ferdinand in the neck and his pregnant wife Sophie in the abdomen. Both died on their way to hospital.

A CLOSER LOOK

Franz Ferdinand's assassin

Fig. 1 *Gavrilo Princip*

Gavrilo Princip (1894–1918) was most likely recruited by the Black Hand to undertake Franz Ferdinand's assassination because he suffered from tuberculosis and was willing to sacrifice his short remaining life for the nationalist cause. Princip was arrested after the shooting before he could commit suicide. Since he was under 21, Princip received a 20-year prison sentence. He died of tuberculosis in 1918.

In this chapter you will learn about:

- the assassination of Franz Ferdinand in Sarajevo

- how and why Austria-Hungary and Germany responded to the assassination

- how and why Russia responded to Austria-Hungary's demands on Serbia following the assassination

- how the July Crisis developed into war with the bombardment of Belgrade.

KEY CHRONOLOGY

Events of 1914

28 June	Gavrilo Princip assassinates Franz Ferdinand
5 July	Austria-Hungary receives 'blank cheque' from Germany
23 July	Austro-Hungarian ultimatum to Serbia
25 July	Serbia's reply to the ultimatum
28 July	Austria-Hungary declares war on Serbia

CROSS-REFERENCE

You can find out more about the aims and origins of the Black Hand in Chapter 8.

The Black Hand's target

The Black Hand, led by Colonel Dimitrijević, had attempted the murder of Franz Joseph in 1911. By 1914, however, his nephew and heir Franz Ferdinand seemed like a far bigger threat to Serbian nationalist aims. The Archduke hoped to instigate political reform, giving the nationalities within the empire far more influence, and incorporating Austria-Hungary's neighbours into the 'United States of Great Austria'. This threatened Serbia's independence, and could also potentially make Slavs within the Habsburg Empire more loyal to Austria and therefore less interested in Slav nationalism. Ironically, if Austria-Hungary's anger with Serbia had been exacerbated by a different crisis, Franz Ferdinand would probably have been one of the strongest voices calling for moderation and the avoidance of war.

Fig. 2 *An artist's impression of the assassination of Archduke Franz Ferdinand*

Explain why Franz Ferdinand was assassinated in July 1914.

The response of Austria-Hungary and Germany to the assassination

Austria-Hungary's options

On a personal level, the Emperor Franz Joseph was far from devastated by the death of his nephew. He did not think Franz Ferdinand was conservative enough and he disapproved of his marriage to the non-royal Sophie Chotek. In general, however, Austrians were appalled by the assassination. Anti-Serb street violence broke out, and for the military chiefs in particular, the murder provided the opportunity some had been looking for to crush Serbia once and for all.

Chief of staff **Franz Conrad von Hötzendorf** led other aggressive anti-Serbs in the Austrian military in advocating the immediate invasion of Serbia. They had no proof that the Serbian government was involved in the Black Hand's plan, but they pointed out that the Serbs had allowed Princip and his associates to cross into Bosnia and they had failed to prevent the activities of the Black Hand. To the minds of Hötzendorf and his colleagues, the rest of Europe would see little problem with an Austrian invasion of Serbia, as Austria-Hungary would merely be taking retaliatory action to what could be viewed as a declaration of war by Serbia.

Indeed, most of Europe's monarchs, including Tsar Nicholas II, expressed their shock at the assassination. But many in Western Europe were indifferent to yet another political assassination in the east, and the Austrian Chancellor Berchtold knew that Russia would be unlikely to stand aside if Serbia, their client state, was attacked without warning. Anticipating an attack by Russia, Austria-Hungary sought a firmer guarantee of German support, which had already been expressed during the Bosnian Crisis and in the aftermath of the Balkan Wars.

The Key Profile for Franz Conrad von Hötzendorf is in Chapter 5, page 35.

Leopold von Berchtold's Key Profile is in Chapter 9, page 72.

From the official minutes of the Austrian ministerial council meeting on 7 July 1914; the meeting was chaired by Austrian Foreign Minister **Leopold von Berchtold**, Prime Minister Count Sturkh, the Hungarian Premier Count Tisza, the Joint Minister for Finance Ritter von Bilinski and the War Minister Ritter von Krobatin:

Berchtold opens the sitting by remarking that the Ministerial Council has been called in order to advise on the measures to be used in reforming the evil internal political conditions in Bosnia and Herzegovina, as shown up by the disastrous event at Sarajevo. In his opinion there were various internal measures applicable within Bosnia, the use of which seemed to him very appropriate, in order to deal with the critical situation; but first of all they must make up their minds as to whether the moment had not come for reducing Serbia to permanent inoffensiveness by a demonstration of their power. The Hungarian Premier agreed that during the last few days the results of our investigations and the tone of the Serbian press had put a materially new complexion on events, and emphasised the fact that he himself held the possibility of warlike action against Serbia to be more obvious than he had thought in the period immediately after the act at Sarajevo.

ACTIVITY

Analysing primary sources

1. What do you think is meant by the phrase 'reducing Serbia to permanent inoffensiveness'?
2. What is the value of Source 1 to an historian investigating Austria's response to the Sarajevo murders?

Although many in the Austrian ministerial council and general staff favoured a military response to the assassination, their response to it was slow – probably too slow to take advantage of the shock felt by the rest of Europe and their immediate sympathy for the Habsburgs. One main reason for Austrian prevarication was that the Dual Monarchy of Austria and Hungary shared the same army and foreign policy, the Hungarian Prime Minister István Tisza had to be consulted. Although he agreed that strong measures should be taken against Serbia, he was not convinced that war was the correct course of action and advocated exhausting all diplomatic options before resorting to conflict.

SOURCE 2

Count Berchtold in a letter to the German government on 4 July 1914, which was hand-delivered to Berlin by Count Hoyos, the trusted secretary of the Austro-Hungarian Chancellor, Berchtold:

→ CAPITAL OF SERBIA.

The Sarajevo affair was a well-organised conspiracy, the threads of which can be traced to Belgrade. Even though it will probably prove impossible to get evidence of the complicity of the Serbian government, there can be no doubt that its policy, directed towards the unification of all the Southern Slav countries under the Serbian flag, is responsible for such crimes and that the continuation of such a state of affairs constitutes an enduring peril for my house and my possessions. Serbia must be eliminated as a factor of political power in the Balkans.

threat of expansion.

PAN SLAVISM.

1908 annexation of Bosnia.

ACTIVITY

Evaluating primary sources

Do any phrases in Berchtold's letter, in Source 2, suggest that Austria was just looking for an excuse to attack Serbia?

Germany's 'blank cheque'

Germany's role in the unfolding crisis was crucial. Since 1912 its military chiefs had advocated war against Russia before the Tsar's armies grew too strong. Meanwhile its alliance with Austria-Hungary had been tested during the Balkan crises which preceded Franz Ferdinand's murder; during the Bosnian Crisis and the more tense moments of the Balkan Wars the German government had declared its continuing support for its ally. The decision to support the Emperor was not to be taken lightly, however: Russia was unlikely to allow its client state Serbia to be attacked without responding, and Russia's involvement would then be likely to prompt French and perhaps British intervention. Despite these probable outcomes, the Kaiser responded to Berchtold's letter through his chancellor, Bethmann Hollweg, on 5 July with a promise that: 'Austria can rest assured that His Majesty will faithfully stand by Austria-Hungary as is required by the obligations of his alliance and of his ancient friendship.'

KEY TERM

blank cheque: a metaphor for Germany's empty promise on 5 July to support Austria in whatever way it chose to respond to the assassination

CROSS-REFERENCE

The details of the Schlieffen Plan are explained in Chapter 5, page 40, and Chapter 9, pages 76–77.

ACTIVITY

Revision

Look back to the terms of the Dual Alliance and Triple Alliance in Chapter 4. Was Germany obliged to support Austria in the circumstances of July 1914?

A CLOSER LOOK

Europe's policymakers and the July Crisis

The July Crisis was the diplomatic crisis arising from the responses of the Great Powers to Franz Ferdinand's assassination. Many of Europe's leaders and foreign policymakers, including Kaiser Wilhelm, went on holiday in the aftermath of the assassination. By mid-July, however, more determined efforts were made by Europe's statesmen to plot a course through the turbulence that would serve their country best. For weeks, the question was whether the conflict would become a Third Balkan War, or one which dragged the rest of the continent with it.

This promise has become known as a '**blank cheque**' because it implied that Germany would back Austria-Hungary in whatever actions the Empire chose to take. No stipulations or provisos were made: Austria-Hungary could make the 'cheque' – its demands – as big as it wanted. Whether Germany realised the full implications of this at the time is an area of debate. It could be that, since the 1912 War Council had believed Germany's best chance of war would be in 1914, Germany too saw this episode as the moment they had been waiting for. The German Chief of Staff, General Helmuth von Moltke, asserted that war was 'unavoidable', and the German High Command was deeply concerned about the growing military strength of Russia; the **Schlieffen Plan** therefore relied on the element of surprise and the rapid mobilisation of troops before the enemy was ready to retaliate.

On the other hand, it is possible that the Kaiser and his advisers believed that when faced with a united Austria-Hungary and Germany, the Russians would back down, just as they had in 1908, and that this declaration of support was nothing more than a way of calling Russia's bluff. The Austrian cabinet debated their action, while in Belgrade, the Austrian envoy, Baron von Wiesner tried, without success, to discover evidence of the Serbian government's complicity in the plot.

The Austro-Hungarian ultimatum

By 14 July, Austria had decided on war and prepared an ultimatum in the following week. It was not despatched, however, until the French President Poincaré, who happened to be visiting St Petersburg at this time, had left Russia. On 23 July, the Austrians sent the ultimatum to the Serbian capital, Belgrade. They demanded a satisfactory answer within 48 hours or Austria-Hungary would declare war on Serbia. However, the Austro-Hungarian government was concerned that the other European powers would view the ultimatum as provocatively harsh, and therefore sent each of them a letter explaining its actions along with copies of the ultimatum itself.

SOURCE 3

From Austria-Hungary's ultimatum to Serbia, which was presented by the Austro-Hungarian government to Belgrade on 23 July 1914 at 6pm:

The history of recent years, and in particular the events of 28 June last, have shown the existence of a subversive movement with the object of detaching a part of the territories of Austria-Hungary from the Monarchy. The movement had its birth under the eye of the Serbian government. The Royal Serbian government shall therefore publish the following declaration:
  'The Royal government of Serbia condemns the propaganda directed against Austria-Hungary and regrets that Serbian army officers participated in it'.
  By 25 July:
- All newspapers and publications hostile to Austria to be suppressed.
- The national Defence Society to be dissolved.
- All schoolteachers hostile to Austria to be dismissed.
- All army officers hostile to Austria to be dismissed.
- Austrian police officials to be admitted to Serbia to investigate the assassination.
- Austrian lawyers to participate in judicial proceedings against suspects.
- Frontier guards to be punished for allowing conspirators to enter Bosnia.
- An apology to be given for anti-Austrian remarks by Serbian government officials since the assassination.

Russia's response to Austria-Hungary's demands on Serbia

Serbia's position was extremely difficult. While it loathed the idea of capitulating to its long-term enemy, its army had been exhausted by the Balkan Wars and it was struggling to repress rebellions amongst its new southern population. Belgrade's strategy, therefore, was to adopt a conciliatory approach and stall for as much time as possible, while enlisting Russian support if Austria-Hungary was not easily satisfied. The health of King Paul of Serbia was failing, so the Serbian appeal to Russia was signed off by his son and regent, Prince Alexander.

ACTIVITY

Evaluating primary sources

Read all the terms of the ultimatum in Source 3. Why do you think each of these terms was made? Do you think they seem unreasonable?

SOURCE 4

The Serbian regent Prince Alexander sent this telegram to Tsar Nicholas II on 24 July 1914, appealing for assistance following the Austrian ultimatum of 23 July:

The demands contained in the Austro-Hungarian note are unnecessarily humiliating for Serbia and incompatible with her dignity as an independent state. Certain of these demands cannot be carried out without changes in our legislation, which require time. We have been given too short a limit. We can be attacked after the expiration of the time-limit by the Austro-Hungarian Army which is concentrating on our frontier. It is impossible for us to defend ourselves, and we supplicate your Majesty to give us your aid as soon as possible. The highly prized good will of your Majesty, which has so often shown itself toward us, makes us hope firmly that this time again our appeal will be heard by his generous Slav heart. In these difficult moments I voice the sentiments of the Serbian people, who supplicate your Majesty to interest himself in the lot of the Kingdom of Serbia.

At first, Russia's response was mixed. Two issues clouded Russian policy at this point: firstly the Tsar displayed classic indecision and appeared to change his mind according to whichever minister or officer he spoke to last; and secondly, the government was mindful that its actions could easily pull France and even Britain into the crisis, and they ought to be consulted. Moreover, Russia's response to the assassination – and the ultimatum – was crucial, especially after Germany's promise to support Austria, as Serbia was far too weak to fight both without a powerful ally. **Sergei Sazonov** (Izvolsky's replacement as Russian Foreign Minister) was shocked by the terms of the ultimatum, and the Russian Council of Ministers met on 24 and 25 July to discuss how to respond. As the deadline for the ultimatum approached, the Russian position became firmer but in practice, still ambiguous: Sazonov stated on 25 July that Russia would 'go to the limit in defence of Serbia.' While this stopped well short of guaranteeing military support, Sazonov and the British Foreign Minister, Edward Grey, put pressure on Austria-Hungary to extend its deadline.

Serbia was prepared to make concessions and initially considered giving way on all counts. Nevertheless, spurred on by Russia, they played for time by rejecting the demands that Austrian police officials enter Serbia and Austrian lawyers participate in judicial proceedings. Such demands were felt to be an unreasonable challenge to Serbian **sovereignty**. They wrote: 'As far as the cooperation in this investigation of specially delegated officials of the Imperial and Royal government is concerned, this cannot be accepted, as this is a violation of the constitution and of criminal procedure.' In Serbia's reply, made on 25 July, they conceded to the ultimatum on every other point. Considering the deliberate harshness of the terms, this was a remarkable concession.

KEY PROFILE

Fig. 3 *Sergei Dmitrievich Sazonov*

Sergei Dmitrievich Sazonov (1860–1927) was Russian Foreign Minister from 1910 to 1916. His support of the Balkan League during the wars of 1912–3 was inconvenient: he could not antagonise the Dual Alliance as the Russian military was too weak to fight a large war. Sazonov advised Serbia to appease Austria in response to the ultimatum, but then advised Nicholas II to mobilise the Russian army. Sazonov was dismissed in 1916 after disagreeing with the Russian Tsarina.

KEY TERM

sovereignty: the authority of a state to govern itself

Fig. 4 *During the Austro-Hungarian bombardment of Belgrade in July 1914, attacking forces rounded up patriotic Serbians and ruthlessly shot them on command*

The bombardment of Belgrade

Most of Europe, including Germany, believed that Serbia's conciliatory response to the ultimatum would be accepted by the Austrians, although Serbia had begun a partial mobilisation in case of an Austrian attack. The prevailing attitude of the Austro-Hungarians, however, was that nothing but complete capitulation would be acceptable. Although talks between Russia and Austria-Hungary were hastily arranged in a final effort to prevent the slide into war, the Germans increasingly regarded conflict as inevitable and advocated decisiveness on the part of its ally so they could keep the military initiative. (Germany was, however, careful to appear ignorant of Austrian intentions in order to avoid blame.) The talks broke down on 27 July.

Austria-Hungary's declaration of war on Serbia on 28 July was made via telegram from Berchtold to Pasič. It stated that as the Serbian government had not 'answered in a satisfactory manner the note of 23 July, the Imperial and Royal Government is compelled to see to the safeguarding of their rights and interests, and, with this object, to have recourse to force of arms. Austria-Hungary consequently considers herself henceforward in a state of war with Serbia.'

As Serbia had already begun to mobilise, all men of military service age had already been conscripted, while many families had fled to the country, leaving Belgrade relatively quiet. Belgrade was in northern Serbia, an area which was woefully ill-prepared for an enemy assault which historically had always come via the south from the Ottomans or Bulgarians.

In the early hours of 29 July, Serbians, under the orders of Black Hand member Major Tankosic, destroyed a bridge over the River Sava which connected Serbian territory to the Austro-Hungarian Empire. The major assault came a week later, but the city was finally taken by the Austrians on 30 November by soldiers under the command of General Potiorek, who had been in the same car as Franz Ferdinand and witnessed his assassination five months earlier.

ACTIVITY

Group work

As a class, divide into different teams representing the foreign offices of Austria-Hungary, Serbia, Germany and Russia. Compose a memorandum of no more than 50 words summing up the bombardment of Belgrade for your respective governments. How different is your reporting of the events of 28–29 July?

Summary

The July Crisis followed the assassination of Franz Ferdinand and involved all of the Great Powers. The responses of Britain and France, and the actions of Germany and Russia following Austria-Hungary's declaration of war on Serbia, are explored in the next chapter.

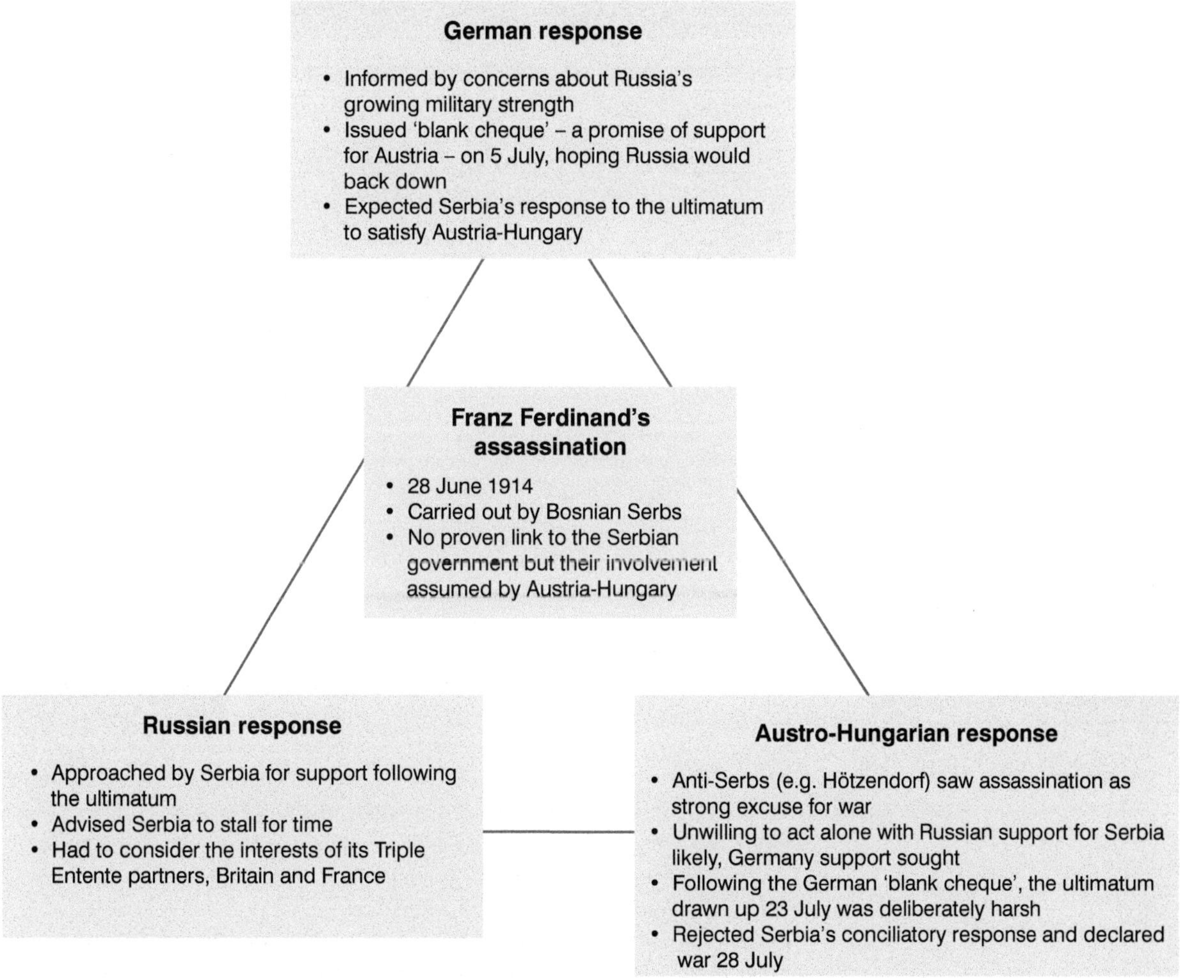

German response

- Informed by concerns about Russia's growing military strength
- Issued 'blank cheque' – a promise of support for Austria – on 5 July, hoping Russia would back down
- Expected Serbia's response to the ultimatum to satisfy Austria-Hungary

Franz Ferdinand's assassination

- 28 June 1914
- Carried out by Bosnian Serbs
- No proven link to the Serbian government but their involvement assumed by Austria-Hungary

Russian response

- Approached by Serbia for support following the ultimatum
- Advised Serbia to stall for time
- Had to consider the interests of its Triple Entente partners, Britain and France

Austro-Hungarian response

- Anti-Serbs (e.g. Hötzendorf) saw assassination as strong excuse for war
- Unwilling to act alone with Russian support for Serbia likely, Germany support sought
- Following the German 'blank cheque', the ultimatum drawn up 23 July was deliberately harsh
- Rejected Serbia's conciliatory response and declared war 28 July

Fig. 5 *Diagram of the July Crisis as covered so far*

STUDY TIP

Consider the content, tone, dates and provenance of each of the sources, and their context. Try to arrive at a balanced judgement, comparing the language used.

PRACTICE QUESTION

Evaluating primary sources

With reference to Sources 1 and 4, and your understanding of the historical context, which of these two sources is more valuable in explaining the pressures faced by Serbia following the assassination in Sarajevo;

STUDY TIP

Remember to consider long-term factors as well, which might suggest several other reasons for the declaration of war. Comparing the importance of short-term and long-term factors will demonstrate a strong understanding of causation.

PRACTICE QUESTION

'Austria-Hungary only declared war in 1914 because of Germany's blank cheque.' Assess the validity of this view.

11 General war in Europe

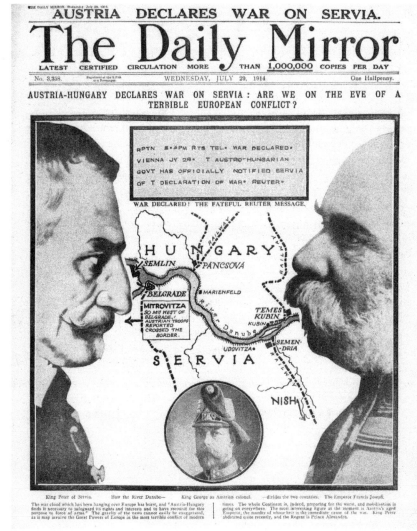

Fig. 1 *Front cover of the* Daily Mirror *on Wednesday 29 July 1914 (the British often spelt and pronounced Serbia as 'Servia')*

The mobilisation of German and Russian forces

By July 1914 it was clear to the Russian government that Russia's influence in the Balkans was at stake, as was the prestige of Russia as a Great Power. By backing down in the **Bosnian Crisis** and not intervening in the **Balkan Wars**, Russia's role as 'protector of Slavs' was at risk, and many in the government, including Sazonov, felt they had little choice but to intervene this time. At first the Tsar toyed with the idea of ordering only partial mobilisation (only readying enough troops to fight Austria-Hungary) in the hope of encouraging Germany to back down. A series of desperate telegrams were sent back and forth from Berlin to St Petersburg as two cousins, Wilhelm II and Nicholas II, tried to persuade each other not to go to war. German ministers and diplomats were also working hard to ensure that Germany would appear to be the victim of aggression. **Chancellor Theobald von Bethmann Hollweg** instructed the German ambassador in St Petersburg on 29 July: 'Kindly impress on Sazonov very seriously that further progress of Russian mobilisation measures would compel us to mobilise and that then European war would scarcely be prevented.' This was Germany's own ultimatum to Russia: either they ceased their military preparations or Germany would mobilise against them.

LEARNING OBJECTIVES

In this chapter you will learn about:

- the reasons for and consequences of the mobilisation of the German and Russian forces

- the implementation of the Schlieffen Plan and the invasion of Belgium

- Britain's reasons for declaring war on Germany

- the motives of the key decision-makers.

KEY CHRONOLOGY

30 July	Russia mobilises its army
1 August	Germany declares war on Russia
3 August	Germany declares war on France and invades Belgium
4 August	Britain and Belgium declare war on Germany

CROSS-REFERENCE

The Bosnian Crisis of 1908 is explored in Chapter 8, pages 62–64.

The causes of the Balkan Wars and their impact on Great Power relations are explained in Chapter 9.

KEY PROFILE

Theobald von Bethmann Hollweg (1856–1921) was German Chancellor from 1909 to 1917. Despite his role in preventing the escalation of the 1912–3 Balkan Wars, by 1914 he was deeply unpopular in Germany and lacked the authority to stop Germany's entry into war. Before and during the conflict he clashed with Admiral von Tirpitz over naval armaments and submarine warfare. He resigned in 1917.

Nicholas' generals, however, asserted that only general mobilisation would give Russia a strong chance of victory against the Dual Alliance, and on 30 July Russia mobilised its army.

SOURCE 1

Adapted from a telegram sent by Kaiser Wilhelm II to Tsar Nicholas II on 31 July 1914. The two monarchs were cousins and had been exchanging telegrams during the July Crisis:

On your appeal to my friendship and your call for assistance I began to mediate between your government and the Austro-Hungarian government. While this action was proceeding your troops were mobilised against Austro-Hungary, my ally. Thereby, as I have already pointed out to you, my mediation has been made almost illusory. I have nevertheless continued my action. I now receive authentic news of serious preparations for war on my eastern frontier. Responsibility for the safety of my empire forces preventive measures of defence upon me. In my endeavours to maintain the peace of the world I have gone to the utmost limit possible. The responsibility for the disaster which is now threatening the whole civilized world will not be laid at my door. In this moment it still lies in your power to avert it. The peace of Europe may still be maintained by you, if Russia will agree to stop the military measures which must threaten Germany and Austro-Hungary.

ACTIVITY

Evaluating primary sources

1. The communications between Kaiser and Tsar are known as the 'Willy–Nicky telegrams' after the affectionate terms in which the two monarchs addressed each other. Find copies of the telegrams online and see if you can identify the stages of the crisis mentioned in them.
2. What is the value of this telegram to an historian investigating the roles of Russia and Germany in the July Crisis?

Nicholas hoped that Russia's mobilisation would act as a threat to Germany and saw it as a last diplomatic effort to maintain peace between the two states. Wilhelm, however, angrily criticised Nicholas for secretly readying his armies while still putting pressure on Wilhelm to negotiate with Austria-Hungary. He interpreted the mobilisation as a declaration of war in itself: from that moment he claimed he had no choice but to declare war on Russia in response. Futhermore, while Russia's mobilisation suited the pro-war ministers in the German cabinet and high command who hoped to defeat Russia in a **preventive war**, it also meant that Wilhelm could later argue that Russia was to blame for the outbreak of conflict, which he did thoroughly with an official statement entitled 'How Russia Betrayed Germany's Confidence'.

KEY TERM

preventive war: a small-scale, quick war planned to avoid a larger, longer war later on

EXTRACT 1

'How Russia Betrayed Germany's Confidence', the official statement of the German government published in August 1914. It was a public statement which the Germans hoped would be read by neutral countries like the USA:

From the beginning of the conflict we assumed the position that there were here concerned the affairs of Austria alone, which it would have to settle with Serbia. We therefore directed our efforts toward the localising of the war, and toward convincing the other powers that Austria-Hungary had to appeal to arms in justifiable self-defence, forced upon her by the conditions. Simultaneously the Austro-Hungarian Government communicated to the Russian Government that the step undertaken against Serbia implied merely a defensive measure against the Serb agitation. The German Government declared that Austria-Hungary had no desire for conquest and only wished peace at her frontiers. After the official explanation by Austria-Hungary to Russia that it did not claim territorial gain in Serbia, the decision concerning the peace of the world rested exclusively with St. Petersburg. The same day the first news of Russian mobilisation reached Berlin in the evening.

ACTIVITY

Many historians, such as Franz Fischer in the 1960s, and Max Hastings more recently, have argued that the German government and military staff demonstrated a 'will to war' and actively welcomed involvement in the conflict. What evidence have you seen so far which supports this view? Revisit your response after studying the actions of Britain and France below.

From 30 July, there was little chance of a wider war in Eastern Europe being avoided. Not only did Germany begin to mobilise in response to Russia's actions, but the German army under Moltke, the Chief of Staff, sent a telegram to the Austrian High Command to encourage them to mobilise against Russia as well as Serbia. This prompted exasperation amongst the Austrian government, as Bethmann Hollweg had been encouraging the Austrian military to scale down its attack on Belgrade, which highlights the significant confusion in Austria over the struggle between military and civilian authority. On 31 July, Emperor Franz Joseph signed the order for Austria-Hungary's full mobilisation, preparing it for war against Russia.

Germany's ultimatum to Russia of 29 July to cease its mobilisation was – aside from Nicholas' telegram justifying the action to the Kaiser – disregarded by St Petersburg. In the meantime, decision-making power in Germany slipped from the Chancellor and Wilhelm (who characteristically hoped to prevent the slide to war now it appeared imminent) and into the hands of the military. Moltke was highly aware that Germany's thoroughly-prepared Schlieffen Plan depended on his army maintaining the initiative and believed that any delay could be fatal. Under great pressure from his generals, Wilhelm signed the order for general mobilisation on 1 August, and on the same day declared war on Russia.

The British and French response

Most people in Britain and France had little interest in the Balkans. Their newspapers barely reported the assassination or its consequences, as both countries were preoccupied with domestic concerns: in France the trial of the wife of the former Prime Minister, Joseph Caillaux, for shooting the editor of *Le Figaro*, captured the public imagination; while in Britain, the growing militancy of the suffragettes and the increasingly volatile debate over Home Rule in Ireland remained top of the government's agenda for weeks. However Grey attempted to mediate between the powers after the Austrian ultimatum. When the Austrians began to mobilise against Serbia on 27 July, Grey called for a conference of the Great Powers, but neither Germany nor Austria were prepared to come to the table.

For days there was intense debate within the cabinet over whether Britain should fight alongside France and Russia once war broke out. The agreements Britain had made with them did not compromise her freedom of action: it was possible for Britain to remain neutral without backtracking on her diplomatic commitments. The secret 1912 Anglo-French Naval Agreement committed the French navy to defending the Mediterranean in a future war with Germany while the British fleet would defend the North Sea and the French Atlantic coast, but **Winston Churchill**, then First Lord of the Admiralty, reminded the French that the Naval Agreement would not be a firm military commitment: Britain would have to declare war on Germany before following this plan. A crucial factor for Britain to consider, however, was whether Germany would enact the Schlieffen Plan, which would involve invading neutral Belgium in order to evade France's strongest defences.

France under **President Poincaré** was already more directly involved if Germany decided to fight. It was committed to offer military support to Russia under the terms of the Franco–Russian Alliance (1894) and realised that Germany was likely to attack France if Germany and Russia went to war against each other.

Fig. 2   *Raymond Poincaré*

The implementation of the Schlieffen Plan and the invasion of Belgium

The Schlieffen Plan

As well as insisting that Russia halted its military preparations, Germany also sent an ultimatum to France which they hoped, again, would encourage the view that Germany was acting defensively, not aggressively. While secretly the German chiefs had no intention of abandoning the Schlieffen Plan, they demanded that the French hand over their fortresses at Toul and Verdun, on the border with Germany, until the defeat of Russia was completed. In addition, the Germans insisted that France should make no military preparations of its own, despite its alliance with Russia.

Like Austria-Hungary's ultimatum to Serbia on 23 July, Germany's demands on France were highly likely to be rejected: although decidedly weaker than Germany in military terms, it was almost unthinkable that Germany would be allowed to effectively dictate French foreign policy. But of course the Germany military did not expect or want France to capitulate if the Schlieffen Plan was to be successful: to make war against Russia effectively, Germany needed France to be totally defeated, not placated. When their ultimatum was ignored, Germany declared war on France on 3 August. In order to keep up the pretence that they were fighting a defensive war, the Germans claimed that French planes had bombed the city of Nuremburg.

STUDY TIP

Several ultimatums were made during the July Crisis. So you can remember the key details of each of them, it may help to construct a grid to record:

- who made the ultimatum and to whom
- what was demanded
- the date it was issued
- the date a satisfactory reply was expected
- the response (if any) of the country receiving the ultimatum
- the consequences.

KEY TERM

reciprocity: the practice of exchanging terms for mutual benefit

ACTIVITY

How would you describe the tone of the German declaration of war on France in Source 2?

CROSS-REFERENCE

The origins of the Schlieffen Plan are explained in Chapter 5.

SOURCE 2

Adapted from Germany's declaration of war with France, presented by the German ambassador to the French government in Paris on 3 August 1914:

The German administrative and military authorities have established a certain number of flagrantly hostile acts committed on German territory by French military aviators. Several of these have openly violated the neutrality of Belgium by flying over the territory of that country; one has thrown bombs on the railway near Karlsruhe and Nuremberg. I am instructed to inform you that in the presence of these acts of aggression the German Empire considers itself in a state of war with France in consequence of the acts of this latter Power. The German authorities will retain French mercantile vessels in German ports, but they will release them if, within forty-eight hours, they are assured of complete **reciprocity**.

The plan devised by Schlieffen had been altered since 1905, but the modifications made speed and the element of surprise even more important. At the last minute, the Kaiser's nerve began to fail, and he asked his military chiefs to alter their plans so that they only attacked Russia, not France. It was, however, far too late: the minute detail of planning could not be reversed.

A CLOSER LOOK

Alan J.P. Taylor's *War by Timetable*

The historian Alan J.P. Taylor argued in his 1969 book *War by Timetable* that the key reason why European leaders failed to prevent war during the July Crisis was the complexity of military planning and the schedules dictating the practicalities of mobilisation. Once heads of state declared war, military chiefs began the process of getting troops and supplies to the front line, and the necessary railway timetables were so carefully planned in advance that it was almost impossible to stop the process once it had begun. Taylor pointed out that just as Wilhelm was about to sign the general mobilisation order on 1 August, Bethmann Hollweg brought the news that the British Foreign Minister Edward Grey had declared that Britain would stay neutral if France was not attacked. Wilhelm was delighted, but his generals told him that this was impossible given that 11,000 trains would then have to be re-routed. Moreover, there was no strategy ready for attacking Russia without defeating France first. Taylor argued that such mundane details prevented a wider European war from being averted at the last minute.

J. P TAYLORS.

Fig. 3 *Map of the theory of the Schlieffen Plan*

The invasion of Belgium

Although Belgium had declared its neutrality on 24 July 1914, the government ordered the mobilisation of its army, and moved to defend its French and German borders in case it could not avoid involvement in the escalating crisis. On 2 August, the German ambassador in Brussels presented the Belgian foreign minister with an ultimatum from Germany which demanded that the German northern army would be allowed to march through Belgium to reach France unresisted. The Belgian cabinet met and discussed the ultimatum into the early hours, and finally decided to reject it. Instead they would fight to defend their neutrality, meanwhile hoping that diplomatic efforts would be successful in avoiding a Western European war. Consequently King Albert of Belgium appealed to King George V of Britain for 'diplomatic assistance', but to keep **Belgium's commitment to neutrality**, orders were given for the army to fire on any French troops – as well as German – who crossed their borders.

On 4 August the Schlieffen Plan was put into action, and the Belgians, as planned, resisted. They were outnumbered by the German army ten to one, but placed their hopes in a series of fortresses around the city of Liège. Huge German guns (nicknamed 'Big Berthas') eventually overcame the Belgian defences. The poor treatment of Belgian civilians by German soldiers as a result of the invasion was turned into powerful propaganda by the British, including posters, the publication of first-hand testimonies and newspaper cartoons with slogans such as 'The rape of Belgium' and 'Once a German, always a German.' This gave the government further justification for their involvement in the war as well as lending emotional appeal to its recruitment campaigns.

Fig. 4 *The invasion of Belgium by Germany began on 3 August as part of the Schlieffen Plan*

Britain's declaration of war

Britain – and Germany – had promised to defend Belgium's neutrality in the 1839 Treaty of London. The Germans thought Britain was highly unlikely to honour this agreement, believing it to be insignificant in 1914: Chancellor Bethmann Hollweg expressed surprise that Britain were willing to go to war based on what he called 'a scrap of paper'. However, there were other factors at play.

Pressure from France

To his colleagues, and to the general public, Grey was careful to emphasise Britain's 'free hand' – its alliances with France and Russia were informal and didn't extend to military support. However, the terms of the secret Anglo-French Naval Agreement – despite Churchill's assertions – did involve a stronger military commitment to the French than the public Anglo-French Entente. If Britain did go to war against Germany, its navy was obliged by the agreement to defend the French Channel ports.

Grey called for the kind of international conference which had effectively contained crises in the past. The French, however, put pressure on Grey and Asquith to declare Britain's full support for its allies if Germany attacked. The Prime Minister was aware though of the political consequences of joining the war – the resignation of his own party members in the cabinet and a coalition government with the Conservatives. Grey stalled for time while making no concrete promises; critics later claimed that if he had clearly stated that Britain would lend France military support, Germany would not have proceeded so far in its mobilisation.

SOURCE 3

Adapted from a letter from the British Ambassador in France to the British government on 31 July 1914. The purpose of the letter was to report on the French attitude to the international crisis:

The feeling here is that peace between the Powers depends on England; that if she declare herself in solidarity with France and Russia there will not be war, for Germany will not face the danger to her of her supplies by sea being cut off by the British fleet. People do not realise or do not take into account the difficulty for the British government to declare England in solidarity with Russia and France in a question such as the Austro-Serbian quarrel. The French, instead of putting pressure on the Russian government to moderate their zeal, expect us to give the Germans to understand that we mean fighting if war breaks out. If we gave an assurance of armed assistance to France and Russia now, Russia would become more exacting and France would follow in her wake. The newspapers but not yet the people are becoming bellicose.

GREY → Foreign
*   mini*
ASQUITH → PM.

The response to the invasion of Belgium

What the British cabinet needed to convince the rest of parliament – and the public – that war was worthwhile was an act of outright aggression by Germany. As late as 2 August, Asquith assured an emotional Prince Lichnowsky, the German ambassador to London, that Britain would not go to war unless Germany invaded Belgium or used the Channel ports to attack France. Although Bethmann Hollweg famously stated his disbelief that Britain would go to war over 'a scrap of paper' (referring to the Treaty of London), the invasion of Belgium gave the British a publically acceptable reason to intervene.

On 3 August, as news reached London of German soldiers massing on the Belgian border, Asquith gave in to increasing pressure and ordered Winston Churchill (then First Lord of the Admiralty) to mobilise the Royal Navy, and Richard Haldane to prepare the British Army for war. That same evening, Grey made his famous observation that 'The lamps are going out all over Europe: we shall not see them lit again in our lifetime.'

Following Germany's invasion of Belgium on 4 August, Britain sent its own ultimatum to the Germans demanding that they withdrew their troops or Britain would declare war. Germany ignored the demand, and Britain declared war on the same day.

British interests at stake

If Germany did go to war against France, it was reasoned, France would fall within months and Britain would then be faced with the prospect of a Europe dominated by Germany. Max Hastings has argued that this would have been hugely detrimental to British interests, and morally questionable given the increasingly autocratic and militaristic character of Germany's government, and that therefore Britain was absolutely justified in intervening in the war. Niall Ferguson, meanwhile, in his work *The Pity of War*, drew the conclusion that Britain could have stayed out of the conflict and the results would not have represented a challenge to Britain's wealth or influence in the world. This appeared to be the initial judgement of Asquith, who on 24 July 1914 said: 'Happily, there seems to be no reason why we should be anything other than spectators.'

ACTIVITY

Revision

Construct a detailed timeline from the assassination on 28 June to Britain's entry into the war on 4 August.

The key decision-makers and their motives

Austria-Hungary

Emperor Franz Joseph

István Tisza (Hungarian Prime Minister)

Leopold Berchtold (Foreign Minister)

Franz Conrad von Hötzendorf (Chief of Staff)

- Long-held desire to crush the 'troublemaker' Serbia
- Believed lack of action would expose Austria-Hungary's decline as a Great Power
- Hötzendorf argued that full mobilisation was needed or Austria would be exposed to a Russian attack while fighting Serbia
- Tisza was initially reluctant to go to war, especially before German support was guaranteed, which slowed Austria-Hungary's response to the assassination
- Tisza sought assurances that Austria-Hungary would not seek to conquer Serbia

Germany

Gottlieb von Jagow (Foreign Minister)

Helmuth von Moltke (Chief of Staff)

Theobold von Bethmann Hollweg (Chancellor)

Kaiser Wilhelm II

- Initially outraged by the assassination, prompting a promise of full support for Austria-Hungary, while expecting Russia not to intervene in early July
- Chiefs of staff wanted a 'preventive' war against Russia before it grew too strong
- Moltke was keen to show his authority within Germany
- Bethmann-Holweg was convinced Britain would not intervene

Britain

Edward Grey (Foreign Secretary)

David Lloyd George (Chancellor of the Exchequer)

Herbert Asquith (Prime Minister)

- Few ministers wanted war, but most viewed the crisis in terms of Britain's wider long-term interests, especially the fate of the Empire
- Grey was mildly anti-German but needed the backing of the Cabinet to proceed with any action; in general he hoped to avoid making any commitments
- Cabinet was divided over whether intervention against Germany was necessary or desirable: Lloyd George was the most senior minister who opposed intervention
- Lloyd George's opposition dropped when Germany invaded Belgium
- Defence of Belgian neutrality was an excuse but not actually binding

France

President Raymond Poincaré

René Viviani (Prime Minister and Foreign Minister)

- Motivated by fear of a strong Germany and desire for *revanche*
- Supported Russia according to the terms of the Franco–Russian Alliance (1894); Poincaré visited the Tsar during the July Crisis
- Poincaré failed to persuade the British to declare military support for France and Russia in advance, which he believed would encouraged Germany to back down

Russia

Ivan Goremykin (Prime Minister)

Sergey Sazonov (Foreign Minister)

Tsar Nicholas II

- Determined not to lose influence over the Balkans by backing down again, as they had done during the Bosnian Crisis
- Concern over the strength of the Russian army may have convinced Sazonov to mobilise before the Central Powers
- The Tsar – moved by Wilhelm's telegrams and fearful of bearing responsibility for war – favoured partial mobilisation, against Austria-Hungary only, but generals asserted that only general mobilisation was feasible according to existing military plans

Fig. 5 *Austria-Hungary, Germany, Britain, France and Russia: the key decision-makers and their motives*

Fig. 6 *This cartoon featured in* Punch *in August 1914; it shows Belgium as a young boy, defending its borders, which are threatened by an aggressive Germany. The caption reads: 'Bravo, Belgium!'*

ACTIVITY

Evaluating primary sources

1. What is the message in this cartoon?
2. The cartoon was created by *Punch* magazine. Why do you think the British government would have approved of it?

Summary

By 5 August, all the Great Powers were at war, the two formidable alliance blocs having been triggered by the assassination of Franz Ferdinand. Christopher Clark has argued that the final declarations of war were the result of complacency amongst the European heads of state, foreign ministers and ambassadors, and that the powers 'sleepwalked' into a catastrophic war. Other historians, such as Alan J.P. Taylor and – more recently – Margaret Macmillan, have hypothesised that it is perhaps more helpful to ask not 'Why did war break out in 1914?' but rather 'Why was peace within Europe allowed

A CLOSER LOOK

The role of diplomats during the July Crisis

Diplomats played a key role in foreign relations: they were the representatives of their country abroad and were vital for effective communication. On 10 July the Russian representative in Serbia, Nicholas Hartwig, died suddenly while visiting Vienna, which proved disastrous: the Russians accused the Austrians of foul play, while Russia and Serbia both proceeded without fully consulting each other. Another example is the disagreement between Edward Grey and Eyre Crowe, Assistant Under-Secretary at the Foreign Office. On 25 July Crowe urged Grey to send a strong signal to France and Russia that Britain would enter the war if Germany attacked, hoping this would deter Germany. Grey thought this unnecessary at this point.

ACTIVITY

Looking at the motivation of the key decision-makers in Fig. 5: do you think it is fair to say that any of them *wanted* war?

to collapse when it had prevailed for so long?' There is also the important distinction between the two questions of why war broke out between Austria-Hungary and Serbia; and why this war escalated to involve Russia, Germany, France, Britain, and their respective empires too.

The second phase of the July Crisis

- War between Russia and Germany was partly provoked by Germany's alliance with Austria-Hungary; by German war plans discussed as early as 1912; and by Russia's need to show resolve in another Balkan crisis.
- France, under threat from German attack due to its alliance with Russia and the Schlieffen Plan, hoped that the promise of British intervention would call Germany's bluff. Ultimately it had no choice but to become involved in the war: it was invaded by Germany.
- Many British ministers, despite growing suspicion of Germany's imperial intentions in the pre-war years, hoped to stay neutral. Concerns over Germany's domination of the continent and then its invasion of Belgium prompted Britain's declaration of war on Germany.

ACTIVITY

Create several of your own, larger versions of the diagram below (one for each of Austria-Hungary, Germany, Russia, France and Britain). For each power, identify and record factors influencing their decision to go to war in the summer of 1914. Discuss in pairs whether they are primary motives (which could have an urgent or direct impact on the country concerned) or secondary motives (less important reasons). Use the suggestions below as a starting point, and use the previous chapters in this book to help you find more.

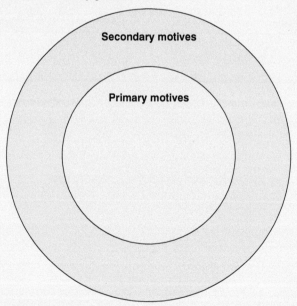

Suggestions for motives
- Fear of war on two fronts
- The need to maintain and protect the Empire
- The need to maintain influence in the Balkans
- Commitments of Franco–Russian Alliance
- Fear of nationalism and pan-Slavism

PRACTICE QUESTION

With reference to Sources 1 and 2, and your understanding of the historical context, which of these two sources is more valuable in explaining why Germany went to war against France in August 1914?

 PRACTICE QUESTION

'The outbreak of war in 1914 was caused by the decisions of generals rather than politicians or statesmen'.
Assess the validity of this view.

KEY CHRONOLOGY

2 August 1914	Italy declares its neutrality
24 May 1915	Italy declares war on Austria-Hungary
7 May 1915	Sinking of the *Lusitania*
16 January 1917	Zimmerman telegram intercepted
2 February 1917	Germany resumes unrestricted submarine warfare
6 April 1917	The USA enters the war on the side of the Allies

Fig. 1 *American opinion had been firmly against involvement in the war; why do you think the USA is portrayed as a sleeping woman in this 1917 recruitment poster?*

The escalation of the conflict

Hopes that the conflict between Austria-Hungary and Serbia would remain localised in the Balkans were soundly and quickly dashed, as it grew into not just a European war, but one which involved the overseas empires of the Great Powers, and was later joined by both Japan and the USA. In Europe itself, British and French forces engaged with German soldiers on the **Western Front**, the German army fought Russia on the **Eastern Front**, and the Austrio-Hungarian armies fought its Balkan opponents and, from 1915, Italy in the south-east.

A CLOSER LOOK

Western and Eastern Fronts

The Western Front refers to the battlegrounds of Belgium and northern France, where British and French troops fought the German army. It is a term synonymous with trench warfare, as both sides 'dug in' to give soldiers protection from machine-gun fire and heavy artillery attacks. The opposing armies were at a stalemate from late 1914. The Eastern Front refers to the conflict between Russia and the forces of Germany and Austria-Hungary. In the east there were more decisive tactical victories for both sides, for example, at Tannenburg and Lutsk, in part due to the far greater length of the front line and conditions which were unsuitable for trench systems to be dug. The Eastern Front was therefore far more mobile than that of the west.

Colonial warfare

By August, Britain, France and Germany had called up their imperial forces to fight for their 'mother' country. As a result, French Algerians and sepoys from the British Indian Army fought in the trenches of the Western Front, while Canadians, West Indians, Australians and New Zealanders also bolstered the Allies' manpower. The imperial powers did not only ship their colonial troops to the European theatres of war, however; colonies themselves became battlegrounds as the rivalries of the Great Powers were played out on the world stage. Fig. 2 shows the huge scale on which the war was fought by identifying the major theatres of war.

Fig. 2 *The key theatres of war in Europe during the First World War*

Africa

Britain's control of South Africa was to prove strategically useful, despite the tenuous loyalty of the mixed South African population towards the Empire. From this base, British South African forces commanded by Jan Smuts launched an attack on German South West Africa in September 1914, and by 1916 South African troops had also defeated German East Africa.

The Allies and the Central Powers

As the war unfolded, the Triple Entente and the colonies and nations that fought alongside it became known as the Allies, while Germany, Austria-Hungary and their allies were known as the Central Powers.

The Pacific

Keen to capitalise on its alliance with Britain under the 1902 Anglo-Japanese agreement, Japan declared war on Germany on 23 August 1914, and on Austria-Hungary two days later. The war was extended to the Pacific when Japanese forces seized Germany's possessions in the Far East – including Tsingtao – to the great disgruntlement of the Kaiser. By the end of September 1914, New Zealand had occupied German Samoa and Australia had invaded part of German New Guinea.

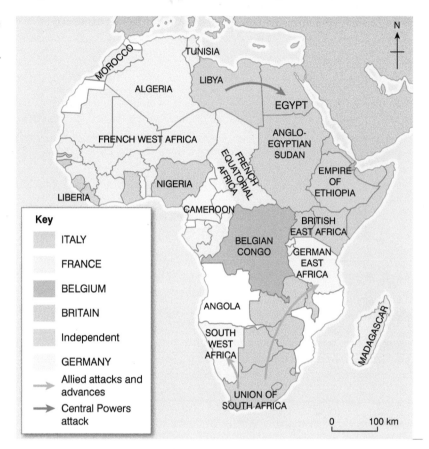

Fig. 3 *The key theatres of war in Africa during the First World War; the green arrows show the Allied attacks and advances*

The Middle East

Five major campaigns were conducted in the Middle East, in Sinai and Palestine, Mesopotamia (modern Iraq), the Caucasus (between Russia and Turkey), Persia (modern Iran), and Gallipoli (in Turkey). The Ottoman Empire allied with Germany and Austria-Hungary in October 1914, and Bulgaria joined the Central Powers in 1915. Bulgaria's entry on the side of Austria-Hungary highlights just how far the Balkan Wars of 1912–3 had reshuffled loyalties within the Balkans: the country had once been one of Russia's loyal client states. Its neighbours Romania and Greece, meanwhile, joined the Allies.

British and French divisions were diverted to the Middle East in 1915 in the hope of relieving the stalemate on the Western Front and limiting Turkish interference with oil supplies in Mesopotamia. The British and French were bolstered by troops from their empires, but this was no guarantee of easy victory: at Gallipoli in April 1915, a disastrous attack by the Allies led to devastating losses of Australian and New Zealand troops. The Germans had established influence over the Turkish forces under the German commander Liman von Sanders in 1912 and 1913, contributing to Kaiser Wilhelm's self-proclaimed role as 'Protector of the Turks' and his friendship with Muslim powers. The Ottoman Empire called for a **military jihad** against the Triple Entente in November 1914, which immediately posed a severe threat to the British Empire's possessions in the Middle East – perhaps even India too. British Empire soldiers, including a large number of Anglo-Indian troops, fought Turkish soldiers under German command in the first months of the war.

Italy's motives for war

By the time Italy declared its neutrality on 2 August 1914, Germany and Austria-Hungary had already anticipated the move as Italy had made no firm gestures of support during the July Crisis. Nevertheless the declaration caused outrage in Berlin and Vienna, where many felt that Italy was breaking the 'spirit', if not the actual terms of the Triple Alliance.

The agreement Italy had signed in 1882 with Germany and Austria-Hungary was specific in terms of the kind of war Italy would join to support her allies: it had to be defensive. As Austria-Hungary had invaded Serbia, Italy was able to avoid committing itself to military involvement. Furthermore, the Italians were concerned that Austria's intentions in the Balkans were expansionist, which went against their own interests in the region: it hoped to gain Dalmatia, a region on the border with Bosnia. Unbeknown to her official 'Allies', Italy had in fact concluded a secret pact with France in 1902 which effectively cancelled out her commitments to Germany and Austria.

SOURCE 1

A telegram from the German Ambassador in Rome to the German Foreign Office in Berlin, sent on 31 July 1914:

Marquis San Giuliano (the Italian Foreign Minister) told me that the Italian Government had considered the question thoroughly, and had again come to the conclusion that Austria's procedure against Serbia must be regarded as an act of aggression, and that consequently a *casus foederis* ('case for the alliance'), according to the terms of the Triple Alliance treaty, did not exist. Therefore Italy would have to declare herself neutral. Upon my violently opposing this point of view, the Minister went on to state that since Italy had not been informed in advance of Austria's procedure against Serbia, she could with less reason be expected to take part in the war, as Italian interests were being directly injured by the Austrian proceeding. All that he could say to me now was that the local Government reserved the right to determine whether it might be possible for Italy to intervene later in behalf of the allies [i.e. Germany and Austria], if, at the time of doing so, Italian interests should be satisfactorily protected.

Negotiations

Most Italians were pleased with their neutral status. To them, fighting alongside Austria appeared to be counterproductive as the Habsburgs were holding onto land inhabited by Italian-speakers which Italy hoped one day to claim, Tyrol and Istria. The Italian government however, particularly after the death of Giuliano in late 1914, grew increasingly nervous about the possible consequences of non-intervention. Anticipating the victory of either side without Italy's involvement appeared risky:

- If the Central Powers won, it was likely that they would exercise harsh, or at least unfavourable, treatment of Italy in a peace settlement, as Italy had reneged on its Triple Alliance commitments.
- If the Allies won, they would be unlikely to grant Italy the territory it coveted around the Mediterranean, specifically the Tyrol and Istria.

KEY TERM

military jihad: a holy war declared by Islamic powers in defence of the Muslim religion

ACTIVITY

Create a timeline of the escalation of the First World War into a global conflict.

CROSS-REFERENCE

Look back at pages 30–31 for the terms of the Triple Alliance.

ACTIVITY

1. According to Source 1, what different reasons did Giuliano make clear to the German ambassador for Italy staying neutral?
2. What is the value of Source 1 to an historian studying the reasons for Italian neutrality at the start of the First World War?

STUDY TIP

The role of ambassadors to foreign countries is to represent the interests of their own country, and to manage relations with their host country in a way that suits the aims of their own country's foreign policy. In communications between ambassadors and their host countries, they need to be tactful rather than direct, and may exaggerate the actions of others or play down the actions of their own country. When reporting back to their own governments, however, they can be far more honest. This is always worth bearing in mind when studying the communications of ambassadors.

Fig. 4 *Conditions for Italian and Austro-Hungarian soldiers fighting in the Alps were atrocious: the weather was often appalling and reliable supply lines were very difficult to establish*

ACTIVITY

1. Germany and Austria-Hungary were furious with Italy's defection to the Allies. To read their statements on the move go to www.firstworldwar.com/source/italiandeclaration.htm.

2. Search for the Italian Prime Minister Antonio Salandra's response to their objections on the same website. Which previous events are referred to by Salandra as evidence of traditionally poor relations between Italy and the Central Powers?

KEY TERM

Risorgimento: The Italian nationalist movement. Risorgimento means 'resurgence' or 'rising again' in Italian

ACTIVITY

Draw a spider diagram to explain why Italy sided with the Allies instead of remaining neutral in 1915.

As intervention appeared to be the best strategy, the Italian government began negotiations with both sides in early 1915, hoping to secure the best arrangement to serve Italian interests. The Central Powers did offer some concessions in terms of territorial claims, but crucially Austria refused to offer Italy Trentino or Trieste. The Allies, meanwhile, offered not only these territories but also lands in southern Tyrol, Dalmatia and Istria, all of which they anticipated seizing from a defeated Habsburg Empire. This offer was sealed with the Treaty of London, signed on 26 April 1915. With these new possessions, Italy would hold considerable influence over the Adriatic Sea. On 24 May, Italy declared war on Austria-Hungary, having formally joined the Triple Entente powers the day before.

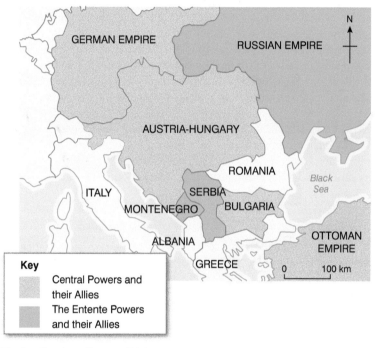

Key
- Central Powers and their Allies
- The Entente Powers and their Allies

Fig. 5 *Southern Europe, 1914*

Dreams of the Risorgimento

Italy's intervention was hardly popular with the majority of its citizens, especially those in the South, many of whom had little interest in gaining extra land when they lived in poverty already. The **Risorgimento**, however, was a Nationalist movement that saw the war as a chance to increase Italy's international standing and to realise their dreams of becoming a world power. In some ways Italy's development was similar to Germany's: both had, in 1871, only united a collection of smaller states into a cohesive nation, and both had domestic problems its leaders hoped could be solved – or at least temporarily forgotten – by going to war.

Despite the unpopularity of the war among many Italians, five million men had served in the Italian army by the end of the war, mostly in atrocious conditions against the Austro-Hungarians on the mountainsides of the Eastern Alps.

The entry of the United States

A CLOSER LOOK

A 'special relationship'?

It is often assumed, given that the USA was a nation of English speakers, that it was a natural ally of Britain and the Triple Entente as the First World War escalated. However, not only were most Americans committed to neutrality, many felt a stronger loyalty towards Germany. Eight million Americans (of a total population of around 100 million) were second- or third-generation German immigrants. Meanwhile Americans of Irish and Eastern European descent had little sympathy for the Allied belligerents.

America's neutrality

The USA had many strong reasons for remaining neutral at the start of the war. Mainstream opinion favoured **isolationism**: the origins of the European war were far removed from most Americans, physically and psychologically. Peace would not only avoid the loss of American lives, but also the economic instability brought by war. Furthermore, interest groups campaigning on domestic issues, such as women's suffrage and the prohibition of alcohol, resented the potential distraction of war. Over the first years of the war, however, mainstream opinion in the USA changed due to a number of developments.

A CLOSER LOOK

Isolationism

It was a common view in America at this time that the US should stay isolated from European affairs and 'entangling alliances', a phrase used by Thomas Jefferson, the third American President, in 1801. Its strongest proponents were **Woodrow Wilson**, who was morally committed to peace, and businessmen who worried about the financial losses entailed in involvement in war.

Wartime boom

Non-intervention allowed America to trade with both the Allies and the Central Powers, fuelling a huge economic boom. Europe's war production meant that countries not only needed large quantities of munitions, but also necessities for the home front as factory production was switched to armaments. American companies filled these gaps in the market: half of Britain's war budget was spent on American materials. In particular, as Britain's chemical industry was in its infancy, it relied on US-produced chemicals to make explosives for the Western Front, having previously traded with Germany. Some American businesses saw their profits increase six-fold from peacetime.

There were many Americans, however, who questioned just how neutral America's neutrality really was. Although the US supplied both the Allies and the Central Powers, the Allies felt a greater benefit thanks to Britain's naval blockade of Germany – British ships were not allowing supplies to Germany to get through to them, even if the carriers were neutral. Furthermore, Britain was borrowing money directly from America, and financial speculators began to gamble increasingly on Allied victories. As the currency reserves of the Allies ran low, they took out large American loans to buy the materials needed for the war effort. If the Allied countries were defeated, they were unlikely to be able to repay their debts: the USA therefore had a considerable financial stake in the Allies winning the war.

Reasons for intervention

Wilson won a second term as president in 1916 with the campaign slogan 'He Kept Us Out of The War'. However three different actions by Germany provided weight for the argument that the USA would have to intervene.

KEY PROFILE

Fig. 6   *Woodrow Wilson*

Woodrow Wilson (1856–1924) was a Democrat who became President in 1913. His commitment to neutrality secured public support and led him to win a second term in 1916. However, he prepared for intervention when Germany resumed its unrestricted U-boat campaign. His **Fourteen Points** programme was a strong influence at the Versailles peace conference in 1919. He died in 1924 after being defeated in the 1920 election by Republican Warren Harding.

CROSS-REFERENCE

Read about Wilson's Fourteen Points programme and its influence over the Versailles peace conference in Chapter 14, page 119.

CROSS-REFERENCE

Dreadnoughts and their importance in the pre-war naval arms race between Germany and Britain are explored in Chapter 5.

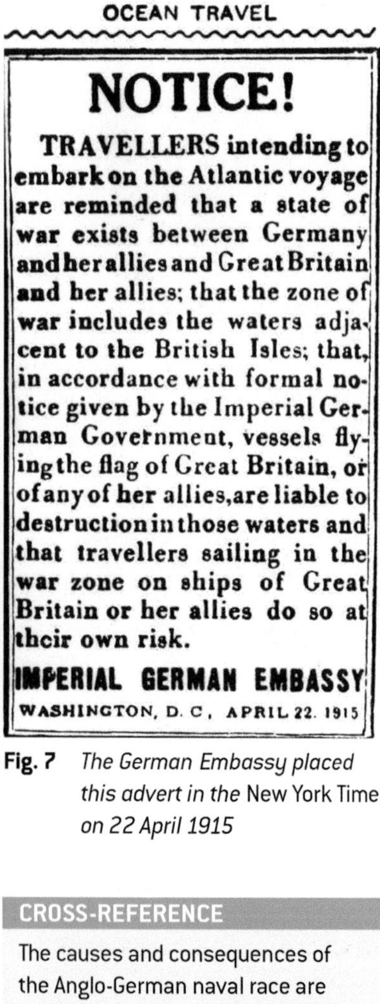

OCEAN TRAVEL

NOTICE!

TRAVELLERS intending to embark on the Atlantic voyage are reminded that a state of war exists between Germany and her allies and Great Britain and her allies; that the zone of war includes the waters adjacent to the British Isles; that, in accordance with formal notice given by the Imperial German Government, vessels flying the flag of Great Britain, or of any of her allies, are liable to destruction in those waters and that travellers sailing in the war zone on ships of Great Britain or her allies do so at their own risk.

IMPERIAL GERMAN EMBASSY
WASHINGTON, D. C., APRIL 22, 1915

Fig. 7 *The German Embassy placed this advert in the* New York Times *on 22 April 1915*

CROSS-REFERENCE

The causes and consequences of the Anglo-German naval race are explored in Chapter 5, pages 38–39.

KEY TERM

home front: the civilian government and people not directly fighting in a war. It is known as a 'front' because, during the two world wars, civilians were under attack from aerial and naval bombardment, and often severely affected by naval blockades

The shift in opinion following the sinking of the *Lusitania*

In February 1915, frustrated by the success of Britain's naval blockade, the Kaiser declared that all waters around Britain were a warzone, so that any ships were liable to be attacked by Germany even if they were neutral. Despite the drama and expense of the Anglo-German naval race, U-boats (submarines) became Germany's naval weapon of choice, not **dreadnoughts**: much of the main German fleet was unable to break the blockade of the numerically superior Royal Navy and stayed close to port on the North Sea coast. The Kaiser's order was a risky one however, and Bethmann Hollweg was concerned about Germany's international reputation if U-boats were to sink merchant vessels without warning, which might make Germany 'the mad dog' in the eyes of the world.

A CLOSER LOOK

Naval blockades

Naval blockades tried to prevent food and supplies reaching the enemy by sea. They had been used in previous wars, but the stalemate in the trenches made them far more significant. When unrestricted submarine warfare was in place, German U-boats tried to sink any vessel carrying supplies to Britain, whereas British tactics involved stopping and searching neutral vessels and seizing any forbidden goods. For this reason, the British blockade of the Central Powers did not significantly damage relations between Britain and the USA, but the use of submarines by Germany to sink ships carrying supplies to the Allies was considered underhand and immoral. The British blockade of Germany and Austria-Hungary was extremely effective, prompting rationing and near starvation of their home fronts by the end of the war.

The Kaiser also shook off his ministers' concerns that unrestricted submarine warfare might give cause for the USA to enter the war. He was already wary of increasing American influence in the Pacific, and judged that a show of naval strength with a determined U-boat campaign might be a deterrent for the US, and therefore worth the gamble.

On 1 May the *Lusitania*, the largest luxury liner in the world with capacity for 2000 passengers, set sail from New York. Ten days earlier, the Imperial German Embassy posted a warning in the *New York Times* stating that any passengers sailing to Britain, France or Russia did so at their own risk; the threat was laughed off by the *Lusitania*'s captain. On 7 May, as the ship approached the Irish coast, she was sunk by a single torpedo from the German U-boat U-20. In total 1198 passengers died, including 128 Americans, prompting outrage on both sides of the Atlantic.

As the sinking occurred almost two years before America's declaration of war, it is questionable how much emphasis we can place upon it as a catalyst for American involvement. It did, however, help to steer public opinion away from their position of neutrality. Wilson's response was to send a threatening message to the German embassy, which resulted in the suspension of unrestricted submarine warfare. The US President, while refusing to end America's neutrality, did launch a 'Preparedness' programme, under which the US Congress approved large-scale shipbuilding in the hope of deterring Germany from further attacks on commercial shipping.

The resumption of unrestricted submarine warfare

By early 1917 the war had begun to tip in the Allies' favour, with the challenge of supplying both the front line and the **home front** a significant factor. The Allies' financial links with the USA gave them a huge economic advantage in this area: when a German U-boat was captured in 1916 and its crew brought onto the British mainland, they were shocked by the healthy condition of British people, compared to the people in Germany, where harsh long-term **rationing** was taking its toll. With this in mind, on 2 February 1917 the Kaiser ordered that U-boats would again be permitted to sink **merchant ships**, perhaps calculating that if the USA had remained neutral thus far, it would continue to do so – and therefore Germany had little option but to take the risk.

The U-boat campaign was now pursued ruthlessly, with the aim of quickly starving the British into submission. The order was made public, which pushed Wilson further towards intervention, but merchant ships could now be sunk without warning. After a panicky few weeks of heavy losses, Britain soon blunted the impact of the U-boats by introducing the convoy system, by which merchant ships sailed together and were protected by warships. The Kaiser's gamble had failed on two fronts.

The Zimmerman telegram

Wilson was already close to preparing the US for intervention, but a telegram intercepted by the British in January 1917 provided the final catalyst. In the telegram, German Foreign Secretary Arthur Zimmerman sent the government of Mexico an extraordinary proposal: to invade the USA in exchange for an alliance with the Central Powers and the reclaiming of land lost to America.

> **SOURCE 2**
>
> From the telegram sent by the German Foreign Secretary to the Mexican government on 19 January 1917:
>
> We intend to begin on the first of February unrestricted submarine warfare. We shall endeavour in spite of this to keep the United States of America neutral. In the event of this not succeeding, we make Mexico a proposal of alliance on the following basis: make war together, make peace together, generous financial support and an understanding on our part that Mexico is to reconquer the lost territory in Texas, New Mexico, and Arizona. The settlement in detail is left to you. You will inform the President of the above most secretly as soon as the outbreak of war with the United States of America is certain and add the suggestion that he should, on his own initiative, invite Japan to immediate adherence and at the same time mediate between Japan and ourselves. Please call the President's attention to the fact that the ruthless employment of our submarines now offers the prospect of compelling England in a few months to make peace.

The British were only too pleased to pass the intercepted message on to the US ambassador. An incitement by the German government to a foreign power to invade the USA was finally, in Wilson's opinion, just grounds for intervening in the war. Events in Russia also tipped him in this direction. In February, a spontaneous revolution resulted in the overthrow of the Tsar – and, more importantly – tsarist autocracy. Wilson could now claim that America was fighting for the cause of democracy, without the inconvenience of an absolutist ally. On 2 April he asked Congress for a declaration of war against Germany. The vote was almost unanimous and the USA went to war on 6 April.

KEY TERM

rationing: a system by which the government allows citizens a restricted amount of food and goods, usually when the production or supply of a commodity is restricted

merchant ships: commercial vessels not belonging to a country's military navy; they did not have guns on-board so they had no means to fight or defend themselves

ACTIVITY

According to the telegram in Source 2, in what ways does Zimmerman try to persuade Mexico to agree to the German plan?

ACTIVITY

Group work

In pairs or groups, discuss whether the main reason that the USA intervened in the war was due to provocation by Germany, or to financial advantages.

Analyse the main reasons why many of the belligerents got involved in the First World War. How many did so because of:

a. alliance commitments?
b. colonial loyalties?
c. provocation by other powers?
d. other factors?

Summary

The seeds of the escalation of what could have been the Third Balkan War into a world war had been sown many years earlier with the imperial ambitions of the Great Powers, while Italy's intervention came as the result of thwarted territorial ambitions around the Mediterranean. The USA was one of only a few powers which joined the war with a moral objective, and President Wilson had high hopes for the post-war world, as he outlined in his address to Congress in April 1917:

SOURCE 3

From President Wilson's speech to the American Congress on 2 April 1917:

It is a fearful thing to lead this great peaceful people into war, into the most terrible and disastrous of all wars, civilization itself seeming to be in the balance. But the right is more precious than peace, and we shall fight for the things which we have always carried nearest our hearts — for democracy, for the right of those who submit to authority to have a voice in their own governments, for the rights and liberties of small nations, for a universal dominion of right by such a concert of free peoples as shall bring peace and safety to all nations and make the world in itself free.

STUDY TIP

Try to write multiple paragraphs on the focus of this question, the sinking of the *Lusitania*, and then balance this factor against a range of others, providing some directed comment and evaluation.

 PRACTICE QUESTION

'The sinking of the *Lusitania* brought the USA into the First World War.' Explain why you agree or disagree with this view.

STUDY TIP

When considering the value of the provenance of the source, especially when analysing the reasons for the actions of a country, it is useful to explore the level of authority of its creator and the audience the source was intended for. Authors will have different levels of authority: the more power and influence a person has, the more likely they are to know the true motivations of their country. However, the audience they are addressing is also crucial. If they are speaking in public and trying to persuade others, they may well have strong reasons not to give an accurate picture, while private correspondence may make their words more trustworthy, depending of course on who they are writing to.

 PRACTICE QUESTION

Evaluating primary sources

With reference to Sources 1, 2 and 3 and your understanding of the historical context, assess the value of these sources to an historian studying the reasons why other countries became involved in the First World War after 1914 in relation to diplomatic exchanges between 1914 and 1917.

4 The end of the First World War and the peace settlement 1917–23

13 The collapse of the autocratic empires

Fig. 1 *Disorder on the streets in Russia, March 1917; the poor living and working conditions of many citizens, exacerbated by war, helped to force the permanent demise of autocratic rule in Russia and Germany*

LEARNING OBJECTIVES

In this chapter you will learn about:

- the reasons for and the events of the Russian and German Revolutions

- why the declining Austro-Hungarian and Ottoman Empires finally collapsed

- nationalist ambitions of Polish, Slav and Arab nationalists and their immediate consequences on international relations and peace-making.

KEY CHRONOLOGY

8 March 1917	Russian Revolution started
15 March 1917	Abdication of Tsar Nicholas II
8 November 1917	Bolsheviks seize power in Russia
8 January 1918	President Wilson announces Fourteen Points peace plan
3 March 1918	Russia and Central Powers sign Treaty of Brest-Litovsk
29 September 1918	Bulgaria asks allies for peace
31 October 1918	Ottoman Empire agrees to armistice
9 November 1918	Kaiser Wilhelm II abdicates
November 1918	Allied forces begin occupation of Constantinople

ACTIVITY

Pair discussion

Using Fig. 1 for initial ideas, discuss in pairs the potential reasons why the First World War led to political revolutions in Germany and Russia.

Revolution in Russia

By March 1917 the war had been going badly for Russia for years. Fighting on the Eastern Front had highlighted the poor training of Russian troops, its inadequate supply lines and the lack of imagination of its generals. To make matters worse, in 1915 the Tsar assumed command of the Russian army himself, which meant that military defeats, such as the Lake Naroch Offensive, were often blamed on Nicholas' poor leadership.

The government in Petrograd (renamed from St Petersburg) was left to the Tsarina Alexandra. Under the influence of the unsavoury Russian mystic Rasputin, the German-born Alexandra was already deeply unpopular with the Russian people. By the winter of 1916–17, conditions on the home front were atrocious: bread rationing was introduced and lack of fuel forced factories to close. Russia was still the most autocratic of all the Great Powers, and as a wide range of acute problems combined to make life intolerable for the Russian people, it was easy for soldiers and citizens alike to focus their anger on Nicholas himself.

The calendar in Russia

Dates in Russian history can be confusing at this point in 1917 because Russia continued to follow the Julian calendar, which was two weeks behind the Gregorian calendar already adopted in the West. Therefore the March Revolution, beginning on 8 March 1917 according to the Gregorian calendar, is often referred to as the February Revolution. Similarly, the November Revolution during which the Bolsheviks seized power is also known as the October Revolution This book uses the Gregorian calendar throughout.

Soviet: Russian word for council, originally meaning (in 1917) a political organisation for and led by the working classes or 'proletariat'

The Bolsheviks later renamed Russia the Union of Soviet Socialist Republics (USSR) in 1922, after which the term 'Soviet' was used to refer to someone or something from the USSR.

Evaluating primary sources

1. Based on your understanding of Source 1 and the historical context, how far would you agree with the statement that the founding principles of the Provisional Government were 'overly ambitious'?

2. How easy do you think it would have been for the government to uphold the principles listed in Source 1, while still continuing with the war?

On 8 March, strikes and rioting broke out in the cities as people demanded first bread, then the abdication of the Tsar. Nicholas, still at the front line, ordered the local Cossack militia to put down the strike, but soldiers balked at shooting citizens protesting their hunger. The mutinies spread, and having lost the support of the army Nicholas abdicated on 15 March, prompting the formation of the Provisional Government.

The Provisional Government and the war

The Provisional Government was severely limited by the compromises it made to retain power. It established its authority over Russia with the support of the Petrograd **Soviet**, which had considerable influence in the capital. The Russian people, sick of the privations of wartime and the appalling loss of life on the Eastern Front, demanded an end to the war.

The Provisional Government could not simply resign from the war, however. Kerensky, the moderate socialist leader of the government from July, realised that doing so would be seen as a deep betrayal by the Allies as well as a strategic disaster, as Germany would then be able to focus all its military muscle on the Western Front. At home, Russia's continued involvement in the war cost the government vital support: the hardships of the war effort and the loss of Western credit made daily life almost indistinguishable from people's misery under the Tsar.

SOURCE 1 SPEECH FROM GOVERNMENT FOLLOWING TSAR ABDICATION

From the proclamation announcing the formation of the Provisional Government, 15 March 1917:

The actual work of the cabinet will be guided by the following principles: → an official pardon.

- An immediate and complete amnesty in all cases of a political and religious nature, including terrorist acts, military revolts and agrarian offences, etc.
- Freedom of speech, press, and assembly, and the extension of political freedom to persons serving in the armed forces.
- The immediate arrangements for the calling on the Constituent Assembly on the basis of universal, equal and direct suffrage and secret ballot, which will determine the form of government and the constitution of the country.
- The substitution of a people's militia for the police, with elective officers responsible to the organs of local self-government.
- Elections to the organs of local self-government are to be held on the basis of universal, equal and direct suffrage and secret ballot.
- The Provisional Government wishes to add that it has no intention whatsoever of taking advantage of the military situation to delay in any way the carrying through of the reforms and the measures outlined above.

The Bolshevik seizure of power

The Bolsheviks, led by Vladimir Lenin, advocated the immediate establishment of Bolshevik control in Russia. They won support from suffering citizens with their simple promise of 'Peace, Land and Bread!', but they did not come to power as a result of a popular uprising. The authority of the Provisional Government was so thin by the autumn of 1917 that the Bolsheviks' storming of the Winter Palace on 8 November met very little resistance. Nicholas II and his family were executed by the Bolsheviks on 17 July 1918.

Fig. 2 *Lenin was the leader of the Bolshevik party and became leader of Russia following the November Revolution*

The Treaty of Brest-Litovsk

Germany was eager to begin peace negotiations with Russia in December 1917. The terms were harsh on Russia, ending its dominion over several Eastern European countries that had been part of the Russian Empire since the eighteenth century. Under the Treaty of Brest-Litovsk, signed on 3 March 1918:

- Russia lost its territorial rights to Poland, Lithuania, Riga, Estonia, Livonia and parts of White Russia (modern-day Belarus). Germany and Austria-Hungary were given the right to decide the fate of these territories.

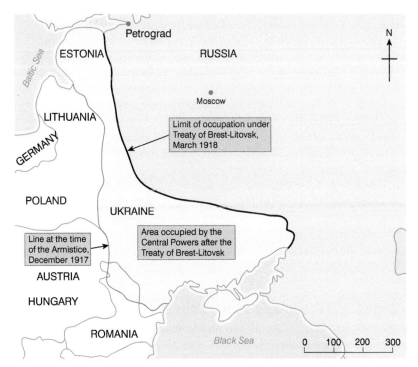

Fig. 3 *This map shows how the Treaty of Brest-Litovsk reduced the territory ruled by Russia*

CROSS-REFERENCE

The German political system prior to the First World War is explored in Chapter 1.

KEY PROFILE

Fig. 4   *Erich Ludendorff*

Erich Ludendorff (1865–1937) was a celebrated German general who exercised considerable power over the Kaiser and the government. As the strain of war increased, colleagues feared for his mental state. After the German Revolution, Ludendorff supported Hitler's Munich Putsch in 1923. He retired in 1928, renouncing his right-wing views for a pacifist outlook.

CROSS-REFERENCE

The reasons for the USA's entry into the war, including Germany's actions, are explored in Chapter 12.

ACTIVITY

Thinking point

Explain why Germany's position was weakened by the position of its allies.

KEY TERM

self-determination: the right of people of the same race or cultural background to be ruled by themselves as a nation

- Russia had to evacuate Finland and recognise the independence of Ukraine.
- Germany was given permission to exploit the rich agricultural land that Russia had given up.

Most Russian soldiers and citizens were war weary and ready for peace, even with such punishing terms. Lenin was also determined to focus on resolving Russia's considerable domestic problems and consolidate his grip on power, rather than continue fighting the war in the hope of a more favourable agreement with Germany. He also believed that revolution in Germany would remove the Treaty.

Revolution in Germany

By the outbreak of war, political power in Germany was almost entirely in the hands of the Kaiser and his military advisers. The Reichstag loyally supported the war effort for most of its duration. The British naval blockade made rationing necessary from 1915, and the German Board of Public Health later claimed that 763,000 died of starvation or disease as a result of the blockade. The winter of 1916–17 marked a turning point, as it had done in Russia. The weather was too cold for the potato harvest, forcing Germans to subsist on a diet of turnips; socialist politicians then acknowledged, and worked to relieve, the Germans' war-weariness. On 19 July 1917 a coalition of socialists and radicals called for a Peace Resolution – negotiations with the Allies – which was passed by 212 votes to 126. It had little effect on the German government, but did mark the sharper division between the will of the Kaiser and the will of elected representatives.

Facing military defeat

With the superior economic assistance provided by the USA to the Allies, a victory for the Central Powers looked increasingly unlikely from 1917. The conclusion of an advantageous peace with Russia in March 1918 provided welcome relief for the German Supreme Command, but it did not last long. The failed gamble of the resumption of unrestricted submarine warfare and the entry of the USA on the side of the Allies made a momentous and decisive breakthrough more necessary than ever. **General Erich Ludendorff** (with **General Hindenburg**, the highest-ranking military officer) realised it was only a matter of time before the American Army provided enough reinforcements for the Western Front to make the war unwinnable for the Central Powers. Germany's Spring Offensive of 1918 won an impressive amount of ground initially, but a series of successful counter-attacks, bolstered by over 1 million American troops, soon forced the Germans into retreat.

On 24 September, Bulgaria asked the Allies to agree to a ceasefire. This was an added disaster for the Central Powers, as it left Austria-Hungary exposed to enemy penetration: Ludendorff was so devastated by the news he collapsed. On 29 September he summoned his military chiefs to a meeting at Spa, at which he admitted that he had no hope in the German army regaining the initiative. Instead he recommended the ending of the war as soon as possible.

The impact of Wilson's Fourteen Points

Wilson's Fourteen Points, announced on 8 January 1918, set out the President's vision for peace. The points became highly influential as the Central Powers began to consider suing for peace, as the USA was expected to offer more lenient terms than either France or Britain. This consideration established democracy and **self-determination** as mainstream ideals.

Once the decision was made by the chiefs of staff to sue for peace, the German government set about preparing the ground. On 30 September a parliamentary government was established, and on 3 October the new Chancellor, Prince Max of Baden, wrote to Wilson asking for an armistice. Wilson, however, had specific criteria with which Germany had to comply first:

- The evacuation of all territory occupied by Germany.
- The end of submarine warfare.
- The guarantee that the new German government would be fully democratic with no military influence.

A CLOSER LOOK

Germany's new government

Germany's new government was a constitutional monarchy similar to that of Britain. The Kaiser remained as head of state, but the government and the chancellor were answerable to the Reichstag instead, which also took control of the army and navy. These constitutional changes have been described as a 'revolution from above', as they were recommended by Ludendorff and sanctioned by Wilhelm with little involvement from the Reichstag, which was in recess between 5 and 22 October. However, in early November unrest amongst civilians and the armed forces – notably the Kiel mutiny – forced more radical change.

Ludendorff resigned when Prince Max made it clear that if Wilson's terms were rejected, Germany would have to surrender rather than negotiate an armistice. On 28 October, Germany became a parliamentary democracy, with the chancellor now answerable to the Reichstag. To the ordinary German citizen, however, little seemed to have changed: the Kaiser was still head of state, the military still had a strong influence in government, strikes were still illegal, and the war continued. Pressure for Wilhelm to abdicate began to mount.

A naval mutiny in Kiel on 3 November, 1918, sparked the German revolution. A meeting of 20,000 sailors called for workers' and sailors' soviets, which were established in Hamburg, Cologne, Frankfurt, Leipzig, Munich and finally Berlin over the next few days. Monarchical authority collapsed, but the revolution was mostly bloodless. Those standing for the old order were either at the front or put up no resistance. In the face of pressure from his ministers, who increasingly saw him as a stubborn obstacle to peace, the Kaiser abdicated on 9 November and went into exile in Holland, where he died in 1940. On the day of the abdication, a German republic was proclaimed from a balcony of the Reichstag and the new government began peace negotiations with the Allies.

ACTIVITY

Summary

Creating a diagram showing the reasons why a republic was declared in Germany in November 1918.

Terms of the Armistice

Representatives from the Allied powers met a German delegation, led by Matthias Erzberger, in a railway carriage in Compiègne in Northern France. Erzberger was visibly shocked by the terms presented to Germany. It would have to immediately evacuate France and Belgium, pay compensation to the Allies and surrender its naval fleet just to obtain peace. Until Germany agreed, Britain would maintain its blockade. With little choice, the German representatives signed the agreement, and fighting stopped on 11 November.

CROSS-REFERENCE

The Fourteen Points are explored in more depth in Chapter 14 as part of Wilson's aims at the 1919 Paris Peace Conference.

KEY PROFILE

Fig. 5   Paul von Hindenburg

Paul von Hindenburg (1847–1934) was a military hero who had been Chief of Staff during the First World War. His popularity helped secure his appointment as German President in 1925. His death in 1934 allowed Hitler to become Führer and receive a personal oath of loyalty from the army.

A CLOSER LOOK

Surrender, armistice, treaty

Armies will generally only surrender if they have no other option and cannot fight any longer; by surrendering they will have little or no influence over the terms by which they stop fighting. Under an armistice the terms under which a truce is called are negotiated between the main belligerents, although the defeated army usually has a far weaker negotiating position. A treaty is the terms by which peace is to be maintained, and is usually concluded weeks or months after fighting stops to allow for longer negotiations.

Fig. 6 *The armistice was signed in a railway carriage in the forest of Compiègne, France*

The disintegration of Austria-Hungary

The nationalities of the Habsburg Empire generally hoped to win concessions by serving loyally in the war. However, as the situation at home and on the front line worsened, the ties linking Austria and Hungary together were increasingly strained. The death of Franz Joseph and the accession of Karl I in 1916 signalled new hope for a change to the status quo.

The deterioration of Austria-Hungary's fortunes in the war began in 1915: Russia had occupied Galicia and Italy had opened up another front in the Alps. By the war's end, 300,000 Austro-Hungarian troops had deserted. The impact of the Allied blockade, coupled with a bad harvest in 1916, encouraged different regions of the empire to operate independently to ensure their economic survival. Karl lacked the authority to restore the bonds of the empire, and in October 1918 he sought an armistice from the Allies in return for granting greater political freedom to the provinces.

ACTIVITY

Evaluating primary sources

What is the value of Source 2 to an historian studying:
a. The collapse of the Austro-Hungarian Empire?
b. The end of the Habsburg monarchy?

SOURCE 2

From Austrian Emperor Karl I's abdication proclamation, made on 11 November 1918:

Since my accession I have incessantly tried to rescue my peoples from this tremendous war. Therefore I have not delayed the re-establishment of constitutional rights or the opening of a way for the people to substantial national development. Filled with an unalterable love for my peoples I will not, with my person, be a hindrance to their free development. I acknowledge the decision recently taken by German Austria to form a separate State. The people has by its deputies taken charge of the Government. I relinquish every participation in the administration of the State. Likewise I have released the members of the Austrian Government from their offices. I sincerely hope the German Austrian people realise harmony from the new adjustment. The happiness of my peoples was my aim from the beginning. My warmest wishes are that an internal peace will soon be able to heal the wounds of this war.

Following Czechoslovakia's proclamation of independence on 18 October 1918, US Secretary of State Robert Lansing informed Austria-Hungary that it could no longer consider offering peace terms on the basis of the Fourteen Points as the Czechs then joined the war against the Central Powers. Heinrich Lammasch became Austrian Prime Minister and was instructed by Karl to organise the peaceful dismantling of the empire. Faced with increasing pressure from nationalists and republicans, Lammasch advised Karl to abdicate, which he did on 11 November. The Habsburg monarchy and its empire were no more. Austria elected a new parliament, and Karl fled to Switzerland where he died in 1922.

The collapse of the Ottoman Empire

Having been 'the sick man of Europe' for over a century, Turkey was forced to give up its territories in the Middle East by a combination of nationalism and Allied military and political campaigns. Arab nationalism had been growing in strength since the beginning of the twentieth century, prompted by fears among Arabs that the once 'light touch' rule of the Ottomans was about to transfigure into unwelcome economic and even military interference. The Hejaz railway, completed in 1908, was seen as a method of facilitating this interference, while the Young Turk revolution a year later alienated Syrians, Mesopotamians and Palestinians with its pan-Turkish agenda. Arab nationalists hoped to detach completely from the Ottoman Empire and form an Arab state stretching from modern-day Syria to Yemen.

Even before the Ottoman Empire allied itself with the Central Powers, Arab nationalist leader **Hussein bin Ali** sought assurances from the British government in Egypt that they would support an Arab uprising. From the very start of the war, the Ottoman Turks had to contend with not only several Allied military campaigns in its Middle Eastern possessions, but also a determined rebellion by the Arabs, led by Hussein bin Ali. A series of loose agreements, each motivated by very different aims – shaped the relations between the Arab nationalists and the Allies:

- In the 1915 McMahon–Hussein correspondence between the British High Commissioner and the Arab leader, Arabs were promised Arabian independence. In return, Arabs would begin an uprising against the Ottoman Empire which would divert the forces of the Central Powers to a third front in the Middle East, thereby providing some relief for the Allies. The question of Palestine was not mentioned by McMahon.
- The 1916 Sykes–Picot agreement between Britain and France – motivated by the desire to settle the region peacefully under the guidance of these two European powers – decided on the division of a defeated Ottoman Empire into British and French spheres of influence, thereby countering the earlier promises made by McMahon.
- The 1917 Balfour Declaration guaranteed Palestine as a Jewish homeland in response to the growing influence of **Zionism**. The Declaration also contravened the McMahon–Hussein correspondence, and made the issue of Palestine extremely contentious.

The latter developments were clearly of concern to the Arab nationalists, but the war was not yet over. Their goal was now to defeat their Ottoman overlords and reach Damascus before the Allies, thereby securing their dominance over the region so they could present their control of the surrounding land as a fait accompli. This was achieved on 1 October 1918, but not without controversy, as Australian troops reached the city at the same moment.

Fig. 7   *Hussein bin Ali*

Hussein bin Ali (1854–1931) was Sharif (steward) and Emir (general) of Mecca and Medina from 1908 to 1917. He led the Arab nationalist cause and was King of Hejaz from 1917. He stopped working with the British after they failed to facilitate the creation of an Arab state at the 1919 Paris Peace Conference; they in turn refused to support him when his kingdom was invaded by the Saudis. He abdicated in 1924.

Zionism: the movement to establish a homeland for Jews in Israel, in response to centuries of persecution in other countries

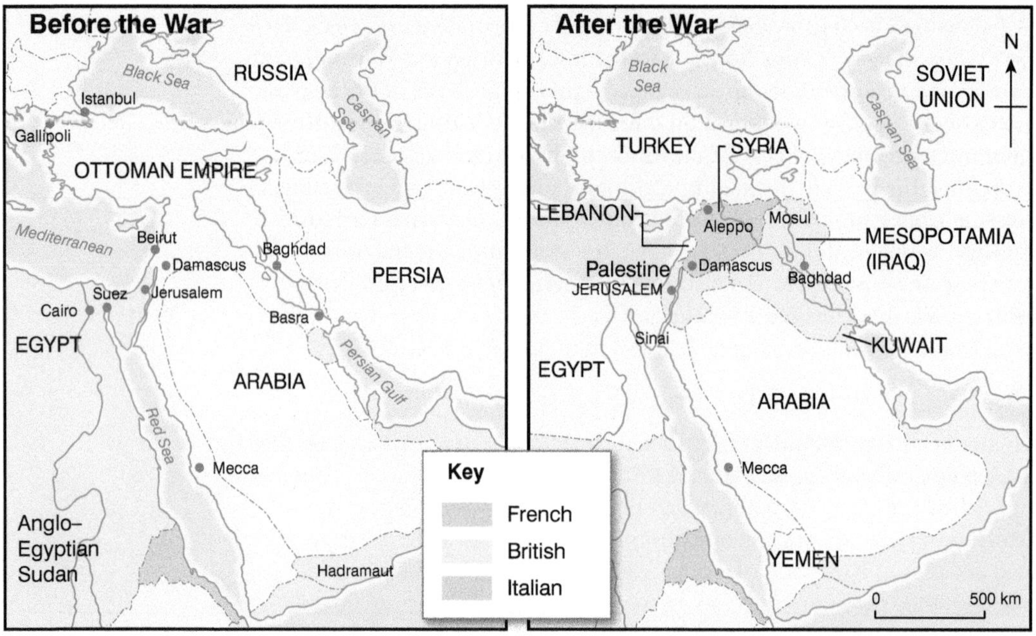

Fig. 8 *These maps show the distribution of power in the Middle East before and after the First World War. The British occupied several key areas towards the end of the war and were given a mandate to continue to do so as part of the peace treaties; France was also granted mandates to administer regions in the north*

The end of the Young Turk government

On 31 October the Ottoman Empire agreed to the Armistice of Mudros with the Allies. By this point, Britain occupied Syria, Palestine and Mesopotamia, while British, French and Greek troops were on the Bulgarian border, threatening the occupation of Thrace and Constantinople. The Young Turk government collapsed in late October. However the Sultan, Mehmed VI, remained in power as the Allies recognised the need to secure post-war stability.

The Allies invaded Constantinople, ostensibly to restore law and order which were in turmoil across the empire, but also to ensure the Turks did not retain control over the whole of Anatolia. Occupation lasted from November 1918 to September 1923. Turkish nationalists, later to be led by Mustafa Kemal – Kemal Atatürk – were horrified by the prospect of losing not only their imperial territories but also parts of Anatolia, which they considered part of the Turkish heartland.

Nationalist ambitions and the impact on international relations and peace-making

The impact of the Russian Revolutions

For nationalists in several areas, revolution in Russia was cause for celebration. Polish nationalists now saw the opportunity to establish an independent Poland, while pan-Slavs were encouraged by the Provisional Government's acknowledgement of 'the right of the nations to decide their own destinies'. Those hoping for political reform were also inspired by the spontaneous uprising that began the March Revolution: surely now authoritarian rulers would grant political concessions to avoid unrest; if not, ordinary Russians had proved that it was possible to force the abdication of a monarch.

ACTIVITY

Thinking point

Using the information in this chapter, including the section on nationalism below and on page 115, compare the reasons why the Habsburg and Ottoman Empires collapsed. How many causes are there in common?

The ambitions of nationalists

Hungarians, eager for some time to end their country's partnership with Austria, began to see an opportunity for independence as the Emperor's authority waned. Slavs in Austria grew restless and disloyal in response to the introduction of martial law. Some months before the war's end, Czechs approached the French to obtain support for the creation of an independent Czechoslovakia, while Serbs and Croats worked together on the birth of Yugoslavia – the goal that had triggered the war in June 1914.

The Congress of Oppressed Nationalities met in Rome in April 1918 seeking self-determination. By this time, the Allies viewed the break-up of the Habsburg Empire as inevitable, and independence from it was positively encouraged. Well in advance of peace negotiations in Versailles, after the Armistice nationalists tended to take matters into their own hands, making self-determination a physical reality with new borders for Poland, Czechoslovakia and Yugoslavia.

SOURCE 3

From the Declaration of Czecho-Slovak Independence by the Provisional Government in Paris, 18 October 1918:

At this grave moment, when the Hohenzollerns are offering peace in order to stop the victorious advance of the allied armies and to prevent the dismemberment of Austria-Hungary and Turkey, and when the Habsburgs are promising the **federalisation** of the Empire and autonomy to the dissatisfied nationalities committed to their rule we, the Czecho-Slovak National Council, realising that federalisation and, still more, autonomy, means nothing under a Habsburg dynasty, do hereby make and declare this our declaration of independence.

We do this because of our belief that no people should be forced to live under a sovereignty they do not recognise and because of our knowledge and firm conviction that our nation cannot freely develop in a Habsburg mock federation, which is only a new form of denationalising oppression under which we have suffered for the past 300 years. We consider freedom to be the first prerequisite for federalisation, and believe that the free nations of central and Eastern Europe may easily federate should they find it necessary.

ACTIVITY

Evaluating primary sources

1. Read Source 3. Why do you think the Czechs and Slovaks were so pessimistic about the prospects of autonomy within the Habsburg Empire?
2. How valuable would Source 3 be to an historian studying the impact of nationalism on the collapse of the Austro-Hungarian Empire?

KEY TERM

federalisation: a system by which individual states are given some powers to govern themselves locally, while remaining within a larger state. The USA has a federal system of government

Summary

The collapse of the autocratic empires could be viewed as expected, but this is to speak with the benefit of hindsight. Nevertheless, the long-term problems faced by each empire were dramatically exacerbated by their involvement in the First World War. The simultaneous end of the Russian, Ottoman and Habsburg Empires also made the issue of nationalism more urgent and more significant, especially as self-determination had been endorsed by Wilson's Fourteen Points programme. It was an issue which would severely test the peacemakers at Paris in 1919.

- The break-up of the Russian Empire and the Treaty of Brest Litovsk encouraged Polish nationalists, who set up an independent state of Poland; its borders would continue to be contested into the 1920s.
- Pan-Slavs in the Balkans, having wished for full independence from Austria-Hungary for many years, had also set up new independent governments in Czechoslovakia and Yugoslavia as the Habsburg Empire collapsed in late 1918.

STUDY TIP

When evaluating the importance of an individual factor, you should consider the significance of other relevant factors too. Evaluate this statement carefully, finding reasons for and against its significance. Making links between this factor and others will show strong analytical skills.

- Arab nationalists hoped to create an Arab state, independent from the Ottomans, in the Middle East. Conflicting aims of the British and French in the region meant that the original promises by McMahon to Hussein in 1915 were unfulfilled.

 PRACTICE QUESTION

'The collapse of the Austro-Hungarian Empire was the result of nationalism'. Assess the validity of this view.

STUDY TIP

When assessing the value of a source's context you should aim to make inferences from the text. What is the author implying with their remarks but not stating explicitly? This should help you show a sophisticated understanding of the text.

 PRACTICE QUESTION

Evaluating primary sources

With reference to the three sources in this chapter and your understanding of the historical context, assess the value of these sources to an historian studying the collapse of the autocratic empires in 1917—18.

14 Peacemaking, 1919–23

The roles and aims of the Big Three

Delegations representing 32 of the nations of the First World War went to the Paris Peace Conference in 1919 to negotiate several peace settlements. Initially, talks were to be led by the Big Five: Britain, France, the USA, Italy and Japan. The Japanese, however, withdrew from a prominent role in negotiations predominantly about the fate of Europe; Italian Prime Minister Vittorio Orlando temporarily withdrew from the conference after he was unable to secure territorial gains for Italy. This left President Wilson of the USA, Prime Minister Clemenceau of France, and Prime Minister Lloyd George of Britain, leaders of the most powerful victorious nations, with a considerable amount of influence over the peace negotiations.

Fig. 1 *Statesmen from around the world gathered in the Hall of Mirrors in Versailles, France, to sign the Treaty of Versailles*

The wreckage of the war was psychological as well as physical. Millions had been killed or wounded. Huge swathes of the French and Belgian landscapes had been utterly destroyed by trench warfare, and vicious fighting still continued in the east as the world leaders met in Paris. The casualty rate and destruction were deeply shocking. As such, Allied statesmen were guided by the desire for revenge and a lasting peace from the public, who were broadly adamant that such loss should never again be tolerated.

Table 1 *Deaths and injuries sustained during the First World War*

Country	Number killed (approximately)	Number wounded
Austria-Hungary	1.4 million	3.6 million
Britain (inc. colonies)	1.1 million	2 million
France	1.4 million	4 million
Germany	2 million	4.2 million
Russia	2 million	4 million
USA	116,000	200,000
Japan	4,000	900
Italy	500,000	950,000
Ottoman Empire	700,000	600,000

LEARNING OBJECTIVES

In this chapter you will learn about:

- the roles and aims of Clemenceau, Wilson and Lloyd George when negotiating the peace treaties

- the key terms of the Treaty of Versailles

- the settlements of Eastern and Southern Europe in the Treaties of St Germain, Neuilly and Trianon

- the settlement with Turkey – the Treaties of Sèvres and Lausanne.

KEY CHRONOLOGY

21 March 1919	Hungarian Soviet Republic established
28 June 1919	Treaty of Versailles signed
June–August 1919	Hungarian communists defeated
10 September 1919	Treaty of St Germain signed
27 November 1919	Treaty of Neuilly signed
10 August 1920	Treaty of Sèvres signed
25 November 1920	Treaty of Trianon signed
24 July 1923	Treaty of Lausanne signed

CROSS-REFERENCE

Negotiations over Italy's territorial gains are explored later in this chapter, on pages 120–121.

Fig. 2   *Georges Clemenceau*

Georges Clemenceau (1841–1929)
entered politics in 1870 when he saw
France defeated and occupied by
Prussians. Nicknamed 'The Tiger', he
had a reputation for toughness and
harboured deep resentment and fear
of Germany. Prime Minister of France
from 1917, Clemenceau also disliked
President Poincaré but was defeated
in the 1920 presidential elections. He
died in 1929 after predicting another
war with Germany.

Fig. 3   *David Lloyd George*

David Lloyd George (1863–1945),
had been British Prime Minister
since December 1916. He was known
for his flexibility but also his integrity.
As a Liberal he had manoeuvred
politically to pass progressive
legislation, and his pragmatism at
the conference meant he acted as
a conciliator between the vengeful
Clemenceau and idealist Wilson. He
later expressed disappointment with
the Versailles Treaty, and became a
critic of the appeasement of Hitler.

As each of the Big Three were also leaders of democratic nations, they had to
reflect the attitudes of their electorates as well as their own personal views;
if the general public did not feel their interests had been represented they
were likely to vote the leaders out of office. This was particularly significant in
Britain, which had a general election in December 1918, and France, which had
a legislative election scheduled for late 1919. As such, the Big Three's aims were:

Georges Clemenceau

- **Clemenceau** had witnessed two German invasions of France, in 1870 and
  1914. He viewed Germany as an inherently dangerous power whose later
  strength would threaten France again unless it was crippled. Amongst the
  general public in France there was also a deep desire for revenge.
- France had suffered by far the worst destruction and casualties of the Allied
  Great Powers, so there was a strong desire for revenge on, and compensation
  from Germany. Twenty-five per cent of the French male population between
  the ages of 18 and 30 were dead or wounded because of the war.
- Clemenceau was sceptical of many of Wilson's Fourteen Points, believing
  Wilson to be too high-minded and idealistic; Clemenceau himself was more
  pragmatic. In particular he wanted Germany to be dismembered, with the
  Rhineland made into a separate state in order to provide a physical barrier
  between France and Germany. He was not convinced that **Lloyd George**
  and Wilson sympathised with the French fear of another German invasion.
- Rather than a neutral location, Clemenceau insisted that the conference be
  held in Paris in recognition of France's sacrifices in the war.

David Lloyd George

- Lloyd George and his government had been elected in late 1918 with
  such campaign slogans as 'Hang the Kaiser' and promises to 'squeeze'
  Germany financially 'until the pips squeak'. Many British citizens expected
  reparations to be imposed on the Germans, not least because the war had
  cost the lives of almost a million British and Empire troops. Lloyd George
  was also determined that Germany would not threaten Britain's command
  of the seas and the security of its empire again.
- Privately, however, Lloyd George believed Britain would benefit most from
  ensuring that long-term peace was secured from the negotiations, not least
  because the war had made a terrible impact on British trade. That the two
  aims of punishing Germany while trying to ensure another war did not
  break out in the future often conflicted with each other – causing bitter
  arguments among the peacemakers – was hugely significant.
- Like Wilson, Lloyd George was concerned that if Germany was punished
  too harshly, it would seek revenge in the near future. He also recognised that
  Germany could be a valuable trading partner for Britain if it was allowed to
  recover economically. Furthermore he was concerned that Germany would
  have a communist revolution if economic conditions were kept poor.
- Like Clemenceau, however, Lloyd George was unenthusiastic about some
  of the Fourteen Points, especially self-determination, which implied Britain
  would have to give up its empire.
- Lloyd George often acted as a mediator between Clemenceau and Wilson
  at the conference. While the British and French leaders considered their
  aims to be more practical than Wilson's, Lloyd George agreed with the US
  President's general aim of securing long-term European peace.

Woodrow Wilson

- Having brought the USA into the war when many Americans continued
  to favour neutrality, Wilson hoped that the results of the Paris Peace
  Conference would convince voters that the war had been worth fighting in.

Therefore the treaties which emerged had to be based on American ideals such as freedom from foreign oppression. This shaped his list of Fourteen Points, announced in January 1918.

- One of the principles behind the increasingly popular policy of isolationism in the USA was that European wars were almost inevitable because of the 'old world' bitterness and rivalry prevalent in Europe – a view particularly prominent amongst Republican senators and congressmen. As a Democrat, Wilson's political career was therefore at stake; a settlement which would produce long-term peace was essential.
- Most important to Wilson was the establishment of a League of Nations which he hoped would prevent further conflict by setting up negotiations and arbitration between countries in the event of disputes.
- Another key principle guiding Wilson in much of the negotiations was self-determination for small states which were formerly part of the Habsburg, Russian and Ottoman empires.

KEY TERM

reparation: a principle of international law which states that it is the obligation of the wrongdoing party to redress the damage caused to the injured party

CROSS-REFERENCE

A Key Profile of Woodrow Wilson can be found in Chapter 12.

A CLOSER LOOK

Wilson's Fourteen Points

In summary, the points were:

1. Peace treaties should be open; there should be no more secret alliances between nations.
2. Absolute freedom of navigation upon the seas.
3. The removal of economic barriers and the establishment of free trade.
4. Disarmament, with just enough weapons to secure domestic safety.
5. Self-determination for colonies.
6. Germany must evacuate all Russian territories and allow Russia to develop politically.
7. The evacuation and freedom of Belgium.
8. All French territory to be freed and Alsace-Lorraine returned to France.
9. Italy's borders should be adjusted to take Italian nationality into account.
10. Autonomy for the nationalities within the Austro-Hungarian Empire.
11. Romania, Serbia and Montenegro to be evacuated; Balkan nationalities to receive independence.
12. Turkey should be consolidated as a state, but the Ottoman Empire to be broken up and its nationalities given independence.
13. Poland to be established as an independent state with access to the sea.
14. The establishment of a general association of nations must be formed to guarantee political independence and territorial integrity for large and small states.

ACTIVITY

1. Are there any clues in the Fourteen Points as to what Wilson thought the causes of the war were?
2. Do you think any of the points would have been unwelcome or inconvenient to Clemenceau or Lloyd George?

As the conference went on, each of the Big Three exerted influence over the aspects of the settlement which they felt most affected the interests of their own countries. After the delegations of the 32 countries represented at the conference, the Big Three discussed the eventual terms of the Treaty of Versailles, which dealt with Germany and the League of Nations, and the subsequent treaties settling disputes in Eastern Europe and Turkey, were shaped by a series of compromises, the result of long and difficult negotiations in the French capital.

Negotiations in Paris

Two crucial powers, however, were not invited to the conference: Germany was not allowed a negotiating position as the defeated side, and Russia was mistrusted and sidelined as a communist state. The conference formally opened on 18 January 1919 and negotiated over the next year.

A CLOSER LOOK

The historiography of Versailles

Historians such as Alan J.P. Taylor – and even the delegates themselves soon after – have traditionally criticised the Versailles Treaty as being too high-minded, or too harsh on Germany. They suggest that it led to the rise of Hitler and the Second World War. Recently, historians like Zara Steiner and Margaret MacMillan have argued that no one could have predicted the set of circumstances that led to the Second World War, and that considering the extremely difficult circumstances the Paris peacemakers did a remarkably fair job.

CROSS-REFERENCE

The term *revanchism* is explained in Chapter 4.

The 'War Guilt' clause is explored later in this chapter, on page 121.

KEY TERM

mandate: territories (particularly overseas colonies) transferred to the control of a different country until they were thought capable of governing themselves

CROSS-REFERENCE

The McMahon–Hussein correspondence, in which Arab nationalists were promised support from the British, is explored in Chapter 13.

The consequences of Italy's experience at the conference are explained in Chapter 19.

Divisions between the Big Three soon emerged. Clemenceau demanded more security for France against Germany, in the form of a barrier in the Rhineland and French control of the Saar coalfields. It is perhaps unsurprising that this demand was rejected by Wilson and Lloyd George: it contradicted self-determination, and Britain and the USA had the seas as a natural barrier against a resurgent Germany. Lloyd George also predicted that confiscating more German territory there would lead to a new *revanchism* and continued bitterness between Germany and France.

By March negotiations reached a stalemate and the conference appeared likely to collapse. At this point Lloyd George issued the Fontainebleau Memorandum, setting out the extent of principles acceptable to the British. He persuaded Clemenceau to accept a more balanced treaty which would not leave Germany unable to recover economically, and convinced him to accept the League of Nations. With Clemenceau's agreement to these key principles secured, Lloyd George then persuaded Wilson to accept the '**War Guilt**' clause.

It was unavoidable that the redrawing of Europe's borders would mean some peoples would now find themselves part of a country they did not want to live in, so the peacemakers tried to ensure protection for minorities, such as freedom of religion and language. Such careful consideration of self-determination did not extend to former empires. For Germany's former colonies, already under the possession of the Allies, as well as the former territories overseas of the Ottoman Empire, a system of **mandates** was introduced. It was widely felt that countries like Cameroon and the Samoan Islands were not yet mature and civilised enough to rule themselves, so they would be governed by Europeans until they had 'matured into nationhood'. According to Wilson, mandates were unnecessary for Europeans when it came to the former Habsburg Empire.

A CLOSER LOOK

Lawrence of Arabia

Thomas Edward Lawrence was a British scholar who was given the job of British intelligence officer in Cairo during the war, on account of his extensive experience in the Middle East and his fluency in Arabic. He felt a deep empathy with the Arab People, and travelled to the Paris Peace Conference to lobby for Arabian self-rule. His efforts earned him the nickname 'Lawrence of Arabia'.

The Arabian delegation led by Prince Faisal and advised by Thomas Edward Lawrence (known to posterity as **Lawrence of Arabia**) arrived in Paris to claim Mesopotamia, but Lloyd George blocked their proposals in favour of British control over the region. Britain's desire for Arabian oil and security around the Suez Canal was prioritised over the promises made to the Arabs in 1915.

Japan hoped their presence at the conference would secure their transition to a world power: they had been a useful wartime ally and now occupied Korea and Manchuria in China. They proposed a racial equality clause in the treaty which would end the ban on Asian immigration in force in the USA and Australia. At first this was blocked; the Japanese then threatened to walk out while China implored the peacemakers not to compromise, as Japan's occupation of Manchuria contravened self-determination. Wilson finally agreed to Japan's demand to prevent the conference collapsing, but the Chinese felt betrayed.

Another power left angry by vetoed proposals was Italy. Under the 1915 Treaty of London the Italians had been promised land around the Adriatic; Wilson now opposed the idea in the name of self-determination. The response of the Italian delegation was to walk out of the conference; the blocking of territorial gains gave rise to increased Italian nationalism and expansionism.

The Treaty of Versailles

In May 1919, while the terms of the Treaty were prepared, the peacemakers wrote to Berlin to request a German delegation to receive the terms. Germany was given no opportunity to change the terms, and had to accept the following:

German military

The German army was allowed only 100,000 regular soldiers; a drastic cut considering Germany mobilised around 4.5 million soldiers in 1914. Its navy was restricted to six battleships and no submarines. In addition, there was to be no conscription, no military aircraft and no armoured vehicles such as tanks. Existing vessels over this limit were to be scrapped or given to the Allies; in protest, German sailors 'scuttled' (deliberately sank) much of their own fleet at **Scapa Flow** in June 1919.

A demilitarised zone in the Rhineland, the rich industrial area of Germany which bordered France, was created and no German soldiers were allowed to occupy this zone. Furthermore Germany was forbidden from allying with Austria.

Territorial changes

The confiscation of territory from Germany had two purposes: to punish Germany and to satisfy France by giving them industrially rich land. Overall Germany lost 10 per cent of its European land (see the map in Fig. 4):

- Alsace-Lorraine was returned to France.
- The Saar coalfields were seized and placed under the League of Nations' control, with a plebiscite allowed after 15 years to allow Saarlanders to decide if they wanted to return to German nationality.
- West Prussia and Posen were given to Poland to give the Poles access to the Baltic Sea.
- North Schleswig was given to Denmark.
- Eupen and Malmédy were given to Belgium.
- All of Germany's overseas colonies were confiscated and put under the control of the League of Nations or former Allies.

Reparations

Article 231 of the Versailles Treaty – known as the 'War Guilt' clause – was hugely significant: it attributed the blame for the war on Germany, which had to accept responsibility 'for causing all the loss and damage'. This article enabled the peacemakers to demand reparations from Germany as compensation for the destruction caused by the war. A split was agreed: 52 per cent would go to France, 28 per cent to Britain, and the rest to other allies, including Italy and Japan. The exact sum of reparations was not decided until 1921, when it was eventually agreed at £66 billion.

SOURCE 1

From French Prime Minister Georges Clemenceau's speech at the Paris Peace Conference on 16 June 1919. It was made following strong objections to the terms of the treaty by the German delegation:

Germany must undertake to make reparation to the very uttermost of her power; for reparation for wrongs inflicted is the essence of justice. That is

---

ACTIVITY

Summary

Compile a list of the grievances and disagreements that surfaced at the Paris Peace Conference. Do any of them appear to be more dangerous than others to long-term peace?

A CLOSER LOOK

Germany's battle fleet had been interned at the Royal Navy's base at Scapa Flow off the coast of Scotland under the terms of Armistice.

A CLOSER LOOK

Germany and reparations

The harshness of the reparations sum has been debated by economists and historians. Immediately after the conference, the economist John Maynard Keynes was furious about the reparations clause, believing it would destroy Germany and cause a collapse of authority in Central Europe. Revisionist historians have recently argued that Germany was more able to pay than its leaders admitted. In 1932 the German government suspended payments amid the economic turmoil of the Great Depression, and Germany finally paid off the sum in 2010.

ACTIVITY

Evaluating primary sources

What is the value of Clemenceau's speech to a historian studying the motives of the peacemakers in 1919?

why Germany must submit for a few years to certain special disabilities and arrangements. Germany has ruined the industries, the mines and the machinery of neighbouring countries, not during battle, but with the deliberate and calculated purpose of enabling her industries to seize their markets before their industries could recover from the devastation thus wantonly inflicted upon them. Germany has despoiled her neighbours of everything she could make use of or carry away. Germany has destroyed the shipping of all nations on the high sea, where there was no chance of rescue for their passengers and crews. It is only justice that restitution should be made and that these wronged peoples should be safeguarded for a time from the competition of a nation whose industries are intact and have even been fortified by machinery stolen from occupied territories.

The League of Nations

Wilson's goal was realised as the new League was established to act as a 'world government', preventing wars by referring international disputes to the League's Council. It was instructed to start the process of worldwide disarmament, and to enforce the Treaty of Versailles. Germay was not allowed to join until it could prove it was a 'peace-loving' nation.

ACTIVITY

1. Do any of the terms of the Treaty of Versailles appear to have their origins in the long-term causes of the war?
2. At what points in the preparation for the treaty of Versailles did the aims of the peacemakers clash? For example, where was there a conflict between preventing another war and allowing self-determination? Note that these kinds of debates affected the negotiations for the other peace settlements too.

Fig. 4 *The border changes affecting Germany in the Treaty of Versailles*

Settlements in Eastern and Southern Europe and Turkey

Putting the theory of self-determination into practice in the east was far more difficult than the peacemakers had anticipated, especially as many of them had little knowledge of the complexities of the regions they were dividing up. In Eastern Europe, the establishment of new states was a fait accompli; the Allies now had the task of affirming or adjusting the exact areas of new states according to international law. Each additional treaty dealt with one of the defeated Central Powers, and the sympathies of the Allies lay with the successor states of the former empires.

Austria – The Treaty of St Germain, 10 September 1919

The St Germain Treaty formally separated Austria and Hungary. It also punished Austria militarily by restricting its army to 30,000 soldiers and forbidding a union – *Anschluss* – with Germany, much to the disappointment of the Austrian people. The principle of self-determination was not applied as Austria was treated as a defeated nation, not a new state. Austria itself was also reduced in size: Bohemia and Moravia became part of Czechoslovakia, Bosnia–Herzegovina became part of Yugoslavia (just as the Serb nationalists who murdered Franz Ferdinand wanted), Galicia went to Poland, and Istria and South Tyrol to Italy. As South Tyrol was home to 230,000 Austrian Germans, this clashed with the self-determination principle, but on this Wilson was prepared to give way to show the Italians he was being reasonable; the British were mindful too of the promises made to Italy under the **1915 Treaty of London**.

Austria, like Germany and later Hungary, was ordered to pay the Allies reparations. Again Keynes and another British representative, James Headlam-Morley, were furious at the idea, but the majority British and French view was that Austrian reparations were justified, despite the damage it would cause to an already impoverished state. Attempts by Austria, Czechoslovakia and Hungary to organise customs agreements between themselves were stifled by the Supreme Economic Council, but food relief was given to prevent starvation. In the words of historian Zara Steiner, Austria was thought 'too small to live but too large to die.'

Bulgaria – The Treaty of Neuilly, 27 November 1919

While Bulgaria too was treated as a defeated enemy, the terms of its treaty were lenient compared to Austria and Hungary's. The country was reduced in size, but on a comparatively small scale: Romania, Greece and Yugoslavia were the beneficiaries. It did, however, lose its access to the Mediterranean, affecting its capacity for trade. The region of Thrace had been strongly contested by the peacemakers, but to Bulgaria's frustration eastern Thrace was eventually awarded to Greece. In addition, Bulgaria's armed forces were limited to 20,000 regular troops and 13,000 military police and border guards.

Hungary – The Treaty of Trianon, 4 June 1920

The treaty dealing with Hungary was negotiated against the backdrop of political turbulence in the country. In March 1919 a communist government, the Hungarian Soviet Republic, was established under Béla Kun in Budapest. This development was of deep concern to the peacemakers, who perhaps drew up terms harsher to Hungary than they would have otherwise been to help prevent the spread of communism. The ambition of the Hungarians also caused disputes with Romania and Czechoslovakia, as they hoped to secure Slovakia as part of the Republic.

After months of conflict, and under the threat of Allied intervention, the communist government was overthrown and a democratic coalition government established in its place. In spite of this change, the terms of Trianon were very harsh: Hungary lost two-thirds of its territory and three million of its people. Transylvania was given to Romania, Slovakia and Ruthenia to Czechoslovakia, and Slovenia and Croatia to Yugoslavia. The new Hungarian government protested against these losses, and against the imposition of reparations, but they had no choice but to sign the treaty.

CROSS-REFERENCE

The 1915 Treaty of London which secured Italy's entry into the First World War is explored in Chapter 12.

SOURCE 2

From a speech by Count Apponyi, a Hungarian politician, to the Supreme Council at the Paris Peace Conference on 16 January 1920:

In the name of the great principle so happily phrased by President Wilson, namely that no group of people, no population, may be transferred from one state to another without being consulted, as though they were a herd of cattle with no will of their own, in the name of this great principle, an axiom of good sense and public morals, we request, we demand a plebiscite on those parts of Hungary that are now on the point of being severed from us. I declare we are willing to bow to the decision of a plebiscite whatever it should be. Of course, we demand it should be held in conditions ensuring the freedom of the vote.

ACTIVITY

1. What grounds did the peacemakers have for ignoring the pleas of Apponyi and other Hungarians? Do you think they were justified?
2. How valuable is Source 2 to an historian studying the motives of the peacemakers when creating the Treaty of Trianon?

Fig. 5 *Border changes in southern and eastern Europe following the Treaties of Neuilly, St Germain and Trianon*

Turkey – The Treaties of Sèvres (1920) and Lausanne (1923)

The treatment of Turkey embodied in the terms of the Treaty of Sèvres reflected the long-term hostility of the Allies to the Turks. Lloyd George compared their 'mismanagement' of the Ottoman Empire to a 'human cancer'; the **Armenian massacre** in 1915–16 further convinced the peacemakers of the Ottoman government's 'evil'. Thus the high ideal of self-determination was mostly ignored, as territories were stripped from Turkey's control and many key strategic areas established as mandates and protectorates. Under the terms of Sèvres:

- Smyrna was given to Greece
- Iraq and Palestine became British mandates; Lebanon and Syria became French mandates
- Morocco and Tunisia became French protectorates
- Hejaz became an independent kingdom
- the Turkish Straits were put under the control of the League of Nations
- British, French, Italian and Greek troops occupied Turkey
- the Turkish army was limited to 50,700 men.

Unsurprisingly, the treaty was deeply unpopular in Turkey and popular discontent sparked an uprising led by the Turk nationalist leader Kemal Atatürk. The Sultan, tainted by his role in signing the Treaty of Sèvres, was deposed and Atatürk's army drove Greek and British troops out of Turkey. Atatürk repudiated Sèvres, and the Allies agreed to renegotiate the settlement.

The Treaty of Lausanne, signed in Switzerland on 24 July 1923, returned all the territories given to Greece back to Turkey – a notable concession given the long-term hostility between Greece and Turkey which had escalated into war in 1897 and 1912. Under the settlement all foreign troops were ordered to leave, and returned control of the Straits back to Turkey, although they had to remain demilitarised. The Republic of Turkey was now recognised internationally as a successor state to the Ottoman Empire.

A CLOSER LOOK

The Armenian massacre was the Ottoman government's systematic extermination of its minority Armenian subjects from their historic homeland within the territory constituting the present-day Republic of Turkey. Hundreds of thousands died from starvation or disease; the exact figure is uncertain.

CROSS-REFERENCE

Atatürk's role in Turkish politics before the war is explored in Chapter 7.

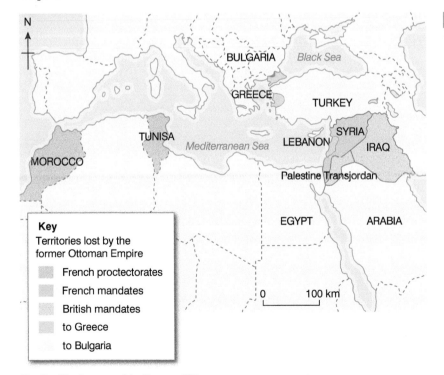

Key
Territories lost by the former Ottoman Empire

- French proctectorates
- French mandates
- British mandates
- to Greece
- to Bulgaria

Fig. 6 *The impact of the Treaty of Sèvres*

Summary

Negotiating the post-war treaties was exceedingly complex and their terms often hindered by the compromises necessary between the 32 nations. Politicians debated the treaties immediately after they were signed as to whether nations had been treated fairly, or whether the terms would actually lead to the long-term peace and stability of Europe further afield. Historians are divided over whether Germany was treated too severely, or should have been given harsher terms, while the other treaties have mostly been criticised for their severity. The map of Central and Eastern Europe had been completely redrawn, millions of people found themselves under the government of a different country, and the Treaty of Versailles had significantly weakened Germany.

Evaluating primary sources

Read Source 3. Using the information in this chapter and your knowledge of the historical context, do you agree with Lansing's assessment of the problems of self-determination?

Be careful to analyse effectively, and avoid a narrative approach. Try to plan your response by thinking about common themes, like self-determination, and examples of similarities and differences, such as those between each treaty. It may help to structure your answer by theme, rather than chronologically.

Try to identify the difficulties the peacemakers faced according to your own knowledge, then you can compare the content of the sources to this outline.

From the comments of Robert Lansing, US Secretary of State, writing on 30 December 1918 before the peace negotiations began:

The more I think about the President's declaration as to the right of 'self-determination', the more convinced I am of the danger of putting such ideas into the minds of certain races. It is bound to be the basis of impossible demands on the Peace Congress and create trouble in many lands. What effect will it have on the Irish, the Indians, the Egyptians, and the nationalists among the Boers? Will it not breed discontent, disorder and rebellion? Will not the Muslims of Syria and Palestine rely on it? The phrase 'self-determination' is simply loaded with dynamite. It will raise hopes which can never be realised. It will, I fear, cost thousands of lives. In the end it is bound to be discredited, to be called the dream of an idealist who failed to realise its danger until too late to check those who attempt to put the principle in force. What a calamity that the phrase was ever uttered. What misery it will cause!

To what extent was the aim of maintaining peace more important than the punishment of Germany to the peacemakers drafting the Treaty of Versailles in 1919–20?

Evaluating primary sources

With reference to the sources in this chapter and your understanding of the historical context, assess the value of these sources to an historian studying the difficulties faced by the peacemakers in 1919–20.

SOURCE 1

From the diary entry of Edward Mandell House, an American diplomat, on 29 June 1919:

I am leaving Paris, after eight fateful months, with conflicting emotions. Looking at the conference in retrospect, there is much to approve and yet much to regret. It is easy to say what should have been done, but more difficult to have found a way of doing it. To those who are saying that the treaty is bad and should never have been made and that it will involve Europe in infinite difficulties in its enforcement, I feel like admitting it. But I would also say in reply that empires cannot be shattered, and new states raised upon their ruins without disturbance. To create new boundaries is to create new troubles. The one follows the other. While I should have preferred a different peace, I doubt very much whether it could have been made, for the ingredients required for such a peace as I would have were lacking at Paris.

Isolationism and the USA

The popularity of isolationism in America increased as a result of its experience of war. Wilson's Fourteen Points were generally very popular with Americans, although some (especially Republicans) were dubious about the idea of a League of Nations and businessmen worried about the impact of free trade, favouring protectionism as the economic embodiment of isolationism. Political developments in the immediate aftermath of the war helped secure the rejection of the Treaty of Versailles and the League by the US Senate.

At the very end of the war the USA held its usual midterm elections, which resulted in the Republican Party gaining the majority of seats in the Congress. Not only was Wilson a Democrat, but the Republicans promoted themselves as champions of isolationism, making the President's ideals appear increasingly at odds with American public opinion. The 66th Congress commenced in March 1919, just as Wilson was negotiating the Treaty of Versailles in Europe.

A CLOSER LOOK

The American political structure

Unlike Britain, the US Constitution embodies the 'separation of powers' principle, which keeps the legislative, executive and judicial branches separate to prevent the abuse of power. This is reflected in the American electoral system: the President is Head of State and voted for in a presidential election every four years. Congressmen are elected every two years to the House of Representatives, while Senators are elected every six years to the Senate. Midterm elections are held two years into a President's term of office. If Americans vote for a Republican majority in Congress during a Democrat President's term of office, or vice versa, the President will find it much more difficult to gain legislative support for his policies, as Wilson experienced. Foreign treaties can be proposed by the President, but need the approval of the Senate, which Wilson failed to obtain in 1919.

Wilson's six-month absence left something of a power vacuum in Washington, just as America was adjusting to the new conditions of peacetime after 20 months of war. The USA was experiencing a post-war slump as industries re-adjusted their output away from munitions, and immigration was of

LEARNING OBJECTIVES

In this chapter you will learn about:

- why the USA returned to isolationism and did not join the League of Nations
- the consequences of the USA's absence at the beginning of the League's existence
- the responses to the post-war settlement in France, Britain and Germany.

KEY CHRONOLOGY

November 1918	Republican Party became the majority party in the US Congress
10 January 1920	League of Nations commenced business
March 1920	US senate refused to ratify Treaty of Versailles or allow the USA to join the League of Nations
January 1921	British and French troops occupy parts of Germany after Germany refused to pay reparations
September 1923	Atatürk repudiates the Treaty of Sèvres

ACTIVITY

Evaluating primary sources

What is the value of House's account in Source 1 to an historian studying the success of the Paris Peace Conference?

CROSS-REFERENCE

Isolationism is explained in more detail in Chapter 12, page 103.

increasing concern to many Americans. The President, preoccupied with international affairs, saw his earlier popularity drain away. If he were to reclaim it, the Treaty of Versailles, when finally agreed, would have to meet with the strong approval of many Americans.

Discontent with the Treaty

Although US public opinion of the Treaty was in general one of disappointment, pro-isolationist Republicans, led by Senator Henry Cabot Lodge, attacked specific points which they felt went most against America's best interests, or contravened the Fourteen Points:

- 'Freedom of the seas' had been abandoned as it had been blocked by Britain.
- Self-determination had not been implemented in all disputed regions. To prevent a walkout by the Japanese delegation in Paris, Wilson had allowed Japan to continue its occupation of Shandong rather than return it to Chinese sovereignty. This was a particular concern to the USA, as Shandong came under the American sphere of influence.
- The League of Nations' mandates in former colonies, as well as the continued existence of the British Empire, offended the long-held American principle of anti-colonialism. Irish Americans, in particular, were disappointed by the lack of self-determination for Ireland.
- Many Americans – especially Republicans, and even Wilson himself – expected a fairer treaty, and worried that Versailles would cause bitterness and a desire for revenge among the defeated powers.
- Many politicians were concerned that agreeing to the Treaty and the League's terms would restrict America's freedom of action: Henry Cabot Lodge argued that they contravened the Monroe Doctrine, in place since the early nineteenth century, which stated that the Americas should remain free from European influence.

Moreover, many American businessmen and Republicans were deeply uncomfortable with the role America would be assigned if it joined the League of Nations. By 1919 the USA was the most influential and economically powerful nation in the world; Wilson's opponents therefore feared the USA would be relied upon more than others to uphold the Treaty and settle international disputes, thereby indefinitely committing itself to troop deployment and long-term involvement in European affairs. Although the USA lost a far smaller number of men than their European allies (116,000 compared to 1.4 million French troops, for example) the conflict was a remote one and many ordinary Americans did not feel that even a small sacrifice was worthwhile.

A CLOSER LOOK

No entangling alliances

When William Edgar Borah spoke of the USA surrendering the policy of 'no entangling alliances', he was referring to President Thomas Jefferson's inaugural speech in 1801, in which he promised to the American people, 'honest friendship will all nations – entangling alliances with none.' Jefferson was in turn referring to President George Washington's retirement letter to the American people, in which he asked, 'Why, by interweaving our destiny in Europe, entangle our peace and prosperity in the toils of American ambition, rivalship, interest, humour or caprice?'

SOURCE 2

From a speech made by Republican Senator William Edgar Borah to the US Senate on 10 November 1919:

What is the result of all this? We are in the midst of all of the affairs of Europe. We have entangled ourselves with all European concerns. We have joined in alliance with all the European nations which have thus far joined the League and all nations which may be admitted to the League. We are sitting there dabbling in their affairs and intermeddling in their concerns. In other words, Mr President, we have forfeited and surrendered, once and for all, the great policy of '**no entangling alliances**' upon which the strength of this republic has been founded for 150 years. There is another and even more commanding reason why I shall record my vote against this treaty. It imperils what I conceive to be the underlying, the very first principles of this Republic. It is in conflict with the right of our people to govern themselves free from all restraint, legal or moral, of foreign powers. Would you purchase peace at the cost of our independence?

Despite the fact that in many of the Treaty's terms, his Fourteen Points had been ignored, Wilson went on a speaking tour of the US in the autumn of 1919, vigorously defending the Versailles settlement. Already overworked in Europe, this proved too much for the President's health and he suffered a stroke in September, further diminishing his capacity to lead the country. After initially proposing to attach their own conditions to the Treaty, in March 1920 the Senate refused to **ratify** it, and refused to allow the USA to become a member of the League of Nations.

Economic isolation

Wilson was succeeded as president by the Republican Warren Harding. His government extended the popular policy of isolationism to immigration policy (banning immigration from Asia and introducing quotas to limit the number of southern and eastern European immigrants) and to the economy. Tariffs were introduced or increased to drive up the cost of foreign imports in order to protect domestic markets. The USA's trading partners responded with 'retaliatory tariffs' which in turn made American imports to their countries more expensive. The result was a decline in global trade, which made international cooperation less important to countries' economies.

Consequences for the League of Nations

The League hoped to foster internationalism – a very different approach to how foreign affairs had been conducted previously, and to how crises and disputes had been resolved before 1914. The League was in many ways 'a great experiment', as Lord Robert Cecil, a British diplomat, put it. Now that the USA was not a member, even its leaders doubted its success.

The leadership of the League was left to Britain and France, giving it a 'European bias' in the words of Zara Steiner. Aside from America, the USSR and Germany were not allowed to join, giving the unfortunate impression that the League was a 'victors' club' which was more likely to defend their own interests than promote international peace. The British and French hardly exuded optimism about the League: Lloyd George labelled it a 'lame duck', believing it to be useless and even counterproductive without America. It was soon clear that Britain would seek to rebuild its own trade and protect its empire, while France was preoccupied with its fear of a German recovery and would never really trust Britain; many French politicians felt the British had little sympathy towards France over the prospect of a future German invasion. Peacekeeping therefore became more Eurocentric as a result of US isolationism, which would damage its credibility when responding to crises in the rest of the world in future years.

The League's leaders knew that without the USA, they lacked not only authority and political influence, but also economic power. As the League did not have an army, one of its strongest sanctions was imposing trade restrictions and boycotts on wayward nations, but the USA, the world's 'biggest' exporter, was under no obligation to observe any such economic sanction, rendering the power of sanctions almost useless. The American economy had fared far better during and after the war than most in Europe. Although there was a slump in US industry as it adjusted to peacetime, recovery was relatively quick, and as such the USA would have been the best-placed power to lend necessary economic assistance and cooperation to the actions of the League of Nations.

ACTIVITY

Evaluating primary sources

Read Source 2 on page 78 and answer the following questions.
1. Why does Borah view membership of the League of Nations as an 'entangling alliance'?
2. What is the value of Source 2 to an historian studying opposition to the League of Nations in the USA?

KEY TERM

ratify: to give the final recognition to a treaty, following its signature by the parties involved

CROSS-REFERENCE

For the aims of the League of Nations see page 122.

ACTIVITY

1. Explain the message of the cartoon in Fig. 1.
2. In groups or as a whole class, discuss and predict the potential longer-term consequences of US isolation by the end of the 1920s. What further effects do you think it might have had on international relations, and in particular the future success of the League of Nations?

THE GAP IN THE BRIDGE.

Fig. 1 *This* Punch *cartoon of December 1919 gives a British perspective on the USA's decision not to join the League*

Responses to the Post-war Settlement

French reaction

The French did not find satisfaction in the post-war settlement either. When the Treaty was discussed in the Chamber of Deputies, it was not quickly ratified as many expected: for six weeks its terms were fiercely debated. The Versailles settlement brought to the surface some of the sharpest divisions in French politics. Socialists argued that the Treaty was too harsh, that Germany was now democratic and that France should cooperate with the new German government. Politicians from the centre and right-wing pointed out that the Treaty contained very few assurances against future German aggression, bemoaning Clemenceau's failure to secure a strong buffer zone in the Rhineland and the fact that Germany was now surrounded by small, weak states. General Foch, who served as Supreme Allied Commander during the war, claimed that the Treaty was 'not peace, but an armistice for 20 years.'

The Treaty was eventually ratified by the French, but Clemenceau, who has been accused by so many since as stubbornly insisting on the punishment of Germany during the Paris conference, found his popularity greatly diminished. He was defeated in a presidential election in 1920; ironically his critics believed he had not been harsh enough on France's former enemy.

SOURCE 3

From Georges Clemenceau's foreword to the book *The Truth About the Treaty* by André Tardieu, published in 1921. Tardieu was part of the French delegation at the Paris Peace Conference and his book aimed to defend the Treaty against French accusations that it was too lenient towards Germany:

The Germans' trouble is that they see the future only through the blood-red mists of a civilisation grafted upon the survival of barbarism. If they can change their perspective, they will, little by little, attain the position to which they are justly entitled in the world. If they cannot, the victors, whether they realise it or not, must continue to mount close guard over lands whose borders have become as President Wilson said, 'the frontiers of freedom'. The maintenance of these frontiers which was the constant aim of French effort at the Conference, is of no small moment.

Vanquished, our lot under Ludendorff would not have differed from that of Rome under Hannibal. Victorious, we have assumed our responsibility in the most noble effort to achieve a lasting peace by the sole forces of Right. To one and all such a state was well worth a general effort of self-restraint instead of the old rush to divide the spoils between those who had overcome the enemy.

ACTIVITY

1. In Source 3, which aspect of the peace settlement does Clemenceau appear to be most proud of and why?
2. What does he mean by the phrase 'our lot under Ludendorff'?

British reaction

Lloyd George expressed concerns over the Treaty of Versailles even before the Germans signed in June 1919. Having been shown the terms, the German delegation published a rebuttal which won Lloyd George's admiration and prompted him to try to convince Wilson and Clemenceau to reconsider key terms in the Treaty, but they refused. However, when Lloyd George returned to Britain from Paris in the summer of 1919, he was greeted as a hero by the British public.

One of the key criticisms of Versailles in Britain was the issue of reparations. Lloyd George's negotiation of Britain's share in Paris was complicated by the fact that Britain had borrowed around £1 billion from the Americans, who were now demanding payment. Nevertheless, British opinion was gradually convinced that the reparations to be extracted on Germany would certainly cause long-term economic misery for the German people, who – many noted – now had a democratic government which could not be held responsible for causing the war. The consequences of a failed German economy would disadvantage Britain – it would at least have a negative impact on British trade, and in the worst case scenario could prompt a communist revolution. This attitude to reparations was fostered by the eloquently-argued work *The Economic Consequences of the Peace* by John Maynard Keynes.

SOURCE 4

From *The Economic Consequences of the Peace* by the economist John Maynard Keynes, published in late 1919. It became a bestseller in Britain and the USA:

The policy of reducing Germany to servitude for a generation, of degrading the lives of millions of human beings, and of depriving a whole nation of happiness, should be abhorrent and detestable. Nations are not authorised, by religion or by natural morals, to visit on the children of their enemies the misdoings of parents or of rulers.

The Treaty includes no provisions for the economic rehabilitation of Europe – nothing to make the defeated Central Empires into good neighbours, nothing to stabilise the new States of Europe, nothing to reclaim Russia. The **Council of Four** paid no attention to these issues, being preoccupied with others – Clemenceau to crush the economic life of his enemy, Lloyd George to bring home something that would pass muster for a week, the President to do nothing that was not just and right.

KEY TERM

Council of Four: this comprised the Big Three (Wilson, Clemenceau and Lloyd George) and Orlando of Italy

Fig. 2 *This British cartoon, published in May 1919, suggests that the Allies were only concerned with squeezing reparations out of Germany*

Germany

When the terms of the Versailles Treaty were shown to the German delegation, Count Brockdorff-Rantzau, the First Minister of the new Weimar Republic, made a defiant speech against it. When the Allies sent a final ultimatum to the Germans on the 16 June, Brockdorff-Rantzau's government resigned in protest, with Chancellor Frederick Scheidemann pronouncing: 'May the hand wither that signs this treaty.' However, the Allies threatened a renewal of conflict and the immediate resumption of the naval blockade if the Treaty was not signed. A new government was formed with Gustav Bauer as Chancellor, and a Reichstag vote was held on the peace settlement. Two-hundred and thirty-seven voted in favour of signing, 138 voted against and five refused to vote (abstained). The Foreign Minister Müller and Colonial Minister Bell were duly sent to Versailles to sign the Treaty on Germany's behalf.

Although Germany's treatment under the Treaty of Versailles was not enough on its own to cause Hitler's rise to power in 1933, the German government's acceptance of the settlement, and adherence to its terms, created a toxic feeling of betrayal among many Germans. Opinion among historians is still divided as to how harsh the Treaty was on Germany; defenders of the settlement often cite the undoubtedly punitive terms the Germans inflicted on Russia in the Treaty of Brest-Litovsk, claiming that Germany protested too much about Versailles by comparison.

For the new socialist government in Weimar, the actual signing of the Treaty was an early and significant blow to its reputation and popularity. Many Germans thought of the Treaty as a 'diktat', as their representatives had had no role in negotiating its terms. Returning troops, who had believed Germany to be making solid gains in the war in autumn 1918 if not actually winning it, often felt a sense of deep betrayal, a mood exploited by right-wing political parties emerging in the newly democratic Republic. As Germany had not been defeated on the battlefield in November 1918 and there had been no Allied invasion, a minority of Germans believed that the German people had been 'stabbed in the back' by a defeatist government.

Fig. 3 *Right-wing Germans used propaganda images like this to argue that German soldiers had been 'stabbed in the back' by their own politicians who had signed the Armistice and the Versailles Treaty*

The main purpose of the 'war guilt' clause of the Treaty, forcing Germany to accept total blame for the outbreak of war, was to give a legal basis for reparations. It was not, however, viewed this way by Germans, who especially resented the clause as many felt that Russia was equally, if not more responsible for the conflict. It dented German pride, as did their exclusion from the League of Nations as a nation not yet 'peace-loving'. This was further exacerbated by the Treaty's military restrictions, which Germans claimed left Germany vulnerable to invasion.

Despite the peacemakers' fears for a new *revanchism* when settling the new borders of central and Eastern Europe, around 6.5 million Germans now lived under foreign rule. There were genuine concerns that ethnic Germans in Poland, Czechoslovakia and other new nations would be persecuted by their new governments, and right-leaning Germans in particular argued that they should be brought back under German jurisdiction.

The most unpalatable element of the post-war settlement was the issue of **reparations**. The strongest opponents of the Treaty claimed that the Allies were deliberately trying to starve German mothers and children. The Weimar government petitioned its creditors to renegotiate both the amount of reparations and the payments schedule. In early 1921, upon Germany's refusal to pay, three cities were occupied by British and French troops; in November the government began making payments as the scale of reparations had been adjusted in Germany's favour.

Summary

The immediate responses to the post-war settlement in the USA, Britain, France and Germany varied considerably, and the mixed feelings of the Americans, British and French did not bode well for the implementation and defence of the Treaty of Versailles' terms in the 1920s and 1930s.

A CLOSER LOOK

November Criminals

Extreme right-wing groups in Germany began propaganda campaigns in the aftermath of the Armistice and the Treaty of Versailles by claiming that the soldiers of the First World War – many of whom returned home frustrated and disaffected – had been betrayed by their government. The politicians involved with signing the Armistice in late 1918 were branded 'November Criminals'. This slogan was adopted by Adolf Hitler in the 1920s, and as his popularity grew, so did this idea; it was among the factors that eroded the credibility of the Weimar Republic.

CROSS-REFERENCE

Russia's role in the outbreak of war is explained in Chapters 11 and 12.

Revanchism is first explored in Chapter 4.

A CLOSER LOOK

The reparations imposed on Germany by the Allies were separate to the war debts that Germany incurred during the war. Both had to be repaid, and together they helped to cause the terrible economic conditions culminating in the 1923 hyperinflation crisis. German propaganda at that time, and Allied critics of the Treaty of Versailles, often blamed the resulting turmoil on the reparations clause, but this is not accurate.

Group work

In pairs, revisit the terms of the Treaty from Chapter 14. Using the information in this chapter on the general response to the terms for extra guidance, write a sentence or two on the individual terms and why many Germans regarded them as unfair.

STUDY TIP

Try to use your existing knowledge of a range of opinions. For example, you might recognise one author as being a representative of a certain political faction, in which case it has a high value because it is typical of a significant viewpoint. You may also be aware of a conflicting view that was influential that is not highlighted by any of the sources, so you can argue that this lessens the value of the sources as a whole. Note also that these particular sources are of different types (diary, speech and in a book) and this may be important in assessing value, as will the dates of their production.

STUDY TIP

It will be important to assess whether the sense of dissatisfaction was equally felt by all the powers referred to.

- **The League of Nations** suffered from its outset due to the absence of the USA. Without America's resources and influence, Britain and France, its reluctant leaders, doubted the League's authority.
- **Self-determination** had not been extended to Germany as over 27,000 square miles of its territory had been confiscated and ethnic Germans placed under foreign control, much to Germany and America's disappointment.
- **Reparations** were actively resisted by Germany; many in Britain feared their impact on Germany would cause long-term misery; and many on the right in France believed that Germany should have paid more to finance France's recovery.
- **Military restrictions** on Germany were considered too lenient by the French and too harsh by the Germans. This, coupled with its loss of territory, created a new *revanchism* in Germany, especially among the right. The post-war settlement among these Germans was a poisonous legacy which caused them to hate not only the Allies who had imposed the terms, but also the socialist democratic government which signed the Treaty.

ACTIVITY

Summary

Create a Venn diagram or similar visual representation of the main criticisms of the post-war settlement and which nations and political parties voiced them. For example, both British and German opinion doubted the fairness of reparations.

 PRACTICE QUESTION

Evaluating primary sources

With reference to Sources 1, 2 and 4 in this chapter, and your understanding of the historical context, assess the value of these three sources to an historian studying the reactions to the post-war settlement.

 PRACTICE QUESTION

'By 1922, the Treaty of Versailles satisfied neither Germany nor the former Allied powers, Britain, France and the USA.'
Assess the validity of this view.

Fig. 1 *The French occupation of the Ruhr was one of the factors that led to a hyperinflation crisis in Germany; for this staged photograph, children were asked to pose with building blocks of money to demonstrate how money had lost so much value*

KEY CHRONOLOGY

November 1917– October 1922	Russian Civil War
February 1919	Beginning of Polish–Soviet War
18 March 1921	Treaty of Riga concluded Polish–Soviet War
12 November 1921– 6 February 1922	Washington Disarmament Conference
16 April 1922	Treaty of Rapallo signed by USSR and Germany
January 1923	French and Belgian occupation of the Ruhr begins
August 1923	Beginning of the Corfu incident

The position of the USA and Russia in world affairs

Despite its formal rejection of the Treaty of Versailles and the League of Nations in 1920, the true extent of the USA's isolationism in the early 1920s has been questioned. The new Republican President, Warren Harding, had been elected with a majority of seven million votes with the promise of a 'return to normalcy', which meant the removal of wartime restrictions and increased government controls. In his inaugural speech Harding reaffirmed the pledges made by early presidents Washington and Jefferson by stating 'we do not mean to be entangled'. However, Harding and his Secretary of State, Charles Evans Hughes, realised that American interests would not be best served by total economic and diplomatic isolationism; but they were concerned about controlling the nature and extent of the USA's involvement in world affairs.

The USA: economics and disarmament

Hughes and the Secretary of Commerce, Herbert Hoover, hoped to encourage the development of European countries. This was a popular idea with US businessmen who saw opportunities for investment abroad; it also increased the ability of debtor nations to repay the total $3 billion lent by the USA during the First World War. After the Paris Peace Conference, America called in its loans to its former allies. Debtor nations Britain, France and Belgium protested: their economic recovery from wartime was slow and Germany was yet to begin paying reparations. The USA's attitude was unsympathetic; Calvin Coolidge, the future US President, reportedly said, 'They hired the money didn't they? Let them pay!'

In addition, the American government introduced protective **tariffs** in 1921 and 1922. US farmers were suffering from the effects of peacetime: during the war they had new markets in Europe and invested in new equipment to increase their production; now Europe could produce more of its own food again, US farmers had too much food and not enough customers. Prices plummeted and Harding passed the Emergency Tariff on imported foodstuffs. This was followed by a more general tariff which cancelled out the lower price of European imports – manufactured by lower-paid workers – to the USA. Consequently, other nations introduced their own retaliatory tariffs, thereby restricting world trade as more consumers bought domestic products.

CROSS-REFERENCE

Tariffs were used by the Great Powers of Europe before the First World War. You can remind yourself of their consequences in Chapter 2.

Fig. 2 *German war materials, like these helmets, were destroyed as part of the process of disarmament under the terms of the Treaty of Versailles*

The Washington Naval Conference

Although the American government was committed to large degree of economic isolation, it still involved itself in international negotiations; however, it operated outside the League of Nations to pursue its own foreign policy objectives. This fitted with the doctrine of isolationism, as it allowed the US to negotiate with other powers to secure American international interests, but without committing it to the 'entanglements' that Republicans were so keen to avoid. Worldwide disarmament was the fourth of Wilson's Fourteen Points, 'to the lowest point consistent with domestic safety'. However, under the terms of the Treaty of Versailles only Germany was to be disarmed; in the subsequent central and Eastern European treaties, Austria, Hungary, Bulgaria and Turkey also had military restrictions placed upon them. Public opinion in many countries was strongly in favour of disarmament, and the unresolved tension between the USA and Japan over their spheres of influence in the Pacific was of growing concern.

The Naval Conference was called by President Harding amid growing concerns about the increasing size of the Japanese navy; meanwhile the Anglo-Japanese agreement signed in 1902 was due to expire in 1922, which would remove a safeguard against an imbalance in naval strength in the Pacific. The leaders of several nations met in Washington DC to conclude on a series of agreements in 1921 and 1922, as outlined in Table 1.

Table 1 *International agreements of 1921–2*

Agreement	Signatories	Terms
Four-Power Pact, 13 December 1921	USA, Britain, Japan and France	• All nations signing the pact would consult each other in the event of a dispute over the Pacific. • Each power would respect others' rights and interests over the Pacific Islands.
Five-Power Limitation Treaty, 6 February 1922	USA, Britain, Japan and France and Italy	• Set a ratio for the number of large warships allowed to each signatory: for every five possessed by the USA and Britain; Japan could have three; France and Italy could have 1.67. • All other military ships were to be scrapped: America, Britain and Japan disposed of 66 ships between them. • The five powers agreed to abandon the building of more large warships for ten years. • This treaty remained force until the 1936 when Japan sought more favourable terms.
Nine-Power Pact, 6 February 1922	USA, Britain, Japan and France, Italy, the Netherlands, Portugal, Belgium and China	• The use of submarines was regulated. • The deployment of poison gas in warfare was banned. • China's independence and borders were reasserted.

The USSR

Liberal leaders were pleased to see the autocratic Tsarist regime overthrown in favour of a provisional government, which promised a Western-style democracy. This was somewhat negated by the Bolshevik seizure of power in November 1917. A communist state, especially one as large as Russia, which openly committed itself to instigating communist uprisings across the world, was a direct threat to the survival of capitalist governments. Communism appealed to the many people of lower classes in advanced capitalist countries like the USA and Britain; therefore those of the middle and upper classes feared a revolution which would strip them of their wealth and privilege, and possibly threaten their lives. Other countries becoming communist would also threaten trade, as communism advocated self-sufficiency, which would in turn make trading with other nations less necessary.

Most countries refused to formally recognise the Bolshevik government led by Lenin; thus Russia was not invited to discuss any of the post-war settlements. By 1922, a series of events meant that the renamed USSR was accepted into the international community, but not the League of Nations, even though most Western leaders continued to express their deep disapproval of the regime.

Western intervention in the Civil War, 1919–22

Almost as soon as the Bolsheviks set up their government, counter-revolutionary forces (known as the Whites, as opposed to the communist Red Army) began their attack. The civil war in Russia was extremely bitter and exceptionally violent; it was not until 1922 that counter-revolutionaries were defeated in Siberia and the Bolsheviks could claim complete control of the country.

The West's attempt to strangle Bolshevism in its cradle by intervening on the side of the Whites was to sour relations between Russia and its former allies for decades to come. British, American, French, Japanese, Czech and Polish forces launched a series of attacks between 1918 and 1921, often separate and uncoordinated, which proved fruitless as the Red Army exploited its home advantages. The 'Red Terror' – the brutal treatment of suspected enemies of the revolution – helped to cement the Bolsheviks' reputation as tyrants in the West (although similar atrocities were committed by the Whites), while the communists never forgave the Western governments for their involvement in the Civil War.

ACTIVITY

Pair discussion

Britain and France were prepared to conduct global affairs and sign international treaties without involving the League of Nations. The Naval Conference suggests they were also very receptive to American influence, even after the USA refused to join the League. Discuss with a partner what inferences you could make about the USA's position in world affairs, bearing these points in mind. Can we also draw any conclusions about the strength of the League of Nations in 1922?

CROSS-REFERENCE

The nature of the Russian revolutions of 1917 is explained in Chapter 13.

ACTIVITY

Evaluating primary sources

How valuable is Source 1 to an historian studying the reasons for foreign intervention in the Russian Civil War?

SOURCE 1

From *Why Have You Come to Murmansk?*, a Bolshevik Party pamphlet written and distributed in 1918 while the First World War was still being fought. Its purpose was to discourage British soldiers from fighting against the Red Army on ideological grounds. During the Civil War, Murmansk, a port city in north-west Russia, was occupied by Western forces:

Why have you come to Murmansk? You have been told in England that the demand for men on the Western front is greater than ever. Yet you are brought here, right in the Arctic Sea, a thousand miles from the battle front. For what purpose? Your government tells us it has no hostile intentions towards us. That it does not desire to occupy our territory. That it will not interfere with our internal affairs. Comrade it is not true! Therefore you are not required to defend us. On the contrary your presence here increases our danger. Why then have you been brought here? You have been brought here to occupy our country in interest of Allied capitalists. You have been brought here to overthrow our revolution and bring back the reign of Tsarism! We ask you, are you going to help crush us? To help to give Russia back to the landlords, the capitalists and Tsar?

A CLOSER LOOK

The New Economic Policy (NEP)

was introduced by Lenin in 1921 following the financial crisis caused by the Russian Civil War. His previous economic policy, War Communism, was so harsh it prompted rebellion, so the NEP allowed peasants to sell their surplus produce for profit, and permitted small private businesses. Although the economy improved, some committed communists believed Lenin had 'sold out' to capitalism and left the Communist Party.

In March 1919, the Bolsheviks established the Third International, the Comintern, to help coordinate and encourage communist parties in other countries to begin a worldwide communist revolution. Despite winning the Civil War, however, Lenin realised the need for pragmatism – well-evidenced by the **New Economic Policy (NEP)** which was deeply unpopular with leftist Marxists. Communist Russia could not survive without re-establishing diplomatic relations with the rest of the world, or creating trade links. Therefore Russian foreign policy in the early 1920s was a strange contradiction between communist ideology advocating world revolution and the spurning of the capitalist and 'imperialist' powers, and the practical need to secure survival through diplomacy and international trade.

Polish–Soviet War and its impact on international relations

War between Russia and its newly independent neighbour began with Poland hoping to extend its eastern border and exploit the weakness of the Bolsheviks in mid-1919, when the Civil War was at its height. Polish troops invaded Galicia and initially made impressive gains, but the Red Army pushed back decisively after the Polish reached Ukraine. The Russian forces were subsequently so successful that they had almost reached Warsaw by June 1920, prompting the Allied leaders to discuss intervention.

The 'Curzon line' was proposed by British Foreign Secretary George Curzon as a demarcation border between the warring states, but this was rejected by the Bolsheviks who were tempted to push on, perhaps to try and spread the communist revolution into Poland and Germany by military means. While the British and French were deeply reluctant to commit troops to the struggle, they did anticipate the blockading of Russian ports, which was enough to make the Bolsheviks consider a peace settlement. On 2 August they published their terms, which were relatively generous to Poland, allowing them more territory than that of the 'Curzon line'. Poland, however, rejected one clause stipulating the creation of a people's militia, so the war continued.

On 13 August the Red Army attacked Warsaw, followed three days later by a successful Polish counter-attack. Six months later, on 16 March 1921, the Treaty of Riga concluded the Polish–Soviet War, restoring both countries' borders to their status before Poland's initial military action. In the same month, Russia signed a trade agreement with Britain. Another agreement, the

ACTIVITY

Summary

Create a Venn diagram to compare and contrast the position of the USA and USSR in world affairs by 1923.

Treaty of Rapallo, was signed by Germany and Russia in April 1922. Under this treaty, normal relations were established after the imbalance of the Treaty of **Brest-Litovsk**, and both states agreed to give up financial claims against one another. Rapallo was of great significance: the agreement between two important powers isolated by the post-war peace settlements worried Western governments and provided the Soviets with economic and military advice from Germany. Germany, meanwhile, gained investment opportunities in the USSR and improved the prospects for a more reasonable amended post-war treaty from the Allies.

CROSS-REFERENCE

The terms of the 1918 Treaty of Brest-Litovsk, under which Germany gained fertile and productive land in the former Russian Empire, are explored in Chapter 13.

SOURCE 2

From Winston Churchill's speech to the Oxford Union on 18 November 1920:

My view has been that all the harm and misery in Russia has arisen out of the wickedness and folly of the Bolsheviks, and there will be no recovery of any kind in Russia or in Eastern Europe while these wicked men, this vile group of cosmopolitan fanatics, hold the Russian nation by the hair of its head and tyrannise over its great population. The policy I will always advocate is the overthrow and destruction of that criminal regime.

ACTIVITY

Do you agree with Churchill's stated view in Source 2 that the Western allies intervened in the Russian Civil War solely to rid Russia and Eastern Europe of Bolshevik 'tyranny'? Explain your answer.

Continuing border disputes

Formalising the boundaries of the new and successor states which emerged at the end of the First World War had been an extraordinarily difficult task for the peacemakers. The Polish–Soviet War was in many ways a border dispute: **Poland** had only just been granted independence from the Russian Empire under the Treaty of Versailles. As Harold Nicholson had predicted (see 'Negotiations in Paris' in Chapter 14), the League of Nations' ability to deal with conflicts caused by the readjustment of the new borders was soon tested. In general their response to many of the disputes arising in the early and mid-1920s was broadly successful.

Vilna, Upper Silesia, and the Aaland Islands

- Vilna (later renamed Vilnius), the capital of Lithuania, was invaded by Poland in 1920. Lithuania appealed to the League for assistance, but Britain and France could not agree on a solution. The League's Covenant stated that troops should have been sent to force Poland's withdrawal, but France was reluctant to offend the Poles, who were potential allies in case of future German aggression, and the British would not act alone. The League ultimately did not respond, and Poland kept control of Vilna.
- Upper Silesia, on the German–Polish border, was disputed by both states who wanted the benefit of its lucrative iron and steel industry. A plebiscite in 1920 was considered contentious enough for the League to send British and French troops to maintain order at the polling booths. The plebiscite revealed a clear split in opinion: voters in industrial areas voted to become German, while those in agricultural areas wanted to remain Polish. The League divided the region accordingly.
- The Aaland Islands were coveted by Sweden and Finland. Geographically the islands were roughly the same distance from each country, so the League's assistance was sought to resolve the dispute. It ruled that the Aaland Islands should become Finnish, which Sweden accepted.

CROSS-REFERENCE

The emergence of Poland as an independent state is explored in Chapters 13 and 14.

ACTIVITY

Extension

Conduct further research into border disputes in Bulgaria and Mosul in the 1920s.

The Corfu Incident

Events in Corfu, an island near the coasts of Greece and Albania, suggested that tension in the Balkans was yet to be resolved after sparking the First

World War. Four years after the peacemaking process began, the Greek–Albanian border was still to be finalised, and in 1923 Italian officials were sent to the area to investigate the two nations' claims. On 27 August, the members of the Italian team led by General Tellini were murdered following Greek claims that they were not act acting impartially.

Fig. 3 *Albania, Greece and Corfu in 1923*

Fig. 4   *Benito Mussolini*

Benito Mussolini (1883–1945) founded the fascist movement in Italy and became Prime Minister in 1922. He transformed Italy into a one-party dictatorship, ruthlessly removing all opposition. He took the country to war on Germany's side in 1940, but was deposed by the King in 1943. Two years later he was executed by anti-fascists.

Mussolini, the new fascist Italian leader, was outraged; a parallel with the aftermath of Franz Ferdinand's assassination emerged as events unfolded. Mussolini demanded that the Greek government – who he believed to be responsible for at least allowing the four murders – meet several demands in an ultimatum on 29 August. This stipulated that the Greeks had to provide Italy with an official apology, have the murderers executed, and pay Italy compensation of 50 million lire. An Italian clause which insisted on Italian involvement in an inquiry into the murders was rejected on the grounds of Greek sovereignty, a move eerily similar to Serbia's rejection of one clause in Austria-Hungary's ultimatum of July 1914. On 31 August, Italy occupied Corfu in retaliation.

Greece appealed to the League, but once again other, unrelated political circumstances looked set to upset the process of peacemaking according to the Covenant: the French were concerned that intervention in Corfu might draw accusations of hypocrisy, as they were at that time occupying the Ruhr in Germany. In this case, however, the League acted quickly, condemning the actions of Italy. Greece would have to pay compensation to Italy, but it would be held by the League and only paid to Italy when the murderers were caught and proved to be Greek. Mussolini was frustrated by the decision and used his influence to persuade the Conference of Ambassadors (one of the League's governing bodies) to alter the judgement. Greece was ordered to pay compensation immediately, and in September the Italians withdrew from Corfu.

SOURCE 3

From the lead article of *The Morning Leader*, a Canadian newspaper, on 2 September 1923. This edition's headline read 'Italy Spurns League':

The lapse of another day finds no decrease in the tension or gravity of the Greco–Italian dispute. A grave aspect of the situation lies in the Italian determination to refuse to recognise the status of the League of Nations in the affair or respect its decision. The British have found consolation in the consideration that in 1914 no international body such as the League of Nations existed, to which the Austro-Serbian dispute might have been submitted with some hope of averting war. This hope will be shattered if Italy refuses to recognise the League. Both Greek and Italian governments are energetically occupying themselves in placing their respective cases before the world. Italy contends that the Greek government has not been recognised by the powers and lacks the status or right of appealing to the League, which ought to repudiate its application, and argues that otherwise Greece will secure recognition through assassination.

CROSS-REFERENCE

Further examples of the League's willingness to act being affected by separate concerns of its member states can be found in Chapters 18 to 20.

The occupation of the Ruhr

The payment of German reparations was suspended in 1922 as Germany experienced an economic crisis. Britain and France agreed to postpone the payments until the German economy recovered, but the German President Ebert prevaricated, hoping for another opportunity to renegotiate payments. The French, under pressure to repay their war debts, grew increasingly impatient with German excuses and invaded the Ruhr, an industrially rich region on the French–German border, in January 1923 with Belgian support.

ACTIVITY

Group work

In pairs, or as two halves of a larger group, research and conduct a debate about why the League did not always act effectively in the early 1920s to settle disputes and maintain peace. One side should argue that it was because the League's member states had too many political concerns of their own; the other side should argue that the League was easy to manipulate.

SOURCE 4

From a letter written by French Prime Minister Raymond Poincaré to Charles de Saint-Aulaire, the French ambassador in London, in December 1922:

Judging others by themselves, the English, who are blinded by their loyalty, have always thought that the Germans did not abide by their pledges inscribed in the Versailles Treaty because they had not frankly agreed to them. We, on the contrary, believe that if Germany, far from making the slightest effort to carry out the treaty of peace, has always tried to escape her obligations, it is because until now she has not been convinced of her defeat. We are also certain that Germany, as a nation, resigns herself to keep her pledged word only under the impact of necessity.

ACTIVITY

1. According to Poincaré, how do the British and French differ in their views about why Germany was not paying reparations in 1922?
2. What is the value of Source 4 to an historian studying the reasons for the occupation of the Ruhr?

A CLOSER LOOK

The role of Poincaré changed during this period. He had been Prime Minister already from 1912 to 1913; then became President until 1920. When his term ended he served as Prime Minister twice, from 1922 to 1924, then from 1926 to 1926.

The occupation

The occupation was legal according to the Treaty of Versailles; the French justified their actions by appropriating what Germany owed in the form of goods and raw materials. Industry in the Ruhr region was severely affected by the occupation: about 60,000 French and Belgian soldiers seized control of

Fig. 5 *A poster encouraging Germans to boycott French and German goods*

Fig. 6   *Gustav Stresemann*

Gustav Stresemann (1878–1929) was a dominant figure in the Weimar Republic, serving as Chancellor for 100 days in 1923, then as Foreign Minister 1923–1929. He was influential in Germany's recovery after the Ruhr occupation and hyperinflation crises and helped engineer détente with France.

factories, mines and railways. With the German army drastically limited by the Treaty, the German government ordered workers in the Ruhr to undertake **passive resistance**, they refused to cooperate with the French soldiers and went on strike. They hoped to cause enough inconvenience to the French that they would abandon their occupation.

The French response to this action was uncompromising. One-hundred and fifty thousand citizens of the Ruhr were expelled from the region for refusing to follow orders. One hundred and thirty-two Germans were killed in eight months, including a seven-year-old boy. Relations between France and Germany dramatically worsened; anti-French protests became a common sight across Germany.

Consequences of the Ruhr occupation

The German economy, already in a period of turbulence, was severely weakened by the occupation. Industrial production in the Ruhr, responsible for a significant proportion of Germany's iron and steel output, ground to a halt, while government support of Ruhr strikers meant they had to pay them **relief money** as long as the dispute continued. In an attempt to cope with these two problems, the government printed more paper money. The effect was disastrous: inflation was already at a dangerous level, but in spring 1923 a period of hyperinflation caused economic chaos for months. The price of bread, still a staple of many German diets, rocketed in price from four marks in 1921 to 200,000 million marks at the height of the crisis in November 1923.

A CLOSER LOOK

The hyperinflation crisis was the period of extreme inflation of prices in 1923. The Weimar government was already faced with the challenge of starting to make reparations payments; then the occupation of the Ruhr put more pressure on its finances as workers went on strike (limiting industrial production) and were paid relief money. As its debts mounted, the government printed more money in an effort to pay them, but this caused the value of the German mark to decrease rapidly. Photographs were taken of workers collecting their weekly wages in wheelbarrows, children playing with stacks of paper money and of people burning bank notes instead of fuel.

The hyperinflation crisis caused real and prolonged suffering to many Germans. Those with savings saw their value wiped out, while workers on a fixed income found it impossible to afford basic goods as their price soared. Although the new Chancellor **Gustav Stresemann** called off passive resistance in the Ruhr in autumn 1923 and stabilised the economy by introducing a new currency, the Rentenmark, the Weimar government's reputation had taken a severe blow. Extremist and reactionary parties, such as the German Communist Party and German National People's Party, gained popularity: parties opposed to the democratic, liberal principles of the Weimar government won 114 out of the 472 seats in the Reichstag in May 1924.

The harsh conditions under which the occupation of the Ruhr was carried out also increased international sympathy for Germany, especially amongst politicians and commentators already critical of the Versailles Treaty. This shift in mood is worth bearing in mind when exploring the appeasement of German aggression in the 1930s, which is introduced in Chapter 21 and discussed further in Chapters 22 and 23.

Summary

By 1923:

- the USA had adopted an isolationist economic policy, but at the Washington Conference did commit itself to agreements with other powers which were aimed at maintaining the peace
- there had been a significant shift in the status of Bolshevik Russia; their victory in the Russian Civil War in conjunction with treaties and trade agreements with Britain signified that the rest of the world was ready to grudgingly accept the Bolsheviks' rule, but mistrust between communism and the West was still significant
- the League of Nations had had some success in resolving disputes, but the incidents in Vilna and Corfu demonstrated that its peacekeeping task would be perhaps even more complex and frustrating than its reluctant leaders feared. The fact that the Washington Conference agreements had been made without the League's involvement showed that cooperation could be achieved in international affairs without it
- the harshness of the occupation of the Ruhr by the French and Belgians helped to change many people's attitudes towards the Treaty of Versailles and question its fairness.

CROSS-REFERENCE

To find out more about the impact of the Ruhr invasion, read about Hitler and the Munich Putsch in Chapter 18, pages 155–156.

ACTIVITY

Group work

In pairs, discuss which of the developments summarised above appears to be most dangerous for maintaining peaceful international relations for the rest of the 1920s and 1930s.

ACTIVITY

Research

The occupation of the Ruhr gave German right-wing critics of the Weimar Republic plenty of material for their propaganda posters. Go online to find examples and sort them according to who was blamed: the French or the Weimar government? Which consequences of the occupation do the posters identify?

 PRACTICE QUESTION

How far were disputes in international affairs between 1920 and 1923 the result of unsatisfactory post-war peace settlements?

STUDY TIP

Try to consider different angles. Plan and consider how you could analyse them to find points to support and challenge the premise of the question.

17 The 'spirit of Locarno'

KEY CHRONOLOGY

September 1923	Britain rejects the draft disarmament treaty at the Assembly of the League of Nations
April 1924	Dawes Plan created
October 1924	Geneva Protocol given preliminary approval by League of Nations
March 1925	New British government refused to ratify Geneva Protocol
August 1925	Last French and Belgian troops withdrew from the Ruhr
October 1925	Locarno agreements signed
August 1928	Kellogg–Briand Pact signed by Germany, France and the USA

SOURCE 1

From a letter written by Austen Chamberlain, British Foreign Secretary, to the King's private secretary on 9 February 1925. Chamberlain was awarded the Nobel Peace Prize in 1925 for his role in the Locarno Treaties, under which Germany recognised its western borders and pledged to resolve disputes peacefully:

I regard it as the first task of statesmanship to set to work to make the new position of Germany tolerable to the German people in the hope that as they regain prosperity under it they may in time become reconciled to it and be unwilling to put their fortunes again to the desperate hazard of war. I am working not for today or tomorrow but for some date like 1960 or 1970 when German strength will have returned and when the prospect of war will again cloud the horizon unless the risks are still too great to be rashly incurred and the actual conditions too tolerable to be jeopardised on a gambler's throw. I believe the key to the solution is to be found in allaying French fears, and that unless we find a means to do this we may be confronted with complete breakdown of our friendly relations with France and an exacerbation of her attitude towards Germany.

[handwritten annotations: "fear of communism", "trade w/ Britain", "Guarantee of French security", "reference to ruhr invasion"]

Attempts at disarmament and conciliation in international relations

Following the resolution – at least in the short-term – of border disputes, and the imposition of the post-war settlements across Europe, the attention of the League of Nations turned to the aim of disarmament, while the issue of reparations needed to be urgently addressed in response to the occupation of the Ruhr.

The draft Treaty of Mutual Assistance, 1923

In 1921 the USA had hosted the Washington Naval Conference to prevent a potential naval race in the Pacific. In the same year, the League of Nations created the Temporary Mixed Commission on Armaments. This commission was charged with the task of developing possible solutions to the disarmament question, and proposed several initiatives including a ban of the bombing of civilians, restricting the amount of artillery and tanks any nation could hold, and prohibiting the use of chemical warfare. However, the delegates could not move past the difficult and contentious issue of how a country would be able to defend itself if it surrendered its weapons.

The League of Nations hoped that the Treaty of Mutual Assistance would act as a severe deterrent against aggression, but the drafted agreement was unpalatable to many nations, especially Britain. The draft Treaty proposed that in the event of conflict, the League would have a deadline of four days to decide which nation was the aggressor and which the victim, after which the League would send armed forces to defend the victim country. All members of the League of Nations would be expected to contribute troops to the peacekeeping effort, which many nations baulked at; the lack of clear guidelines on how the League would judge victim from aggressor in such a short timespan was also discouraging. Britain put up the strongest resistance, objecting to the use of its troops in the manner proposed when they were needed to defend the Empire. The drafting of the Treaty was the most determined effort to date of the League to resolve many of the grey areas in its Covenant and processes relating to peacekeeping, but the Treaty was never enacted.

The Dawes Plan, 1924

Harsh treatment at the hands of the Ruhr occupiers had changed other nations' perspectives of the post-war settlement. Germany was no longer the 'bogeyman' of Europe; this title passed to Communist Russia. Germany was therefore viewed by Britain and France as a potential bulwark against Russian aggression; meanwhile some economists and politicians – especially in Britain – feared that without an urgent review of Germany's ability to pay reparations and service its war debts, an internal revolution would ensure it became a communist state on its own terms.

France, however, was bitter about the relative failure of the Ruhr occupation, and especially the lack of support from Britain. The invasion had provoked an economic downturn in France and, as the French economy was increasingly bolstered by American loans, it could not afford to court the hostility of its creditor by refusing to review the reparations question or the occupation.

In November 1923 Britain, France and the USA agreed to discuss reparations again. A commission was created under the chairmanship of US economist Charles Dawes, and comprised two financial experts each from the USA, Britain, France, Belgium and Italy. The aim was to restructure reparations and support the German economy in such a way that would encourage German recovery so that it could afford to make payments to the Allies, who would then have no need to take them by force, as France and Belgium had done.

The terms of the Dawes Plan

The Plan was completed in April 1924. The following points were agreed:
1. German reparations were restructured. In the first year of payment, Germany would pay 1 billion marks, increasing to 2.5 billion in subsequent years.
2. The Reichsbank (the German national bank) would be restructured under the supervision of the Allies.
3. Germany would resume control of the Ruhr and French and Belgian troops would withdraw to allow Germany to regain key industrial resources, facilitating its recovery.
4. Sanctions against Germany were only to be used if it deliberately failed to honour these commitments.

Alongside the Plan, although not part of its official provisions, the USA agreed to loan 800 million marks to Germany. After the Plan's approval, American investors rushed to invest in Germany's recovery.

CROSS-REFERENCE

For the agreements made in Washington in 1921, see Chapter 16.

ACTIVITY

Summary

Write a short statement from the point of view of a British politician defending your government's decision not to agree to the Treaty of Mutual Assistance. Which factors will you emphasise most, bearing in mind that it would go against Britain if their motives appeared selfish to other nations?

CROSS-REFERENCE

The willingness of the USA to cooperate economically with Europe, despite its professed isolationism, is explained in Chapter 16.

ACTIVITY

Thinking point

Why do you think that the Allies wanted the Reichsbank to be reorganised with their help?

Fig. 1   *Édouard Herriot*

Édouard Herriot (1872–1957) was a left-wing politician who became Prime Minister of France in 1924. He aimed to improve relations with other powers by agreeing to end the Ruhr occupation and accepting the Dawes Plan. He recognised the threat posed by Nazi Germany, and was taken prisoner when Germany invaded France in 1940. After his release he continued in French politics.

honest brokers: arbitrators in a dispute or potential disputes who remain neutral and consider points made by all parties concerned

The USA sent Parker Gilbert to Germany as 'General Reparations Agent' to supervise payments. This guarantee was key to French acceptance of the deal: despite the amount of reparations being lowered, the French were relieved to have international support to ensure that Germany did not default on its payments again. The Dawes Plan was to last five years before being reviewed again.

The German economy and politics in the mid-1920s

With two new appointments, Wilhelm Marx as Chancellor and Hjalmar Schacht as the Reichsbank President, the new Rentenmark was finally introduced in November 1923. This slowly brought inflation under control, but not before the price of bread hit 165 billion marks per loaf. British and American funding helped Schacht to make economic reforms, including a credit freeze, to create stability. However, hyperinflation had already caused considerable damage to the Weimar government's popularity. Political turbulence led President Ebert to pass Schacht's reforms by emergency decree under Article 48 of the constitution, instead of them being passed by the Reichstag.

As the Dawes Plan involved a review of the terms of the Treaty of Versailles, an international conference was convened in London in the summer of 1924. Two delegations were of particular significance: the USA hoped to act as **'honest brokers'** for Europe; and Germany, which was treated as an equal for the first time since 1919. Although Poincaré's personal disapproval was no longer a factor, the new French Prime Minister **Édouard Herriot** tried to secure compensation for France in the form of payment in return for their withdrawal from the Ruhr. He was persuaded, however, to agree to evacuate his troops within a year.

The consequences of the Dawes Plan

As well as helping to finance its recovery – which continued until the Wall Street Crash in 1929 – Germany's international standing greatly improved as a result of the Plan. **Ramsay MacDonald**, the new British Prime Minister, was optimistic about the long-term consequences of this development: 'We are now offering the first really negotiated agreement since the war. This agreement may be regarded as the first Peace Treaty, because we sign it with a feeling that we have turned our backs on the terrible years of war and war mentality.'

Ramsay MacDonald (1866–1937) was Britain's first Labour Prime Minister, serving for 10 months in 1924 and again between 1929 and 1935. He had opposed Britain's involvement in the First World War, and favoured internationalism in world affairs. MacDonald led the Conservative-dominated National Government formed in the midst of the Great Depression, which damaged his reputation amongst left-wing supporters.

Fig. 2   *Ramsay MacDonald*

However, the Dawes Plan was a matter of concern for French politicians, who saw their position as isolated and vulnerable. The British and Americans had strongly discouraged another occupation to secure reparations, while the terms of the plan superseded the existing Reparations Commission in which France had greater influence. It highlighted the shift to a more conciliatory approach to Germany, but undermined the Treaty of Versailles in the process by revising its terms; while the French had learned that it could not successfully enforce the Treaty's terms without the explicit support of Britain.

The Geneva Protocol, 1924

Under its Covenant, the League of Nations promised to 'preserve' its members against acts of aggression, but the Covenant did not define what an act of aggression was. In the event of disputes the League had to make a decision on whether aggression had taken place before taking action, making its response slow and exposing it to claims of partiality. This situation helped to muddle its response to the Corfu incident. MacDonald, Herriot and the Czech leader Edvard Beneš advocated a solution to this problem in 1924.

The plan to refine the term 'act of aggression' was termed the 'Protocol for the Pacific Settlement of International Disputes' but became known as the Geneva Protocol after the Swiss city in which it was negotiated. The word 'protocol' was used deliberately to signal that it was not intended to contravene the Covenant of the League of Nations, but was designed instead to support it. Ultimately, however, the Geneva Protocol undermined the League, as the international reaction was lukewarm; Britain chose not to ratify it, highlighting the unpopularity of collective security, and the ability of the League to arbitrate was called into question.

Fig. 3 *The delegates of the Geneva conference meeting in 1924*

The terms of the protocol stated that in the event of a dispute, countries would submit their case to the League and not go to war while the case was arbitrated by the Permanent Court of International Justice. An 'aggressor' was thereby defined as any power making war during the process of arbitration; the League could then take action against them. A further term of the protocol involved all of its members in a pledge to attend a conference to limit armaments.

Britain's refusal to fully ratify the Geneva Protocol was due to two factors: firstly, it was unpopular amongst the new Conservative government, following

Fig. 4   Austen Chamberlain

Austen Chamberlain (1863–1937)
was the half-brother of future Prime
Minister Neville and served as
Foreign Secretary 1924–29. Though
a Francophile, he was determined to
engineer revisions to the post-war
settlement in Germany's favour in
order to guarantee future European
security.

Fig. 5   Aristide Briand

Aristide Briand (1862–1932)
served 11 terms as French Prime
Minister before becoming Foreign
Minister 1925–1932. He had a
more conciliatory style than his
predecessors, accepting the need for
France to cooperate with Germany.
His idealism was encapsulated in his
initiation of the Kellogg–Briand pact.

Rhenish: of the Rhineland

a general election in November 1924; and secondly, Britain remained wary
of committing itself to any entangling treaty agreements. The protocol could
easily have committed the British to sending troops to intervene in a distant
conflict via the League of Nations.

Consolidation of the Post-war Settlement at Locarno

Several new realities were recognised by the time of the Locarno agreements
of 1925:

- The Dawes Plan had eased the pressure of reparations by temporarily
  shelving them as a potential catalyst for disputes. A focus for statesmen
  was now the question of how to balance the German desire for revisions
  to the Treaty of Versailles with French demands for security. The French in
  particular were pleased that a stronger international commitment had been
  agreed to ensure Germany would pay reparations, and that France's own
  post-war reconstruction had significantly progressed.
- The Dawes Plan marked the first time Germany had been included in
  international negotiations since the war, thereby improving its international
  status.
- Foreign secretaries were now centre stage again in international affairs:
  immediately after the war, presidents and prime ministers had tended
  to take the lead. From 1925, **Austen Chamberlain** of Britain, Gustav
  Stresemann of Germany and **Aristide Briand** of France represented the
  foreign interests of their respective nations. All three were to receive Nobel
  Peace Prizes for their peacekeeping work.
- Disarmament seemed more achievable: there was firm public support for it
  in many European countries and America, and a more concerted effort was
  made to limit weapons stored.

Although French and Belgian troops were due to withdraw from the Ruhr
in August 1925, other Allied troops continued to occupy Rhineland cities,
including Cologne. During the occupation crisis, the French had fostered
hopes of **Rhenish** separatism, anticipating that Rhinelanders would grow tired
of the disadvantages of being part of Germany and become the buffer state
that France wanted.

From the diary entry of Gustav Stresemann, German Foreign Minister, on
19 July 1925:

Peace between France and Germany is not merely a Franco–German but a
European affair. The last world war in my opinion produced no victors who could
rejoice in their victory. The war, and the continuation of the war by other means,
were responsible for social, political, and economic upheavals in Europe which
have directly confronted the older civilised nations with the question of their
future material existence. Currency and trade are, not merely in this country but
in others, the supporters of the idea of the State, the most steadfast pillars of the
present order. The collapse of the currency has spread from East to West, and has
hitherto not stopped at any national frontier. I do not belong to those who expect
any advantages for Germany from the continuance of this currency fall in France.
I can envisage no political or even economic advantages if this fall goes on.

The Locarno negotiations

At Locarno, Switzerland, in February 1925, Stresemann revealed a proposal
to the Allies: Germany would issue voluntarily a guarantee of its current
western border, thereby giving up its claims to Alsace and Lorraine,

and to Eupen and Malmédy, which would relieve France and Belgium respectively. The advantage for Germany in such a plan was that France could never legally invade the Ruhr or Rhineland again on the pretext of recovering its reparations, and the prospect of a Rhenish state would disappear. Britain showed enthusiasm for this initial proposal, but the French pointed out that Germany should acknowledge its eastern borders too. Similarly, Italy hoped to secure a guarantee of Germany's southern border to protect Austria.

For several months, negotiations in Locarno continued. There was far more at stake than the confirmation of existing borders: by making key compromises with its former enemies, Germany expected to finally become a member of the League of Nations, thereby confirming its acceptance as an equal in world affairs. Eventually a series of agreements, which became known as the Locarno Treaties, were initialled in October by Britain, France, Germany, Italy and Belgium, and signed in full in December after they had been discussed by the signatories' governments.

The Locarno members agreed the following:
1. A Treaty of Mutual Guarantee was established, which guaranteed the borders of Germany, France and Belgium to Germany's west, and guaranteed the demilitarisation of the Rhineland.
2. Germany, France and Belgium agreed not to go to war against each other unless the terms of the Mutual Guarantee Treaty were broken, or unless the League of Nations called for action against one of them as an aggressor. The guarantors would act immediately, without the League, in the event of a 'flagrant' abuse of these terms.
3. Germany agreed four separate treaties, one each with France, Belgium, Czechoslovakia and Poland, to resolve any disputes between them peacefully.

After the agreements at Locarno, Germany duly took its place on the Permanent Council of the League of Nations in September 1926. Its role in the negotiations was not a simple matter, however, and the Allies grew frustrated at Stresemann's attempts to secure an even better deal for Germany. First of all, the Germans tried to make the Allies repudiate the 'war guilt' clause in the Treaty of Versailles as a condition of its attendance at Locarno. This request was ignored though, and the German delegation still attended. Towards the end of the negotiations, Stresemann made more demands, including a faster evacuation of Allied troops from the Rhineland and an earlier **Saar** plebiscite. Although the British, French and Belgians promised to consider these proposals, Germany's suggestion that it should police its own disarmament rather than allow it to be done under Allied supervision infuriated Austen Chamberlain; the plans were quickly dropped.

Reactions to Locarno

Britain had much to celebrate in the Locarno terms. The Franco–German détente increased European security, much to the approval of the Foreign Office, and Chamberlain was hailed as a hero of the peace. Notably, however, Britain had contrived to avoid some of the entanglements that it feared in the Geneva Protocol: it had refused to commit itself to possible border disputes in Eastern Europe, while possible intervention required on Germany's western border would be managed by the League of Nations.

In Paris, the treaties were also given a warm welcome. French fears of isolation following the creation of the Dawes Plan were alleviated, as Britain and other powers had agreed to defend France in the event of a German invasion. The French did not achieve the guarantee of Germany's eastern borders; France's existing agreements with Poland and Czechoslovakia were recognised at Locarno, but made more difficult to enforce without France violating Germany's border itself. Again, France's acceptance of the Locarno

ACTIVITY

Read Source 2 and then answer the following questions:
1. What are the advantages and disadvantages of using the diary entries of statesmen for historians studying international relations?
2. What do you think Stresemann was referring to with the phrase 'the continuation of the War by other means'?

ACTIVITY

Summary

As you read through the terms of the Locarno Treaties here, make a chart to show which aspects represented revisions to the Treaty of Versailles, and which merely confirmed one or more of the terms.

CROSS-REFERENCE

The fate of the Saar coalfields was decided at the Paris Peace Conference, explored in Chapter 14.

KEY TERM

unilateral: the action of one country alone; bilateral action would involve two countries

KEY PROFILE

Fig. 6   *Joseph Stalin*

Joseph Stalin (1879–1953) was the son of a Georgian cobbler. He took the name 'Stalin' (man of steel) after being frequently arrested and exiled to Siberia in the last years of the Tsarist regime. He became editor of *Pravda*, the communist newspaper in 1917 and asserted himself as leader of the USSR after Lenin's death. A deeply paranoid individual, he launched several 'purges' of 'disloyal' Russians, including military staff, which weakened the USSR's fighting strength. Stalin foresaw war with the West and launched programmes of industrialisation and militarisation. He died in 1953 after helping to start the Cold War with the USSR's former wartime ally, the USA.

ACTIVITY

Rank the following powers in order in terms of how positive the Locarno agreements were for them: Britain, France, Germany, Belgium, Italy and the USSR. Give reasons for the order you place them in.

terms highlighted the new attitude towards Germany: instead of acting **unilaterally** to control and punish Germany, the French now pursued the conclusion of international agreements which would make German adherence to their terms an international concern.

Despite the clear gains achieved by Stresemann, the reaction in Germany was hardly enthusiastic. The foreign minister tried to convince the government that it had little choice but to re-affirm its western border given its limited army, but the largest nationalist party, the DNVP, stormed out of the Reichstag in protest. On 27 November 1925 the Reichstag passed the Locarno agreements by 292 votes to 174.

Belgians and Italians were also disappointed by the provisions of the treaties. Belgium remained dependent on France for its security, while Italy secured no gains for itself despite its presence at the negotiations. Similarly, there were few guarantees of security for Poland and Czechoslovakia, both of whom also looked to France for support against future German aggression, but now France had less freedom of action. The reaction in Eastern Europe and the USSR was lukewarm: little was settled for the eastern nations, and **Joseph Stalin** viewed Locarno as having a hidden anti-Soviet agenda. To this end, he pursued a separate agreement with Germany in addition to the Treaty of Rapallo signed in 1922. In April 1926 the USSR and Germany signed the Neutrality and Non-Aggression Pact, under which both would remain neutral if either was attacked by a third power, and Germany pledged not to join an (imagined) anti-Soviet plot.

A CLOSER LOOK

Germany and the USSR

Relations between Germany and the USSR were close during the 1920s. Both had the common experience of bitterness of not having been included in the post-war peace negotiations, and having lost some of their territory to the newly independent Poland. Germany never accepted its new borders in Eastern Europe; indeed Poland viewed the agreements between Germany and the USSR as a real threat to its security. The Soviet Union also gained the continued benefit of trade agreements with Germany as well as help to modernise its industry.

The Kellogg–Briand pact

The new mood of conciliation in international relations, which came to be known as the 'spirit of Locarno', was extended in 1928 with the conclusion of the Kellogg–Briand pact, under which 62 nations pledged never to go to war again. The idea was first mooted by Briand to the US Secretary of State Frank B. Kellogg as a peace pledge between France and the USA. Despite America's declared isolationism, there was a growing demand among its people for the 'outlawry' of war, and many politicians looked for ways to ensure that war would never break out again.

Of the nations invited to sign the pact, only Brazil and Argentina declined. The almost unanimous acceptance of the peace pledge is perhaps best explained by the careful wording of the agreement: its terms were deliberately compromised to ensure that no existing treaties or agreements, including the League of Nations Convenant, were undermined or contravened. This alone watered down the high ideal of the agreement, but the added disadvantage that no sanctions were specified in the pact's terms rendered it practically pointless. Nevertheless, it is viewed as the high point of post-war conciliation.

SOURCE 3

From the terms of the Kellogg–Briand pact, signed by the USA, Germany and France on 27 August 1928, and signed by other states, including Britain and Italy, in 1929:

The signatories of the Kellogg–Briand pact sign it:

- deeply sensible of their solemn duty to promote the welfare of mankind;
- persuaded that the time has come when a frank renunciation of war as an instrument of national policy should be made to the end that the peaceful and friendly relations now existing between their peoples may be perpetuated;
- convinced that all changes in their relations with one another should be sought only by pacific means and be the result of a peaceful and orderly process, and that any signatory Power which shall hereafter seek to promote its national interests by resort to war should be denied the benefits furnished by this Treaty;
- hopeful that, encouraged by their example, all the other nations of the world will join in this humane endeavour and by adhering to the present Treaty as soon as it comes into force bring their peoples within the scope of its beneficent provisions, thus uniting the civilised nations of the world in a common renunciation of war as an instrument of their national policy;
- decided to conclude a Treaty.

ACTIVITY

Evaluating primary sources

1. Read Source 3. Do you think the Pact's critics were justified in believing it to be weak or useless?
2. Do you think the most important factor undermining the effectiveness of the Pact was its need to compromise?

Summary

The 'spirit of Locarno' which resulted in the hopeful international agreements of 1924–28 have been described as overly optimistic, even naïve. Certainly, there are elements of the pacts made which suggest that they had little chance of succeeding, but there were positive signs too.

Draft Treaty of Mutual Assistance, 1923	
• Aimed to clarify and speed up the League's response to conflict	
• Tried to commit members to contribute to League peacekeeping forces	
• Rejected on the grounds of member contribution and lack of clarity on procedure	
Dawes Plan, 1924	**Geneva Protocol, 1924**
• Made German reparations more affordable	• Aimed to make the work of the League easier
• Promoted German recovery with American loans	• Rejected on the basis of committing countries to faraway conflicts
• France one of the signatories	
Locarno Pacts, 1925	**Kellogg–Briand Pact, 1928**
• Recognised Germany's western borders only	• High idealism of international relations
• Reduced significant area of tension and promoted French security	• A large number of signatories
• Left eastern border concerns open	• No sanctions decided if nations broke the pact

STUDY TIP

Remember to consider the nature of a source to fully evaluate its provenance. Private letters and diary entries, for example, may sometimes be more useful than a public speech because they are more likely to reveal the truthful, innermost thoughts of the author as they don't need to worry about the reaction of a wider audience. However in some cases, especially if the issue discussed is deeply controversial, privately communicated sources may be more subject to bias or emotion.

STUDY TIP

Try to consider both the actual problems that existed in international relations as a result of the post-war settlements, and the successes and failures of the conferences in resolving them. Be careful, though, not to drift from the focus and remember to consider the effectiveness of the conferences; plan and time your response accordingly.

ACTIVITY

Group work

Debate in pairs, or as two sides of your class, which judgement of the Locarno years (1924–28) is the more accurate:
1. The treaties and agreements made at this time were naïvely optimistic. They were doomed to fail no matter what circumstances emerged later.
2. The treaties and agreements were hopeful but achievable given the public mood. Only with hindsight can we see that a global depression was set to ruin their chances of success.

 PRACTICE QUESTION

Evaluating primary sources

With reference to Sources 1, 2, and 3, and your understanding of the historical context, assess their value to an historian studying the reasons for the change in the international attitude to Germany from 1924 to 1928.

 PRACTICE QUESTION

How successful were the international conferences between 1924 and 1928 in resolving the problems remaining from the post-war peace settlements?

18 The Depression and its impact on international relations

From German Chancellor Von Papen's address to the Lausanne Conference, called to discuss the issue of reparations, on 16 June 1932:

Nothing can prove more clearly the catastrophic upheaval which has occurred during this period than a comparison between the world as it was in 1929 and the situation today. Then there existed a system of international credit and a fruitful exchange of capital from one country to another. Commercial relations between almost all countries seemed to be regulated by a well-organized system of commercial treaties. Governments, parliaments, economic circles and public opinion condemned any policy of isolation. Every country welcomed the goods of other countries in well-ordered exchanges. Banks granted credits to foreign countries. Investors entrusted their savings to foreign governments. In the majority of countries unemployment was still an unknown problem. Those were the features of the period during which the Young Plan was conceived. What an abyss between the glowing optimism of those days and the pessimism and despair of today! The desperate situation today is evidenced by the number of 25 million unemployed. In Germany this state of things has most strongly shaken the confidence of the masses in the good functioning of the capitalist system.

The Great Depression from 1929

After the cautious optimism of the Locarno pacts and reparations plans of the 1920s, the 1930s were characterised by a shift away from internationalism and towards national, isolationist economic policies as every country struggled to cope with the impact of the **Great Depression**. The League of Nations continued with its goals of disarmament and resolving the reparations issue, but the consequences of the global **downturn** made its problems even more intractable. As the seriousness and long-term nature of the economic crisis became more apparent, the role of the USA as the leading creditor nation became increasingly important in Europe. One of the earliest casualties of the Depression was the **Young Plan**.

A CLOSER LOOK

The Young Plan was created in 1929 to succeed the Dawes Plan of 1924, which had a five-year term. The Young Plan, named after American lawyer Owen D. Young, reduced Germany's final repayment sum and linked British and French debts to reparation amounts. Germany would complete its payments by 1988. The plan committed the USA to continued economic involvement in Europe, despite its official policy of isolationism.

The causes of the Great Depression were complex, but one of the major factors behind the economic crisis was a loss of confidence in the American economy. The stock market boom of the 1920s saw increased investment in shares, which had artificially raised the value of US companies, and a rise in the use of credit. When share prices plummeted during the **Wall Street Crash** of 1929, investors and banks lost billions of dollars ($8 billion was wiped off the price

CROSS-REFERENCE

The Lausanne Conference is discussed in this chapter, pages 156–157.

ACTIVITY

1. Read Source 1. Can you find any exaggerations or omissions relating to the world economy in Von Papen's speech?
2. In what ways might the context of this source potentially weaken its reliability?

A CLOSER LOOK

The Great Depression was a severe economic decline affecting the majority of countries. It started in 1929, the year of the Wall Street Crash (although it would be too simplistic to say the Crash caused the Depression) and its effects continued in many nations until the late 1930s. It was characterised by mass unemployment and a decline in world trade.

KEY TERM

downturn: a decrease in economic activity; the Great Depression was an extreme, long-term example

A CLOSER LOOK

The Wall Street Crash was the sudden and dramatic loss of share value in the USA's financial centre, Wall Street in New York. As the price of shares decreased, investors sold their shares in a panic. Thousands were ruined overnight, and the Crash resulted in a banking crisis in the US which also affected their debtor nations.

of shares on 29 October alone). Banks began to fail as ordinary people rushed to withdraw their savings – 659 banks failed in 1929, 1352 in 1930 and 2294 in 1931. The Great Depression set in as US companies closed down or limited their production and unemployment in the USA soared.

The economic crisis in America quickly spread to the rest of the world. US investors had lent $6 billion dollars abroad between 1924 and 1928, in particular to its former wartime allies, Britain and France, and of course to Germany in conjunction with the Dawes plan. As American banks were struggling – with many on the brink of collapse – most of these loans were recalled, but debtor nations were unable to pay.

Fig. 1   *Unemployed men queuing outside a soup kitchen in Chicago in 1931; the Depression had a devastating impact on many people's lives, which in turn affected the priorities of world leaders*

The 'tariff war'

In one example of how governments abandoned international cooperation in order to secure their own interests, **protectionism** increased. The USA had already introduced the Emergency Tariff and the Fordney-McCumber Tariff in the early 1920s to protect its domestic markets from foreign competition; in 1930 it imposed the Smoot-Hawley Tariff which extended the protective tariff to over 20,000 imported goods. Other nations had already introduced retaliatory tariffs, and in response to the Depression these tariffs increased in number and in severity. Britain turned to a strategy first mooted at the end of the nineteenth century: favourable trade arrangements within the Empire and between its colonies and **dominions** (now increasingly known as the Commonwealth). The 1932 Import Duties Act ended the British policy of free trade, imposing a 10 per cent tariff on imported goods except those from India, South Rhodesia and the Dominions. France soon followed suit with a similar arrangement with its own colonies.

KEY TERM

dominions: countries united by their common allegiance to the British Crown but free to run their own domestic and foreign affairs; together they comprised the British Commonwealth

CROSS-REFERENCE

The use of protectionism – the use of tariffs to protect domestic producers – in America is explained in Chapter 15.

The abandonment of the gold standard

Having been suspended during the First World War, the gold standard was restored in Britain by then Chancellor Winston Churchill in 1925. In the wake of falling prices and the slump in world trade, Britain was the first leading economy to remove itself from the gold standard as a result of the Great Depression. In September 1931 Britain made it clear that this would be a longer-term decision, despite many subsequent attempts by the Americans and the French to woo the British back to it. This strategy had immediate benefits for Britain as it had more freedom to stimulate its own economy, but it came at America's cost. The value of the pound decreased compared to the US dollar (from $4.86 to $3.50) which helped British industry by making US imports more expensive, and their own exports cheaper.

Within a month, several countries followed Britain's example, including Denmark, Sweden and Canada. Two blocs emerged amongst the leading world economies: those that remained on the gold standard – including France, Czechoslovakia, Belgium, Poland, and Italy – and those whose currencies were linked to the value of sterling (the British pound). These 'sterling bloc' nations included the Commonwealth and Norway, Sweden and Denmark. On 27 July 1933 the British Commonwealth Declaration was signed. Its aims were to raise prices, plan an eventual return to the gold standard, and to ensure the stabilisation of exchange rates within the sterling bloc.

A CLOSER LOOK

The gold standard

The gold standard linked a currency's exchange rate to a specified amount of gold. The advantage of countries staying on the gold standard was that their currencies would remain stable; this would also make them favourable trading partners as their exchange rate was tied to a steady measure. A potential disadvantage of the gold standard, however, was that it restricted the freedom of individual economies, but as being on the gold standard was a kind of 'quality mark' for an economy, it was worth tolerating. In the event of a depression though, countries often risked coming off the gold standard in order to free up the economy: it allowed them to increase their supply of money and encourage exports.

ACTIVITY

Thinking point

In what ways might economic collaboration lead to political collaboration in international affairs?

The Depression in Germany

One of the most significant consequences of the Great Depression was the inability of the Weimar government to resolve the catastrophic effects of the economic crisis in Germany. As unemployment increased, support for the moderate ruling parties – and even for democracy itself – sharply declined. The popularity of the KPD (the German Communist Party) and the fascist Nazi Party soared: many previously moderate Germans supported the Nazis due to their fear of communism. Others, meanwhile, were impressed by the impression of order and stability that the Nazis offered with Hitler as a strong decisive leader and the military-style uniforms and marches of the Nazi *Sturmabteilung* (the 'Brownshirts'). Hitler also promised to provide jobs and support small business owners.

A CLOSER LOOK

Nazism

National Socialism, shortened to Nazism, was a political ideology based on **fascism**. It advocated the resurgence of Germany as a world power in defiance of the post-war settlement, blaming the German defeat on supposed 'enemies' such as communists and Jews and urging their removal from public life. Nazis also believed that the German race (known as Aryans) were biologically superior to others, especially Slavs.

CROSS-REFERENCE

Fascism is defined in the Introduction to this book, page xiii.

A CLOSER LOOK

The rise of Hitler and the Nazi Party

In an attempt to seize power by force, in November 1923 Hitler and his supporters attempted a march through the streets of Munich, demanding the overthrow of the government. After an extremely lenient prison sentence, Hitler decided to make his bid for power through election success, not a *coup d'état*. Although his time in prison allowed Hitler to write about his ideology and foreign policy aims in *Mein Kampf*, by the time he was released the economy had recovered and the Weimar government's popularity increased. It was only a short-term recovery, however: the political landscape of Germany changed drastically in 1929 following the Wall Street Crash.

KEY PROFILE

Fig. 2 *Adolf Hitler*

Adolf Hitler (1889–1945) joined the fledgling German Workers' Party in 1919, becoming its leader in 1921. Partly inspired by Italian Fascism, he at first hoped to seize power in the failed 1923 Munich Putsch, but then committed the renamed National Socialist (Nazi) Party to electoral success. He became Chancellor in 1933, and Führer in 1934. Hitler committed suicide in April 1945 when Germany's defeat in the Second World War became inevitable.

KEY TERM

moratorium: a temporary suspension of debt repayment grants, with the agreement of the creditor

Nazis claimed to embrace socialism; but once in power; many of the socialist aspects of their early programme were quietly forgotten.

The Nazis promised Germans a return to economic stability and an end to unemployment. Even before **Adolf Hitler** became Chancellor on 30 January 1933, the increasing popularity of right-wing ideas made Weimar politicians more assertive in their dealings with other nations, as their behaviour in the early stages of the Lausanne and World Disarmament and Conferences highlighted.

The effect on international relations

The optimism seen amongst countries in the 1920s did not immediately disappear with the onset of the Depression. Although the economic crisis made internationalism less appealing to statesmen, who had to prioritise their own countries' financial and domestic interests more highly, concerted and high-minded efforts continued to be made to resolve the more difficult issues of the post-war world.

The Hoover moratorium on reparations, 1931

In October 1930, Germany asked President Herbert Hoover of the USA to consider a **moratorium** on reparations due to the impact of the Depression on the German economy, a request it was entitled to make under the terms of Versailles. The proposal had the support of Wall Street investors, who were concerned about Germany's ability to honour loan repayments without it. Hoover agreed to the moratorium, but only as a short-term measure, and only if the savings Germany made were not used for armaments; it was eventually agreed that the money would be invested in railways. The moratorium began in June 1931 for a year-long period in the ambitious hope that the impact of the Depression in Europe would be short-lived. The deal earned harsh criticism from the French, who viewed it as yet another Anglo-American agreement to help Germany at France's expense.

Lausanne Conference on reparations, 1932

By the summer of 1932 it was clear that Hoover's expectation of European recovery within a year of the start of the moratorium was far too optimistic (this chimed with his promise to the American public that prosperity was 'just around the corner'). In June a conference was convened in Lausanne, Switzerland, to resolve the ongoing issue of reparations. It was attended by Britain, France, Germany, Belgium and Italy, and it is unsurprising that the German and French delegates (Chancellor **Franz von Papen** and Prime Minister **Édouard Herriot**, respectively) made their opposing goals clear from the outset. Papen claimed that reparations were dangerous and unrealistic, while Herriot continued the previous French argument that Germany could afford them but repeatedly chose not to.

Progress was made at Lausanne, however. Like Hoover, the British Prime Minister Ramsay MacDonald was in favour of linking the abandonment of reparations with the process of disarmament. As the World Disarmament Conference was already underway in Geneva (just over 60 kilometres away on the other side of Lake Geneva), the Lausanne Conference itself was somewhat overshadowed by the objective of limiting armaments.

In contrast to the terms of the Young Plan, at Lausanne it was agreed that reparations would end, with Germany paying a final 3000 million Marks as a lump sum – just 10 per cent of its outstanding debt – to the Bank of International Settlements, which had been established in 1930. The Lausanne

Protocol was not ratified because all creditor nations agreed not to proceed until they had decided how to compensate the USA for remaining war debts. This 'gentlemen's agreement' was of particular importance to Britain and France, but its secret details were leaked to Washington, which took a dim view of the arrangement: ultimately it amounted to its debtors agreeing to cancel their own debts. The delegates at Lausanne hoped to soothe American objections by organising a world conference to address the economic crisis and restore international cooperation, which would meet in London the next year. In France, too, the Lausanne Protocol received a frosty reception, and the proposal by the government to pay its own final lump sum to America was rejected by the National Assembly.

SOURCE 2

From the British publication the *Spectator*, a right-wing magazine, published on 16 July 1932:

As a result of the Lausanne Conference, reparations are dead. What is more, the issue is swept finally from the international arena by an agreement both fair and friendly. That is an achievement of immense value. There is a good deal to be said for the decision, accepted by the German delegation, that Germany shall make an ultimate payment of £150,000,000 in final discharge of her obligations under the reparations chapter of the Treaty of Versailles. On the other hand, provision for this final payment has enabled **M. Herriot** to demonstrate convincingly to a still restive public that there is no question of repudiation on Germany's part. The French Prime Minister has deserved well of his country and of the world. The Paris Press was suspicious and hostile. The real temper of the country was hard to gauge. It is a testimony to the changed outlook of France and to M. Herriot's personal courage that the Prime Minister should have set his name to the Lausanne agreement and at the end gained the general approval of his countrymen.

The agreements made at Lausanne in 1932 finally cancelled out the economic terms of the Treaty of Versailles; its terms also effectively cancelled out those of the Young Plan. France's role in the Lausanne Protocol served to distance it further from the USA, while the last one-off payment scheduled to be made by Germany never materialised. The abandonment of reparations was very popular in the USA and most of Europe, but it did little to help the beleaguered Weimar government. Despite the success of its politicians in ensuring another key aspect of the Versailles settlement was abolished, the Nazi party used the fact that it still had some debts and that it had not yet secured the right to re-arm to level of other nations as propaganda. Its proportion of seats in the Reichstag had doubled by the end of the conference.

The London Conference 1933

The promise of the USA's debtor nations, to discuss world debts in return for the Lausanne agreements, was fulfilled when a conference took place between 12 June and 27 July 1933. The World Economic and Monetary Conference took place in the newly-built Geological Museum in London and 66 nations were represented. The aims of the conference were to:
- restore economic confidence and raise prices
- encourage more economies back to the gold standard
- halt the spread of protectionism
- increase world trade.

KEY PROFILE

Franz von Papen (1879–1969) was a right-wing German statesman and diplomat who began his career as a professional soldier. He was appointed Chancellor in June 1932 at a time of increasing political turbulence in Germany. He resigned in November to be replaced by Kurt von Schleicher, but in January 1933 Papen and Schleicher recommended to Hindenburg that Adolf Hitler be appointed Chancellor due to Schelicher's inability to control the Reichstag. Papen was swiftly marginalised by the Nazis.

CROSS-REFERENCE

A profile of Édouard Herriot can be found in Chapter 17, page 146.

ACTIVITY

1. In the view of the *Spectator*'s article in Source 2, how successful were the negotiations at Lausanne?
2. Revisit von Papen's speech at the beginning of this chapter and list what he claimed had changed between 1929 and 1932 in global economic affairs.

Fig. 3   *Franklin Delano Roosevelt*

Franklin Delano Roosevelt (1882–1945), a Democrat, became US President in a landslide victory against Republican Herbert Hoover. He promised Americans a 'New Deal' to solve the Depression and introduced several policies to reduce its domestic and international consequences. Roosevelt's plans were not completely successful but his popularity saw him re-elected three times. He died in 1945 after taking America into the Second World War.

KEY TERM

autarky: economic self-sufficiency

ACTIVITY

Evaluating primary sources

What reasons does Roosevelt give in Source 3 for his rejection of the stabilisation proposals?

Coincidentally, three of the major powers had new leadership by the time of the conference: Hitler became German Chancellor in January; in the same month, Édouard Daladier became French Prime Minister; and **Franklin Roosevelt** had replaced Hoover as US President in March. MacDonald still led the British government, but as it was a coalition – the National Government – Conservatives such as Stanley Baldwin and Neville Chamberlain were gaining more influence. Once again, disagreements between the French and the British were to be a recurring theme in London. France was desperate for Britain to return to the gold standard and blamed Britain's departure for the slump in world trade. Britain's main concern, meanwhile, was the abolition of war debt.

Cancelling war debt set the USA against its European debtors. Although the impact of the Depression was felt globally, America remained one of the worst-affected, while the British economy and that of others in the 'sterling bloc' had improved relatively quickly.

Other key proposals made at the conference involved the stabilisation of currencies. The question of Roosevelt's approval was to prove decisive; he had already given an indication of his views towards stabilisation with his cautious moves to take the USA off the gold standard in April. With the hope of returning Britain to the gold standard, British and American bankers floated the idea of fixing the value of the US dollar at a low rate, and further steps were taken towards currency stabilisation. However, on 3 July Roosevelt sent the conference a 'bombshell message', repudiating attempts at stabilisation and accusing the delegates of bad faith. His mind had changed several times since becoming President, but Roosevelt finally made it clear that he would not consider any stabilisation proposal which limited America's freedom to recover from the Depression.

Without the President's approval, the conference was all but over. The delegates tried to continue their discussions, but only to keep up appearances: no agreements were made on protectionism or industrial recovery. While many lay the blame for the conference's failure squarely on Roosevelt's shoulders, historian Zara Steiner has argued neither Britain nor France were ready for an international solution to the Depression. At the Imperial Economic Conference in Ottawa in the summer of 1932, the British made it clear they had no intention of returning to the gold standard or abandoning their tariff arrangements with the Commonwealth, while France continued to pursue currency stabilisation. Once again, the leading world powers had chosen to pursue their own national interests ahead of global cooperation. The last international effort to resolve the consequences of the Depression had ended in failure, a point duly noted by nationalist governments like Hitler's Germany, which went on to adopt a policy of **autarky** – economic self-sufficiency – and Hirohito's Japan, which had already turned to aggression and empire-building in an effort to improve its own economic circumstances.

SOURCE 3

From President Roosevelt's telegram to the London Conference on 3 July 1933:

I would regard it as a catastrophe amounting to a world tragedy if the great Conference of Nations, called to bring about a more real and permanent financial stability and a greater prosperity to the masses of all Nations, should, in advance of any serious effort to consider these broader problems, allow itself to be diverted by the proposal of a purely artificial and temporary experiment affecting the monetary exchange of a few Nations only. Insistence on such action would be an excuse for the continuance of the basic economic errors that underlie so much of the present **worldwide depression**. The sound internal economic system of a Nation is a greater factor in its well-being than the price of its currency in changing terms of the currencies of other Nations. Let me be frank in saying that the United States seeks the kind of dollar which a generation hence will have the same purchasing and debt-paying power as the dollar value we hope to attain in the near future. That objective means more to the good of other Nations than a fixed ratio for a month or two in terms of the pound or franc.

CROSS-REFERENCE

The effects of the Great Depression on the economies and foreign policy of Germany, Japan and Italy are explored in Chapters 19 and 20.

ACTIVITY

Are there any common features which help to explain the failure of both the Lausanne and London Conferences?

The World Disarmament Conference, 1932–4

In its earlier stages, the failure of the Lausanne and London conferences hardly provided solid ground for optimism or cooperation, while the actions of Japan in Manchuria from 1931 (see Chapter 20) clouded the issue of disarmament and helped to split opinion. The enthusiasm for limiting weapons amongst governments was weak despite public pressure for disarmament.

Germany had huge moral bargaining power at the conference. They had been forced to disarm to the levels prescribed by the Treaty of Versailles; now they could accuse other powers of hypocrisy if levels of disarmament were not made equal. Furthermore, the impact of the Depression ensured that countries were seeking national, isolated solutions to problems by 1932.

On 2 February 1932, 59 states were represented at Geneva, including all the major powers. Support for the meeting from the general public was strong and widespread: prayers were said for its success and public meetings held. On 1 November 1931 the League of Nations' members had agreed to a truce on armaments, and a pledge was made to freeze the production of weapons while the disarmament conference was in progress.

The high hopes of the November agreements continued in Geneva, at least in the initial months. By July, **resolutions** were created to place limits on the size of artillery and tanks, and to ban the bombing of civilians and the use of

KEY TERM

resolution: in international relations, a formal commitment to achieving an objective

Fig. 4 *A peace movement campaigns in 1932*

chemicals in warfare. As so often with the initiatives of the League of Nations, however, these resolutions contained very little detail on how these objectives would be secured. For instance, despite the popularity of the resolution prohibiting the bombing of civilian populations, nations were reluctant to give up the right to build planes with the capacity to drop bombs.

A CLOSER LOOK

Rearmament and Germany

The Weimar government had already started a secret rearmament programme by 1928: a five-year plan to expand the army, build tanks and aircraft. In July 1932 German delegates in Geneva introduced proposals for all countries to disarm to the level it had been forced to in 1919. When this was rejected, the Germans left the conference. It was not until January 1933 when 'equality of armaments' was accepted that Germany returned to negotiate. When Hitler became Chancellor on 30 January, however, he began to secretly rearm on a far more ambitious scale than his predecessors. He withdrew Germany from the disarmament conference in October 1933 and then from the League of Nations itself. The conference finally ended in 1934.

ACTIVITY

1. Prepare for a class debate on the reasons for the failure of the World Disarmament Conference. One side should argue that Germany was the most responsible, while the other should argue that the reluctance of the other powers was more to blame.
2. Use a line graph to plot the changes in Germany's relationship with the rest of the world (excluding France) from 1918 to 1934. On the y axis label 10 at the top, representing 'trust and equality', and 0 at the bottom representing 'mistrust and inferiority'. On the x axis label the years. In the graph itself you should also label the events which caused or represented a change, in or out of Germany's favour.

Summary

The Great Depression had severe consequences for international relations, and ultimately led to the end of the dream of global disarmament. To encourage countries' economic recovery from the Depression, the financial terms of the Treaty of Versailles had been significantly watered down, but the tariff war and its impact on world trade damaged the prospects for greater international cooperation. The increasing tendency of countries to prioritise their own domestic recovery was to have significant consequences in the 1930s.

ACTIVITY

Summary

Draw up a table to summarise the meetings and agreements made on economic issues in this chapter. You should include the following categories: names (and any alternatives), dates, location, delegates, overall aims, any individual countries' aims, terms agreed, immediate successes and failures.

PRACTICE QUESTION

'The actions of the USA were the most important reason for the failure of the economic conferences in the early 1930s.'
Assess the validity of this view.

STUDY TIP

If you are considering the role of a country in causing a particular outcome, remember to consider not just the role of other nations, but also of other forces or issues. For example, almost every world power was reluctant to pursue an international approach to solving the Great Depression, which was a major factor in the failure of the conferences and not the action of just one nation.

 PRACTICE QUESTION

Evaluating primary sources

With reference to Sources 1, 2 and 3, and your understanding of the historical context, assess the value of these three sources to an historian studying the problems faced by statesmen negotiating international agreements between 1929 and 1933.

STUDY TIP

It is important that you take different dates and contexts into account when evaluating not just their provenance, but their tone as well. For example, in Source 1 Von Papen is addressing an international conference with the purpose of persuading his fellow statesmen to treat Germany more favourably; back in Germany the political situation was increasingly turbulent, with Nazi ideas winning considerable support. There is, therefore, a large degree of exaggeration in his speech which you need to consider carefully. All three sources refer to the importance of the domestic political issues at the time they were produced. Note also that Source 2, whilst referring to statesmen, is a newspaper article. How does this affect its value?

19 Changing balance of power

LEARNING OBJECTIVES

In this chapter you will learn about:

- Mussolini's impact on foreign relations

- the changing ambitions of Japan in the 1930s

- Hitler's impact on foreign relations

- relations between Italy and Germany and the Western powers before 1935.

KEY CHRONOLOGY

October 1922	Mussolini becomes Prime Minister of Italy
25 December 1926	Accession of Emperor Hirohito in Japan
18 September 1931	Japanese-owned railway in Manchuria bombed
30 January 1933	Hitler becomes German Chancellor
July 1933	Four Power Pact agreed
July 1934	Italy prevents *Anschluss*
April 1935	Stresa conference

KEY TERM

leverage: a strong negotiating position; a person who has good leverage is able to influence others

CROSS-REFERENCE

The reasons for Italy's entry into the war in 1915 are explored in Chapter 12.

The ambitions of three powers – Italy, Japan and Germany – significantly challenged the post-war balance of power in the 1930s. As seen in Chapter 18, the new realities of the global economic situation in the aftermath of the Depression encouraged the revision of key terms in the post-war peace settlements. The Western democracies continued to conduct international relations as they had in the 1920s, as they began to accept the grievances of the defeated powers. Although Mussolini cooperated with the democracies in the 1920s and even up to 1935 with the Stresa Pact, the expansionist aims of Hitler and the Japanese provided a strong catalyst for significant changes in the global balance of power.

Fig. 1. *Hitler and Mussolini, the fascist leaders of Germany and Italy, at a meeting in 1937*

The ambitions of Italy

Before and after the First World War, Italy aspired to Great Power status, but was not treated as an equal by Britain and France. The importance of Italy to European peace, however, grew in response to the growing threat of both Nazi Germany and the communist USSR, giving Italy's dictator, Mussolini, considerable **leverage** in the 1920s and 1930s.

The rise of fascism

Italy had intervened in the First World War on the side of the Allies, but found itself heavily defeated by Austria in the Battle of Caparetto in 1917. The armistice of 1918 was a relief for Italy, but Mussolini referred to it as a 'mutilated victory' when it became clear that the promises made in the Treaty of London in 1915 would not all be fulfilled. The mood in Italy was one of anger and fear of revolution: strikes, looting, demonstrations and riots were commonplace. In 1919 Mussolini and other disillusioned former soldiers formed a new movement, the *Fasci di Combattimento* (loosely translated as 'league of combat'), later shortened to fascism. Support for the fascist movement increased, and by 29 October 1922, **King Victor Emmanuel** invited Mussolini to form a government. Mussolini had transformed Italy into a one-party state.

Mussolini's foreign policy

Mussolini's foreign policy aims

Mussolini hoped to gain greater control over Italy's spheres of influence in the Balkans and around the Mediterranean. His foreign policy also involved claiming the 'unredeemed' territory around the Adriatic which was promised to Italy in 1915 but not granted under the 1919 treaties. Some historians have argued that Mussolini's increasingly aggressive policies were meant to serve as a distraction from domestic problems (a charge also levelled at the leaders of the Great Powers before the First World War). More recently, historians have concluded that he was in fact responding to circumstances as they arose, such as the impact of the Great Depression and the growing strength of Nazi Germany.

The nature and consistency of Italy's foreign policy aims under Mussolini are contested by historians but it is unlikely that he had to stick to a pre-defined set of objectives, unlike Hitler. The fascist commitment to strength and violence demanded a foreign policy with concurrent values: Mussolini himself declared 'it is a crime not to be strong', which explains Italy's involvement in Libya from 1922 onwards. Libya had been an Italian colony since 1912, but revolts by the native population were frequent and often severe, and the previous liberal government had been unable to keep the area under control. Upon Mussolini's rise to power, Italian troops began to regain control with a more decisive and aggressive course of action, but still **guerrilla** troops stopped Italy from being able to claim full power over Libya. In 1928, Mussolini escalated his army's involvement, and Libyans were subjected to barbaric treatment including the rounding up of civilians into concentration camps, the desecration of mosques and the use of chemical weapons. In January 1932, the Italian governor of the region declared the 'Pacification of Libya' complete.

Fig. 2   *Victor Emmanuel III*

Victor Emmanuel III (1869–1947) was King of Italy from 1900. As Mussolini turned Italy into a dictatorship, Victor Emmanuel became little more than a figurehead. By 1943 Italy was facing defeat in the Second World War and he had Mussolini arrested. He abdicated in favour of his son in 1946 but the Italians voted to become a republic instead. The last King of Italy died in exile.

Guerrilla tactics are explained in Chapter 3.

Fig. 3   *Italian soldiers in Libya in 1930*

The first agreement made between Britain, France and Italy, in July 1933, included Germany: at this stage Hitler was still trying to gain approval as a statesman by cooperating with his foreign counterparts, while attempting to keep his rearmament plans secret. The Four Power Pact agreed between the states involved the promise for each of them to keep the peace for ten years, which Germany broke almost immediately by withdrawing from the Disarmament Conference in 1933, and publicly announcing Germany's rearmament programme on 16 March 1935. The Pact was never ratified, but it alienated the USSR, which was still being excluded from major agreements 15 years after the Bolshevik Revolution. In January 1935 Italy and France agreed to respect each other's European and colonial borders under the Rome Agreements, a move championed by the pro-Italian Foreign Minister of France, Pierre Laval.

Germany's first attempt to take over Austria (see below) in 1934 alarmed Mussolini: Italy shared a border with Austria and he was concerned that the Italian sphere of influence around the Balkans was being threatened. Mussolini joined the Stresa Conference which assembled in April 1935. As part of the 'Stresa Front', Britain, Italy and France agreed to oppose 'by all practical means, any unilateral repudiation of treaties, which may endanger the peace of Europe'. While the paperwork did little to discourage Hitler, Mussolini felt assured that Britain and France would not intervene in his planned invasion of **Abyssinia**.

CROSS-REFERENCE

Italy's planned invasion of Abyssinia is detailed in Chapter 20, page 172.

A CLOSER LOOK

Italy's relations with Britain and France

It was not until Hitler rose to power that Britain and France began to see Mussolini as a valuable ally: Sir John Simon, British Foreign Secretary even described Italy as 'the key to European peace'. Fascism was repugnant to the liberal democracies of Britain and France, but Italian foreign policy was less dangerous than Hitler's. (Ironically, Nazism was nonetheless preferable to Soviet communism, which was one of many reasons why Hitler was appeased until 1939.) By working with Italy, its former allies hoped to maintain the balance of power in Europe.

ACTIVITY

How much evidence is there to suggest that Italian foreign policy under Mussolini was inconsistent?

Fig. 4 *Map of south-east Europe in 1924*

SOURCE 1

From the 'Joint Resolution of the Stresa Conference', the agreement made by Italy, Britain and France on 14 April 1935:

The representatives of Italy, France and the United Kingdom have examined the general European situation in the light of the decision taken on the 16th March by the German Government. In approaching the problem of armaments, the Representatives of the three Powers recalled that the London communiqué envisaged an agreement to be freely negotiated with Germany to take the place of the relevant clauses of Part V of the Treaty of Versailles. It was regretfully recognised that the method of unilateral repudiation adopted by the German Government, at a moment when steps were being taken to promote a freely negotiated settlement of the question of armaments, had undermined public confidence in the security of a peaceful order. The three Powers, nevertheless, reaffirm their earnest desire to sustain peace by establishing a sense of security, and declare for themselves that they remain anxious to join in every practicable effort for promoting international agreement on the limitation of armaments.

The ambitions of Japan

Japanese government in the 1920s and 1930s

Japan was ruled by an Emperor, a hereditary title which bestowed upon the incumbent huge power and the status of *arahitogami*, making him a god to his people, according to the teachings of the State Shinto religion founded in 1868. **Emperor Hirohito,** who came to the throne in 1926, was the head of both the government and the army. The Japanese political system had been established in 1889 under the Meiji Constitution, and comprised two parliamentary houses along similar lines to European governments. Although the constitution contained some liberal elements and the Emperor did not have absolute power, he appointed prime ministers and had the power to dissolve the lower house, and he was able to allow his 'inner circle' of advisers to wield considerable influence.

Hirohito's enthronement in 1928 provided a sharp contrast between the lavish court ceremony and the grinding poverty of the Japanese countryside. The mood was, however, patriotic, and about to be exploited by nationalists who were becoming increasingly influential. Japanese nationalism had clear expansionist aims: in a reflection of its extremely hierarchical society, Japanese school children were taught that they were the superior race, and racist attitudes towards the Chinese were encouraged. (There was also to be a backlash against Westernisation, sparking a particular hatred towards the USA.) This 'master race' ideology became particularly prevalent in the army, which by the late 1920s enjoyed a strong influence on government policy.

Japanese expansionism

The Depression hit Japan very hard. With its population growing by 1 million per year, the government soon found itself unable to feed its people: even subsistence farmers struggled to feed their families. As a small nation with scarce natural resources, Japan relied on imports, and also necessarily relied on exports to maintain a balance of trade. After 1929, rice had to be imported to prevent starvation, and Japan's main export, silk, suffered a collapse in prices. To make matters worse, tariffs were imposed by America and much of Europe, Japan's exports sank to their lowest ever level, dropping by 40 per cent between 1929 and 1930. Government ministers hoped to solve Japan's

Fig. 5 *Emperor Hirohito*

Emperor Hirohito (1901–1989) inherited the title of Emperor in 1926. The Meiji Constituion of 1889 gave Japanese emperors great power, but Hirohito rarely opposed the policies of his ministers and military chiefs. Historians are divided over his true role in Japan's foreign policy in the 1930s and 1940s. He was forced to relinquish much of his power after 1945, but remained Emperor until his death.

problems with emigration, but this failed and the prospect of expansion became a popular alternative.

To the minds of nationalists in the Japanese army, the solution was obvious: colonise China, exploit its natural resources and relieve the overcrowding in Japan. An excuse for an invasion was ready – China appeared to be in desperate need of stable government. Its Emperor had been overthrown in 1911 and much of China was under the volatile control of local warlords. The Japanese were already in a strong position in one of China's closest provinces, **Manchuria**: most Japanese immigrants (70 per cent of all foreigners in China) lived there, and 35 per cent of foreign investment in China was provided by the Japanese, mostly in Manchuria, including the South Manchurian Railway which had helped to spread Japanese political and economic influence in the region.

Japanese relations with other world powers in the early 1930s also seemed to provide good reasons for expansion into China. Victory in the Russo–Japanese War (see Chapter 6) helped Japan to world power status, ended rivalry with Russia in the Far East and allowed Japan to annex Korea, increasing its sphere of influence. After the Bolshevik Revolution, Japan was appreciated by the West as an ally against communism, but the **Washington Naval Treaty of 1921–2** restricted Japanese naval development to 70 per cent of Britain and America's. In 1930 the London Naval Treaty helped widen the existing division between the civilian and military authorities in Japan, as the latter believed that government ministers had not done enough to achieve equality of naval armaments with the West.

CROSS-REFERENCE

The terms agreed at the Washington Conference of 1921–2 are explained fully in Chapter 16.

The beginning of the Japanese invasion of Manchuria is explored in Chapter 20.

SOURCE 2

From the diary, written 1945–48, of Hedeki Tojo, a Japanese army official who became a major general in 1933 and later Prime Minister of Japan. In this extract, he sought to defend Japan's foreign policy and involvement in the Second World War:

Before the Second World War, Japan's peaceful commercial relations were successively obstructed, primarily by the American rupture of commercial relations, and this was a grave threat to the survival of Japan… Even military ministers have no more than a certain amount of control. It is customary that they have the right and the power to participate, from a political and military point of view, in the planning of actual operations… I would point out that Japan's proposal at the Versailles Peace Conference on the principle of racial equality was rejected by delegates such as those from Britain and the United States… I would point out that the cultural advance of the Japanese people has been suppressed in the past… It goes without saying that when survival is threatened, struggles erupt between peoples, and unfortunate wars between nations result… Justice has nothing to do with victor nations and vanquished nations, but must be a moral standard that all the world's peoples can agree to.

ACTIVITY

Evaluating primary sources

What arguments does Tojo use to make Japan's actions appear reasonable?

There was serious talk of a *coup d'état* by the nationalist movement, but it was decided instead to force the government's hand in relation to the Manchurian project.

The ambitions of Germany

As Germany's Chancellor, Hitler made no secret of his intention to dismantle democracy and abandon Germany's adherence to the post-war settlement. On 30 June 1934, Hitler declared himself **Führer** und Reichskanzler ('leader and chancellor') and made the army swear a personal oath of allegiance to him. In

KEY TERM

Führer: German for 'leader'; in Nazi ideology it took on the connotation of undisputed dictator

1933 he rapidly expanded the rearmament programme begun in 1928 by the Weimar government, but did not formally withdraw Germany from the World Disarmament Conference until October. Hitler made Germany's rearmament public with a rally in March 1935.

SOURCE 3

Hitler's letter to Colonel Walther von Reichenau, on Germany's international position on 4 December 1932. Reichenau was already a Nazi supporter, but in the letter Hitler sought to explain his strong hostility to the von Schleicher government:

While our political and military strategists regard German rearmament as a technical or organisational matter, I see the precondition for any rearmament as the creation of a new German national unity of mind and of will. Without the solution of this problem all talk of 'equality of rights' and 'rearmament' is superficial and idle chatter. This creation of a unity of ideology, mind, and will among our people is the task which I set myself fourteen years ago and which I have struggled to achieve ever since. No great ideas and reforms of humanity have ever come from the professionals. Why should it be any different today? However, recognition of this historical truth does not relieve the person who has taken the measure of this question in all its enormous significance from the duty of working to resolve it. I must, therefore, however regretfully, make a stand against, indeed must combat, any German government which is not ready and determined to carry out this inward rearmament of the German nation. All other measures follow from it.

CROSS-REFERENCE

The impact of the Depression on Germany is explained in Chapter 18.

Fig. 6 *Soldiers in Berlin swearing the oath of loyalty to Adolf Hitler, 1934*

ACTIVITY

Evaluating primary sources

1. According to Hitler, what key ideological principles were essential to Germany in 1932?
2. Which phrases does Hitler use in Source 3 to persuade Reichenau that rearmament is essential to the success of Germany?
3. How valuable is Source 3 to an historian studying the reasons why Germany rearmed in the 1930s?

Relations between Germany and Italy

Mussolini had much to fear from an aggressive Germany:

- Hitler had made his aim of achieving *Anschluss* with Austria clear. German expansion into Austria would potentially threaten Italy's north-east border.
- If Germany continued to expand, Italy's sphere of influence in the Balkans would be endangered.

The first fear was realised within a year of Hitler's chancellorship, although its initial impetus came from Mussolini himself. He encouraged Engelbert Dollfuss, the fascist but anti-Nazi Chancellor of Austria, to establish an authoritarian regime with Italy's support. In response, Austrian Nazis murdered Dollfuss in an attempted *coup d'état* on 25 July 1934. Mussolini was outraged, and mobilised his troops on the Italo–Austrian border at the Brenner Pass to dissuade Germany from taking Austria by force. Hitler backed down, but would attempt an *Anschluss* again in 1938 with very different results.

By concluding the Rome Agreements in January 1935 with France (by which the two nations agreed to respect each other's European and colonial

CROSS-REFERENCE

The union of Germany and Austria was forbidden by the Treaty of Versailles; see Chapter 14 for details.

The development of Italo–German relations, including the Rome–Berlin Axis, are explored in Chapter 22.

The consequences of Italy's alignment with Germany, and of Britain and France's appeasement of Hitler are explained in Chapters 22 and 23.

borders) and the Stresa Front with France and Britain, Mussolini hoped to secure the support of Italy's former allies in the event of German aggression threatening its interests. Within two years, however, Italy had made two agreements with Hitler which brought the two fascist powers closer together.

Summary

By 1935, the changing ambitions of Italy, Japan and Germany presented severe, and eventually insurmountable, challenges to the post-war settlement:

- Italy had committed itself to a dynamic foreign policy under Mussolini. It was to make its bid for Great Power status by invading Abyssinia.
- Japan had a strong emperor but a weak government, which had been unable to resolve the problems of the Great Depression and was then powerless to prevent the Japanese Army from invading Manchuria, a move designed to relieve Japanese over-population and secure raw materials.
- Germany had abandoned democracy for Nazism, and Hitler wasted little time in abolishing the Treaty of Versailles by rearming Germany, and helping to provoke an attempted *coup d'état* in Austria.

ACTIVITY

Summary

Construct a timeline of the events in this chapter, with a line in the middle of the page. On one side, record the events affecting the individual countries of Italy, Japan and Germany, and on the other record the international events or agreements.

STUDY TIP

Considering the author and purpose of sources is always essential when judging their use, but dictators or members of authoritarian governments can pose particular issues. Take into account what stage of their political career they are at, and who they are addressing; this will affect the level of propaganda evident in their viewpoint. You should also take account of the 'diplomatic language' evident in Source 1. Also, note carefully the times and contexts of various sources.

 PRACTICE QUESTION

Evaluating primary sources

Study Sources 1 and 2. With reference to these sources and your understanding of the historical context, assess the value of these three sources to an historian studying the reasons for threats to world peace in the early 1930s.

20 The collapse of collective security

Collective security was the underlying principle of the League of Nations: the idea that states should cooperate and support each other if one was threatened by another power. The security of each country was therefore – in theory – far stronger than if they acted alone. The pursuit of collective security had been broadly successful in the 1920s but was significantly challenged by the changing balance of power brought about by the new ambitions of Germany, Italy and Japan. By the time Stanley Baldwin made the speech below, the principle of collective security was under threat due to the practicalities of enforcing it.

SOURCE 1

From a speech by British Prime Minister Stanley Baldwin to the House of Commons on 23 June 1936:

Where there is an aggressor it would be quite impossible for the nations that wished to exercise the power of military sanctions against the aggressor or a group of aggressors to do it unless they are in a position to do it at once and together. Collective security failed ultimately because of the reluctance of nearly all the nations in Europe to proceed to what I might call military sanctions. The real reason, or the main reason, was that we discovered in the process of weeks that there was no country except the aggressor country which was ready for war. If collective action is to be a reality and not merely a thing to be talked about, it means not only that every country is to be ready for war; but must be ready to go to war at once. That is a terrible thing, but it is an essential part of collective security.

ACTIVITY

Evaluating primary sources

What does Baldwin identify as the major problems with the principle of collective security?

The Manchurian Crisis, 1931

In response to Japan's internal problems (see pages 165–166), influential nationalists in the Japanese army were determined to colonise China. In 1931 the **Kwantung army** was stationed in Manchuria, a province of China over which Japan already had political and economic influence. Kwantung officers exploded a bomb on the Japanese-owned South Manchurian Railway on 18 September 1931 and blamed it on local Chinese troops. Within hours, the town of Mukden had been taken over by Japanese forces. Four days later, Kwantung troops occupied towns within a 200-mile radius of Mukden.

A CLOSER LOOK

The **Kwantung army** was the largest and most influential military group of the Japanese army. It had an increasingly strong influence over civilian government in the 1930s

LEARNING OBJECTIVES

In this chapter you will learn about:

- reasons for the failure of the League of Nations in the Manchurian and Abyssinia Crises

- the consequences of the failure of the League of Nations in Manchuria and Abyssinia and the collapse of collective security.

KEY CHRONOLOGY

18 September 1931	Bomb explodes on Chinese-owned railway in Manchuria
21 September 1931	China appeals to League of Nations following Manchurian incident
10 December 1931	Lytton Commission established to investigate
January 1932	Japanese army operations spread to Shanghai
10 October 1932	Lytton report published
March 1933	Japan withdraws from the League
3 October 1935	Italy invades Abyssinia
December 1935	Hoare–Laval Pact discussed
May 1936	Italy declares victory in the conquest of Abyssinia

CROSS-REFERENCE

The League of Nations is first introduced in Chapter 14; you can find an analysis of its work in the 1920s in Chapter 16.

The League of Nations' response

On 21 September, the Chinese appealed to the League of Nations under Article 11 of the Covenant, which stated that any war or threat of war necessitated an emergency meeting of the Council, summoned by the Secretary General. The Japanese were ordered to withdraw by the next council meeting on 16 November 1931, but Kwantung officers ignored this deadline.

On 10 December, a commission was ordered to investigate the claims of China and Japan in Manchuria and recommend solutions. This was chaired by the British politician Victor Bulwer-Lytton and made up of French, Italian, German and American representatives, with Chinese and Japanese advisers. The commission landed in China on 29 February 1932, but progress towards a thorough investigation was painstakingly slow, exacerbated by deliberate Japanese obstruction.

Britain, with its commercial interests in China and former alliance with Japan, became a reluctant focus of the West's reaction to the Manchurian incident. The timing, however, was unfortunate: the economic effects of the Great Depression were yet to be resolved, and Britain simply could not afford to send a peacekeeping force to such a remote conflict. Public opinion was correspondingly pessimistic. The prospect of imposing economic sanctions on Japan to force her withdrawal – one of the few 'weapons' in the League's arsenal – was a non-starter as the USA, Japan's main trading partner, had already refused to engage in an international response to the crisis, despite being a member of the Lytton Commission.

Fig. 1 *The Lytton Commission, who published a report on the Manchurian Question for the League of Nations*

A CLOSER LOOK

The roles of Simon and Stimson

The British Foreign Secretary at the time of the crisis, John Simon, attracted criticism from contemporaries, and later from historians. Simon's speech at Geneva in December 1932, in which he failed to criticise the actions of the Japanese, appeared very conciliatory, and set a precedent for the appeasement of aggressors.

US secretary of state Henry Stimson's role was also significant. Although a US delegation was present at council meetings of the League for the first time in response to the crisis, Stimson soon grew frustrated with attempts to make Japan and China recognise the Kellogg–Briand Pact. In January 1932 America published the Stimson Doctrine. This stated that the USA would refuse to recognise any agreement between China and Japan which threatened American interests, or to recognise any territorial changes as a result of aggression. The doctrine alienated the Japanese, as it was now highly unlikely to have American approval for its expansion into China.

With no firm deterrent from the international community, the Japanese forces in China extended their strategic objectives. By the end of 1932 the invasion forces had pushed on to Shanghai, the largest port in Asia, and all of Manchuria was under Japanese control. To emphasise this development, the province was renamed Manchukuo in March, and the former Chinese Emperor, Henry Pu Yi, was installed as a puppet ruler under Japanese direction.

Fig. 2 *Chinese resistance to the Japanese invasion made the conflict long and often brutal*

The consequences of the League's decisions

Despite the escalation of the Japanese invasion throughout 1932, the 139-page Lytton report was not published until 10 October. It condemned the creation of Manchukuo as a Japanese protectorate, which directly contravened the principle of self-determination, and insisted on the withdrawal of Japanese forces from the region. The Japanese delegation led by Matsuoka was furious: he argued angrily that China was equally to blame for the conflict. All member states of the Council voted in favour of the Lytton report, except Japan; upon hearing the result of the vote, Matsuoka led his delegation in a walk-out.

From Matsuoka's address to the League Council on 6 December 1932 in response to the Lytton report compiled by League of Nation's investigators into the Japanese invasion of Manchuria:

Japan is a loyal supporter of the League of Nations. In conformity with the principles of peace, on which the League is founded, we have striven to avoid war for many years under provocations that, prior to the drafting of the Covenant, would certainly have brought it about. Our adherence to the Covenant has been a guiding principle in our foreign policy for the thirteen years of the League's existence.

Our Government was still persisting earnestly in efforts to induce the Chinese Government to see the light of reason when the incident of September 18th, 1931, took place. We wanted no such situation as has developed. We sought in Manchuria only the observance of our treaty rights and the safety of the lives of our people and their property. We wanted from China the right to trade, according to existing treaties, free from unwarranted interference and molestation. But our policy of patience and our efforts at persuasion were misinterpreted by the Chinese people. Our attitude was regarded as weakness, and provocations became persistently more unbearable.

ACTIVITY

Study Source 2 and answer the following questions:
1. How does Matsuoka justify Japan's actions and make it appear that Japan had acted reasonably?
2. What is the value of Matsuoka's speech to an historian studying Japan's reasons for leaving the League of Nations?

Discussions on what action to take were no easier following Japan's withdrawal from the process. Talks continued in late 1932 and early 1933

KEY TERM

Abyssinia: an alternative name for the Ethiopian Empire in the 1930s

CROSS-REFERENCE

The Scramble for Africa, which set a precedent for Italian actions in North Africa, is explored in Chapter 3.

KEY PROFILE

Fig. 3   *Haile Selassie*

Haile Selassie (1892–1975) became Emperor of Ethiopia in 1930. As regent, he had progressive policies and achieved Ethiopia's entrance into the League of Nations. In 1931 he introduced Ethiopia's first written constitution. He fled the country following Italy's invasion but was restored as Emperor in 1941. Selassie became a popular and respected figure but was deposed in 1974 following a revolution.

CROSS-REFERENCE

The details of the Stresa Pact can be found in Chapter 19.

with very little agreement. In February, the issue was referred to the Assembly, which contained stronger anti-Japanese sentiments and more member states. A new report was drafted, incorporating Lytton's findings and insisting on both the Japanese army's withdrawal from Manchuria and Japanese recognition of China's rights to the region. It still fell short of condemning Japan, but was adopted on 24 February by 42 votes to one. The Japanese ignored both reports, and left the League altogether in March 1933.

The Abyssinian Crisis

Italy's planned invasion

Having completed the 'Pacification of Libya' (see page 163), Mussolini turned his attention to establishing an empire in East Africa. **Abyssinia** was a ripe target: ruled by **Haile Selassie**, the country was one of the only two remaining independent states in Africa, but was economically underdeveloped and had no modern military capabilities. Also the status of the borders of Abyssinia was not clear; it would be easy for Italy to turn a border dispute into the justification for an invasion.

Italian troops began to occupy positions around Abyssinia's ambiguous borders, and the hoped-for provocation occurred in December 1934 in Walwal. In a skirmish between Italian and Abyssinian soldiers, 30 Italians were killed. Mussolini insisted on a thorough apology from the Abyssinians and ordered that they pay heavy compensation. Abyssinia appealed to the League of Nations to arbitrate and an enquiry was set up. Nothing practical, however, was done to prevent a full-scale Italian invasion in October 1935.

The League's response

Mussolini sought assurances that neither Britain nor France would strongly oppose his Abyssinian ambitions. The Rome Agreements with France in January 1935 convinced him of French support, which was further reinforced by the **Stresa Pact** in April. The Italian dictator correctly calculated that both Britain and France would be far more concerned by Hitler's rearmament and the possible consequences for the peace in Europe for them to risk Italy's friendship by obstructing the Abyssinian invasion. Germany's rearmament also worried Italy, however; sending 650,000 troops to Africa could expose Italy to potential German aggression. Again, the Stresa Pact convinced Mussolini that the risk was low.

The invasion was thoroughly executed: Mussolini insisted on ten army divisions rather than the three recommended by his generals, and the Italian army made full use of their modern equipment – tanks, planes and poison gas – against often barefooted Abyssinians who fought defiantly with rifles and spears. The Italians captured the capital Addis Ababa, forced Haile Selassie to flee, and declared victory in May 1936.

The League of Nations was quick to respond to Italian aggression: within a week of the invasion it declared Italy to be the aggressor and condemned Italy's action as an unprovoked invasion in contravention of the Covenant. Britain led the call to impose economic sanctions on Italy, but as world trade was yet to fully recover following the Depression, there was little international enthusiasm for the move. Committing their own troops, however, was even less palatable to member states, and a series of economic restrictions was imposed on Italy. The nature of the sanctions, though, was once again compromised by nations asserting their own interests.

Thinking point

Of the sanctions avoided, which one do you think did the most damage to the effectiveness of the League's response?

Sanctions imposed	Sanctions avoided
• The sale of armaments to Italy was banned • Trading some other goods, including gold, rubber, tin and textiles, with Italy was banned • Loans to Italy were prohibited • League members could not import Italian goods	• Oil exports to Italy were not banned; it was argued that Italy would simply get oil from the USA, making the sanction useless • Coal exports to Italy were not banned; it was argued that British coal-mining would be adversely affected – 30,000 could lose their jobs • The Suez Canal, jointly owned by Britain and France, was not closed to Italian ships

ITALY GROWS CLOSER TO GERMANY.

The fear held by Britain and France that Italy would abandon the Stresa Front and ally with Germany – and perhaps provoke war immediately afterwards – is highlighted by the weakness of the sanctions that were eventually decided upon. Allowing oil and coal into Italy helped to resource its war machine,

THE AWFUL WARNING.

FRANCE AND ENGLAND
(*together ?*).
{ "WE DON'T WANT YOU TO FIGHT,
  BUT, BY JINGO, IF YOU DO,
  WE SHALL PROBABLY ISSUE A JOINT MEMORANDUM
  SUGGESTING A MILD DISAPPROVAL OF YOU."

Fig. 4 *A Punch cartoon, 1935, of Britain and France wagging their fingers at Mussolini in an ineffective protest*

The Hoare–Laval Pact

In December 1935 British Foreign Secretary Samuel Hoare and French Prime Minister Pierre Laval secretly discussed a way to end the fighting in Abyssinia with a settlement strongly in Italy's favour. They proposed that Italy should acquire the best farming land in Abyssinia and its richest mineral resources; Abyssinia would be left with one-third of its territory before the invasion, and mostly barren land. The details of the Hoare–Laval Pact, however, were leaked to the French press and there was public outcry against the plan.

while keeping the Suez Canal open meant that the Italian army had an uninterrupted and convenient supply line to continue its campaign. In many ways the sanctions imposed were the worst of both worlds: they weren't strong enough to convince Mussolini to abandon the invasion, but they were frustrating enough to turn Italian opinion against the League of Nations and towards an alliance with Germany.

The Hoare–Laval Pact, a secret proposal between the British Foreign Secretary and the French Prime Minister, was an attempt to reconcile the conflicting priorities of the League Council, but without its involvement. The terms of the pact (see A Closer Look) were discussed privately, but the details were leaked to the public. Many citizens of the Western democracies viewed the plans as clear appeasement of an aggressor, making the Pact deeply unpopular: the League would have been undermined by a separate agreement outside its jurisdiction; it would also have rewarded Italy with land at the expense of the victim nation, Abyssinia. The Pact was soon dropped; meanwhile, the painfully slow speed of the discussions over whether or not to pursue a ban on oil exports to Italy also took its toll: by February 1936, when it was decided that a prohibition would be worthwhile, even with American supplies, Italy had almost completed its conquest of Abyssinia.

ACTIVITY

Summary

Create a Venn diagram to show the differences and similarities between the Manchurian and Abyssinian crises. Consider causes, the League's response, and consequences.

ACTIVITY

Evaluating primary sources

1. Which nation do you think Haile Selassie is referring to which the phrase 'the attitude of a certain government'?
2. After studying the remainder of this unit, search for the full text of Haile Selassie's speech online, in which he makes a number of predictions about the consequences of the League's failure in Abyssinia. How accurate are his forecasts?

SOURCE 3

From Haile Selassie's speech to the League of Nations in June 1936. Selassie was in exile and the League's attention was focused on Germany, not Abyssinia:

In December 1935, the Council made it quite clear that its feelings were in harmony with those of hundreds of millions of people who, in all parts of the world, had protested against the proposal to dismember Ethiopia. It was constantly repeated that there was not merely a conflict between the Italian Government and the League of Nations; I was defending the cause of all small peoples who are threatened with aggression. What has become of the promises made to me in October 1935? I noted with grief, but without surprise that three Powers considered their undertakings under the Covenant as absolutely of no value. Their connections with Italy impelled them to refuse to take any measures whatsoever in order to stop Italian aggression. On the contrary, it was a profound disappointment to me to learn the attitude of a certain Government which, whilst ever protesting its scrupulous attachment to the Covenant, has tirelessly used all its efforts to prevent its observance.

The consequences of the failure of the League of Nations' responses to Manchuria and Abyssinia

The Manchurian and Abyssinian crises, and the League's response to them, damaged the League's reputation as an effective conciliator. The USA's decision not to join the League – a considerable weakness since 1920 – was not reversed by the experience of Japanese and Italian aggression; in fact America was further put off by the perceived 'dodgy dealing' of the Hoare–Laval Pact and the potential impact of world trade caused by Italian sanctions, while the Stimson Doctrine cemented its isolationism in response to the Manchurian crisis. The USSR also noted the League's inability to deter or halt aggression, making it far less likely to engage with collective security.

The Manchurian Crisis highlighted the League's inherent weaknesses and the self-interest of countries as a result of the Depression. It had failed to prevent a member state from invading and occupying another. The subsequent loss of Japan as a member suggested that even a Council colleague could commit an act of aggression and then withdraw with no meaningful consequences. Britain, due to its economic restraints and public opinion, felt it had no grounds for imposing any sanctions against Japan, and France was unwilling to upset the status quo in the Far East. While Mussolini calculated that his own quest for imperial glory would receive as little practical censure as Japan's had, the smaller states, particularly of Europe, could only be worried by the precedent set by Japan.

Ultimately, perhaps the most damaging outcome of the Manchurian and Abyssinian Crises was the simple point that both Japan and Italy had got away with acts of aggression against member states, which the League had been powerless to stop. This suggested that collective security would fail in the 1930s, and that nations were better off pursuing private arrangements with other powers just as they had done before the First World War. It also suggested to Hitler that any protests the League made against the pursuit of his own foreign policy goals would be weak and easily ignored.

A CLOSER LOOK

Historians' debates on the failures of the League

The two major debates surrounding the Manchurian and Abyssinian crises are: to what extent each crisis was responsible for the League's collapse; and to what extent the Second World War was due to the League's collapse. Before either crisis was over, Oxford history professor H.A.L. Fisher argued that the core objective of the League of Nations was doomed to failure, as it was impossible for all countries to commit themselves to a permanent peace: 'League or no League, a country which is determined to have war can always have it.'

Historian Alan J.P. Taylor claimed that the refusal to consider, much less to adopt, the Hoare–Laval Pact was foolish, as it differed little in nature from the League's tacit acceptance of Japan's occupation of Manchuria. In *The Origins of the Second World War* (1961) Taylor asserted that the Pact would 'end the war; satisfied Italy; and left Abyssinia with a more workable, national territory.' He also argued that it was the Abyssinian crisis which caused the League's ultimate demise: 'One day it was a powerful body imposing sanctions, the next it was an empty sham, everyone scuttling from it as quickly as possible. Hitler watched.'

Historians including James Joll and T.A. Morris took a similar view to Taylor, but recently it has been argued that the League's inherent weaknesses and the far more difficult circumstances of the 1930s were more to blame. History professors Zara Steiner and Susan Pederson are proponents of this view, with Pederson asserting that 'Diplomacy requires leaders who can speak for their states; it requires secrecy; and it requires the ability to make credible threats. The Covenant's security arrangements met none of these criteria.'

FISHER – core objective of LoN doomed to fail.

TAYLOR – Abyssinia was L ultimate demise.

JOll & MORRIS –

Summary

In the cases of both Manchuria and Abyssinia, both aggressor nations had some degree of support from the leaders of the League: the Japanese because of existing spheres of influence in China and Indochina; and the Italians because of their potential as an ally against Germany. The methods used by the Japanese and Italian armies to achieve their goals attracted justified criticism,

STUDY TIP

Try to focus on the key words; in this case, 'response', 'decisive' and 'ineffective'. Consider each crisis carefully on its own merits, but ensure you include several comparisons. Remember that simply mentioning both crises in the same paragraph doesn't necessarily mean you are comparing: try to use useful phrases like 'in contrast' and 'by comparison'.

but the League was unable or unwilling to enforce meaningful sanctions. It was highly unlikely that the next use of aggression would be effectively stopped, and the cause of internationalism was more or less abandoned after Abyssinia. The League itself continued to operate, with far less support from either the public or it member states, until the outbreak of war in Europe in September 1939.

 PRACTICE QUESTION

'The League of Nations' response to the Abyssinia crisis was more decisive than its action over Manchuria, but just as ineffective.'
Assess the validity of this view.

STUDY TIP

The sources, written at different times, illustrate different problems which the League faced. Examine the extent to which the sources suggest that self-interest was the key to the League's failure, but also note the dates and context.

 PRACTICE QUESTION

Evaluating primary sources

With reference to Sources 1, 2 and 3 and your knowledge of the historical context, assess the value of these sources to an historian studying the problems faced by the League of Nations in the early 1930s.

21 Germany's challenges to the Treaty of Versailles

Fig. 1 *In Hitler's first direct challenge to the Versailles Treaty, German soldiers enter the Rhineland on 7 March 1936*

Hitler's aims

There has been intense debate amongst historians (see page 179) over the consistency of Nazi foreign policy aims, their origins and indeed whether Germany's foreign policy ought to be attributed solely to Hitler's own views; additionally a variety of different sources have been emphasised to support the various interpretations of Hitler's aims, as well as the tactics he used. However, there are areas of broad agreement as to Hitler's intentions in foreign policy.

Long-term aims

Since the early stages of his political career, Hitler had asserted that:
- the terms of the Treaty of Versailles should be abolished – land given to Poland and Czechoslovakia should be restored to Germany and union with Austria should be allowed
- all German-speaking peoples must be united under one Reich
- Germany must acquire **Lebensraum** in Eastern Europe and the USSR. According to Nazi ideology, the German people (Aryans) were superior to other 'races' and deserved to conquer their territory
- the USSR, believed by Hitler to be a communist state run by Jews, should be destroyed.

Hitler's book *Mein Kampf* contains much evidence of his foreign policy objectives; in the opening chapter he insisted on the achievement of an *Anschluss* with Austria, which had been a goal of many German and Austrian nationalists since the 1848 revolutions. Bismarck, whom Hitler greatly admired, had opposed German union with Austria-Hungary due to its ambitions in the Balkans. Hitler, however, who was born in Austria, was inspired by the idea of a glorious, united Germanic empire.

ACTIVITY

What reasons does Hitler give in Source 1 for his criticism of Germany's foreign policy before the First World War?

KEY TERM

Teutonic Knights: a medieval religious and military order. 'Teutonic' is a word describing the German people

A CLOSER LOOK

National Socialism

While the Nazis and the Bolsheviks both use the term 'socialism' to describe their own political philosophies, they meant very different things to each group. National Socialism (also known as Nazism) promoted greater social equality (except for groups considered undesirable by the Nazis, such as Jews, Gypsies and the disabled) and some state control over the economy, but they also committed themselves to the protection of private property. There was a minority within the Nazi movement who advocated more of a true socialist system in economic terms.

ACTIVITY

Thinking point

How might the Hossbach Memorandum – and its timing – be used as evidence of Hitler's foreign policy aims? Which school of historians might include it in their arguments?

SOURCE 1

From *Mein Kampf*, written by Hitler while in Landsberg Prison in 1924:

If land was desired in Europe, it could be obtained by and large only at the expense of Russia, and this meant that the new Reich must again set itself on the march along the road of the **Teutonic Knights** of old, to obtain by the German sword earth for the German plough and daily bread for the nation. Germany will either be a world power or there will be no Germany. And so we National Socialists consciously draw a line beneath the foreign policy tendency of our pre-war period. We stop the endless German movement to the south and west and turn our gaze towards the land in the east. At long last we break off the colonial and commercial policy of the pre-war period and shift to the soil policy of the future. If we speak of soil in Europe today, we can primarily have in mind only Russia and her vassal border states. This colossal empire in the east is ripe for dissolution, and the end of Russia as a state.

Hitler later asserted on a great number of occasions that *Lebensraum* was Germany's most important goal and that the country would collapse altogether if new land was not acquired. After coming to power in January 1933, he told a group of army officers that together they would achieve 'the conquest and ruthless Germanisation of new living space in the East'. This aim was to be vigorously reasserted at the Hossbach conference in 1937, after a number of foreign policy victories for Germany.

Short-term aims

Hitler sought to weaken existing international alignments which could serve as a barrier to his long-term aims, such as French influence in Eastern Europe.

However, following Hitler's early success with the Saar plebiscite, the Anglo-German Naval Agreement and the public announcement of Germany's remilitarisation without punishment by the League of Nations, his confidence increased and his tactics – if not his original aims – became more ambitious. 'Intentionalist' historians, however (see page 179) argue that Hitler was working to a long-term plan (*Stufenplan*) to implement his foreign policy from the moment he took power.

Evidence exists from the 'Four Year Plan' document (1936) and the **Hossbach Memorandum** (1937) that strongly suggests that Hitler wanted a European war as soon as possible. Some historians claim that he hoped to use military action as a method of alleviating domestic problems, especially the 'overheating' of the German economy caused by rearmament.

A CLOSER LOOK

The Hossbach Memorandum was named after the officer who made a recording of the meeting. In November 1937 Hitler met with three commanders-in-chief, War Minister Blomberg and Foreign Minister Neurath. Hitler claimed Germany needed to go to war to ensure its survival and that *Lebensraum* must be pursued as early as possible. After Blomberg and Field Marshal Fritsch voiced doubts over Germany's ability to fight a war in 1940 and questioned the assumed non-intervention of Britain and

France, Hitler had them removed, and appointed himself as Commander-in-Chief of the German army in February 1938.

Tactics

Between 1933, when he took office, and 1938, the year of the *Anschluss* with Austria, Hitler was careful to make his foreign policy objectives appear reasonable and palatable to the Western democracies, and therefore to appear diplomatic in pursuit of his aims. The Saar plebiscite was conducted (for the most part) according to international law; he accused other countries (with some justification) of hypocrisy in terms of disarmament, arguing that Germany had a moral right to rearm itself to the same level as its neighbours; and he was careful to emphasise the perceived injustices of the Treaty of Versailles. Hitler and the Nazis knew that all-out aggression was likely to invite retaliation from Britain and France – despite the failure of the League of Nations to take firm action in the Abyssinian and Manchurian Crises – due to Germany's location and reputation since the First World War as an aggressive state. Furthermore, Hitler had to be careful not to antagonise the German military leaders, many of whom had long been concerned that the Nazis' radical foreign policy aims would lead the country into a disastrous war.

The historical debate

The 'Intentionalist' school of thought (and the most popular immediately after the Second World War) is that Hitler was a 'driven' dictator who planned and caused the Second World War almost single-handedly with his unstoppable thirst for more land to add to his Reich; *Mein Kampf* and the Hossbach Memorandum are often used in support of this view. This was challenged in 1961 by Alan J.P. Taylor, who argued in *The Origins of the Second World War* that Hitler was a fairly conventional statesman who was given several opportunities by the other powers to achieve his goals, and that he chose to exploit these chances as they arose rather than planning every step carefully. This fits broadly with the 'Functionalist' interpretation of Hitler's intentions, which asserts that he was opportunistic and often used foreign policy to further consolidate his power; furthermore that his aims and actions should be viewed in broader context to be fully understood.

majority of historians now disagree.

The publication of Taylor's work attracted a storm of criticism from other historians, most vehemently Hugh Trevor-Roper, who argued against Taylor in a televised debate. Taylor's critics pointed to *Mein Kampf* as strong evidence against his assertions. More recently, historians have evaluated Nazi foreign policy with a greater consideration of its domestic policies, especially its commitment to 'purifying' and strengthening the German race. David Kaiser asserts that these core aims could not have been achieved without war, therefore Taylor's claim that Hitler almost accidentally sparked conflict in September 1939 is invalid.

Hitler's actions

Three days after becoming Chancellor, Hitler ordered the secret rearmament of Germany. By 1939, German military spending had increased from 1 per cent of the government budget in 1932 to 23 per cent. In his first months as leader, however, Hitler continued to play the reasonable statesman, and German delegates continued to attend the **World Disarmament Conference**. He correctly calculated though that the French would refuse to disarm immediately, and used this as the excuse to withdraw in October 1933. On 14 October Germany also withdrew from the League of Nations: it was now free to pursue **bilateral agreements** with other powers.

ACTIVITY

1. Look back to Chapter 14 which explores the terms of the Treaty of Versailles. Do any of Hitler's foreign policy objectives overlap with each other?
2. Which of the foreign policy aims do you think would have required the most force to achieve?

ACTIVITY

Extension

Watch the debate between Alan J.P. Taylor and Hugh Trevor-Roper in the programme *Did Hitler Cause the War?*, originally broadcast in 1961. What points does each historian make?

CROSS-REFERENCE

The reasons for the collapse of the World Disarmament Conference are explored in Chapter 18.

KEY TERM

bilateral agreements: agreements between two powers, rather than a wider international understanding

The German–Polish Non-Aggression Pact, January 1934

German rearmament and Hitler's publicly declared intention to reclaim East Prussia was a direct threat to Poland, its eastern neighbour. By 1934 Poland had a strong army of its own, bordered as it was by two potentially aggressive neighbours: Germany and the USSR. The Poles considered a **pre-emptive** strike on Germany before it could remilitarise any further, but support from its Locarno ally France was not forthcoming. Nevertheless, Polish military manoeuvres in Danzig convinced Germany to negotiate: with its rearmament programme in its infancy, it was not ready for war. The Non-Aggression Pact between Germany and Poland was concluded in January 1934, under which each power promised not to go to war with the other for at least ten years. It had two major consequences – Germany's eastern border was now secure and remilitarisation could be pursued, French diplomatic influence in Eastern Europe was severely reduced, and it also reinforced the idea of Hitler's 'reasonableness'.

SOURCE 2

From the secret Cabinet memorandum of John Simon, British Foreign Secretary, written in April 1934. Here he is discussing the aims of Germany's Non-Aggression Pact with Poland:

It may be asked how this apparent digression on Poland affects the question whether the **Defence Requirements Committee** was justified in describing Germany as the ultimate potential enemy so far as this country is concerned. The answer is twofold: that, despite agreements or pauses, it is Germany's eventual aim to execute her full and original programme, which includes points bound to affect us; and that Hitler's assurances must be regarded with scepticism. I recall a recent memorandum from our representative at Munich: 'I was at a social gathering attended by German army officers. They were overjoyed to notice that foreigners could be so easily duped by the so-called intensive peace campaign and occasional peace propaganda from the mouth of the German Chancellor.' It would be difficult to have a clearer indication that this. I am fully justified in thinking it possible that Herr Hitler probably wishes to create abroad an impression of the peaceful nature of German foreign policy and thereby, if possible, further to divide the remnants of the war coalition.

[handwritten margin notes:]
Austrian Catholics did not like Hitler.
Austrian Gov't against Anschluss.

[handwritten note:] right wing, Austrian, Catholic.

The attempted *Anschluss*, July 1934

One event which appears to demonstrate Hitler responding to events as they arose was the first attempt to create a union between Germany and Austria under Nazi control. Following Mussolini's attempt to install Engelbert Dollfuss as an anti-Nazi Austrian Chancellor, German Nazis encouraged their Austrian counterparts to murder Dollfuss on 25 July 1934 in an attempted *coup d'état*. To prevent Germany seizing control of Austria, Mussolini sent Italian troops to the Austrian border. The German military was not ready for such potential conflict, so Hitler abandoned the immediate plan for *Anschluss*, but not the long-term goal. Over the next two years Nazi foreign policymakers cultivated a friendlier relationship with Italy to avoid another confrontation.

[handwritten note:] river itself.

The Saar plebiscite, January 1935

The Saarland, or Saar, bordered France and contained rich resources of coal. It had been placed under the protection of the League of Nations, but at the end of 1934 the planned plebiscite was approaching. Many anti-Nazis had fled to the Saar when Hitler came to power, and there was a sizeable French minority living in the area. For Hitler, the Saar plebiscite was a test of the popularity of the Nazi regime, and he couldn't risk a poor result. Local Nazis were instructed to harass potential opponents, but this attracted too much attention for Hitler's liking and the pro-Nazi campaign was scaled down. The plebiscite on 13 January 1935 was overseen by foreign officials who declared that the voting was conducted fairly, and the overwhelming result of 90 per cent in favour of returning to German control was perceived as a huge success for the Nazis. [↦ by LON]

[handwritten: o majority french.]
[handwritten: o 90% vote in favour of German control.]

The plebiscite convinced many foreign powers of Hitler's moral authority: in a free election, people had chosen not just German rule, but Nazi rule. Given that he later intended to unite German-speakers in Austria and the Sudetenland, the Saar result provided a confidence boost. However, the affair had not been easy, and the Nazi propaganda campaign had alarmed the British and the French.

[handwritten: o Justified later policies of appeasement to Germany]

Rearmament and conscription, March 1935

Having commenced the secret build-up of German armaments from 1933, in March 1935 the Nazis felt confident enough to announce their remilitarisation aims publicly. On 9 March, Minister of Aviation Hermann Goering announced the existence of a German air force, the Luftwaffe; a week later Hitler declared that Germany was to reintroduce conscription. British, French and Russian rearmament following the failure of the Geneva Conference was cited as the reason for this further breach of the Versailles Treaty: Germany would need 550,000 troops for defence, which would increase to 750,000. In a display of Germany's increasing optimism and ambition, a 'Freedom to Rearm' rally was held on 16 March.

Fig. 2 *Rallies were commonplace in Nazi Germany. They emphasised the Nazi ideals of militarism, discipline and order*

Wehrmacht: the armed forces of Germany from 1935; it was disbanded by the Allies in 1945

ACTIVITY

Evaluating primary sources

How does Hitler attempt to justify Germany's rearmament in Source 3?

KEY PROFILE

Fig. 3   *Joachim von Ribbentrop*

Joachim von Ribbentrop (1893–1946) was a committed Nazi and diplomat, trusted by Hitler to negotiate hugely significant agreements with other powers including the naval agreement with Britain and the Nazi–Soviet Pact in 1939. He became Foreign Minister in 1938, replacing Neurath who had questioned Hitler's foreign policy. Ribbentrop was hanged for war crimes after the Second World War.

CROSS-REFERENCE

The Stresa Front – the agreement between Britain, France and Italy – is explored in Chapter 20.

KEY TERM

appeasement: the method of keeping peace by making compromises. Here it refers specifically to the policy of Britain and France towards Germany in response to Hitler's actions. It was, and remains, a very controversial policy

SOURCE 3   *recent world disarmament confrence.*

From Hitler's public statement in Berlin on 16 March 1935 announcing German rearmament to the world

[margin note: SIMILAR TO PROMISE OF LON]

What the German Government desires, as protector of the honour and the interests of the German nation, is to secure the measure of power essential not only for upholding the integrity of the German Reich but also for Germany's international respect and esteem as a co-guarantor of general peace. For in this very hour, the German Government renews its resolve before the German Volk [*people*] and before the entire world that it will never step beyond the bounds of preserving German honour and the freedom of the Reich and in particular shall never make of the German national arms an instrument of warlike aggression but an instrument confined exclusively to defence and thereby to the preservation of peace. Bearing this in mind, the German Reich Government has passed the following Law on the Establishment of the **Wehrmacht:** *armed forces.*
1. Service in the Wehrmacht shall be effected on the basis of general conscription.
2. The German peacetime army, is comprised of twelve corps and thirty-six divisions. (10-15,000 soldiers)   → 2¢ S divisions.

[handwritten note: 4x army that Tov allowed.]

The Anglo-German Naval Agreement, June 1935

In 1935, foreign office adviser **Joachim von Ribbentrop** was sent to Britain to negotiate an agreement on Germany's naval rearmament. Hitler surmised that Britain, with its superior navy and overseas empire, would be far more concerned with naval remilitarisation than military preparation in Europe, just as Wilhelm II had done before the First World War. Therefore he sought permission from the British to increase Germany's battle fleet. Under the terms of the Washington and London naval treaties (1921–2 and 1930) Britain's own naval rearmament was pegged to that of the USA and Japan, so an opportunity to set restrictions on Germany's navy in Britain's favour was welcome in London despite it breaking both the Treaty of Versailles and the **Stresa Front**.

The Anglo-German Naval Agreement signed in June 1935 restricted the German navy to 35 per cent of the size of Britain's. Hitler was very pleased to have reached an agreement with the British, whom he much admired, as it increased the Nazi regime's international prestige.

Summary

Within three years Hitler had overturned some of the key tenets of the Treaty of Versailles:
- The Non-Aggression Pact with Poland was not in direct defiance, but as a bilateral agreement it undermined the principles of collective security.
- Remilitarisation and conscription flouted the military restrictions imposed on Germany, particularly the creation of the Luftwaffe and the planned increase of soldiers to 750,000. The Anglo-German Naval Agreement also suggested an important shift in British policy towards German rearmament.

Hitler could not have achieved these foreign policy successes if his potential opponents were not so divided and unwilling to oppose Germany. This apathy, if it can be so called, was a direct response to the difficulties of the Great Depression which in turn helped ensure the abandonment of the League of Nations. As the chances of an international response to German aggression had truly faded away, Britain in particular sought to limit Hitler's progress in a policy known as **appeasement**.

"the straw that broke the camels back".

ACTIVITY

Summary

Match Hitler's actions up to the *Anschluss* with his four core aims outlined at the beginning of this chapter. Some did, of course, fulfil more than one objective.

 PRACTICE QUESTION

Evaluating primary sources

Study Sources 1, 2 and 3. With reference to these sources and your understanding of the historical context, assess the value of these three sources to an historian studying Hitler's aims to the end of 1935.

22 The international response to German, Italian and Japanese aggression

[handwritten: → labour → PM of national government]
[handwritten: → opposition mp]
[handwritten: → more likely to be critical]

SOURCE 1

[handwritten: → PRO ACTIVE STANCE]

From Winston Churchill's speech broadcast on BBC Radio on 15 November 1934. Churchill was a firm critic of the policy of appeasement and argued that the aggressive nations would not be satisfied until they had started the next world war:

[handwritten side note: Emphasis danger of common citizen]

- There is a nation which is in the grip of a group of ruthless men preaching a gospel of intolerance and racial pride unrestrained by law, by Parliament or by public opinion. In that country all pacifist speeches are forbidden or suppressed and the authors rigorously imprisoned. They are rearming with the utmost speed, and ready to their hands is this new lamentable weapon *[handwritten: Useless against airforce]* of the air against which a navy has no defence and before which women and children, the weak and the frail, the warrior and the civilian, all lie in equal peril. Worse still, for with the new weapon has come a new method – the possibility of compelling the submission of races by torturing their civil population. And worst of all, the more civilised the country is, the larger, more splendid its cities, the more intricate the structure of its social and economic life, the more it is vulnerable, the more it is at the mercy of those who may make it their prey. These are facts, and I ask again, 'What are we to do?'

The Rhineland Crisis and *Anschluss*

[handwritten: → directly contravened TOV & Locarno]

The remilitarisation of the Rhineland, March 1936

The remilitarisation of the Rhineland was a key objective for the Nazis, linking together their rearmament plans and the restoration of Germany to Great Power status. By 1936, the **Stresa Front** had been more or less abandoned following the Abyssinian invasion and the Anglo-German Naval Agreement, and as Mussolini's troops were about to claim victory over the Abyssinians the League of Nations was distracted from German actions.

On 7 March 1936, 32,000 German soldiers marched into the Rhineland, but officers had been given orders to retreat if they met with French resistance. Hitler had an excuse if challenged: a new Franco–Soviet alliance (the Treaty of Mutual Assistance), ratified in February 1936, directly threatened German security and he claimed that remilitarising the Franco–German border was necessary for defence. It was, nevertheless, a huge gamble for Hitler: if the French did send in troops, Germany's retreat would be humiliating.

[handwritten side note: Collective responsibility]

[handwritten: no public disagreement]

SOURCE 2

[handwritten: → no public disagreement]

From the meeting minutes of the British Cabinet on 11 March 1936, four days after the remilitarisation of the Rhineland. The Foreign Minister at this point was Anthony Eden, who was later to resign in protest at Britain's policy of appeasing Hitler: *[handwritten: decision making has to be unified]*

The Foreign Minister gave the Cabinet an account of the conversations he had held with representatives of the French, Belgian and Italian Governments in Paris on the previous day. He was alarmed by the complexity and gravity of the situation which confronted Europe, and more especially our own country as one of the guarantors of Locarno. On the outcome of the present situation depends the course of events in Europe over the next ten years, and it must be remembered that our influence is greater than that of any other nation.

[handwritten: allow Germany to pursue policy of aggression]

Our policy of condemning the German action and then developing a constructive policy to re-establish the European situation has no chance of acceptance. He thinks it inevitable that the French and Belgians will both announce their intention – if Germany cannot be persuaded to evacuate the demilitarised zone – to ask the Council of the League to make a pronouncement. If Germany is still unwilling, they will proceed to military measures and ask us to do the same. In that case we will have to decide whether we intend to fulfil our Treaty obligation – and we will be in an impossible position if we refuse.

HOC - pro- German, fear of war.

The response to the remilitarisation of the Rhineland

Britain's reaction to the Rhineland Crisis was indifferent because Lord Lothian, an outspoken critic of the Treaty of Versailles, argued that the Germans were doing no more than walking 'into their own back garden'. For the British government, the remilitarisation was a welcome solution to an outdated problem.

The reaction in France was very different: its government was deeply troubled but struggled to agree on an effective response. A number of factors prevented the French from taking action:

- The government was deeply divided in March 1936. With a general election looming, no party wanted to advocate intervention for fear of losing votes.
- French generals overestimated the strength of the German army: France could have successfully used force to make the Germans retreat.
- The French felt unable to act alone without the support of the British. This reliance on Britain when considering their response to German aggression, despite the greater threat to France, weakened the international response as a whole.

The result for French security would later prove to be disastrous. At the time the French military stepped up its defences on the **Maginot Line**, which consisted of a series of fortifications running along its eastern borders with Belgium, Luxembourg and Germany. From 1936 onwards, France's military strategy was defensive, not offensive. When Belgium declared its neutrality in 1937, France's position became even more perilous.

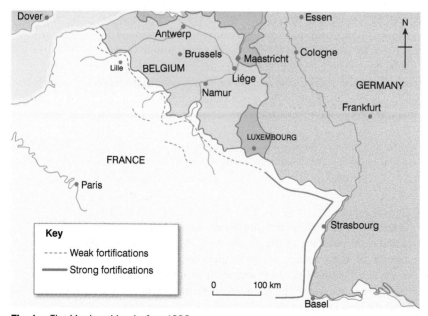

Fig. 1 *The Maginot Line before 1939*

ACTIVITY

Read Source 2 and answer the following questions:

1. What pressures on Britain did Eden highlight during this meeting?
2. What options are open to the British Cabinet in response to German rearmament, according to Eden?

CROSS-REFERENCE

The aims and the method of remilitarising the Rhineland are explored in Chapter 21.

A CLOSER LOOK

The response to German rearmament

Before the remilitarisation of the Rhineland, France and Britain asked Hitler to limit Germany's rearmament. Hitler was still cautious at this point and did not reject the proposal immediately, but instead played for time. Neither France nor Britain trusted Hitler's intentions; however on 4 March 1935 the British government used German rearmament to justify its plans to expand the air force. That same month, France increased its conscription period from 12 to 18 months. The League of Nations condemned German militarisation but planned a reactive, not proactive, response.

KEY TERM

Maginot Line: The defensive line of fortifications built in France from 1929 to protect against a German invasion

ACTIVITY

Research the Maginot Line in more depth. How far do you think its planners were influenced by memories of the Schlieffen Plan, Germany's strategy at the beginning of the First World War?

ACTIVITY

Evaluating primary sources

1. What can we infer about Flandin's expectations of the other powers from Source 3?
2. How valuable is Source 3 to a historian studying the reaction to the remilitarisation of the Rhineland?

CROSS-REFERENCE

The aims and terms of the Locarno treaties are explained in Chapter 17.

The reasons for Germany's failed attempt to unite with Austria in 1934 are explained in Chapter 19. For an exploration of the pacts and agreements made by Germany which helped the success of the 1938 *Anschluss*, see Chapter 22.

KEY PROFILE

Fig. 2   *Kurt Schuschnigg*

Kurt Schuschnigg (1897–1977)
was a right-wing but anti-Nazi Austrian politician who became Austrian Chancellor in 1934. Deeply committed to Austrian independence, he attempted to appease Nazi Germany until the *Anschluss*, after which he was imprisoned by the Nazis in concentration camps for opposing the union. He survived the war and emigrated to the USA.

The USSR had finally been accepted as a member of the League of Nations in September 1934. When the League's council met to discuss the Rhineland, the Soviet delegate Maxim Litvinov was the only one to advocate sanctions against Germany, despite the general acceptance that Germany's actions contravened both the Versailles and **Locarno** treaties.

SOURCE 3

From a public statement by Pierre-Étienne Flandin, French Foreign Minister, on 10 March 1936:

What has been violated is a treaty into which Germany has freely entered. It is a violation of a territorial character, a violation following upon repeated assurances by Hitler that he would respect the Locarno Treaty. If such violations are tolerated by members of the League, and in particular by the Locarno Powers, there is no basis for the establishment of international order, and no chance for the organisation of peace through a system of collective security under the Covenant. Once the breach has been declared by the Council, the French Government would put at the disposal of the Council all their moral and material resources (including military, naval and air forces) in order to repress what they regarded as an attempt upon international peace. The French Government expected that the Locarno Powers, in virtue of their formal obligations to render assistance, and the other members of the League would act with the French Government in exercising pressure upon the author of this action.

[handwritten annotations: unlike Tov.; breakdown of collective security.; Military.; expect aid of allies.]

The *Anschluss*, March 1938

The first attempt to unite Austria with Germany in 1934 had failed, but just four years later the prospects for *Anschluss* were transformed by several international developments. With rearmament and the success of the German economy, at least according to Nazi claims, Germany had grown stronger than Italy, which was now less likely to protest; meanwhile the collapse of the Stresa Front and the League of Nations' reputation made the prospect of determined opposition to Austro–German union very unlikely.

Austrian Nazis were still active in stirring up agitation and opposition to **Kurt Schuschnigg**, who had replaced Mussolini's favourite Dolfuss as Austrian Chancellor after the latter's assassination. Schuschnigg was suspicious of Nazi Germany and committed to Austrian independence. He was summoned to meet Hitler on 12 February 1938 to discuss the worsening situation in Austria: rioting by the Austrian Nazis was causing considerable problems for the government. Schuschnigg was given a set of demands: the appointment of fanatical Nazi Seyss-Inquart as minister of the interior; and the coordination of economic and foreign policy with Germany's. If Schuschnigg refused, Germany would invade. In what amounted to the partial loss of Austria's sovereignty, the stunned Schuschnigg agreed to Hitler's demands.

Back in Vienna, however, Schuschnigg became more defiant. He planned a plebiscite for 13 March, believing Austrians would vote to remain independent. Hitler ordered his army to prepare for the invasion of Austria and instructed Seyss-Inquart to demand the postponement of the plebiscite. Schuschnigg gave way, to be met with another demand from Hitler: he must resign and be replaced by Seyss-Inquart.

The new Chancellor Seyss-Inquart then sent a telegram requesting German intervention to 'restore order' in Austria, and the Nazis sent an invasion force crossing the border on 12 March. The successful *Anschluss* was declared on 14 March, and the subsequent plebiscite was held. With the German army already on Austrian land, 80,000 opponents locked up and the *Anschluss* already a fait accompli, a scarcely believable 99.75 per cent of Austrians voted in favour of union with Germany. Hitler now had 70 million people under his rule, and borders with Italy, Yugoslavia and Hungary. Czechoslovakia was dangerously exposed to German aggression, but once again there had been little protest in response to Hitler's actions.

Fig. 3 *Invading Nazi troops were generally given an enthusiastic reception by the Austrian crowds*

KEY PROFILE

Fig. 4 *Edward Wood*

Edward Wood, First Earl of Halifax (1881–1959) was a senior Conservative politician in the 1930s and Foreign Minister 1938–40. He became Viscount Halifax in 1934 and was an influential voice in favour of appeasement. In 1940 he advocated negotiating a peace settlement with Germany after the Dunkirk evacuation when a German invasion of Britain seemed imminent. Halifax later served as British ambassador to the United States.

The response to the *Anschluss*

In the midst of the *Anschluss* crisis, Austrian Chancellor Schuschnigg had appealed to the Western powers for help, but Britain in particular was reluctant to intervene. In November 1937 **Viscount Halifax** had visited Germany on a 'goodwill mission'. He was impressed by Germany's recovery from the desperate years of the Depression, and agreed that Germany was 'the bulwark of the West against Bolshevism'. Crucially, Halifax privately sympathised with Hitler's aims of overturning the Versailles settlement and reuniting German speakers in Austria, Czechoslovakia and Danzig. He supported the policy of appeasement, and suggested that Britain wouldn't oppose these aims as long as they were carried out peacefully, and that 'methods likely to lead to far-reaching disturbances' were avoided. As Source 1 demonstrates, not everyone approved of this proposal.

The French, meanwhile, were incapacitated by a government crisis: four days before the German invasion, Camille Chautemps had resigned as Prime Minister, and his successor Leon Blum had not yet assumed office. Italy, having signed up to the **Stresa Front** against German expansion in April 1935, had since aligned itself with Germany. The *Anschluss* was still more of a concern to Mussolini than to the British and French, but by 1938 Italy was already committed in Abyssinia and the Spanish Civil War, so Mussolini had little choice other than to accept the German annexation.

CROSS-REFERENCE

The Stresa Front is discussed in Chapter 19, pages 164–165.

The details of Italy's political alignment with Germany in 1936 is detailed later in this chapter, page 190.

Fig. 5   *This map of central Europe in April 1938 shows the extent of the German Reich following the* Anschluss

The Spanish Civil War, 1936–9

Civil war erupted in Spain in 1936 when right-wing nationalists rebelled against the Republican, left-wing government, the Popular Front. The intervention of Germany and Italy was to prove decisive in securing the victory of Nationalist leader **General Franco**, while the Western democracies committed themselves to non-intervention.

Germany and Italy's assistance to the Nationalists

General Franco, who led the Nationalist campaign against the Republican Government, appealed to the German and Italian governments for help getting his troops from their base in Morocco to the Spanish mainland. Hitler and Mussolini were keen to oblige by sending transport planes, thereby involving their countries in the war from its earliest stages. There were several possible reasons for this:

- Ideologically, the Nationalist side pledged to resist communism, which was a core aim of fascism (Nazism was based on aspects of fascist ideology).
- The Civil War was a useful 'testing ground' of new weapons, equipment, personnel and strategy. Hitler wanted to see how the new Luftwaffe performed.
- It provided an opportunity to forge alliances: Hitler hoped to lure Italy firmly away from the Stresa Front; Mussolini was beginning to view Germany as a more beneficial ally than Britain and France, who were likely to object to Italian expansion; and both hoped that a victorious Franco would ensure Spain became a useful partner.

The contributions of both Germany and Italy to the Nationalist cause were significant. Germany provided over 100 fighter aircraft and 12,000 soldiers. German and Italian planes, the Condor Legion and Aviazone Legionaria respectively, gave the Nationalists a huge advantage. Heavy bombing was used with devastating effects: the Condor Legion utterly destroyed the town of

Fig. 6   *Francisco Franco*

Francisco Franco (1892–1975) was Chief of Staff in the Spanish army before the outbreak of the Civil War. When he led the revolt against the Popular Front he became the leader of the Nationalist movement in the war. Franco ruled Spain as a dictator after his victory in 1939, but refused to get involved in the Second World War, recognising the weakness of post-Civil War Spain. He died in office in 1975.

Guernica on 26 April 1937, killing between 200 and 300 civilians (the exact number is heavily disputed).

The Non-Intervention Committee

In September 1936, two months after the outbreak of hostilities, Britain set up the Non-Intervention Committee (NIC) to try to stop foreign powers aiding either side in the Civil War. In total, 24 countries joined the NIC, including Germany and Italy who then directly and openly contradicted it. Britain, France and the USA stayed broadly loyal to the agreements of the NIC and even forbade their citizens from fighting in the war on their own initiative. Tens of thousands of left-wing sympathisers, however, ignored this ban and joined the International Brigade, travelling to Spain and fighting for the Republicans.

Without official and practical support from the liberal democracies, the Republicans turned to the USSR for help, but Stalin was unwilling to commit himself as fully as Hitler and Mussolini did: it was far more difficult for the USSR to move supplies into Spain, and he did not want to leave Russia's western border open to German aggression. The Nationalists had a distinct advantage, despite the legitimate Republican government having the natural support of the Western democracies.

Italy and Albania, 1939

Two defence agreements, the Treaties of Tirana, were signed between Italy and Albania in 1924 and 1926. Italian control over Albania steadily increased, but its king, Zog I, refused to bow to pressure from Mussolini to give away even more of Albania's independence. In 1931 Zog refused to renew the Tirana treaty, and in 1934 he signed trade agreements with Yugoslavia and Greece. Mussolini threatened invasion by sending warships to the Albanian coast, but was then distracted by the invasion of Abyssinia. After Hitler's invasion of Czechoslovakia in March 1939 (see Chapter 23) Mussolini felt compelled to act, or risk being totally eclipsed as a partner in the fascist alignment.

The invasion and international response

Mussolini sent an ultimatum to Zog on 25 March, demanding that Italy be allowed to annex Albania. Zog broadcast his resistance to the ultimatum on Albanian radio on 6 April, but the next day 100,000 Italian troops and 600 planes began the invasion, which took just five days to complete. Two days after the Italians' arrival, Zog and his family fled the country, and on 12 April the Albanian parliament voted to depose Zog and offer the throne to Victor Emmanuel of Italy. Italy and Albania were united in a 'personal union' under the Italian crown.

International attention was once against distracted, this time by German expansion in Eastern Europe, as governments reeled from Hitler's invasion of Czechoslovakia despite the promises made at Munich (see Chapter 23). Although they did nothing to reverse Italy's actions, the Albanian invasion prompted Britain and France to extend the guarantee they made to Poland to defend its independence to Greece and Romania as well on 13 April.

War in China, 1937–41

The beginning of an all-out war between China and Japan (the second Sino-Japanese War) was triggered by an exchange of fire between Chinese and Japanese troops in July 1937 at the Marco Polo Bridge near Beijing. The Japanese army claimed that the Chinese had started the trouble, and used this as an excuse to mount a full-scale invasion. The 'Marco Polo Bridge incident' galvanised Chinese resistance, which had previously been weak.

Fig. 7 *The town of Guernica was devastated by the German Condor Legion's bombing campaign*

CROSS-REFERENCE

The beginning of Japan's Manchurian invasion is explained in Chapter 20.

KEY TERM

Nanjing: China's administrative capital at the time of the Japanese invasion

Fig. 8 *Shanghai damaged by Japanese bombing, 1932*

ACTIVITY

Summary

Rank the powers of Britain, France, the USA and USSR in order of how involved they became in the Sino-Japanese War. Give a summary of the reasons for the position of each.

CROSS-REFERENCE

An outline of the early relations between Italy and Hitler's Germany is given in Chapter 19.

As Manchukuo (formerly **Manchuria**) was under the full control of the Japanese, this became a useful military base for the Kwantung army. Shanghai fell to the Japanese in November 1937 and **Nanjing**, a month later. The treatment of Nanjing citizens and surrendered soldiers was appallingly brutal, with up to 250,000 killed and many mutilated by Japanese troops. The 'Rape of Nanjing' and the devastation of Shanghai turned Western liberal public opinion firmly against Japan.

As a result, Britain, France and the US provided financial assistance to China. While they felt unable to directly support China militarily, the future Allied Powers recognised the importance of Chinese resistance, even though they were not strong enough to drive out the Japanese. The United States, standing by its isolationist policy, refused to intervene directly in the Sino-Japanese War, particularly as it did not wish to risk its profitable trade with Japan. The USSR involved itself the most, partly prompted by the signing of the Anti-Comintern Pact by Germany and Japan on 25 November 1936: the Soviets saw the war in China as a useful distraction from Japanese designs on Siberia. In September 1937 the Sino-Soviet Non-Aggression Pact between China and the USSR was signed. As part of Operation Zet, a volunteer Russian air force was formed and Soviets provided assistance to the Chinese air force.

By the end of 1937, all of China's major cities had fallen to the Japanese but the vast expanse of Chinese territory was not completely conquered. Japan's resources could not support any further advance and there seemed to be little strategic importance in doing so. By 1941, 2 million Japanese troops were stationed in China, and they had two kinds of Chinese enemies: the visible Kuomintang army which fought with traditional methods, and guerrilla fighters led by the communist leader Mao Zedong. Faced with these problems, the Japanese invasion stalled and a stalemate was reached in 1938.

Alliances between the aggressors

The Rome–Berlin Axis, October 1936

The Berlin Agreement signed by Italy and Germany on 25 and 26 October 1936 provided useful strategic guarantees for each country. As a result of the Abyssinian invasion, Italy was isolated from the liberal democracies but feared the remilitarisation of Germany. The Germans, meanwhile, were keen to secure their southern border and free up the military for Hitler's planned operations elsewhere. The two fascist powers agreed a series of protocols in October 1936, which later became known as the Rome–Berlin Axis. The agreements consolidated the alignment between Germany and Italy politically and militarily: they were to follow a similar foreign policy. This was a frustrating development for the British, who had hoped to keep Mussolini as a counterbalance against the potential threat of Germany. It also created the threatening prospect of a Fascist partnership dominating Europe if both followed their expansion plans.

The Anti-Comintern Pact, November 1936 and November 1937

Germany and Japan feared the growing military strength of the USSR, and reached an agreement in November 1936 to oppose and limit the activities of the Comintern. The Anti-Comintern Pact also recognised the similar interests of Germany and Japan in their strong ideological opposition to communism: this was, in some ways, reassuring to the liberal democracies who also opposed the spread of communism, highlighting one key reason why Britain,

France and the USA did not respond decisively to the threat posed by the aggressors before 1939.

Italy joined the pact on 6 November 1937, as did Spain and several non-fascist powers including Finland and Denmark. As the Rome–Berlin Axis had already been agreed, Tokyo was added to the alignment of the Axis Powers.

Given its ideological nature, the **Anti-Comintern Pact** was of greatest concern to the USSR. It intensified the division between the Western powers and the Soviets, which had been growing since the remilitarisation of the Rhineland. The influence of communism was a domestic as well as a foreign policy concern to Britain and France; the Anti-Comintern Pact forced them to consider their ideological allegiances. Hitler was generally considered a lesser threat than the long-term danger of communism, a judgement which helped to justify appeasement, especially to British politicians. France's position was further complicated by the instability of its government and the greater popularity of its own communist party.

The Pact of Steel, 1939

On 22 May 1939 the loose terms of the Rome–Berlin Axis were formalised into a fully military alliance, named the Pact of Steel to emphasise its aggressive nature. The Pact committed both powers to 'permanent contact' with each other; consultation in the event of unfavourable international developments; close economic and military cooperation; and most importantly, support for each other in the event of attack from another power 'with all its military might on land, at sea, and in the air.' Japan did not join the Pact of Steel because it wanted to maintain its focus on the Far East, hoping to complete its invasion of China and continue to resist any Soviet expansion. Thus the Pact of Steel was European in its intentions and could be viewed as directed against Britain and France, although neither country was mentioned in its terms.

Summary

By 1938, a number of developments convinced the Western democracies that war was growing more likely. Britain, for instance, began to prepare for conflict by increasing war production and planning for rationing and evacuation. The much bleaker prospects for peace in 1938 compared to just three years before were not helped by the lack of a coordinated response by the liberal democracies and the USSR to the aggression of Germany, Italy and Japan:

- Many British politicians and citizens no longer believed that the Treaty of Versailles was fair or appropriate. Leading figures like Lothian and Halifax privately asserted that Hitler was addressing imbalances with its rearmament programme and remilitarisation of the Rhineland.
- The French government was severely hampered by its own instability: with considerable domestic concerns and frequent ministerial changes, following a consistent and decisive foreign policy was challenging. Many were pessimistic about the strength of the French army compared to Germany's and France's ability to stand against German actions alone.
- The commitment of the American public to neutrality remained firm, especially as the US was still resolving domestic problems caused by the Great Depression in the late 1930s. Despite Roosevelt's personal belief that war between the democracies and the dictatorships seemed increasingly likely, his passing of the Neutrality Acts re-affirmed the American commitment to isolationism.

Comintern is short for 'Communist International', a commitment by the USSR to organise communist movements abroad and facilitate communist revolutions in other countries. It was formed in 1919 with the aim of encouraging 'by all available means, including armed force, for the overthrow of the international bourgeoisie and for the creation of an international Soviet republic as a transition stage to the complete abolition of the State'.

Summary chart

Create a chart to record the key points of each of the alliances in this section. Include signatories, dates signed, aims, terms, and the responses of other nations.

American isolationism in the 1930s

US governments prioritised domestic concerns as they tried to resolve the problems of the Depression. Isolationism grew more popular in this environment and a series of Neutrality Acts were passed between 1935 and 1939 which limited the sale of armaments to warring nations. Roosevelt made the 'Quarantine Speech' in 1937 in response to Japanese and Italian aggression, arguing that aggressor states should be politically isolated. The speech was so poorly received in America that Roosevelt soon backed down from this stance. As a result, the USA's fellow liberal democracies could not depend on its cooperation, much less its leadership, in responding to the threat of aggression.

ACTIVITY

Class debate

Conduct a class debate with the aim of deciding which of the developments explored in this chapter was most threatening to world peace. See how much of an agreement you can come to.

- All the liberal democracies saw communism as a long-term threat to the stability of their own countries. For much of the 1930s many Western statesmen believed that despite the aggression of the dictators, communist revolution was the bigger threat.
- The USSR had been the most openly threatened by the Anti-Comintern Pact. Stalin, already mistrustful of the Western democracies due to their intervention in the Russian Civil War and their initial refusal to allow the USSR into the League of Nations, increasingly lost faith in them as a result of the Rhineland Crisis. He gloomily predicted war with Germany and focused on building up Soviet industry in preparation, rather than trusting in any form of collective security.

STUDY TIP

Pay close attention to countries and dates given in this question, and try to focus your thinking on the key phrase 'turning point' and what this means. Consider the extent to which the foreign policies of the two countries changed as a result of the Spanish Civil War. You could develop a list of key differences in the policies before and after, then consider whether this can be attributed to their intervention in Spain.

A LEVEL **PRACTICE QUESTION**

To what extent was involvement in the Spanish Civil War a turning point in the foreign policies of both Germany and Italy in the years 1934 to 1938?

fear of airforce.

23 The outbreak of war in Europe

Appeasement

After the Manchurian and Abyssinian Crises, faith in the principle of collective security was extremely low. Protecting individual countries' interests had severely hampered the work of the League of Nations when settling international disputes; British and French policymakers pursued a policy of appeasement instead. Identifying exactly when appeasement began can be tricky. As Britain negotiated with Germany to produce the Anglo-German Naval agreement in June 1935 and Hitler was rearming anyway, this could be considered an early example of appeasement, but it is not entirely accurate to do so, as Hitler was not making demands to go to war at this time. Before Italy's conquest of Abyssinia in May 1936, Britain and France had not yet abandoned collective security, or completely lost faith in the League of Nations. In the event of the Czech Crisis in September 1938, however, a policy of Appeasement was certainly pursued.

ACTIVITY

Research

The cartoons created by David Low for British newspapers in the 1930s are excellent for studying reactions to Hitler's foreign policy. Look up some examples online and see if you can work out the message of each one.

Support for appeasement

In hindsight, it is easy to criticise appeasement and its chief proponent, **Prime Minister Neville Chamberlain**. However, the policy was popular with the British public, for several reasons:

- By the late 1930s, the Treaty of Versailles appeared increasingly irrelevant. Hitler had directly flouted many of its terms with little resistance. Therefore there was little enthusiasm for applying strong sanctions – much less going to war – to defend the Versailles settlement.
- While support for many terms of the Versailles Treaty – especially the strong punishment of Germany – had faded, the horror of the Western Front had not been forgotten. The destruction of the First World War was only tolerable if it really was 'the war to end all wars'. Almost any settlement seemed preferable to another large war.
- The failure of the World Disarmament Conference had allowed Germany to remilitarise; in comparison, by 1938 British and French rearmament had fallen behind.
- There was a deep fear of aerial bombing following the devastation of Shanghai and Guernica. Fighter plane technology had progressed since the First World War; the dropping of poison gas by enemy aircraft was also an expected and dreaded development.
- The communist USSR was regarded as the greatest threat to Western democracy, despite deep mistrust of Nazism. Strategically a strong anti-Soviet Germany was a potentially useful bulwark against communism, but some in Britain doubted the military capacity of the USSR, which in part explains why a defensive agreement was not reached with the Soviets in 1939.
- Until the remilitarisation of the Rhineland, Hitler had convinced many statesmen that he was 'a reasonable man with reasonable grievances'. Even as his methods (and aims) became more aggressive, Chamberlain expected to negotiate with him and – crucially – that Hitler would stick to his word

LEARNING OBJECTIVES

In this chapter you will learn about:

- why Britain and France pursued a policy of appeasement towards German aggression

- the outcome of the Czech crisis and why Britain and France made guarantees to Poland

- the reasons for the Nazi–Soviet Pact

- how Germany's invasion of Poland led to the outbreak of the Second World War in Europe

- Italy's reaction to the outbreak of war.

KEY PROFILE

Fig. 1 *Neville Chamberlain*

Neville Chamberlain (1869–1940) was increasingly influential in British foreign policy and became Prime Minister in May 1937. He remained committed to appeasement until Germany's invasion of Czechoslovakia in March 1939. After the Allies failed to stop the German invasion of Norway, and with France about to be invaded, Chamberlain resigned in May 1940 and died six months later.

KEY PROFILE

Fig. 2   *Édouard Daladier*

Édouard Daladier (1884–1970) had already been Prime Minister of France twice before being elected again in April 1938. He supported appeasement out of concern for France's ability to defeat Germany, rather than believing Hitler's demands were reasonable. Daladier resigned in March 1940, two months after delivering a defiant speech arguing that Hitler was intent on European domination.

and uphold agreements. **Édouard Daladier** was far more sceptical of Hitler's intentions, but knew France was not ready to fight in 1938.

A CLOSER LOOK

The historiography of appeasement

Initially appeasement was popular amongst the British public, but within months of the invasion of Poland criticism of Chamberlain's actions grew. Three journalists published a bestselling work entitled *Guilty Men* in July 1940 when France had fallen to Germany. The book altered people's perception of appeasement, declaring that the policy amounted to the 'deliberate surrender of small nations in the face of Hitler's blatant bullying'.

Russians also blamed the appeasers for allowing war to break out. The Munich agreement and the USSR's lack of involvement in the conference have been cited as the reasons Stalin concluded the Nazi–Soviet Pact (see below). Soviet historians during the Cold War between capitalist and communist nations, attacked the Western powers for negotiating with Hitler in their selfish desire to have a buffer against communism.

The British view of appeasement changed around the 1970s as 'revisionist' historians pointed out that Britain couldn't have fought Germany and defended its empire simultaneously, so Chamberlain skilfully bought valuable time by negotiating. More recently, historians and politicians have been more sensitive to the idea of aggression being tolerated in attempts to keep the peace, as global terrorism has become a greater concern.

The Czech Crisis

Czechoslovakia consisted of several divided and competing nationalities. As ethnic Germans, German-speakers in the Sudetenland region were highly influential in the old Austro-Hungarian Empire, but since 1919 were a minority group. Czech resentment of the ethnic Germans' former high status led to some repressive policies against them: **Edvard Beneš**, later President of Czechoslovakia, explained to the British that its policy of 'Czechification' was designed to 'teach the Germans a lesson.'

Fig. 3. *The languages and ethnicities of Czechoslovakia in September 1938*

Hitler's designs on the Sudetenland

One of Hitler's core aims, to overturn the post-war settlement, would be served by eliminating Czechoslovakia as a nation. Czechoslovakia's awkward geographical location, jutting into the German Reich, also made it an obvious step towards Hitler's achievement of *Lebensraum*. It contained economic assets like the **Skoda** factories and rich coalfields, both of which would benefit the German war effort. *leading Sudeten German politician.*

The excuse Hitler used to justify his intended actions was the treatment of Sudeten Germans by the Czech government. Local Nazis, led by Konrad Henlein, were encouraged to stir up trouble and make demands on the government – just as Austrian Nazis had before the invasion of Austria – and on 12 September 1938 riots broke out. When they were crushed by the Czech authorities, Hitler threatened war.

This was Hitler's greatest gamble yet. **Czechoslovakia** had a strong and professional army. Moreover, the Czechs had a defensive alliance with France dating back to January 1924. As the likelihood of a European war grew, governments stepped up their preparations, but German military chiefs were sceptical. They doubted Germany would be able to defeat Czechoslovakia and France, and worried that the British would intervene to support the French if Germany invaded the Sudetenland.

Chamberlain's meetings with Hitler and Berchtesgaden and Godesberg, September 1938 – *immediate & clear appeasement.*

Chamberlain requested a meeting with Hitler on 15 September, very soon after the crushing of the Sudeten Nazi riots. The first meeting between Chamberlain and Hitler took place at Hitler's mountain retreat in the Bavarian Alps, Berchtesgaden. Chamberlain's bold and dynamic idea appeared to work; Hitler tempered his demands and claimed that he would be satisfied with certain parts of the Sudetenland – those areas where the majority of the population were German-speakers. He also agreed to a plebiscite. On 19 September, after Chamberlain had briefed Daladier, the British and French approached the Czech government with the proposals. The Czechs reluctantly agreed.

Chamberlain met with Hitler again on 22 September at Godesburg in western Germany. Chamberlain triumphantly informed Hitler of Czechoslovakia's agreement, only to find the dictator had changed his mind: he demanded that all of the Sudetenland be ceded to the Reich. Again he used the mistreatment of ethnic Germans by the Czechs as justification, but grossly exaggerated the details. Hitler even set a date – 1 October – for the invasion of the Sudetenland and once again war seemed imminent. Orders for German mobilisation were given on 28 September and the British fleet was mobilised in response.

The Munich Conference, 29 September 1938

At this point, Mussolini intervened as an unlikely conciliator. He persuaded Hitler to hold a four-power conference in Munich, attended by Britain, France and Italy, on 29 September. Chamberlain was less optimistic on his third flight to Germany in a fortnight, calling it the 'last desperate snatch at the last tuft of grass on the very verge of the precipice'. Significantly, neither Czechoslovakia nor the USSR was invited to the conference: the Czechs were expected to raise strong objections; the Soviets would also object to the threat to the security of their sphere of influence in Eastern Europe. With Mussolini acting as mediator between the fascist and democratic powers, an agreement was quickly concluded. The Sudetenland would become part of Germany immediately and the German army were given permission to occupy the region.

Peace had been secured – for the time being. Daladier and Chamberlain had the task of informing the Czech government of the agreement which it could only acquiesce to. Before he left Munich, Chamberlain persuaded Hitler

Fig. 4   *Edvard Beneš*

Edvard Beneš (1884–1948) was instrumental in the founding of Czechoslovakia in 1919, becoming its Foreign Minister. A strong supporter of the League of Nations, he grew frustrated with its limited response to aggression in the 1930s. Beneš went into exile after the Munich agreement and led Czechoslovakia's government-in-exile, becoming Czechoslovakian President in 1945 after the Nazis' defeat.

to sign a rather loose pledge that Germany and Britain would never go to war with each other. On his return to London, Chamberlain, waving the 'piece of paper' as the pledge as come to be known, was greeted as a hero.

ACTIVITY

Summary

Create a timeline of the Munich Crisis (also known as the Sudeten Crisis) including the changes in Hitler's demands.

ACTIVITY

Class debate

Conduct a class debate on the interpretations of Britain and France's role in the Munich Crisis. One side should argue that the agreement was a triumph; the other, that it was a sell-out.

SOURCE 1

From a report the British newspaper, the *Manchester Guardian*, published on 1 October 1938. The paper had left-wing leanings and was generally critical of the policy of appeasement:

No stranger experience can have happened to Mr Chamberlain during the past month than his reception back home in London. He drove to Buckingham Palace, where the crowd clamoured for him, and within five minutes of his arrival he was standing on the balcony with the King and Queen. The cries were all for 'Neville,' and he stood waving his hand and smiling. Another welcome awaited the Premier in Downing Street. Every window of No. 10 was open and filled with faces. The windows of the Foreign Office were equally full – except one, which was made up with sandbags. Everywhere were people cheering. One of the women there found no other words to express her feelings but these, 'The man who gave me back my son'. Mr Chamberlain went to a first-floor window and leaned forward happily smiling on the people. 'My good friends,' he said – it took some time to still the clamour so that he might be heard – 'this is the second time in our history that there has come back from Germany "peace with honour". I believe it is peace for our time.'

The invasion of Czechoslovakia, March 1939

During his initial discussions with Chamberlain, Hitler had twice promised that after the Sudetenland, he had no further territorial demands. However, the annexation of the Sudetenland by Germany severely weakened Czechoslovakia's north-western defences, and it also encouraged its eastern and southern neighbours to make their claims to Czech territory. Poland was able to seize land in the north-east in October 1938, and Hungary took a larger amount of territory in the south-east in November. Even Slovaks, the other majority ethnic group comprising Czechoslovakia, began to demand greater rights.

Fig. 5. *After the Munich Conference and the ceding of the Sudetenland to Germany, Czechoslovakia's other neighbours took territory from it too. This is the country by the end of 1938*

In March 1939, with the country badly weakened and facing internal divisions, Hitler invited the new Czech president Emil Hacha – Beneš had gone into exile – to Berlin to discuss the situation. He kept Hacha waiting until 2am; when Hitler finally saw the Czech premier, it was to inform him that the German army was on the border ready to invade. Bowing to the inevitable, the beleaguered Hacha signed a document that conceded Czechoslovakia to Germany. On 15 March German soldiers marched into Prague.

Although France was bound by the 1924 treaty to defend Czechoslovakia, Hacha's role in signing his country over to the Nazis made the invasion technically legal. However, Chamberlain and Daladier were now convinced that appeasement had failed and that Poland would be the next target for Hitler's aggression.

The crisis over Poland and the Nazi–Soviet Pact, 1939

Britain and France's guarantee to Poland

Hitler resented the 'Polish corridor' which gave Poland access to the sea by giving it land in East Prussia; as an eastern Slavic nation Poland was also the focus of *Lebensraum*. After the invasion of Czechoslovakia it became obvious to Britain and France that the Polish corridor would be Hitler's next objective, if not the invasion of the whole of Poland. In fact, Hitler drew up plans for the latter as early as April 1939. He was convinced Britain and France would not intervene.

Chamberlain made no more negotiations with Hitler after Czechoslovakia's invasion. With appeasement abandoned, Chamberlain (who viewed the Czech invasion as a personal betrayal) and Daladier changed tack and offered a guarantee to assist Poland if it was attacked by Germany. Chamberlain publicly announced Britain's intention to defend Poland on 31 March, which was to be followed by a full military alliance. By this he hoped that Hitler might reconsider his plan to attack Poland, and to demonstrate to the USSR (with whom an alliance was still possible in the spring of 1939) that the Western democracies could take firmer action. The agreement, known as the Polish–British Common Defence Act, was ratified on 25 August, two days after the conclusion of the Nazi–Soviet Pact. In reality, however, there was little useful military assistance that Britain or France could provide to Poland, as their troops would have to travel through enemy territory to reach it.

ACTIVITY

Research

Compare the takeovers of Austria, the Sudetenland and Czechoslovakia. How similar were the three crises?

CROSS-REFERENCE

To refresh your memory of the situation of Poland following the First World War, see Chapters 13 and 14.

Chapter 22 explains why Britain and France extended this guarantee to Greece and Romania.

SOURCE 2

From Chamberlain's address to the House of Commons on 31 March 1939:

I am glad to take this opportunity of stating again the general policy of the British government. They have constantly advocated the adjustment, by way of free negotiation between the parties concerned, of any differences that may arise between them. Certain consultations are now proceeding with other governments. In order to make perfectly clear the position of this government in the meantime before those consultations are concluded, I now have to inform the House that during that period, in the event of any action which clearly threatened Polish independence, and which the Polish government accordingly considered it vital to resist with their national forces, this government would feel themselves bound at once to lend the Polish government all support in their power. They have given the Polish Government an assurance to this effect. I may add that the French Government have authorised me to make it plain that they stand in the same position in this matter as do His Majesty's Government.

Reasons for the Nazi–Soviet Pact

The Nazi–Soviet Pact, signed on 23 August 1939, was an agreement between Hitler and Stalin. This pact was shocking because it was a commitment between Hitler and his sworn enemy. The pact committed each power to non-aggression against the other. In a secret clause they also agreed to invade Poland and divide it between themselves. This was a masterstroke on Hitler's part as it immediately weakened Britain and France's guarantee to Poland by ensuring that Poland now had aggressors on its western and eastern borders, therefore making its British and French military support almost impossible. It also gave Hitler ample time to prepare for the full-scale invasion of the USSR he still fully intended to undertake.

Fig. 6 *The signing of the Nazi–Soviet Pact on 23 August 1939*

ACTIVITY

1. Which of the reasons given here do you think was Stalin's main reason for signing the Nazi–Soviet Pact?
2. Several cartoons were created about the Nazi–Soviet Pact for British and American newspapers. Look up some examples online. How far do they agree in their interpretations of the agreement?

Stalin, however, was only convinced that the Pact was a prudent idea in summer 1939. He had hoped that he would be able to form an alliance with the democracies to encircle Germany, and in April 1939 had engaged in discussions with the British to this effect. However, British policymakers procrastinated as they were reluctant to ally with a communist state, which they distrusted almost as much as Nazi Germany. Stalin, increasingly frustrated with Britain and France's inability or unwillingness to stand up to the aggression of Japan, Italy and Germany, no longer believed the Western democracies would be useful allies. Stalin was also outraged that he had not been included in the Munich Conference, and believed that Britain and France were using the USSR to divert Hitler's attention away from Western Europe. He deeply distrusted Hitler and welcomed the opportunity to build up his armed forces before war began.

A CLOSER LOOK

The historiography of the Nazi–Soviet Pact

Stalin's motives for signing the Nazi –Soviet Pact continue to be debated amongst historians. Many historians, such as Alan J.P. Taylor, view the Soviet Union's decision to conclude a non-aggression pact with Germany to have been the only realistic option open to it at this stage: despite formidable long-term economic plans to boost industrial output, the USSR was not ready for war. Stalin's purges had also removed many high-ranking and experienced Soviet military officers.

Other historians point to the advantages the Soviets gained from the agreement. Max Hastings has criticised the tendency of historians immediately after the war to accept the USSR's claim to be neutral in the war before 1941. Instead Hastings describes the Soviet Union as 'co-beneficiaries of Nazi aggression'. Indeed, the Soviets gained not only half of Poland in September 1939, but were also able to invade Finland.

The outbreak of war

SOURCE 3

From the minutes of a meeting recording a speech by Hitler to his military advisers on 27 August 1939:

The following special reasons strengthen my resolve. There is no actual rearmament in England, just propaganda. The construction programme of the Navy for 1938 has not yet been fulfilled. Little has been done on land. England will only be able to send a maximum of three divisions to the continent. A little has been done for the Air Force, but it is only a beginning. England does not want the conflict to break out for two or three years. England's position in the world is very precarious. She will not accept any risks. France lacks men due to the decline in the birth rate. Little has been done for rearmament. The artillery is antiquated. France did not want to enter upon this adventure. The enemy had another hope, that Russia would become our enemy after the conquest of Poland. The enemy did not count on my great power of resolution. Our enemies are little worms. I saw them at Munich.

ACTIVITY

Evaluating primary sources

What is the value of this source to an historian studying the reasons for the invasion of Poland?

The invasion of Poland, 1 September 1939

Ironically, Poland's involvement in the land-grabbing in Czechoslovakia that followed Germany's acquisition of the Sudetenland weakened its own security. In April 1939, Hitler laid claim to Danzig, the port city which had been administered by the League of Nations since 1920, claiming that ethnic Germans in the region were being mistreated. Britain and France, knowing that their military preparations were not yet adequate, and in a final effort to postpone war, tried to persuade the Poles to allow Danzig to be annexed by Germany in the last week of August, but Poland resisted.

In turn however, Hitler's deceit had made Britain and France less likely to back down again. They were encouraged by Mussolini's announcement on 25 August that Italy wasn't ready to fight. Using the pretext of 'border violations' by Polish troops, Germany invaded Poland on 1 September 1939. The attack had been postponed from 26 August because Hitler was trying to persuade the Italians to intervene in a potential war against Britain and France.

Britain and France's declaration of war, 3 September 1939

A day after learning of the invasion of Poland, Britain and France issued Germany with an ultimatum. It stated that Germany must withdraw its troops from Poland immediately or both powers would intervene. The deadline of 11am on 3 September was ignored by Germany, and Britain and France declared war. Realistically, however, there was very little Britain and France could do to assist Poland: an amphibious landing would take several weeks to organise; attacking through Germany would have been almost impossible and neither had an air force yet capable of taking on the Luftwaffe. On 7 September, ten French army divisions advanced into Saarland, but only by five miles: token resistance to Germany's invasion was all the Allies offered.

ACTIVITY

Thinking point

The British guarantee to Poland on 31 March 1939 and the Polish–British Common Defence Act of 25 August were by far the firmest commitments made to a country threatened by German aggression. Why do you think Hitler ignored them?

CROSS-REFERENCE

For an explanation of how German–Italian relations developed up to 1939, see Chapter 22.

Italy's reaction to the outbreak of war

The May 1939 Pact of Steel committed Italy to supporting Germany, even if Germany was the aggressor. Historians are unsure as to why Mussolini was prepared to commit Italy to such extreme terms. It is possible that Mussolini did not read the actual terms of the agreement with Germany or was never really serious about them; his advisers were more alarmed. At the end of May, Foreign Minister Ciano persuaded Mussolini to make Germany aware of Italy's woeful lack of military preparation. Hitler was told that to support Germany, Italy would need at least three years to prepare. He ignored the appeal.

Mussolini's reasons for non-intervention

Mussolini knew that a European war would be deeply unpopular with the Italian people, and so tried to free Italy from the Pact. He argued it could fight immediately if Germany supplied it with large quantities of petrol, coal and steel to fuel its war effort – totally unrealistic quantities that Mussolini knew Germany would refuse. Hitler angrily accused Mussolini of behaving like the 1914 liberal Italian government when it refused to honour the Triple Alliance.

When war did break out in September, Mussolini claimed that its ally's behaviour was 'treacherous' and that the Pact of Steel would be abandoned. He announced that Italy would be a 'non-belligerent', to the relief of most Italians.

Italy's declaration of war on Britain and France, June 1940

Mussolini soon despised neutrality: it advertised Italy's weakness and made him appear hypocritical after all his speeches glorifying war. He was envious of the Nazis' breathtaking success waging war across Europe, and as German

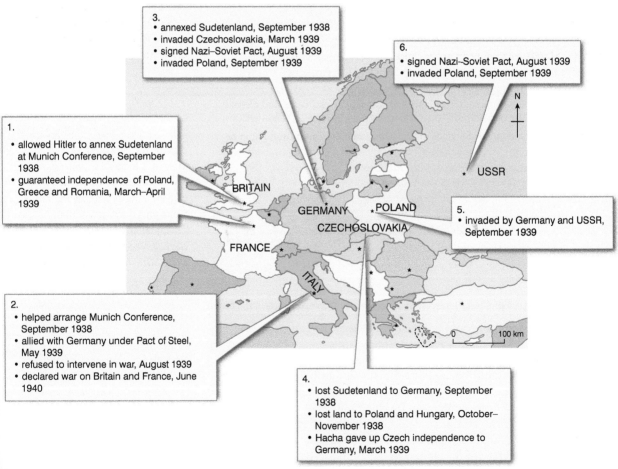

Fig. 7 *Europe in October 1939*

Blitzkrieg tactics proved increasingly effective, Mussolini baulked at the idea of a Nazi-dominated continent and an all-powerful Nazi government vengeful towards Italy for its lack of faith. Joining Nazi Germany offered the potential reward of dominance over the Mediterranean. Convinced the conflict was almost over, Mussolini argued that if Italy wanted to secure such gains it would need to sustain 'a few thousand dead' to earn respect at the post-war conference table. On 10 June 1940, Italy declared war on Britain and France.

KEY TERM

Blitzkreig: translates as 'lightning war'. The use of aerial bombing to 'soften up' targets, followed by swift and heavy tank and infantry advances had a devastating effect in 1939–40

Summary

ACTIVITY

Summary

On a large piece of paper, record the main developments leading to war in Chapters 22 and 23 in separate boxes. Draw arrows to show links between the events and agreements that help explain Hitler, Chamberlain, Daladier, Mussolini and Stalin's actions from September 1938 to June 1940; e.g. a link between the Munich agreement, invasion of Czechoslovakia and Polish guarantee – the first two explain why Britain and France were determined not to allow Hitler another foreign policy victory.

ACTIVITY

Summary chart

Draw up a table of two columns to record the reasons for and against Italian involvement in the Second World War, according to Mussolini. You may want to consider longer-term factors from previous chapters.

 PRACTICE QUESTION

Evaluating historical extracts

With reference to Sources 1, 2 and 3 in this chapter, and your understanding of the historical context, assess the value of these three sources to an historian studying the reasons for Britain's abandonment of appeasement by September 1939.

STUDY TIP

Try to evaluate the provenance and context of the sources. Your own contextual knowledge can be applied in order to explain and comment on the source detail.

 PRACTICE QUESTION

How important was the Nazi–Soviet Pact in causing the outbreak of war in Europe in September 1939?

STUDY TIP

Consider and analyse the various reasons for the outbreak of war. Try to avoid writing an answer which is narrative and descriptive. Remember to explain clearly and thoroughly how each of the various causes led to the final outcome of war between Germany and Britain and France in September 1939.

- the reasons for the escalation to world war

- why the USSR joined the war against Germany

- the position of the USA

- why the Japanese attacked Pearl Harbor in December 1941 and the entry of the USA into the War.

KEY CHRONOLOGY

17 September 1939	The USSR invades Poland
21 June 1940	The French sign an armistice with Germany
22 June 1941	Germany invades the USSR
7 December 1941	The Japanese attack Pearl Harbor
26 May 1942	Anglo-Soviet Treaty signed

ACTIVITY

What does Churchill mean by 'the New World' in Source 1?

SOURCE 1

From Winston Churchill's speech to the House of Commons on 4 June 1940:

The British Empire and the French Republic will defend to the death their native soil, aiding each other like good comrades to the utmost of their strength. Even though large tracts of Europe and many old and famous States have fallen or may fall into the grip of the odious apparatus of Nazi rule, we shall not flag or fail. We shall go on to the end, we shall fight in France, we shall fight on the seas and oceans, we shall fight with growing confidence and growing strength in the air, we shall defend our Island, whatever the cost may be, we shall fight on the beaches, we shall fight on the landing grounds, we shall fight in the fields and in the streets, we shall fight in the hills; we shall never surrender, and even if this Island or a large part of it were subjugated and starving, then our Empire beyond the seas, armed and guarded by the British Fleet, would carry on the struggle, until, in God's good time, the New World, with all its power and might, steps forth to the rescue and the liberation of the old.

The escalation to World War

War in Europe broke out on 3 September 1939 when Britain and France declared war on Germany following its invasion of Poland. This section gives a brief outline of the Second World War's development.

Blitzkrieg and the 'Phoney War', September 1939 to March 1940

The rapid conquest of Poland in September 1939 was mostly due to the success of German 'Blitzkrieg' tactics. Blitzkrieg translates as 'lightning war' and involved the fast, devastating use of modern technology: the Luftwaffe would begin attacks by bombing railway lines and communication links; then tanks and infantry moved in in large numbers to fight off resistance and secure the area. Britain and France did very little to assist Poland, but did hope to prevent the German invasion of Norway as Scandinavia supplied 51 per cent of Germany's iron ore. The 'Phoney War' was a phrase coined at the time to describe the lack of firm action taken by the Allies until Norway was threatened in March 1940. When it was clear that British attempts to secure Norway against a Nazi attack had failed, Neville Chamberlain resigned and was replaced by Winston Churchill, who refused to give in to influential figures pressing for an agreement with Germany.

The fall of France, the Battle of Britain and the Blitz, June 1940 to May 1941

Blitzkrieg tactics were again used with devastating effect against the Netherlands, Belgium and France. The British Expeditionary Force (BEF) dispatched to support the French was forced back to the beaches of Dunkirk in northern France and only escaped back to Britain with a hastily-organised evacuation in May and June 1940. After the Wehrmacht swept through France, and with Italy having declared war against it on 12 June, the French surrendered on 21 June. Britain and its empire stood alone against the German war machine.

Hitler had never aimed to invade and subjugate Britain: unlike his conquests in Eastern Europe, he respected the British as imperialist role models and natural allies against communism. This may explain what was, by German military standards, a half-hearted attempt to prepare for an invasion of Britain in the summer of 1940. Under Operation Sealion, Hitler instructed the Luftwaffe to eliminate the Royal Air Force (RAF) in the Battle of Britain. The RAF's superior planes and home-front advantages helped secure the first Allied victory against the Nazis in September 1940, prompting a change in German strategy. The Blitz, which began on 7 September, targeted civilians in their homes with heavy bombing for eight months.

Fig. 1 *The extent of the German Reich by the end of 1940 (until 1942 only northern and western France were occupied by the Nazis: the rest was nominally neutral with the town of Vichy as its capital)*

The Battle of the Atlantic, 1939–44

As in the First World War, a key objective of each side was to prevent supplies from reaching the enemy. Canada joined the war on Britain's side in September 1939, and from November 1939 the USA sold supplies to Britain under the Cash and Carry scheme. This replaced the earlier American Neutrality Acts as Roosevelt was adamant that the Western democracies should receive some assistance, but the Cash and Carry legislation stipulated that goods must be transported by the purchasing nation who assumed all the incumbent risks in doing so (remembering that German submarine attacks on American commercial shipping were a reason for the USA's involvement in the First World War).

As the conflict in Europe developed, Britain's ability to pay upfront for necessary war materials decreased. Roosevelt was alarmed by the swiftness of the Wehrmacht's conquest of Europe and, while aware that most Americans were still in favour of neutrality, advocated more support for the democracies and proposed the Lend–Lease scheme. From March 1941, this enabled the USA to supply the materials necessary for the war against the Axis powers, including weapons, military transport vehicles and food, to Britain, China and **France's government-in-exile**. The scheme extended to the Soviet Union after its invasion by Germany. Over $50 billion of supplies were shipped to these countries under Lend–Lease, and were provided on the condition that they be returned where possible, or paid for after the war. Roosevelt attempted to convince the public of the necessity of Lend–Lease by comparing the situation to that of someone lending a garden hose to a neighbour whose house was

A CLOSER LOOK

France's government in exile

On 22 June 1940, unable to resist the Wehrmacht's Western Offensive, the French government signed an armistice with Germany. France was divided into occupied and non-occupied zones, the latter known as Vichy France after its makeshift capital. A French government in exile, 'Free France', was established by Charles de Gaulle in London. It supported the French Resistance movement working secretly against the Nazis.

on fire: 'What do I do in such a crisis? I don't say, 'Neighbour, my garden hose cost me $15; you have to pay me $15 for it'! I don't want $15 – I want my garden hose back after the fire is over.'"

Under the Lend–Lease scheme food and raw materials arrived in Britain via shipping routes in the North Atlantic, without which it could not have continued to resist Germany. Again, German U-boats played a key role in disrupting British supply lines. Initially they were so badly affected that Churchill admitted later: 'the only thing that ever really frightened me was the U-boat peril'.

War in North Africa and the Mediterranean

Italy's declaration of war on Britain in June 1940 prompted fighting between Italian and British troops in Libya, as British soldiers were stationed in neighbouring Egypt. Despite being heavily outnumbered, General O'Connor led a British force into Libya and met little determined resistance from the Italians. Tobruk and Tripoli fell to the British, and in January 1941 the British Army attacked Abyssinia. In May 1941, Haile Selassie was restored to power, five years after he was forced into exile. Italian fortunes in North Africa were only reversed with the intervention of Germany, which in turn decreased Germany's resources.

CROSS-REFERENCE

The reasons for Italy's intervention and its early campaigns in the war are explained in Chapter 23.

Mussolini ordered the invasion of Greece on 28 October, in the hope of realising his long-held dream of securing dominance in the Balkans, but the assault was a disaster. To prevent the failure of the fascist attack in the Mediterranean arena, Germany invaded Yugoslavia in April 1941 and completed the conquest of Greece within a month. Crete was attacked on 20 May 1941 and its government surrendered within eight days. The island of Malta, of great strategic importance to the Allies, resisted sustained German attacks and was awarded the George Cross by Britain.

War in the Pacific

When Japan joined the war on the side of the Axis Powers (see page 191), Western colonial possessions in the Far East were under threat. British colonial troops from across the empire were deployed to defend its colonies, especially Burma, Britain's longest campaign of the war. Many islands in the Philippines fell following Japanese invasions in the first

Fig. 2 *British and Italian forces in North Africa, where much of the British military action took place after Dunkirk and before D-Day*

half of 1942, as did New Guinea in 1943. US submarine warfare was increasingly used to disrupt Japanese shipping, and by 1943 the Japanese were in retreat.

The entry of the Soviet Union

The secret clause of the Nazi–Soviet Pact – the division of Poland – was enacted on 17 September when the USSR invaded Poland from the east. Poland's army was ill-equipped, and as the invasion of Germany by Britain and France the Poles hoped for never materialised, the country fell: Warsaw surrendered to the invaders on 27 September. The Germans and Russians had already agreed how to divide up Poland into their respective spheres of influence under the Treaty of Friendship, Cooperation and Demarcation, signed on 28 September.

Red Army operations

The Nazi–Soviet Pact allowed Stalin to establish a sphere of influence in nations on the Soviet Union's western border: Estonia, Latvia and Lithuania. These states had declared their independence from Russia between 1918 and 1920, but Stalin was determined to match the Tsarist possessions in Eastern Europe. By October 1939, the Red Army had overthrown their independent governments.

The success of the German *Wehrmacht* at the start of the war proved that the Nazi–Soviet Pact had been a necessary and prudent precaution: by contrast, the **Red Army's** operations were far less effective. This was not only because the USSR was not ready to fight at the same strength as Germany, but because of Stalin's damaging political **purges** which saw the dismissal, imprisonment and even execution of the Soviet Union's most experienced military officers on the grounds of 'disloyalty'. This severely weakened Soviet military strategy, and Hitler took note of the USSR's botched invasion of Finland during the 'Winter War' from October 1939 to March 1940. The Finns put up brave resistance to the Red Army invasion, but the large numbers of reserves ordered by Stalin eventually tipped the balance in the Soviets' favour. On 12 March 1940, Finland signed an armistice with the Soviet Union.

The German invasion of the USSR

The Nazi–Soviet Pact had fulfilled its objectives in an astonishingly short space of time: Poland had been eliminated as an independent state and divided; both parties had allowed each other to pursue their other war aims; and still neither Britain nor France had launched any real assault to stop Germany, despite having declared war on 3 September. However, Hitler ordered the German army to invade the Soviet Union on 22 June 1941. He had several reasons for doing so:

- Attacking the USSR remained a key objective. It fulfilled Hitler's long-term aims of crushing communism and obtaining *Lebensraum*, but was also a clear manifestation of the Nazi belief that the Russian Slavs were an inferior race.
- Hitler was aware of Japan's planned attack on the USA (see below). Keeping Stalin occupied with an invasion from the west would allow the Japanese to throw its full force behind the Pacific War.
- Hitler anticipated that Stalin would soon find Germany's sphere of influence in Eastern Europe intolerable and seek to challenge it.

Soviet military leaders expected an attack from Germany, but not until 1942 or 1943; the Wehrmacht's initial success in Operation Barbarossa (the invasion of the USSR) proved that while the Nazi–Soviet Pact had bought the Soviets time to remilitarise, it wasn't enough. On 22 June 121 Wehrmacht divisions invaded,

ACTIVITY

Summary

Create a timeline recording the developments in the Second World War up to 1943. You could also label a blank map of the world, highlighting the main theatres of war.

KEY TERM

Red Army: the land military forces of the Soviet Union

purge: in the Stalinist sense, the removal of disloyal or potentially disloyal personnel

Fig. 3 *The Soviet invasion of Finland was fiercely resisted by the Finns*

A CLOSER LOOK

The Eastern Front of the Second World War

The nature of fighting in the USSR was particularly savage on both sides. German soldiers were encouraged to think of their Soviet enemies as racially and politically inferior: Jews and Russian prisoners of war faced brutal treatment ranging from summary execution by *Einsatzgruppen* (death squads) to forced labour on pitiful rations. Civilians were shown little mercy: during the siege of Leningrad the local population faced mass starvation but refused to surrender.

ACTIVITY

Evaluating primary sources

What can be learned from Source 2 about what the USSR expected from its new allies?

supported by the Luftwaffe. Opinion was divided, however, on how to proceed: generals recommended a full-scale attack on Moscow, but Hitler insisted on assaults on Leningrad and Ukraine as well, to cut off Finnish aid by way of the Baltic Sea and prevent Soviet use of industrial and agricultural areas.

The Nazi–Soviet Pact had seen Nazi Germany and the communist USSR become unlikely bedfellows; Operation Barbarossa forced the Soviets into another 'unnatural' alliance. The USA and Britain – two capitalist democracies – were (publicly, at least) committed to assist the USSR against Germany until the end of the war. For the first months after the German invasion, the Soviet Union's primary objective was survival; only in the winter of 1941 did the Russians begin an effective counter-offensive. At first the alignment between the USSR and the Western democracies was informal, and based on the existence of a common enemy. The British Foreign Secretary, Anthony Eden, and Soviet Foreign Minister, Vyacheslav Molotov, concluded the Anglo-Soviet Treaty on 26 May 1942, under which both powers agreed to a political and military alliance for a period of 20 years. By this point the Soviets were challenging the Wehrmacht's early success with Barbarossa: the Battle of Moscow fought between October 1941 and January 1942 was a decisive Russian victory.

SOURCE 2

From Molotov's address to Soviet party members on 19 June 1942, describing the Anglo-Soviet Treaty of May 1942:

The entire tenor of the treaty bears out its great political importance not only for the development of Anglo-Soviet relations but also for the future development of the entire complex of international relations in Europe. Both the Anglo-Soviet treaty and the results of the negotiations which I conducted on instructions of the Soviet Government in London and Washington testify to the substantial consolidation of friendly relations between the Soviet Union, Great Britain and the United States of America. The importance of this fact to the peoples of the Soviet Union, who are bearing the main brunt of the struggle against Hitlerite Germany, will increase in such measure as it helps expedite our victory over the German invaders. The treaty, like other results from the negotiations in London and Washington, should hasten the defeat of Hitlerite Germany and its associates in aggression in Europe. At the same time these results will serve as a basis for further development of friendly relations between the USSR and Great Britain, as well as between both these countries and the United States of America.

Western assistance to the beleaguered USSR was greatly enhanced by the entry of the USA into the war in December 1941 (see below). With its formidable industrial resources, America was able to supply its allies with huge quantities of armaments, equipment and food. Under the Lend–Lease agreement, half a million motor vehicles were sent to the USSR; while Soviet figures state that the US supplied the Red Army with 2 per cent of its artillery, 10 per cent of its tanks and 12 per cent of its planes. However, the contribution of food and transport vehicles was of far greater significance to the Soviet war effort than armaments.

CROSS-REFERENCE

The Neutrality Acts are explored in Chapter 22.

Japan, Pearl Harbor and the entry of the USA

The end of American isolationism

The USA's 1937 **Neutrality Act** outlawed the selling of weapons or loaning of capital to all belligerents in a future war, and prevented the president from distinguishing between aggressor and victim in the event of a conflict and giving support to the latter. Despite his reservations at the time, Roosevelt agreed to the act as he was already embroiled in a dispute with the Supreme Court over his plans to alleviate the continuing effects of the Great Depression.

In May 1941 a poll of US public opinion revealed that 79 per cent were opposed to entering the war voluntarily, but news of Nazi atrocities in the conquered territories began to change the mood. Having won a third term as president in 1940, Roosevelt carefully steered the Lend–Lease Act through Congress in early 1941. Like his predecessor Woodrow Wilson, Roosevelt believed US intervention in the war to be morally justifiable and increasingly inevitable, and was willing to subvert America's proclaimed neutrality to support its future allies. However, he expected and hoped that US intervention would be limited to the European and Atlantic arenas, and viewed a war in the Pacific against Japan as involving unwelcome risks.

SOURCE 3

From Roosevelt's broadcast to the American people on 29 December 1940. Roosevelt often explained his policy in radio broadcasts in what became known as his 'fireside chats'. In this one, he was answering his critics who argued that the Lend–Lease Act would definitely drag the USA into an unwanted war:

Some of our people like to believe that wars in Europe and in Asia are of no concern to us. Does anyone seriously believe that we need to fear attack anywhere in the Americas while a free Britain remains our most powerful naval neighbor in the Atlantic? Does anyone seriously believe, on the other hand, that we could rest easy if the Axis powers were our neighbors there? If Great Britain goes down, the Axis powers will control the continents of Europe, Asia, Africa, Australasia, and the high seas – and they will be in a position to bring enormous military and naval resources against this hemisphere. It is no exaggeration to say that all of us, in all the Americas, would be living at the point of a gun – a gun loaded with explosive bullets, economic as well as military. We should enter upon a new and terrible era in which the whole world, our hemisphere included, would be run by threats of brute force. To survive in such a world, we would have to convert ourselves permanently into a militaristic power on the basis of war economy.

ACTIVITY

Are there any phrases in Source 3 which suggest Roosevelt saw US intervention as inevitable?

The Atlantic Charter, 1941

Roosevelt and Churchill met in Newfoundland on 9 and 10 August 1941 to discuss the development of the war and outline plans for the post-war world. The Atlantic Charter – eight 'common principles' drafted by the two leaders – including the restoration of independent government to all countries occupied by foreign powers during the war. Churchill and Roosevelt shared many aims with regards to the war, and many post-war ideals, but they also shared the disappointment that the Charter failed to convince the American people that intervention in the war was necessary or prudent. Nevertheless, the Charter was significant despite not resulting in a formal treaty. It acknowledged the USA's sympathy with the British against the aggression of the Axis powers, and demonstrated that Roosevelt's vision for peace was similar to the one outlined in Wilson's Fourteen Points in 1918.

Motives behind the Japanese attack

Japan – and in particular its military, which held increasing influence over the government in Tokyo – sought to establish itself as the dominant power in the Far East: the invasion of Manchuria and war on China were one step towards this goal. The USA was therefore an inconvenience: although most Americans were committed to isolationism, many would object to the abandonment of

Fig. 4 *Hideki Tojo*

Hideki Tojo (1884–1948), a committed nationalist, served as a general in the Japanese Army before becoming War Minister in 1940 and Prime Minister in 1941. As he ordered the Japanese attack on Pearl Harbor, he was held responsible for initiating war with the USA. After the war he was sentenced to death for war crimes, and hanged in 1948.

Research

Create a news report or broadcast informing the American people of the Japanese attack. Include some background information on US neutrality up until the bombing of Pearl Harbor. Will you take a critical tone?

China to an aggressor with a track record in brutality, so the US government appeared increasingly likely to interfere with Japanese expansion. As the Sino-Japanese war dragged on, the US decided to block the Japanese from accessing war materials needed to complete its invasion. By the summer of 1941, the American embargo prevented the Japanese from getting rubber, oil and iron, just as its trade tariffs in 1931 had prompted Japan to seek new markets for its exports by building an empire.

On 27 September 1940, Germany, Italy and Japan signed the Three Power Pact, by which they would 'assist one another with all political, economic and military means when one of the three parties is at war with a power at present not involved with the European war of the Chinese–Japanese conflict.' The USA may not have been mentioned explicitly, but it was clear that was the 'power' alluded to: the signatories hoped to deter Roosevelt from intervening on the side of the Allies in Europe by suggesting it would invite war with Japan. Germany also wanted to reaffirm principles behind the Anti-Comintern Pact, despite the non-aggression agreement in the Nazi–Soviet Pact.

On 16 October 1941, **General Tojo** became Prime Minister of Japan, which emphasised the military's dominance over Japanese policy. Tojo formulated plans for war against Britain and the USA. The Japanese didn't expect to be able to invade and conquer America; instead they hoped that a surprise attack would allow them to defend their interests in the western Pacific. Admiral Yamamoto was instructed to prepare a force to attack the US fleet at Pearl Harbor, its base in Hawaii. Early in December 1941, Washington received intelligence that a Japanese attack was imminent, but believed that the Philippines would be the most likely target. On 7 December, 300 Japanese planes launched a bombing raid on Pearl Harbor, deliberately attacking on a Sunday so the Americans were caught off-guard. The next day, Congress voted to declare war on Japan; on 11 December Germany declared war on the USA, according to the Three Power Pact.

Fig. 5 *The Japanese bombing of the US fleet at Pearl Harbor, Hawaii, 7 December 1941*

Summary

The entry of the United States, and the failure of the German invasion of the USSR tipped the balance of the war away from the Axis powers and in favour of the Allies. The war comprised theatres all over the world: Europe, North Africa, the USSR, and the Atlantic and Pacific Oceans. The Germans and Japanese overstretched themselves by attacking the USSR and USA respectively. Both assaults were prompted by ideological goals and – indirectly, in Japan's case – the desire to create an empire which subjugated 'inferior races'. Many in the West viewed the war as a battle between dictatorship and democracy; between totalitarianism and freedom. However, the awkward alliance with the Soviet Union made this an inaccuracy, and would have formidable future consequences as the Second World War ended and the Cold War began.

ACTIVITY

Summary

1. For each assault or theatre of combat explored in this chapter, summarise the motives of the aggressors in a series of bullet points.
2. Using your list, the maps in this chapter and the opening timeline, identify the key reasons why the conflicts in Europe and the Far East escalated (and sometimes overlapped) to create a global war.

 PRACTICE QUESTION

How important was the attack on Pearl Harbor to the USA's decision to declare war on Germany and Japan?

STUDY TIP

Try to distinguish between causes and catalyst. While it might have been the attack that prompted the declaration of war, the fact that the USA declared war on both Japan and Germany could have been indicative of other reasons which you should try to explore in this answer.

Conclusion: an overview of international relations by 1941

Fig. 1 *British soldiers being evacuated from Dunkirk in May 1940 after being forced to retreat from mainland France by the Nazis*

The outbreak of two devastating world wars in 1914 and 1939 suggests that international diplomacy in the years 1890 to 1941 failed to contain the rivalries and aggression of the Great Powers, and therefore failed to keep the peace. This is to assume that a consistent aim of all statesmen was to avoid going to war, an assumption disproved by men like Conrad von Hotzendorf and Leopold von Berchtold in 1914, and Adolf Hitler and the Japanese High Command in the 1930s. It is, of course, a matter of debate as to how wide a war the more aggressive policymakers planned for, or expected.

Using the examples of the First and Second World Wars to argue that international diplomacy was a failure also overlooks the ability and willingness of statesmen to manage and resolve (at least temporarily) a wide range of crises before decisions were taken to declare war and mobilise troops. Britain and France resolved two centuries of colonial rivalry with the 1904 Anglo-French Entente; Russia and Serbia decided against war in the wake of the 1908 Bosnian Crisis; and, despite strong objections, Germany backed down in the 1905 and 1911 Moroccan Crises. This is not to say, of course, that any of these solutions were permanent: each caused or exacerbated rivalries between the powers, but they do suggest that a European war was far from a foregone conclusion in the early twentieth century.

Between the wars, and especially after the onset of the Great Depression, there were even greater internal and external pressures on most governments to avoid war, often – ironically – at the expense of the terms of the post-war peace settlements. Despite such pressures, and the ultimate failure of the appeasement of German, Italian and Japanese aggression, there were united attempts to resolve the world's problems under the principle of collective security: among them the League of Nations' successful resolution of disputes in the 1920s (with obvious exceptions, such as the Corfu Incident), the World Disarmament Conference, the Locarno Treaties and the Stresa Pact. Although the last three would eventually collapse, they point to the efforts – often determined and well-meaning – of statesmen, to avoid the horrors of the Great War, well into the 1930s.

In an analysis of the causes of the two World Wars, however, some key themes emerge to help us understand why these attempts by the world's governments to avoid large-scale conflict failed in 1914 and again in 1939.

Nationalism

Two strands of nationalism existed between the 1890s and 1940s: the more general, political form of patriotism felt by the majority of civilians, which often encouraged governments to prioritise national prestige over peaceful relations with its rivals. The nationalism felt by many British, French and German citizens in the early 1900s was the product of insecurity too: the German challenge to the supremacy of the British navy could not go unchecked despite the plans of the Liberal government of the time to prioritise social reforms, while the French alliance with Russia was born out of the former's humiliating defeat, and subsequent diplomatic isolation, by Germany in 1870.

The second strand of nationalism, however, proved to be a far greater destabilising factor in the early twentieth century. The Eastern Question, having been a source of concern for European statesmen since the early 1800s, came into sharper focus as the collapse of the Ottoman Empire in Europe accelerated in the last years of the century. As Russia and Austria-Hungary advanced their ambitions to create spheres of influence in the Balkans, the addition of a restless and increasingly ruthless pan-Slav nationalism, led by Serbia, created a dangerously precarious situation in which tension grew. The ideal of creating a South Slav nation independent from Ottoman authority or Austro-Hungarian domination incurred the deep suspicion of Austria-Hungary, which had enough difficulty containing nationalist feelings within its borders. Thus the assassination of Franz Ferdinand in June 1914 provided the excuse Austria-Hungary needed to justify crushing the nationalist threat.

With the pursuit of self-determination for Europeans during the Paris Peace Conference of 1919 several new nation states were created or recognised officially. The simultaneous collapse of the Austro-Hungarian, Ottoman and Russian Empires, as well as the confiscation of some German territory, dramatically altered the map of Europe. Several new states however, such as Czechoslovakia, still contained a wide variety of ethnicities and, with their new democratic governments, would prove to be vulnerable to aggression from their neighbours.

As a result of the Great Depression, nationalism again became a potentially dangerous force in the 1930s as governments were forced to prioritise their own economic recoveries over the principle of collective security. This not only deterred member states of the League of Nations from sending troops or imposing economic sanctions during the Manchurian and Abyssinian Crises, but also encouraged Nazi Germany and Japan to use aggression to increase their own resources, resulting in the German pursuit of *Lebensraum* and the Japanese invasion of China.

The balance of power

Maintaining the balance of power was probably the most important foreign policy priority for most governments in the years 1890 to 1941. For the European countries before the First World War this meant ensuring that no power was in a position to dominate the continent as the French had done under Napoleon in the early nineteenth century. This policy explains the suspicion aroused in Britain, France and Russia by Germany's rapid economic development from the 1880s, and what drove the British government to declare war in August 1914. Fears about the military strength of rival powers helped to create the two alliance systems in place by 1914, while the military staff of Germany, Austria-Hungary and Russia gained increasing influence over the civilian government.

Restoring the balance of power was a key principle of the 1919 Paris peace conference, and along with the desire for revenge most keenly felt by France, explains the treatment of Germany according to the Treaty of Versailles. The limited membership of the League of Nations, however, was one of the main reasons for its later failure, as it did not initially include Germany or Soviet Russia, and the USA was never persuaded to abandon its isolationism. Britain and France reluctantly assumed the leadership of the League which lacked real power due to the absences on the Council, and was not able to defend the balance of power into the 1930s.

The restoration of German economic and military strength under the Nazi government in the 1930s was a direct challenge to the balance of power in Europe, just as Japanese expansion threatened the status quo in Asia and the Pacific. The USA made some determined efforts to limit Japanese ambition, not because it saw itself as a global police force, but because its own security and commercial interests were threatened. British policy towards Nazi Germany centred around appeasement, partly because Hitler was seen as a lesser threat than the communist USSR until the very late 1930s, and partly to postpone the outbreak of another European war for as long as possible. As Austria, the Sudetenland and Czechoslovakia were subsumed into the German Reich, the maintenance of the balance of power became entirely distorted and British and French preparations for war increased accordingly.

Fig. 2 *A German crowd responds to news of Britain's declaration of war against Germany in August 1914*

The causes of war

The assassination of an Austrian archduke by a Bosnian Serb gave Austria-Hungary a justifiable reason to attack Serbia, whose pan-Slav ambitions threatened the security of the Habsburg Empire. The involvement of the other powers was brought about by the system of alliances. Militarism in Germany, Austria-Hungary and Russia also played a part: their military staffs had created war plans (as had France) which hinged on the necessity to attack quickly before the enemy was thoroughly prepared; as these were highly developed by 1914, chiefs-of-staff argued that to delay while diplomats tried to negotiate would be militarily disastrous. Many governments also believed, due to the popularity of nationalism which was partly fostered by the imperial tensions of the late nineteenth century, that their citizens would support a war against its traditional rivals. Militarism, nationalism, and the existence of alliance systems are therefore all key to understanding the complex events of the July Crisis.

The causes of the Second World War are less straightforward, as the conflicts between Japan and China, and those between Germany and Britain and France, between Germany and the USSR, and between Japan and the USA all had separate but interlinked origins. Militarism was again a factor in Japan's invasion of China, but the need to acquire raw materials was also important, while the shortcomings of the League of Nations, as well as the weakness of the Chinese government, allowed the invasion to escalate. British appeasement of Germany was a dubious policy due to the misunderstanding of a Hitler as a 'reasonable man with reasonable grievances' who would be satisfied once the 'wrongs' of Versailles had been addressed. The League's failure to take any action against Germany's violation of the Treaty demonstrated its ultimate failure. The German invasion of the USSR in 1941 was one of the longest-held Nazi aims in foreign policy as Hitler sought to crush communism and acquire *Lebensraum* for the German people. The Japanese attack on Pearl Harbor in the same year was the result of increasing Japanese distaste for Western influence and frustration with American attempts to limit Japanese military strength.

Wars can only be fully understood with an appreciation of their longer-term origins, leading some historians to conclude that the Second World War arose out of the unsuitability of the post-war peace treaties, and growing dissatisfaction with them by the late 1930s. In support of this argument, it is the case that the restrictions and reparations imposed on Germany helped Hitler to gain support, and that the Japanese and Italians were deeply dissatisfied with their treatment by the 1919 peacemakers. However, this interpretation overlooks the serious challenge to collective security – which had achieved some notable successes and still had broad support in the 1920s – posed by the Great Depression. The American commitment to isolationism severely undermined the effectiveness of the League of Nations, as did the exclusion of the USSR and Germany at its inception. It could also be argued that the horror of the First World War, vividly remembered by so many European civilians, caused governments to try to avoid further conflict for as long as possible, inadvertently encouraging Mussolini and Hitler to take advantage.

Fig. 3   *The invasion of Czechoslovakia by Nazi Germany proved that appeasement was no longer working, and nor was it morally justifiable*

To evaluate fully the success or failure of international diplomacy, there are several factors to consider. The mainstream values and attitudes of the general public have a bearing on a government's foreign policy, especially if it is broadly democratic. This affected a number of decisions in the years 1890 to 1945 to go to war, to continue negotiating, or to pursue non-military means to conduct foreign policy at the expense of a rival power: examples include the popularity of pan-Slavism in Russia when Serbia was facing Austro-Hungarian attack; Britain's involvement in the naval arms race with Germany; and the

French desire for the punishment of Germany at the Paris Peace Conference. Another factor is the internal and external pressure faced by statesmen when conducting foreign policy: the new realities of the Great Depression were probably the strongest example of this. Furthermore, the capabilities of statesmen and diplomats, as well as their own views and ambitions, were often crucial in determining the success of a country's foreign policy. Personal relationships – even misunderstandings – could have a significant impact, as did Edward Grey's hedging of British intentions in 1914 and Neville Chamberlain's feeling of betrayal following the invasion of Czechoslovakia in 1939. There is certainly some truth in the suggestion that in both 1914 and 1939, statesmen made key mistakes and in many ways stumbled into war. It would also be true to add, however, that the origins of both conflicts had been born decades earlier.

Comparing the state of international relations between 1890 and 1941, many changes become apparent. At the beginning of the period, international relations had been dominated by the Great Powers of Europe, most of which were empires with control over several nations, and with autocratic or at least conservative political systems. By 1941 this had changed significantly. The autocratic empires had collapsed, to be replaced in Germany and Russia by conflicting totalitarian systems. Furthermore, in 1890 neither Japan nor the USA acted decisively or significantly in international relations. By 1941, the USA was developing into a dominant global power, and the rise of Japan had been very significant in the geopolitics of the Far East.

Glossary

A

Abyssinia: an alternative name for the Ethiopian Empire in the 1930s

Anglo–French Entente: agreement between Britain and France, signed in 1904; often referred to as the Entente Cordiale, which translates as 'cordial understanding'

appeasement: the method of keeping peace by making compromises. Here it refers specifically to the policy of Britain and France towards Germany in response to Hitler's actions. It was, and remains, a very controversial policy

arms race: a competition between countries to produce the most armaments. This often included the rapid development of military technology. The same concept applies to a naval race: battleships were produced, often with increasingly destructive capabilities

Ausgleich: German for 'concession' or 'compensation'; the Ausgleich of 1867 was the result of Hungarian attempts to win independence from the Habsburg Empire in 1848–49

autarky: economic self-sufficiency

autocracy: system of government by which all power is concentrated in the hands of the ruler and officials whom they appoint; absolute monarchies are also autocracies

autonomous: able to do what you want without reference to other authorities; in this case the Reichstag and civilian authorities

B

battleship: A large, armoured war vessel equipped with heavy weaponry

bilateral agreement: an agreement between two powers, rather than a wider international understanding

blank cheque: a metaphor for Germany's promise to support Austria in whatever way it chose to respond to the assassination of Franz Ferdinand

Blitzkreig: translates as 'lightning war'; the use of aerial bombing to 'soften up' targets, followed by swift and heavy tank and infantry advances had a devastating effect in 1939–40

Boers: the descendants of the Dutch who had settled in South Africa in the eighteenth century

C

Cabinet: a group of ministers, such as Foreign Secretary and Chancellor of the Exchequer, appointed by the Prime Minister

censorship: involves the restriction or banning of public material (such as news media), usually by governments

Chancellor: the German chief minister

chiefs of staff: high-ranking army officials responsible for military planning and tactics

client states: smaller nations given economic, political and often military assistance by larger countries in return for their loyalty

communism: a political and economic system under which the means of production (farms, factories, etc.) are owned and run by the state, and wealth and resources shared equally

Council of Four: comprised the Big Three (Wilson, Clemenceau and Lloyd George) and Orlando of Italy

coup: a violent seizure of power

conscription: the compulsory drafting of all men of military age into the armed forces

constitution: a set of rules on how a country should be governed; most constitutions limit the power of the monarchy in some way

D

Defence Requirements Committee: a British government committee established in 1933 to assess the potential need for rearmament in response to growing international insecurity

democracy: political system in which the people choose their own rulers; in modern states this is usually by electing representatives to sit in a National Assembly or Parliament

demobilisation: the process by which armed forces are disbanded

democratisation: the process by which armed forces are disbanded

depression: a downturn in economic activity, causing nations' economies to shrink, leading to large-scale unemployment, and often a reduction in trade

détente: improvement in relations between countries which had previously been strained

Diet: Hungarian parliament

dominions: countries united by their common allegiance to the British Crown but free to run their own domestic and foreign affairs; together they comprised the British Commonwealth

downturn: a decrease in economic activity; the Great Depression was an extreme, long-term example

Dual Monarchy: rule of Austria and Hungary by a single monarch, under whom the two states had equal political status

E

electoral college: an elected body which votes on behalf of a larger group of voters

émigré: a person who has fled their country for fear of oppression

entente: an understanding. It is not an alliance and does not bind either party to support the other in the event of a general war

F

fait accompli: an action already completed, and therefore must be accepted, even if inconvenient

fascism: a radical political ideology embracing the values of nationalism and authoritarianism; it is an extreme right-wing viewpoint and its traditional enemy is communism, the extreme left-wing equivalent

federalisation: a system by which individual states are given some powers to govern themselves locally, while remaining within a larger state

foreign policy: a government's strategy in dealing with other nations

franchise: the right to vote in elections, or the portion of the population which is entitled to vote

Führer: German for 'leader'; in Nazi ideology it took on the connotation of undisputed dictator

G

Geneva: a city in Switzerland where the League of Nations' headquarters were situated

grand vizier: a long-established position in the Ottoman government, roughly equivalent to a British prime minister

guerrilla: fighting involving 'undercover' methods of attacking a stronger enemy

H

home front: the civilian government and people not directly fighting in a war

honest brokers: arbitrators in a dispute or potential dispute who remain neutral and consider points made by all parties concerned

I

imperialism: the policy of creating and expanding an empire, or the desire to do so

intellectualism: the pursuit of intellectual development and learning

J

July Crisis: a diplomatic crisis among the major powers of Europe in the summer of 1914 that led to the First World War

K

Kaiser: the German Emperor

Kwantung army: the largest and most influential army group of the Japanese army

L

Lebensraum: translates as 'living space'; part of Nazi ideology that dictated Germany should expand and colonise land belonging to 'inferior races' such as Slavs

leverage: a strong negotiating position; a person who has good leverage is able to apply influence on others

liberalism: political view advocating greater freedoms for civilians, including freedom of speech and of the press, and limits to the power of rulers

M

Maginot Line: the defensive line of fortifications built in France from 1929 to protect against a German invasion

mandate: territories (particularly overseas colonies) transferred to the control of a different country until they were thought capable of governing themselves

Maxim machine gun: invented in 1884, and could fire up to 600 rounds per minute

merchant ships: commercial vessels not belonging to a country's military navy; they did not have guns on board so they had no means to fight or defend themselves

military jihad: a holy war declared by Islamic powers in defence of the Muslim religion

mir: a peasant commune

mobilised: mobilisation is the process of moving soldiers and military equipment to the front line in preparation for war

moratorium: temporarily suspends a debt repayment grants, with the agreement of the creditor

N

nationalism: a strong, politicised form of patriotism; many nationalists' goals in the late nineteenth century were focused on gaining independence from an empire or dominant state

Night of the Long Knives: between 30 June and 2 July 1934 the SS murdered around 400 of Hitler's perceived opponents

P

pan-Slavism: the nationalist ambition to unite all Slavs and win independence from non-Slav empires; South Slav nationalism refers to pan-Slavism in the Balkans

pan-Turkism: a movement advocating the union of Turkish-speaking peoples within and outside the borders of the Ottoman Empire

parliamentary bill: the draft version of an Act of Parliament, often revised before receiving approval

peace footing: the status of an army whose country is needed only for defence; usually the number of active soldiers is reduced

passive resistance: a form of non-violent protest; often such protesters will aim to cause as much inconvenience as possible

preventive war: a small-scale, quick war planned to avoid a larger, longer war later on

protectionism: ensuring that goods are cheaper for consumers than imported products

protectorate: territory over which a foreign power has political authority

purge: in the Stalinist sense, the removal of disloyal or potentially disloyal personnel

R

ratify: the final recognition of a treaty, following its signature by the parties involved

rationing: a system by which the government allows citizens a restricted amount of food and goods, usually when the production or supply of a commodity is restricted

reactionary: policies which demonstrated a negative response to change

reciprocity: the practice of exchanging terms for mutual benefit

reparation: a principle of international law which states that it is the obligation of the wrongdoing party to redress the damage caused to the injured party

representative government: a government that is elected to serve the needs of its citizens

Red Army: the land military forces of the Soviet Union

relief money: paid to workers on strike to ensure they can afford to live without receiving a wage

resolution: in international relations, a formal commitment to achieving an objective

revanchism: French for 'revenge'; a policy that aimed to overturn the losses to French territory incurred as a result of the Franco–Prussian War

Rhenish: of the Rhineland

Risorgimento: the Italian nationalist movement

S

self-determination: the right of people of the same race or cultural background to be ruled by themselves as a nation

Shinto: the state religion of Japan until 1945; centuries old, it involved the worship of ancestors, natural spirits, and the Emperor

Skoda: a Czech manufacturing company which produced armaments

socialism: political school of thought advocating the fair distribution of wealth

sovereignty: the authority of a state to govern itself

Soviet: Russian word for council, meaning a political organisation for and led by the working classes or 'proletariat'

Splendid Isolation: the British policy of remaining aloof from foreign affairs in Europe; it was viewed as splendid by British ministers as it avoided disadvantageous agreements with other countries and emphasised the British Empire's strength

Sublime Porte: the location of the central government of the Ottoman Empire

suzerainty: a status under which a country has control over its own domestic affairs, but its foreign policy is under the influence of another state, to which it owes formal allegiance

T

Teutonic Knights: a medieval religious and military order; 'Teutonic' is a word describing the German people

Third Republic: the government established in France after the fall of Napoleon III in September 1870 while the Franco–Prussian War was still being fought; it ended in 1940 following the invasion of Nazi Germany

trade union: workers' organisations which campaign for better pay and conditions; the severest action trade unions could take to influence their employers was to go on strike and refuse to work

tribunal: a committee set up to settle a dispute

U

unilateral: the action of one country alone; bilateral action would involve two countries

universal suffrage: extending the right to vote in elections to all adult men and women

V

veto: the power to prevent a law being passed

W

Wehrmacht: the armed forces of Germany from 1935; immediately disbanded by the Allies in 1945

Y

Yugoslav Empire: a country for the southern Slavs

Z

Zionism: the movement to establish a homeland for Jews in Israel, in response to centuries of persecution in other countries

Bibliography

Books for students

Aldred, John, *British Imperial and Foreign Policy 1846–1980*, 2004

Bromley, Jonathan, *Russia 1848–1917*, 2002

Dailey, Andy, and Williamson, David, *Peacemaking, Peacekeeping: International Relations 1918-36*, 2012

Gildea, Robert, *Barricades and Borders: Europe 1800–1914*, 2003

Goldstein, Erik, *The First World War Peace Settlements 1919–1925*, 2002

Henig, Ruth, *Origins of the Second World War 1933–1939*, 1985

Henig, Ruth, *Versailles and After, 1919–1933*, 1995

Hite, John and Hinton, Chris, *Weimar and Nazi Germany*, 2000

Layton, Geoff, *From Bismarck to Hitler: Germany 1890–1933*, 1996

Lowe, John and Pearce, Robert, *Rivalry and Accord: International Relations 1870–1914*, 2001

Mason, John, *The Dissolution of the Austro-Hungarian Empire, 1867–1918*, 1996

McDonough, Frank, *The Origins of the First and Second World War*, 1997

Morris, Terry and Murphy, Derrick, *Europe 1870–1991*, 2004

Neville, Peter, *France 1914–69: The Three Republics*, 1995

Overy, Richard, *The Origins of the Second World War*, 1987

Peaple, Simon, *European Diplomacy 1870–1939*, 2002

Pelling, Nick, *The Habsburg Empire 1815–1918*, 1996

Robson, Mark, *Access to History: Italy – the Rise of Fascism 1915–1945*, 2006

Waller, Sally, Waugh, Steven and Peaple, Simon, *Russia and Germany, 1871–1914*, 2009

Williamson, David, *War and Peace: International Relations 1878–1941*, 2009

Wilmot, Eric, *Great Powers, 1814–1914*, 1992

Books for teachers and extension

Albertini, Luigi, *Origins of the War of 1914*, 1953

Bergamini, David, *Japan's Imperial Conspiracy: How Emperor Hirohito led Japan into war against the West*, 1971

Brogan, Hugh, *The Penguin History of the United States of America*, 2001

Bullock, Alan, *Hitler: A Study in Tyranny*, 1990

Burkman, Thomas, *Japan and the League of Nations: Empire and World Order, 1914-1938*, 2008

Carr, William, *A History of Germany 1815–1990*, 1991

Clavin, Patricia, *Securing the World Economy: The Reinvention of the League of Nations 1920–1946*, 2013

Clark, Christopher, *Iron Kingdom: The Rise and Downfall of Prussia 1600–1947*, 2007

Clark, Christopher, *How Europe Went to War in 1914*, 2013

Duggan, Christopher, *The Force of Destiny: A History of Italy since 1796*, 2008

Ferguson, Niall, *The Pity of War*, 2009

Finkel, Caroline, *Osman's Dream: The Story of the Ottoman Empire 1300–1923*, 2006

Fischer, Fritz, *Germany's Aims in the First World War*, 1961

Gildea, Robert, *France 1870–1914*, 1996

Glenny, Mischa, *The Balkans 1804–2012: Nationalism, War and the Great Powers*, 2012

Hastings, Max, *Catastrophe: Europe Goes to War 1914*, 2013

Henig, Ruth, *The Origins of the First World War*, 1989

Hobsbawm, Eric, *The Age of Empire: 1875–1914*, 1989

Joll, James and Martel, Gordon, *The Origins of the First World War*, 2006

Kennan, George, *The Fateful Alliance: France, Russia and the Coming of the First World War*, 1984

Kennedy, Paul, *The Rise and Fall of the Great Powers: Economic Change and Military Conflict from 1500–2000*, 1989

Kershaw, Ian, *Hitler 1936–1945: Nemesis*, 2001

Keynes, John Maynard, *The Economic Consequences of the Peace*, 1919

Kinross, Patrick, *The Ottoman Centuries: The Rise and Fall of the Turkish Empire*, 1979

Lee, Stephen J., *Aspects of European History 1789–1980*, 1988

Lowe, C.J. and Marzari, F., *Italian Foreign Policy 1870–1940*, 1975

Macmillan, Margaret, *Peacemakers: Six Months that Changed the World*, 2003

Macmillan, Margaret, *The War that Ended Peace: How Europe Abandoned Peace for the First World War*, 2013

Martel, Gordon, *The Origins of the Second World War Reconsidered: The A.J.P. Taylor Debate after Twenty-Five Years*, 1986

Martel, Gordon, *The Origins of the First World War*, 1987

Martel, Gordon, ed., *A Companion to Europe 1900–1945*, 2010

Massie, Robert, *Dreadnought: Britain, Germany and the Coming of the Great War*, 2007

Mazower, Mark, *Dark Continent: Europe's Twentieth Century*, 1999

Mazower, Mark, *The Balkans: From the End of Byzantium to the Present Day*, 2002

McMeekin, Sean, *The Russian Origins of the First World War*, 2011

McMeekin, Sean, *July 1914: Countdown to War,* 2014

Mitter, Rana, *China's War with Japan 1937–1945: The Struggle for Survival,* 2013

Mombauer, Annika, *The Origins of the First World War: Controversies and Consensus,* 2002

Pakenham, Thomas, *The Scramble for Africa,* 1992

Ponting, Clive, *Thirteen Days: Diplomacy and Disaster, the Countdown to the Great War,* 2003

Randell, Keith, *France: The Third Republic 1870–1914,* 1996

Service, Robert, *The Penguin History of Modern Russia,* 2009

Simms, Brendan, *Europe: The Struggle for Supremacy, 1453 to the Present,* 2013

Steiner, Zara, *The Lights that Failed: European International History 1919–1933,* 2007

Stone, Norman, *Turkey: A Short History,* 2012

Taylor, A.J.P., *The Origins of the Second World War,* 1961

Taylor, A.J.P., *War by Timetable: How the First World War Began,* 1969

Taylor, A.J.P., *The Struggle for Mastery in Europe: 1848–1918,* 1971

Taylor, A.J.P., *The Habsburg Monarchy 1809–1918,* 1990

Tooze, Adam, *The Deluge: The Great War and the Remaking of Global Order,* 2014

Wright, Gordon, *France in Modern Times: From the Enlightenment to the Present,* 1995

Zuber, Terence, *Inventing the Schlieffen Plan: German War Planning 1871–1914,* 2014

TV documentaries – Part One

'On the Idle Hill of Summer', Episode 1 of *The Great War,* BBC, 1964

The Necessary War, BBC, 2014

Royal Cousins at War, BBC, 2014

'Munich 1938', Episode 1 of *Summits,* BBC, 2009

'The Wrong War', Episode 3 of *The Nazis: A Warning From History,* BBC, 1997

The Road to War, BBC, 1989

Podcasts

'The Spanish Civil War', *In Our Time,* BBC Radio 4, 2003

Alexander Watson, 'The German View on the First World War', History Extra, 2014

Adam Tooze, 'The Legacy of the First World War', History Extra, 2014

Tim Butcher, 'The Man Who Started the First World War', History Extra, 2014

Richard Sanders, 'Royal Cousins at War', History Extra, 2014

Margaret Macmillan, 'The Path to the First World War', History Extra, 2013

Christopher Clark, 'The First World War', History Extra, 2012

Acknowledgements

The publisher would like to thank the following for permission to use their photographs:

cover: Mary Evans/Interfoto; **pxii**: Art Archive; **pxiii**: AKG-images; **pxv**: North Wind Picture Archives/Alamy; **pxvi**: Interfoto /Alamy; **p1**: Illustrated London News Ltd./Mary Evans Picture Library; **p4**: (t) Fine Art Images/Getty Images, (b) 2011 Gamma-Rapho/Getty Images; **p7**: Franz von Hanfstaengl/ullstein bild/Getty Images; **p9**: Popperfoto/Getty Images; **p10**: Hulton Archive/Getty Images; **p12**: Hulton Archive/Getty Images; **p13**: The Art Archive/Alamy; **p14**: War Archive/Alamy; **p20**: Mary Evans Picture Library; **p21**: The Art Archive/Alamy; **p29**: The Print Collector/Heritage-Images/Getty Images; **p30**: Apic/Getty Images; **p33**: Private Collection/Peter Newark Military Pictures/Bridgeman Art Library; **p35**: (l) Bain News Service/The Library of Congress, (r) AKG-images; **p37**: Interfoto/Alamy; **p43**: (l) Mirrorpix.com, (r) W. & D. Downey/Getty Images; **p46**: (t) Hulton Archive/Getty Images, (b) Roger-Viollet/TopFoto; **p48**: Leonard Raven-Hill/Mary Evans Picture Library; **p51**: Grenville Collins Postcard Collection/Mary Evans Picture Library; **p52**: DeAgostini/Getty Images; **p55**: Keystone/Getty Images; **p57**: Zooid Pictures; **p63**: Illustrated London News Ltd./Mary Evans Picture Library; **p64**: Mary Evans Picture Library/Alamy; **p70**: DEA/A. Dagli Orti/Getty Images; **p72**: (l) Imagno/Austrian Archives/Getty Images, (r) AKG-images; **p73**: UPPA/Photoshot; **p77**: Zooid Pictures; **p79**: Time Life Pictures/Getty Images; **p80**: De Agostini A. Dagli Orti/Age Fotostock; **p83**: Interfoto/Alamy; **p84**: Underwood & Underwood/Buyenlarge/Getty Images; **p87**: John Frost Newspapers/Alamy; **p89**: ullstein bild/Getty Images; **p92**: General Photographic Agency/Getty Images; **p95**: Zooid Pictures; **p98**: James Montgomery Flagg/The New York Historical Society/Getty Images; **p102**: Illustrated London News Ltd./Mary Evans Picture Library; **p103**: Stock Montage/Getty Images; **p104**: Interfoto/Sammlung Rauch/Mary Evans Picture Library; **p107**: Sovfoto/UIG/Getty Images; **p109**: Image Asset Management/Age Fotostock; **p110**: Haeckel collection/ullstein bild/Getty Images; **p111**: Prisma Bildagentur AG/Alamy; **p112**: DeAgostini/Getty Images; **p113**: The Print Collector/Heritage-Images/Getty Images; **p117**: GL Archive/Alamy; **p118**: (t) Pictorial Press Ltd./Alamy, (b) The Art Archive/Alamy; **p130**: Chronicle/Alamy; **p132**: Interfoto/Alamy; **p133**: AKG-images; **p135**: AKG-images; **p136**: Heritage Image Partnership Ltd./Alamy; **p141**: Pictorial Press Ltd./Alamy; **p142**: (t) Chronicle/Alamy, (b) Interfoto/Alamy; **p146**: (t) imagebroker/Alamy, (b) Apic/Getty Images; **p147**: 1924 Keystone-France/Getty Images; **p148**: (t) GL Archive/Alamy, (b) Archive Pics/Alamy; **p150**: AF archive/Alamy; **p154**: Corbis UK Ltd.; **p156**: David Cole/Age Fotostock; **p158**: GL Archive/Alamy; **p159**: Epic/Tallandier/Mary Evans Picture Library; **p162**: ullstein bild/Getty Images; **p163**: (l) Florence/Alinari/Getty Images, (r) The Print Collector/Age Fotostock; **p165**: Image Asset Management/Age Fotostock; **p167**: Herbert Hoffmann/ullstein bild/Getty Images; **p170**: Fox Photos/Getty Images; **p171**: 1937 The Asahi Shimbun/Getty Images; **p172**: ullstein bild/Getty Images; **p173**: Punch Cartoon Library; **p177**: Hulton Archive/Getty Images; **p181**: World History Archive/Ann Ronan Collection/Age Fotostock; **p182**: Sueddeutsche Zeitun/Mary Evans Picture Library; **p186**: ullstein bild/Getty Images; **p187**: (l) Popperfoto/Getty Images, (r) Associated Newspapers/Rex Features; **p188**: ullstein bild/Getty Images; **p189**: Bettmann/Corbis UK Ltd.; **p190**: Glasshouse Images/Alamy; **p193**: Corbis UK Ltd.; **p194**: ullstein bild/Getty Images; **p195**: 2013 Culture Club/Getty Images; **p198**: Sovfoto/UIG/Getty Images; **p204**: Bettmann/Corbis UK Ltd.; **p205**: Mark Redkin/FotoSoyuz/Getty Images; **p208**: (l) Culver Pictures/Art Archive, (r) Fine Art Images/Age Fotostock; **p211**: Interfoto/AKG-images; **p213**: Interfoto/AKG-images; **p214**: 1939 Keystone-France/Getty Images

We are grateful to the authors and publishers for use of extracts from their titles and in particular to the following:

Luigi Albertini: *The Origins of the War of 1914* translated by Isabella M Massey (OUP, 1952), reproduced by permission of Oxford University Press; **Winston S Churchill**: 'Speech to the Oxford Union', Oxford University, 18 Nov 1920; 'We lie within...striking distance', BBC Radio broadcast, 15 Nov 1934; and 'Wars are not won by evacuations' speech to House of Commons, 4 June 1940, copyright © The Estate of Winston S Churchill, reproduced by permission of Curtis Brown Ltd London, on behalf of the Estate of Winston S Churchill; **Adolf Hitler**: *Mein Kampf* translated by Ralph Manheim (Hutchinson, 1974/Pimlico, 1992), reproduced by permission of The Random House Group Ltd; **John Maynard Keynes**: *The Economic Consequences of the Peace* (1919) in *Collected Writings of John Maynard Keynes* (Cambridge University Press for the Royal Economic Society, 1978, 2013), reproduced by permission of Cambridge University Press; **Margaret MacMillan**: *The War that Ended Peace* (Profile Books, 2013), reproduced by permission of Profile Books; **The *Spectator***: 'Lausanne and After', The *Spectator* 16 July 1932, reproduced by permission of The Spectator; **Hedeki Tojo**: *The Prison Diary 1945–1948*, translation from *The Journal of Historical Review,* Vol 12, No 1, Spring 1992, copyright © IHR 1992, reproduced by permission of Institute for Historical Review.

We have made every effort to trace and contact all copyright holders before publication, but if notified of any errors or omissions, the publisher will be happy to rectify these at the earliest opportunity.

We have made every effort to trace and contract all copyright holders before publication, but if notified of any errors or omissions, the publisher will be happy to rectify these at the earliest opportunity.

From the author: everyone I've worked with at OUP – Janice, Sarah, Kirsty and Becky – and Sally Waller, whose patience and advice have been invaluable; my colleagues at George Abbot School for their understanding and support; my parents for their constant encouragement; Bath Spa University's history department for their long-term inspiration; and not least my husband Sean for his kindness and unflagging provision of tea.

The publisher would like to thank the following people for offering their contribution in the development of this book: Roy Whittle and Sally Waller.

Index

Topics available from
Oxford AQA History for A Level

...arist and Communist
...ussia 1855-1964
...8 019 835467 3

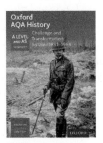

Challenge and
Transformation: Britain
c1851-1964
978 019 835466 6

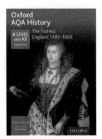

The Tudors: England
1485-1603
978 019 835460 4

Stuart Britain and the
Crisis of Monarchy
1603-1702
978 019 835462 8

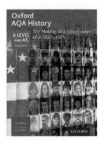

The Making of a
Superpower: USA
1865-1975
978 019 835469 7

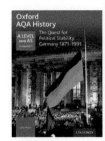

The Quest for Political
Stability: Germany
1871-1991
978 019 835468 0

...e British Empire
...857-1967
...8 019 835463 5

Industrialisation and
the People: Britain
c1783-1885
978 019 835453 6

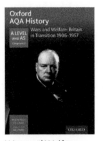

Wars and Welfare:
Britain in Transition
1906-1957
978 019 835459 8

The Cold War
c1945-1991
978 019 835461 1

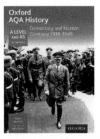

Democracy and Nazism:
Germany 1918-1945
978 019 835457 4

Revolution and
Dictatorship: Russia
1917-1953
978 019 835458 1

...ligious Conflict and
...e Church in England
...529-c1570
...8 019 835471 0

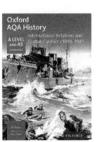

International Relations
and Global Conflict
c1890-1941
978 019 835454 3

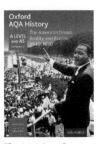

The American Dream:
Reality and Illusion
1945-1980
978 019 835455 0

The Making of Modern
Britain 1951-2007
978 019 835464 2

The Crisis of
Communism: the USSR
and the Soviet Empire
1953-2000
978 019 835465 9

The English Revoluti...
1625-1660
978 019 835472 7

...ance in Revolution
...74-1815
...8 019 835473 4

The Transformation of
China 1936-1997
978 019 835456 7

Also available
in eBook format eBook
Available